I0821306

JAMES

Zondervan Exegetical Commentary Series: New Testament

JAMES

ZONDERVAN

Exegetical Commentary on the New Testament

CRAIG L. BLOMBERG

MARIAM J. KAMELL

CLINTON E. ARNOLD
General Editor

ZONDERVAN ACADEMIC

James

Published in Grand Rapids, Michigan, by Zondervan. Zondervan is a registered trademark of The Zondervan Corporation, L.L.C., a wholly owned subsidiary of HarperCollins Christian Publishing, Inc.

Requests for information should be addressed to customercare@harpercollins.com.

Zondervan titles may be purchased in bulk for educational, business, fundraising, or sales promotional use. For information, please email SpecialMarkets@Zondervan.com.

ISBN 978-0-310-59017-2 (ebook)

Library of Congress Cataloging-in-Publication Data

Blomberg, Craig.
James / Craig L. Blomberg and Mariam J. Kamell.
p. cm. — (Zondervan exegetical commentary series on the New Testament ; v. 16)
Includes bibliographical references and indexes.
ISBN 978-0-310-24402-8 (hardcover)
1. Bible. N.T. James — Commentaries. I. Kamell, Mariam J. II. Title.
BS2785.53.B56 2008
227'.9107 — dc22 2008026376

Interior design: Beth Shagene

Printed in the United States of America

---

25 26 27 28 29 30 31 32 33 34 35 36 /TRM/ 24 23 22 21 20 19 18 17 16 15 14 13

For Bill Klein

Contents

Series Introduction

This generation has been blessed with an abundance of excellent commentaries. Some are technical and do a good job of addressing issues that the critics have raised; other commentaries are long and provide extensive information about word usage and catalog nearly every opinion expressed on the various interpretive issues; still other commentaries focus on providing cultural and historical background information; and then there are those commentaries that endeavor to draw out many applicational insights.

The key question to ask is: What are you looking for in a commentary? This commentary series might be for you if

- you have taken Greek and would like a commentary that helps you apply what you have learned without assuming you are a well-trained scholar.
- you would find it useful to see a concise, one- or two- sentence statement of what the commentator thinks the main point of each passage is.
- you would like help interpreting the words of Scripture without getting bogged down in scholarly issues that seem irrelevant to the life of the church.
- you would like to see a visual representation (a graphical display) of the flow of thought in each passage.
- you would like expert guidance from solid evangelical scholars who set out to explain the meaning of the original text in the clearest way possible and to help you navigate through the main interpretive issues.
- you want to benefit from the results of the latest and best scholarly studies and historical information that helps to illuminate the meaning of the text.
- you would find it useful to see a brief summary of the key theological insights that can be gleaned from each passage and some discussion of the relevance of these for Christians today.

These are just some of the features that characterize the new Zondervan Exegetical Commentary on the New Testament series. The idea for this series was refined over time by an editorial board who listened to pastors and teachers express what they wanted to see in a commentary series based on the Greek text. That board consisted of myself, George H. Guthrie, William D. Mounce, Thomas R. Schreiner, and Mark L. Strauss along with Zondervan senior editor at large, Verlyn Verbrugge, and former Zondervan senior acquisitions editor, Jack Kuhatschek. We also enlisted a board of consulting editors who are active pastors, ministry leaders, and seminary professors to help in the process of designing a commentary series that will be useful to the church. Zondervan senior acquisitions editor David Frees has now been shepherding the process to completion.

We arrived at a design that includes seven components for the treatment of each biblical passage. What follows is a brief orientation to these primary components of the commentary.

Literary Context

In this section, you will find a concise discussion of how the passage functions in the broader literary context of the book. The commentator highlights connections with the preceding and following material in the book and makes observations on the key literary features of this text.

Main Idea

Many readers will find this to be an enormously helpful feature of this series. For each passage, the commentator carefully crafts a one- or two- sentence statement of the big idea or central thrust of the passage.

Translation and Graphical Layout

Another unique feature of this series is the presentation of each commentator's translation of the Greek text in a graphical layout. The purpose of this diagram is to help the reader visualize, and thus better understand, the flow of thought within the text. The translation itself reflects the interpretive decisions made by each commentator in the "Explanation" section of the commentary. Here are a few insights that will help you to understand the way these are put together:

1. On the far left side next to the verse numbers is a series of interpretive labels that indicate the function of each clause or phrase of the biblical text. The corresponding portion of the text is on the same line to the right of the label. We have not used technical linguistic jargon for these, so they should be easily understood.
2. In general, we place every clause (a group of words containing a subject and a predicate) on a separate line and identify how it is supporting the principal assertion of the text (namely, is it saying when the action occurred, how it took place, or why it took place). We sometimes place longer phrases or a series of items on separate lines as well.

3. Subordinate (or dependent) clauses and phrases are indented and placed directly under the words that they modify. This helps the reader to more easily see the nature of the relationship of clauses and phrases in the flow of the text.
4. Every main clause has been placed in bold print and pushed to the left margin for clear identification.
5. Sometimes when the level of subordination moves too far to the right — as often happens with some of Paul's long, involved sentences! — we reposition the flow to the left of the diagram, but use an arrow to indicate that this has happened.
6. The overall process we have followed has been deeply informed by principles of discourse analysis and narrative criticism (for the Gospels and Acts).

Structure

Immediately following the translation, the commentator describes the flow of thought in the passage and explains how certain interpretive decisions regarding the relationship of the clauses were made in the passage.

Exegetical Outline

The overall structure of the passage is described in a detailed exegetical outline. This will be particularly helpful for those who are looking for a way to concisely explain the flow of thought in the passage in a teaching or preaching setting.

Explanation of the Text

As an exegetical commentary, this work makes use of the Greek language to interpret the meaning of the text. If your Greek is rather rusty (or even somewhat limited), don't be too concerned. All of the Greek words are cited in parentheses following an English translation. We have made every effort to make this commentary as readable and useful as possible even for the nonspecialist.

Those who will benefit the most from this commentary will have had the equivalent of two years of Greek in college or seminary. This would include a semester or two of working through an intermediate grammar (such as Wallace, Porter, Brooks and Winberry, or Dana and Mantey). The authors use the grammatical language that is found in these kinds of grammars. The details of the grammar of the passage, however, are only discussed when it has a bearing on the interpretation of the text.

The emphasis on this section of the text is to convey the meaning. Commentators examine words and images, grammatical details, relevant OT and Jewish background to a particular concept, historical and cultural context, important text-critical issues, and various interpretational issues that surface.

Theology in Application

This, too, is a unique feature for an exegetical commentary series. We felt it was important for each author not only to describe what the text meant in its various details, but also to take a moment and reflect on the theological contribution that it makes. In this section, the theological message of the passage is summarized. The authors discuss the theology of the text in terms of its place within the book and in a broader biblical-theological context. Finally, each commentator provides some suggestions on what the message of the passage is for the church today. At the conclusion of each volume in this series is a summary of the whole range of theological themes touched on by this book of the Bible.

Our sincere hope and prayer is that you find this series helpful not only for your own understanding of the text of the New Testament, but as you are actively engaged in teaching and preaching God's Word to people who are hungry to be fed on its truth.

Clinton E. Arnold, general editor

Authors' Preface

When Clint Arnold, general editor of the Zondervan Exegetical Commentary Series on the New Testament, first sent out his prospectus to potential authors in 2002, he described his experience of having vowed never to participate in another commentary series, only to have his mind changed by the unique features that the publishers were proposing for this one. I (Craig) had to chuckle, recalling that I had made similar declarations in the past. Surely, especially for the New Testament and especially in the United States, there is such a glut of commentaries at every level and from every angle imaginable that it could not be good stewardship of time to work on yet one more series just to compete with all of the resources already available.

Then I read the bulk of the prospectus. Not only was the format distinctive, but it truly captured the variety of information and collection of insights that a busy preacher or teacher needs for a "one-stop shopping" approach to adequate sermon preparation or lesson planning. All that remains is for speakers to tailor their messages to their specific audiences and organize whatever audio-visual aids or interactive activities they want to add.

A second thought hit me at almost the same time. The proposed ZECNT format was remarkably close to what the Denver Seminary New Testament department had asked exegesis students to utilize for their major papers for fourth-semester Greek (or its equivalent when we were on the quarter system) for nearly three decades. Because my students have translated and exegeted the entire epistle of James each of the twenty times I have taught the class over my years at the seminary, I have had to study this epistle more intensively than any other book of the Bible. Writing on James was the natural slot in the commentary series for me to fill. I wrote Clint back and asked if I could be assigned this volume, and he quickly agreed. The due date for the manuscript that I negotiated (the end of 2007) was far enough into the future to make the task seem manageable, so I committed myself to the project.

In the spring of 2003, when it was time to choose my research assistant for the coming academic year, it dawned on me that the person I was already very much hoping would agree to the job (Mariam Kamell) was writing her M.A. thesis on aspects of the epistle of James. She had also taken my section of our Exegesis of James requirement. I had been aware of colleagues at other institutions who had coauthored works with graduate students or recent graduates of their programs, and they testified to the mutual benefits that such collaboration can afford. I had been wanting to try out the process for quite awhile, so I wondered if that time might be approaching.

I invited Mariam to be my research assistant for the 2003 – 2004 school year, even as she finished her degree with us. In early 2004, when it was clear she planned on staying in Denver at least one more year and I had seen the caliber of work of which she was capable, I asked if she'd like to keep the job for a second year and use most of her hours to work on this commentary with me. She jumped at the chance. Stan Gundry, chief academic books editor at Zondervan, was open to the idea of a coauthored work, so I tore up my contract as he replaced it with two, splitting the work and the royalties evenly between the two of us.

By the summer of 2005, Mariam had a first draft of all the "Explanation of Text" sections complete, and I had a first draft of everything else in the passage-by-passage body of the volume finished. We had already been reading and commenting on each other's material as we completed smaller segments, but now we needed to revise and supplement. The 2005 – 2006 school year saw Mariam produce her revisions even as she began her Ph.D. work in New Testament in St. Andrews in still further aspects of James's epistle. I had other projects with more pressing deadlines to occupy what time I had for research and writing, so my revisions had to await the 2006 – 2007 school year. Again, we read and revised each other's material as it progressed, worked on uniformity of style, and hashed out the few exegetical differences of opinion that remained. The introduction emerged as a fully collaborative effort.

That left the second half of 2007 for last readings and final editing. By this time it was only occasionally possible to discern who was responsible for the precise thought or wording of the manuscript at any particular point. The volume is genuinely a "team-taught" rather than merely a "tandem-taught" product, if we may borrow that analogy from the world of education.

The use of the third-person singular generic pronoun in English remains a minefield of controversy, much more than it merits. Does one uniformly employ "he" for both genders as was nearly universal in the English-speaking world prior to about 1970? Although some continue to claim to be surprised to learn it, it is a fact that a large number of twenty-first century Americans find the language jarring, odd, sexist, or old-fashioned, and a few genuinely misunderstand it. Yet it seems pedantic to be constantly explaining one's meaning. "He or she" (or "she or he") works well as an occasional substitute but becomes cumbersome when one has to use it too frequently. Using "he" once and "she" the next time works nicely with parallel structures but seldom elsewhere. Thus we have opted for what has become the almost universal solution of choice in oral conversation, though not yet as consistently in print, namely, the third person plural "they" when its antecedent is a generic singular.

Craig would like to thank Keith Wells, Denver Seminary librarian, and his staff for continuing to make our library, especially on the new campus onto which we moved in the summer of 2005, so congenial an atmosphere, so helpful in service, and so rich in resources. I must similarly thank Kim Backlund (now Kim Claire), former Denver Seminary bookstore manager, and her staff, who also took a personal interest in the work of their colleagues and friends and went out of their way to encourage them in that work. I am grateful to Mike Hemenway, my research assistant for 2005 – 2006, for tracking down and assembling for me a number of primary references in the ancient Jewish and Greco-Roman literature. I am thankful to the administration and trustees of the seminary for providing me with the distinguished professorship position that I hold, which makes it noticeably easier for me both to pursue and to fund the amount of research and writing to which I seem continually to find myself committing. Finally, I am particularly appreciative of our department's graduate assistant, Jennifer Foutz, for compiling the list of abbreviations, putting the manuscript into Zondervan's house style, and checking the quotations throughout the manuscript for accuracy — all under a fairly condensed timetable at the last minute!

I (Mariam) would like to thank Craig for inviting me to be a part of this project and always encouraging me onward. I would also like to thank Professor Richard Bauckham for his continued support of my staying involved in other writing projects alongside my dissertation. His encouragement to never stop writing and caring for the church as well as the academy is exemplary not only of his career but one I hope to have, and I appreciate his grace even when my thesis has slowed at times because of these "distractions." I am grateful for my prayer group and my other friends in St. Andrews who ground me in reality and help me keep my sense of humor amidst this degree process, and for the Scum of the Earth Church in Denver where I learned hands-on the cost — and the joy — of loving "the least of these." Finally, I am thankful for a godly family who has always loved and supported me, and more importantly, taught me by example a religion that is pure and acceptable to God (Jas 1:27).

While the two of us could each have selected one or more individuals to whom to dedicate this volume, we have chosen to single out Dr. William W. Klein for a joint dedication. Bill was responsible for recommending Craig to be hired for his first teaching job in New Testament studies at Palm Beach Atlantic College (before it became the university that it is today) in 1982, and took an active role on the Faculty Affairs Committee (before it became "Concerns" rather than "Affairs") at Denver Seminary, lobbying for his candidacy for the position here that Craig took in 1986. He has been as supportive and congenial a colleague and friend over the twenty-two years they have worked together as anyone could ever hope for.

But Bill has also served as New Testament department and Biblical Studies division chair in recent years, so that he was most directly responsible for inviting

Mariam to begin her theological teaching career as a Denver Seminary adjunct Greek instructor in 2004–2005. He also initiated the conversations that led to Mariam and Craig getting to team-teach a New Testament survey course during the summer of 2006, giving her additional, valuable vocational experience. It is not an exaggeration to say that more than any other individual, Bill is responsible for launching both of our professional ministries. For this we are profoundly grateful, and for this reason we dedicate this commentary to Bill with much appreciation. But to God be all the glory.

Abbreviations

AB	Anchor Bible
ASV	American Standard Version
AThR	*Anglican Theological Review*
AUSS	Andrews University Seminary Studies
BDAG	Bauer, W., F. W. Danker, W. F. Arndt, and F. W. Gingrich. *A Greek-English Lexicon of the New Testament and Other Early Christian Literature,* 3rd ed. Chicago, 2000.
BDF	Blass, F., A. Debrunner, and R. W. Funk. *A Greek Grammar of the New Testament and Other Early Christian Literature.* Chicago, 1961.
BECNT	Baker Exegetical Commentary on the New Testament
Bib	*Biblica*
BSac	*Bibliotheca Sacra*
BT	*Bible Translator*
BTB	*Biblical Theology Bulletin*
BTS	Bible Speaks Today
Byz.	Byzantine
BZ	*Biblische Zeitschrift*
CBQ	*Catholic Biblical Quarterly*
CBR	*Currents in Biblical Research*
CCDA	Christian Community Development Association
CTR	*Criswell Theological Review*
CUP	Cambridge University Press
CurBS	*Currents in Research: Biblical Studies*
DRev	*Downside Review*
EDNT	*Exegetical Dictionary of the New Testament.* Edited by H. Balz, G. Schneider. English translation. 3 vols. Grand Rapids, 1990 – 1993.
ESV	English Standard Version
ETL	*Ephemerides theologicae lovanienses*
ETR	*Etudes théologiques et religieuses*
EvJ	*Evangelical Journal*
EvQ	*Evangelical Quarterly*
ExpTim	*Expository Times*

FoiVie	*Foi et vie*
GNB	Good News Bible
GTJ	*Grace Theological Journal*
HCSB	Holman Christian Standard Bible
HTR	*Harvard Theological Review*
ICC	International Critical Commentaries
Int	*Interpretation*
IRM	*International Review of Missions*
IVP	InterVarsity Press, Inter-Varsity Press (England)
JBL	*Journal of Biblical Literature*
JETS	*Journal of the Evangelical Theological Society*
JOTT	*Journal of Translation and Textlinguistics*
JPT	*Journal of Pentecostal Theology*
JSNT	*Journal for the Study of the New Testament*
JSNTSup	Journal for the Study of the New Testament Supplement series
JSOT	*Journal for the Study of the Old Testament*
JSOTSup	Journal for the Study of the Old Testament Supplement series
JTS	*Journal of Theological Studies*
KJV	King James Version
LS	*Louvain Studies*
LUP	Leuven University Press
NAB	New American Bible
NAC	New American Commentary
NASB	New American Standard Bible
NCBC	New Cambridge Bible Commentary
NEB	New English Bible
Neot	*Neotestamentica*
NET	New English Translation
NICNT	New International Commentary on the New Testament
NIDNTT	*New International Dictionary of New Testament Theology*. Edited by C. Brown. 4 vols. Grand Rapids, 1986.
NIGTC	New International Greek Testament Commentary
NIV	New International Version
NIVAC	NIV Application Commentary
NJB	New Jerusalem Bible
NLT	New Living Translation
NovT	*Novum Testamentum*
NRSV	New Revised Standard Version
NTLT	New Testament in the Language of Today
NTS	*New Testament Studies*
OED	*Oxford English Dictionary*

Presb	*Presbyterion*
PRSt	*Perspectives in Religious Studies*
RB	*Revue biblique*
REB	Revised English Bible
RevExp	*Review and Expositor*
RevistBib	*Revista bíblica*
RHPR	*Revue d'histoire et de philosophie religieuses*
RivBib	*Rivista biblica italiana*
RSR	*Recherches de science religieuse*
RSV	Revised Standard Version
RV	Revised Version
SAP	Sheffield Academic Press
SBFLA	Studii biblici Franciscani liber annuus
SBJT	*Southern Baptist Journal of Theology*
SBL	Society of Biblical Literature
SBLSP	*Society of Biblical Literature Seminar Papers*
SBT	Studia Biblica et Theologica
SCM	Student Christian Movement
SJT	*Scottish Journal of Theology*
SNTSU	*Studien zum Neuen Testament und seiner Umwelt*
SP	Sacra Pagina
ST	*Studia theologica*
TCNT	Twentieth Century New Testament
Them	*Themelios*
TJ	*Trinity Journal*
TNIV	Today's New International Version
TNTC	Tyndale New Testament Commentary
TRu	*Theologische Rundschau*
TTE	*The Theological Educator*
TynBul	*Tyndale Bulletin*
UBS	United Bible Societies' *Greek New Testament*
VE	*Vox evangelica*
WBC	Word Biblical Commentary
WJKP	Westminster John Knox Press
WTJ	*Westminster Theological Journal*
WW	*Word and World*
ZKT	*Zeitschrift für katholische Theologie*
ZNW	*Zeitschrift für die neutestamentliche Wissenschaft*

Introduction

- Count it all joy when you encounter many kinds of trials.
- Faith without works is dead.
- Let not many of you become teachers because you know you will incur stricter judgment.
- You adulteresses, don't you know that friendship with the world is enmity with God?
- Come now, you rich, weep and wail for the miseries coming over you!
- The prayer of faith will heal the sick person.

All these and similarly challenging pronouncements punctuate the short epistle of James.[1] Little wonder that many Christians have avoided this book in their studies or at least given it short shrift. Martin Luther wondered if it belonged in the canon because he thought it preached so little of Christ.[2] Modern skeptics have repeatedly charged James with flatly contradicting Paul on the relationship of faith and works. Liberationist theologians have argued that Northern and Western scholars have "intercepted"[3] the letter, avoiding the full force of its teaching on wealth and poverty. Prosperity gospel advocates have appealed to apparently "blank check" promises to promulgate their teachings of "name it and claim it." What *should* the Christian preacher or teacher do with this first of the so-called catholic or general epistles or, as one of our friends once dubbed them, "the forgotten books in the back of the New Testament"?

The format of the Zondervan Exegetical Commentary series does not permit lengthy, detailed introductions to the biblical books it analyzes. Those are readily available elsewhere.[4] But no exposition of any Scripture should begin without an understanding of the basic issues of the original context in which it emerged: authorship, audience, date, provenance, circumstances, theology, structure, and the

1. See Jas 1:2; 2:26; 3:1; 4:4; 5:1, 15, respectively.

2. See *Luther's Works*, vol. 35: *Word and Sacrament I* (Philadelphia: Fortress, 1960), 396. But he never rejected it and included many positive things in his writings about James alongside his concerns. See Gerhard Maier, *Der Brief des Jakobus* (Wuppertal: Brockhaus, 2004), 26–28. On the Reformers' approaches to James more generally, see Timothy George, "'A Right Strawy Epistle': Reformation Perspectives on James," *RevExp* 83 (1986): 369–82.

3. Elsa Tamez, *The Scandalous Message of James: Faith without Works Is Dead*, rev. ed. (New York: Crossroad, 2002), 1.

4. See esp. Luke T. Johnson, *The Letter of James* (AB; New York: Doubleday, 1995), 3–164.

like. With the letters of Paul, many of these details prove discernible without great effort. With the remaining NT epistles, however, we often lack sufficient data to declare with confidence that we know as much. In most instances, both external and internal evidence disclose less information. In the case of James, where we lack secure information about the background but clearly have the text, one of the most secure pieces of information involves the constituent elements or building blocks of the letter. Unlike many commentaries on many biblical books, therefore, we begin with a discussion of James's structure.

Outline

The Individual Passages

Commentators have achieved a reasonable consensus that James is comprised of a dozen or so passages of preachable length, with a few, shorter introductory, transitional, and/or concluding sections.[5] James 1:1 obviously forms the letter's opening address and greeting. Chapter 1:2 – 11 (or 12) comprises the thematic foundation of the letter, introducing topics that will recur throughout: a Christian response to trials, the source of true wisdom, and a right attitude to poverty and riches. Most scholars acknowledge that 1:2 – 11 subdivides into three shorter paragraphs (vv. 2 – 4, 5 – 8 and 9 – 11) on these three topics. Some see v. 12 as rounding out the pericope, while others see it as introducing the next one. Less unanimity surrounds the subdivision of 1:12 (or 13) – 27, but a wide swath of scholars would accept a major break at v. 18, viewing vv. 12 – 18 as pursuing the theme of trials and temptations, and vv. 19 – 27 as stressing the need to "do" as well as "hear" God's Word.

Chapter 2 divides clearly into vv. 1 – 13 and 14 – 26 (though some would set off vv. 12 – 13 as a separate, transitional paragraph). The first half of the chapter warns against discriminating against the poor in favor of the rich, while the second generalizes from the need for believers to exhibit works of mercy to the necessity of good works in general as the demonstration of true, saving faith.

Chapter 3 elicits almost no disagreement over its major subdivisions: vv. 1 – 12 wax eloquent on the power of the tongue for both good and evil, while vv. 13 – 18 contrast "wisdom from above" with that which stems from the world, the flesh, and the devil.

Chapter 4 likewise divides into two units of disproportionate size, with vv. 1 – 12 united by warnings against verbal quarrels and in-fighting among people in James's audience, and vv. 13 – 17 rebuking those who boast in their planning and fail to

5. For a full survey of approaches, see Mark E. Taylor, "Recent Scholarship on the Structure of James," *CBR* 3 (2004): 86 – 115.

6. See throughout Martin Dibelius, *James*, rev. Heinrich Greeven (Hermeneia; Philadelphia; Fortress, 1975 [Germ. orig. 1921]). The commentary went through five German editions, the last of which, in 1964, led to this English translation.

declare their humble dependence on God's sovereign will. Not all commentators keep all of 4:1 – 12 together; vv. 11 – 12 could again form a short transition between sections or introduce vv. 13 – 17. Some link 4:1 – 3 or 4:1 – 10 (or 12) more closely with 3:13 – 18 than with 4:13 – 17, but the basic units of James's material still remain visible.

James 5 raises the most questions among those who analyze this letter's structure. Does 5:1 – 6 end the body of the letter, tying back in with 4:13 – 17 as James discusses in turn the merchants in his community and the wealthy (probably non-Christian) landlords oppressing his readers? Does 5:1 – 11 belong together as problem (vv. 1 – 6) and solution (vv. 7 – 11)? Is v. 12 an isolated piece of wisdom or does it conclude 5:1 – 11 or introduce 5:13 – 20? Can vv. 19 – 20 be understood as a letter closing or does James simply break off his epistle without any proper ending? Notwithstanding all these questions, there is little dispute that vv. 1 – 6, 7 – 11, 12, 13 – 18, and 19 – 20 form the building blocks of chapter 5; the only debate surrounds how, if at all, to group them together.

The Overall Structure

The significant agreement among scholars concerning the constituent elements of James quickly gives way to radical diversity with respect to an overall outline. Four broad clusters of approaches may nevertheless be discerned.

First, championed particularly by Martin Dibelius in the mid-twentieth century in the heyday of form criticism, James may have had *no* overarching outline in view. Like those approaches to the Gospels that saw them as compiled by the Evangelists like strings of pearls — discrete pericopes linked loosely together — or like Pr 10 – 29 and numerous other extrabiblical examples of Jewish wisdom literature, James may have simply grouped together small "thematic essays" without having more linear, Greco-Roman structures in mind. The frequency of "catchwords" throughout the epistle — key words or concepts appearing in one verse and repeated in the next to move the line of thought on to a somewhat separate but partially related topic — can be viewed as supporting this approach. For example, 1:2 introduces the theme of tests or trials (πειρασμοί), which v. 3 repeats (though with the different word δοκίμιον). V. 3 commends endurance (ὑπομονή), which v. 4 pursues further. V. 4 talks about not lacking (from λείπω), while v. 5 tells us what to do if we lack wisdom, namely, to ask (from αἰτέω) God. V. 6 qualifies asking by insisting that we eschew doubt. Vv. 7 – 8 explain why and introduce a partial synonym for the doubter, one who is literally "double-souled" (δίψυχος). Except for sentences that introduce or conclude the larger pericopes already identified, a sizable majority of James's verses contain similar catchwords.[6]

Second, James may have intended a broad topical or thematic structure. Catchwords that link the internal segments of a passage in no way preclude an author from having a different kind of outline overall. A majority of recent studies of James have opted for this approach. Simon Kistemaker finds one key theme per chapter: perseverance, faith, restraint, submission, and patience, respectively.[7] Ralph Martin divides the letter, after the opening greeting, into "enduring trials" (1:12 – 19a), "applying the word" (1:19b – 3:18), and "witnessing to divine providence" (4:1 – 5:20).[8] But each of these headings is so broad that one wonders if it really captures the *distinctive* emphasis of the section it labels and if several other parts of the letter could not have been subsumed under the identical heading with equal ease.

Luke Johnson finds seven main segments after the greeting, which he entitles, "epitome of exhortation" (1:2 – 27), "the deeds of faith" (2:1 – 26), "the power and peril of speech" (3:1 – 12), "call to conversion" (3:13 – 4:10), "examples of arrogance" (4:11 – 5:6), "patience in time of testing" (5:7 – 11), and "speech in the assembly of faith" (5:12 – 20).[9] This improves on Kistemaker and Martin, but are all seven of these sections/themes truly of equal weight? Johnson himself recognizes the complexity of 1:2 – 27 and the simplicity of 5:7 – 11. And is a seven-part outline that much of an improvement over the eleven-part version attainable simply by listing the passages of preachable length identified in the body of our commentary?

A third approach resembles more the recent phase of gospel redaction criticism. James, like the gospel writers, can be seen as a purposeful theologian, carefully weaving his smaller units together into larger fabrics of thought and using his overall structure to prioritize his key themes. One of the best-known examples of this approach comes from Peter Davids. Davids identifies three key themes in the epistle. James introduces each briefly in 1:2 – 11: testing (vv. 2 – 4), wisdom (vv. 5 – 8), and poverty and wealth (vv. 9 – 11). He then repeats the cycle in vv. 12 – 27 with some elaboration: testing compared with temptation (vv. 12 – 18), wisdom particularly in the area of speech (vv. 19 – 21), and the generosity that socioeconomic disparity requires (vv. 22 – 27, with vv. 26 – 27 functioning also as a summary and transition). James 2:1 – 5:6 then unpacks each of these three clusters of topics further, but in reverse order (2:1 – 26; 3:1 – 4:12; and 4:13 – 5:6). Davids calls 5:7 – 20 the letter's "closing statement," with vv. 7 – 11 summarizing the three major themes before vv. 12 – 20 proceed to the more formal closing.[10]

Robert Wall likewise believes that James 1 presents "two introductory statements" on the themes of the testing of faith, the wisdom of God, and a great reversal (1:2 – 4, 5 – 8, 9 – 11; 1:12 – 15, 16 – 18, 19 – 21). But he finds 1:19 programmatic for the body of

7. Simon J. Kistemaker, *Exposition of the Epistle of James and the Epistles of John* (Grand Rapids: Baker, 1986), 21 – 22.

8. Ralph P. Martin, *James* (WBC; Waco, TX: Word, 1988), xcviii – civ.

9. Johnson, *The Letter of James*, 11 – 16. Cf. Douglas J. Moo (*The Letter of James* [Pillar; Grand Rapids: Eerdmans, 2000], 43 – 46), who likewise finds seven main sections after 1:1, even while making slightly different subdivisions.

10. Peter H. Davids, *The Epistle of James* (NIGTC; Grand Rapids: Eerdmans, 1982), 22 – 28. Davids was initially influenced particularly by Fred O. Francis, "The Form and Function of the Opening and Closing Paragraphs of James and 1 John," *ZNW* 61 (1970): 110 – 26.

the letter, with its triad of commands to be "quick to listen, slow to speak and slow to become angry"[11] dictating James's overall structure. The theme of being quick to hear accounts for 1:22 – 2:26, slowness of speech unifies 3:1 – 18, and slowness to anger determines 4:1 – 5:6. The letter closing then mirrors the letter opening with two tripartite sections cycling through an exhortation to endurance, an OT example, and a confirmation of wisdom (5:7 – 8, 9 – 11, 12; 5:13 – 16a, 16b – 18, 19 – 20).[12]

An impressive contingent of recent commentators has agreed with Davids and Wall concerning a two-part introduction with three key themes, with a majority seeing the introduction spanning all of ch. 1. A fair number have also agreed that these three themes are then elaborated in the body of the epistle, even if many doubt that the sections can be delineated as precisely as Davids or Wall did. The majority of disagreement surrounds the demarcation of the end of the letter body and how 5:7 – 20 should be subdivided in more detail.

A final group of scholars tries to fit James's letter into Greco-Roman rhetorical structures[13] or modern discourse analysis. The most promising of these has been outlined in several places by Mark Taylor and George Guthrie.[14] These scholars follow Davids reasonably closely in seeing ch. 1 as a twofold introduction to the key themes of the book and in viewing 5:7 – 20 as a tripartite conclusion. But their key to unlocking the secrets of James's internal structure involves discerning an inclusio in 2:12 – 13 and 4:11 – 12, which reiterates the central commands of speaking and behaving properly in light of the Law and its coming judgment. This inclusio enables Taylor and Guthrie to identify 2:1 – 11 as the body opening and 4:13 – 5:6 as the body closing. The heart of the epistle then emerges in 2:14 – 4:10 and its sustained emphasis on right and wrong acting and speaking in community, with the stark contrast between righteous and worldly wisdom in 3:13 – 18 at the center of a chiastic (in this case, A B C B' A') structure that subdivides what we can call the body of the letter body.

Even with just this brief overview of approaches, we might be inclined to despair of discerning James's outline or to side with those who have been convinced that he has none. Nevertheless, the various points of partial agreement among a significant number of scholars persuade us that we can still make progress. James 2:12 – 13 and 4:11 – 12 read more naturally to us as conclusions to smaller units of thought than as forming a grand inclusio around fairly disparate material. Davids's identification

11. Quotations from Scripture that are not our own translations directly from the Greek are taken from the TNIV unless otherwise indicated.

12. Robert W. Wall, *Community of the Wise: The Letter of James* (Valley Forge, PA: Trinity Press International, 1997), 34 – 38.

13. See esp. Lauri Thurén, "Risky Rhetoric in James," *NovT* 37 (1995): 262 – 84.

14. Mark E. Taylor, *A Text-Linguistic Investigation into the Discourse Structure of James* (London: T&T Clark, 2006); Mark E. Taylor and George H. Guthrie, "The Structure of James," *CBQ* 68 (2006): 681 – 705; George H. Guthrie, "James," in *The Expositor's Bible Commentary*, ed. Tremper Longman III and David E. Garland, rev. ed. (Grand Rapids: Zondervan, 2006), 13:209.

of the three key themes, cycled through twice in ch. 1 and then unfolded in reverse order in chs. 2–5, seems most adequately to account for the main topics that unite the smaller pericopes, though we are modifying his verse divisions in a few key places. The largest of these modifications comes at the end of his outline. If, as we will suggest, 5:19–20 can stand alone as the letter closing, then the door is open to extending the section in the letter body on the theme of trials and temptations all the way through 5:18. After all, 5:7–12 clearly commands how the believers tried or tested by their landlords' oppression (vv. 1–6) should respond, while vv. 13–18 introduce an equally common and related first-century trial—physical suffering and illness.

We would be the first to grant that we may still be imposing more structure on the text than James had in mind. We readily concede that the major themes remain intertwined at several places. Still, even if this outline enables us merely to identify the three dominant themes of the letter, it seems worth generating. Irrespective of controversies over verse divisions, if there is at least *some* form of inverse parallelism along the lines we have sketched, then the central theme of a right approach to wealth and poverty turns out to be the dominant concern. This by itself makes our endeavor worthwhile, because this is precisely the topic that, until quite recently, has not received adequate attention in studies of James. For further details concerning our rationale, readers will have to consult the sections on the Literary Context of each passage in the commentary proper. Meanwhile, we present our working outline here and move on to other introductory considerations:

- I. Greetings (1:1)
- II. Statement of Three Key Themes (1:2–11)
  - A. Trials in the Christian Life (1:2–4)
  - B. Wisdom (1:5–8)
  - C. Riches and Poverty (1:9–11)
- III. Restatement of the Three Themes (1:12–27)
  - A. Trials/Temptations in Relation to God (1:12–18)
  - B. Wisdom in the Areas of Speech and Obedience (1:19–26)
  - C. The "Have-Nots" and the Responsibility of the "Haves": The Thesis of the Letter (1:27)
- IV. The Three Themes Expanded (2:1–5:18)
  - A. Riches and Poverty (2:1–26)
    - 1. Favoritism Condemned (2:1–13)
    - 2. The Problem of Faith without Works (2:14–26)
  - B. Wisdom and Speech (3:1–4:12)
    - 1. The Power of the Tongue (3:1–12)
    - 2. Wisdom from Above and Wisdom from Below (3:13–18)
    - 3. The Misuse of Speech in Quarrels and Slander (4:1–12)
  - C. Trials and Temptations (4:13–5:18)

1. Planning apart from God's Will (4:13 – 17)
2. Responding to Oppression (5:1 – 12)
3. Anointing Prayer for Serious Illness (5:13 – 18)

V. Closing (5:19 – 20)

Circumstances

The nature of a letter's detail often discloses a lot about the circumstances of its composition. As when one listens to just one side of a telephone conversation, there is always the danger of making wrong inferences about the views of the other party or parties. Particularly with wisdom and exhortational literature, we dare not infer that every command or proverb reflects a serious problem afflicting the audience in question. But when issues recur more often than might otherwise be expected and when situations are explicitly described and addressed, we can usually make valid inferences. A section-by-section, or at times even verse-by-verse, analysis of James proves particularly productive in this respect.

The first verse of the letter refers to the author by name as James.[15] The NT contains three men by this name of some prominence. Two are apostles: James, the brother of John and son of Zebedee, and James the less (or younger) and son of Alphaeus (if these are the same individual). The third one is Jesus' (half-)brother,[16] who early in the church's life became the lead elder of the church in Jerusalem (Ac 12:17, 15:13, 21:18).[17] Early church tradition largely supports this last James as the author of this letter,[18] which makes most sense, because James the son of Zebedee was martyred by Herod Agrippa I already by AD 44 (Ac 12:2), the year in which Agrippa died (Jos., *Ant.* 19.343 – 50; cf. Ac 12:20 – 23), and no one else we know in

15. Unrelated to the interpretation of James, but likely to come up in any extended discussion of the man behind the letter, is the controversy over the ossuary from Jerusalem with the Hebrew inscription, "James, son of Joseph, brother of Jesus," that came to public attention in 2002. If it did in fact contain the bones of this James, then it is one of the greatest archaeological finds and corroborations of NT history ever. But enough doubt surrounds the authenticity of the second part of this inscription that we must tread cautiously. For a full account, see Hershel Shanks and Ben Witherington III (*The Brother of Jesus: The Dramatic Story and Meaning of the First Archaeological Link to Jesus and His Family* [San Francisco: HarperSanFrancisco, 2003], 3 – 87), who conclude that the find is authentic. For the strongest arguments against this conclusion, see Jodi Magness, "Ossuaries and the Burials of Jesus and James," *JBL* 124 (2005): 121 – 54.

16. A number of views developed in the early church concerning the identity of the "brothers and sisters" of Jesus (see Mark 6:3 par.): that they were really cousins, that they were children of Joseph by a previous marriage, or that they were children of Joseph and Mary after Jesus' birth. The most natural meaning of the Greek words, coupled with the grammar of Mt 1:25, supports the last of these options. See esp. John P. Meier, *A Marginal Jew: Rethinking the Historical Jesus,* vol. 1: *The Roots of the Problem and the Person* (New York: Doubleday, 1991), 318 – 32.

17. On this James's rise to prominence, see esp. Richard Bauckham, "James and the Jerusalem Church," in *The Book of Acts in Its Palestinian Setting,* ed. Richard Bauckham (Grand Rapids: Eerdmans, 1995), 415 – 80.

18. See esp. Eusebius, *H.E.* 2.23.25; 3.25.3; see also Origen, Jerome, Augustine, and the Council of Carthage. For the fullest compilation of the relevant external evidence, including numerous direct quotations and probable allusions to the letter by patristic authors, see Joseph B. Mayor, *The Epistle of St. James,* 3rd ed. (London: Macmillan, 1913), lxvi – lxxxiv.

the early church by the name of James attained to the prominence normally needed for penning a letter of this nature.

Later Christian tradition about James, the elder in Jerusalem, regularly portrays him as "James the Just," excelling in piety — especially in prayer, fasting, and the practice of Nazirite purity.[19] He is claimed by the second-century Jewish-Christian Ebionites as providing precedent for a Torah-observant form of Christianity, but both gnostic and mainstream Christian appropriations of James contradict this claim.[20] It is almost impossible to separate fact from fiction in all these later traditions, while the Jerusalem Council of Ac 15 clearly concludes with James speaking authoritatively in defense of Paul's understanding of a law-free gospel, even if he requests that Gentile Christians voluntarily refrain from certain practices particularly offensive to the Jews and consistently bound up with pagan idolatry (vv. 28 – 29; cf. also the probably earlier caucus in Gal 2:1 – 10).[21] More certain is James's skepticism concerning the identity of his famous brother during his lifetime (Mk 3:21; Jn 7:5). James may have come to believe in Jesus only after a special resurrection appearance to him (1Co 15:7), though of course he could have been coming to faith more gradually as well.[22]

James 1:1 further identifies the recipients of this letter as "the twelve tribes in the dispersion." The most natural reading of this phrase understands James to be addressing Jewish Christians outside of Israel. First Peter 1:1, it is true, will apply similar language to churches of predominantly Gentile background, but the only way we learn this is from references later in the letter. Nothing in James overturns the assumption that most or all of his readers are literal, ethnic Jews. A few scholars have argued for a setting within Israel but outside Jerusalem and have taken the dispersion of James's audience to refer to the scattering of believers after Stephen's stoning (Ac 8:1, 4),[23] but nothing in the letter points to this more specific dispersion.

"Diaspora" (διασπορά) so commonly referred to Jews scattered throughout the Roman empire, heirs to the exiles of their ancestors living under the Assyrian, Babylonian, Persian, and Greek empires, that it is best to take it in this way here too. Dale Allison has recently resurrected a view frequently held in the seventeenth

19. See esp. Bruce Chilton and Craig A. Evans, eds., *James the Just and Christian Origins* (Leiden: Brill, 1999).

20. For a good overview of canonical and extracanonical traditions about James, see esp. Shanks and Witherington, *The Brother of Jesus*, 89 – 223. Cf. Patrick J. Hartin, *James of Jerusalem: Heir to Jesus of Nazareth* (Collegeville: Liturgical, 2004). Voluminous but highly idiosyncratic is Robert Eisenman, *James the Brother of Jesus* (New York: Viking, 1996). For a full survey of recent scholarship on James the man, see Matti Myllykoski, "James the Just in History and Tradition: Perspectives of Past and Present Scholarship," *CBR* 5 (2006): 73 – 122; 7 (2008): 11 – 98.

21. See esp. Ben Witherington III, *The Acts of the Apostles: A Socio-Rhetorical Commentary* (Grand Rapids: Eerdmans, 1998), 460 – 67.

22. The latter is defended by John Painter, *Just James: The Brother of Jesus in History and Tradition* (Columbia: Univ. of South Carolina Press, rev. 2004), 11 – 41.

23. E.g., David P. Scaer, *James: The Apostle of Faith* (St. Louis: Concordia, 1993), 28 – 30.

24. Dale C. Allison, Jr., "The Fiction of James and Its *Sitz im Leben*," *RB* 108 (2001): 529 – 70.

through nineteenth centuries that James was addressing both Christian and non-Christian Jews in his letter,[24] a view that merits serious consideration especially if we think of people interested in but not yet committed to Christ as one segment of the groups that formed James's "communities."

Several contemporary scholars, most notably Manabu Tsuji, have argued that the letter should be understood as a pastoral encyclical or "apostolic letter to the diaspora" to all Jewish-Christians throughout the empire.[25] But the little evidence we have contradicts the suggestion that any first-generation Christian leader had that kind of authority over or access to all Christians, even just of one ethnic or religious background, throughout the then-known world. Even the much larger non-Christian Jewish community did not have leaders who wielded that much influence (cf. Ac 28:21).

Indeed, the very genre proposed is somewhat problematic. Scholars often point to Jer 29; 2Ma 1:1–9; 1:10–2:18; the Epistle of Jeremiah; *2 Bar* 78–86; the *Paraleipomena Jeremiou* 6:19–25; 7:24–34; three letters from Gamaliel I; two letters from Simeon ben Gamaliel and Johanan ben Zakkai; Aramaic Papyri 21 and 30; and/or epistles from the time of bar Kochba from the Judean wilderness as analogies. But these are "letters" within larger documents and/or letters written only to one small part of the diaspora.[26] Indeed, numerous features of James, particularly the early and late rains of 5:7, suggest a setting limited to the Eastern (Greek-speaking) half of the empire because of geographical realities. Jewish Christianity, like Judaism more generally, was strongest toward the Eastern end of the Mediterranean basin, and so many scholars have envisioned congregations in and around Syria as the most probable recipients of this epistle. The fact that "certain people came from James" to Syrian Antioch (Gal 2:12), precipitating Peter's withdrawal from table fellowship with the Gentiles and the resulting confrontation with Paul, has made that community a commonly suggested target audience.[27]

James 1:2–11 clearly addresses trials of many kinds (v. 2), and vv. 9–11 could certainly have applied as a generalization about how rich and poor were to view their earthly circumstances. By the end of the letter, however, the frequency with which James returns to the issue of wealth and poverty suggests that socioeconomic disparities were causing problems for his congregations.[28] So, too, 1:12–27 contains much timeless, proverbial wisdom. But the pointed summary or conclusion in

25. Manabu Tsuji, *Glaube zwischen Vollkommenheit und Verweltlichung: Eine Untersuchung zur literarischen Gestalt und zur inhaltlichen Kohärenz des Jakobusbriefes* (Tübingen: Mohr, 1997), 5–50. Cf. Richard Bauckham, *James* (London: Routledge, 1999), 11–28; Donald J. Verseput, "Genre and Story: The Community Setting of the Epistle of James," *CBQ* 62 (2000): 96–110; Karl-Wilhelm Niebuhr, "Der Jakobusbrief im Licht Frühjudischer Diasporabriefe," *NTS* 44 (1998): 420–43.

26. Cf. further Margaret M. Mitchell, "The Letter of James as a Document of Paulinism?" in *Reading James with New Eyes: Methodological Reassessments of the Letter of James*, ed. Robert L. Webb and John S. Kloppenborg (London: T&T Clark, 2007), 84–85, n. 33.

27. Christoph Burchard, *Der Jakobusbrief* (Tübingen: Mohr, 2000), 6, and the literature there cited.

28. See esp. Pedrito U. Maynard-Reid, *Poverty and Wealth in James* (Maryknoll, NY: Orbis, 1987).

vv. 26–27 appears to indicate that James's churches may have been engaged in too many inappropriate forms of speech and may not have been recognizing the central need of care for the most dispossessed in their communities.

Chapter 2 reinforces these suspicions.[29] The example of discrimination in 2:1–4 could have been hypothetical and/or deliberately extreme. The illustration in 2:14–17 of ignoring the starving, ill-clad fellow believers, even while wishing them well, strikes many as intentionally extreme. The demography of the first-century Mediterranean world, nevertheless, suggests that up to 10 percent of the population could well have been poor and/or sick enough at any given time for their lives to be in actual jeopardy.[30] These percentages would have carried over into James's churches as well, so that those who could count on regularly receiving more than just their "daily bread" needed to share some of it with those who often lacked enough to eat.

Economic need thus drives theology in 2:14–26. James's teaching on faith and works (vv. 18–26), which has caused so many debates in the history of NT interpretation, grows out of the reality of life in a world far closer to today's Two-Thirds or Majority World than to "the West" (vv. 14–17). No theological controversy has necessarily precipitated it, as with Paul's need to rebut the Judaizers in Galatia and elsewhere. Much more appears below on the relationship between James and Paul on this issue, but here the question becomes whether James is more likely to have written with the vocabulary and diction that he has chosen (a) independent of and therefore prior to Paul's views, (b) deliberately responding to and rebutting Paul's views, or (c) consciously correcting a misunderstanding or distortion of Paul's views. Once one understands the way James uses his key terms, (b) becomes unlikely (see below). Option (c) remains possible,[31] but one wonders whether James would have continued to use language so susceptible to being interpreted as contradicting Paul. With a growing number of recent scholars, therefore, we would opt for (a).[32]

Given that Galatians may well have been written as early as AD 48 or 49 and that James the elder is not mentioned in early Christian literature as playing a prominent role until the death of his namesake in 44, we suspect that the most likely date for this epistle is in the mid-to-late 40s. Patrick Hartin offers six additional reasons for so early a date: (1) the author's self-description in 1:1 as if he is readily known, without any reference to his relationship to Jesus or any leadership office; (2) his intimate relationship with Israel's heritage; (3) the way in which he loosely cites the Jesus tradition, less likely after it was written down; (4) the closeness of his spirit and

29. See esp. David H. Edgar, *Has God Not Chosen the Poor? The Social Setting of the Epistle of James* (Sheffield: SAP, 2001). Cf. Wesley H. Wachob, *The Voice of Jesus in the Social Rhetoric of James* (Cambridge: CUP, 2000).

30. The classic study is Gerhard Lenski, *Power and Privilege: A Theory of Social Stratification* (New York: McGraw-Hill, 1966). See the helpful chart labeled Fig. 1 on p. 284.

31. The strongest recent defense appears in Mitchell, "The Letter of James as a Document of Paulinism?" 75–98.

32. E.g., Davids, *The Epistle of James*, 22; Douglas Moo, *The Letter of James* (Pillar; Grand Rapids: Eerdmans, 2000), 25–26; Guthrie, "James," *EBC*, 13:201–2.

vision to Christ; (5) the complete absence of any mention of Gentiles; and (6) the lack of any reference to the temple's destruction in AD 70.[33] For those unconvinced by this line of argumentation but who still see James as author, the date of the letter must at least precede his martyrdom in 62 (see Jos. *Ant.* 20.200).[34]

James 3:1 warns against too many wanting to become teachers, a desire probably due to the status that it would afford them. This reinforces the impression that many, if not most, in James's communities were poor. Rabbis were not necessarily much better off financially than other Jews, particularly in the smaller villages, but they were accorded far greater honor.

The anger, selfishness, and quarrelling that is rebuked in 3:13 – 4:12 could readily have embodied these Christians' common response to the socioeconomic oppression they were experiencing. Modern psychologists may have first created labels like "projection" and "displacement," but the phenomenon of infighting when one's true opponents are inaccessible is a timeless one. If one follows Ralph Martin in taking the references to "wars and fightings" in 4:1 or to "murder" in 4:2 literally, then we may discern here the beginnings of more organized Zealotry in the early 60s (or later, if James be deemed pseudonymous).[35] But the vast majority of commentators appears correct in taking this language as metaphorical and the quarrels as primarily verbal, which we will defend below.

Chapter 4:13 – 17 reveals the presence of at least a small community of traveling merchants. Most likely these are the minority of better-off Christians in James's churches. It seems unlikely that he would rebuke them for not taking the Lord's will into account (4:15) if they were unbelieving outsiders.

By contrast, 5:1 – 6 is best taken as a literary apostrophe, addressing the absentee landlords, Roman or Jewish, who were persecuting James's church members and withholding their daily wages. The landowners would come from the handful of very rich outsiders, not any kind of Christians, who were making life miserable for many of the believers they put to work on their farms. The details of this passage (esp. in v. 4) identify these oppressed Christians as day-laborers who depended on being paid their wages at the end of each workday in order to buy enough food to feed their families and themselves that evening or the next. "Migrant workers" may form the closest North American analogy today. The murder mentioned in v. 6 is probably de facto. By not paying the "farmhands" a livable wage and/or not paying it on time, some may well have starved to death. More commonly, others would have been forced to borrow money that they could never repay. They were then thrown

33. Patrick J. Hartin, *James* (SP; Collegeville: Liturgical, 2003), 24.

34. See James S. McLaren, "Ananus, James, and Earliest Christianity: Josephus' Account of the Death of James," *JTS* 52 (2001): 1 – 25. For theories of pseudonymity, see below. An intermediate option, of course, is to argue that a compiler of James's authentic traditions or sermons organized them as we now have the letter after his death.

35. Martin, *James*, lxii – lxxii.

into debtors' prison and, without anyone to look after their physical needs, they would eventually die there.

Most Westerners have little sense of how frequently a significant percentage of pre-industrial-age populations were sick and without adequate health care.[36] James 5:13 – 18 need not suggest that James's community experienced a disproportionate amount of illness by the standards of its day, but those standards alone ensured that these verses would remain relevant. The number of ethical areas that James had to address throughout his letter makes 5:19 – 20 far more than hypothetical. Many would have needed restoration and turning from their errant ways.

The barrage of imperatives that dominates James qualifies it for the broad literary and rhetorical genre of paraenesis or exhortation.[37] The letter emerges out of a background of wisdom literature[38] but with clear prophetic overtones as well.[39] In form, it partly resembles an epistle (letter), partly a homily (sermon), and primarily a protreptic discourse (exhortation that develops by means of extended argumentation).[40] Much of this discourse is dialectic, as James frequently contrasts good and bad behavior, often with illustrations (ships, clothing, fire, water, fruit, farming, etc.) susceptible to both positive and negative development.[41]

Objections to James as Author and/or to a Date during His Lifetime

All that we have deduced thus far has assumed that the letter of James is not pseudonymous. But what if "James" is not the actual author of this epistle? Debate still swirls around the legitimacy of pseudonymity as a literary device in antiquity. It seems beyond reasonable doubt that a significant swath of pre-Christian Judaism recognized the technique as something other than forgery with the intent to deceive,[42] but the Christian evidence that we have, beginning in the mid-second

36. But see Peter G. Bolt, "Life, Death, and the Afterlife in the Greco-Roman World," in *Life in the Face of Death: The Resurrection Message of the New Testament*, ed. Richard N. Longenecker (Grand Rapids: Eerdmans, 1998), 51 – 79.

37. See esp. Luke L. Cheung, *The Genre, Composition and Hermeneutics of James* (Carlisle: Paternoster, 2003), 15 – 52. Cf. Leo G. Perdue, "Paraenesis and the Epistle of James," *ZNW* 72 (1981): 241 – 56.

38. Hubert Frankemölle ("Das semantische Netz des Jakobusbriefes: Zur Einheit eines umstritten Briefes," *BZ* 34 [1990]: 161 – 97, with a foldout chart at the end of the fascicle) demonstrates in detail the amount of vocabulary in James characteristic of intertestamental Jewish Wisdom literature, particularly the Wisdom of Jesus ben Sira(ch). Cf. Ernst Baasland, "Der Jakobusbrief als neutestamentliche Weisheitsschrift," *ST* 36 (1982): 119 – 39.

39. See the range of perspectives surveyed in Todd C. Penner, "The Epistle of James in Current Research," *CurBS* 7 (1999): 275 – 80.

40. Hartin, *James*, 10 – 16; Johnson, *The Letter of James*, 16 – 24.

41. Kenneth D. Tollefson, "The Epistle of James as Dialectical Discourse," *BTB* 27 (1997): 62 – 69.

42. See esp. David G. Meade, *Pseudonymity and Canon: An Investigation into the Relationship of Authorship and Authority in Jewish and Earliest Christian Tradition* (Grand Rapids: Eerdmans, 1986). Karen H. Jobes (BECNT; *1 Peter* [Grand Rapids: Baker, 2005], 15 – 17) notes, however, that although the practice appears to have been accepted when the putative author had died centuries earlier, it was not deemed legitimate if the author had died comparatively recently.

century, reasonably uniformly rejects it as morally unacceptable.[43] Given Christianity's origins in Judaism, there must have been some time at which certain Jewish Christians changed their minds about this device. Was this before or after the production of any or all of the NT documents? To date we simply lack the data that enable us to answer this question.

The four main reasons why some reject Jamesian authorship of this letter are as follows:

1. The style represents more elegant Greek and the concepts more sophisticated Hellenism than the son of a Jewish carpenter could have been expected to master.
2. The contents of the letter are not distinctively Christian enough. References to Jesus appear only in 1:1 and 2:1, while there is no unambiguous mention of the Holy Spirit anywhere ("S/spirit" [πνεῦμα] appears only in 4:5). Take away these two verses and a non-Christian Jew could have written the entire document.
3. The letter is not distinctively *Jewish*-Christian enough. Little represents the unique theology of the second-century Ebionites, an early Jewish-Christian sect that assiduously kept the Mosaic law and questioned the divinity of Jesus.
4. The comparatively slow acceptance of James into the emerging NT canon during the first three centuries of Christian history suggests early doubts about the genuineness of this letter's claims for authorship.

Each of these four points can be fairly readily countered. Because of centuries of Hellenistic influence in Israel, particularly in Galilee, it is impossible to pontificate on how much Greek language and culture any given Jew could or could not have learned. Nazareth lay a scant five miles from Sepphoris, the second largest city in Galilee and the former provincial capital. With a building boom in the 20s, Sepphoris could easily have afforded both James and Jesus numerous carpentry opportunities over a number of years, where they could also have picked up a quantity of Greek language and culture.[44] Martin and Davids have also suggested that James shows some signs of the use of a smoother Greek redaction overlying a more Jewish original,[45] though the criteria for determining such stages of composition prove far too subjective for us to assess such theories with any verdict other than "possible."

While Jesus appears by name only twice, James regularly alludes to his teachings,

43. See esp. Terry L. Wilder, *Pseudonymity, the New Testament, and Deception: An Inquiry into Intention and Reception* (Lanham, MD: Univ. Press of America, 2004).

44. Cf. Richard A. Batey, *Jesus and the Forgotten City: New Light on Sepphoris and the Urban World of Jesus* (Grand Rapids: Baker, 1991).

45. Martin (*James*, lxxii – lxxvii), citing Jerome's remark that "James wrote a single epistle and some claim that it was published by another under his name" (*De Vir. Illust.* 2); Davids, *The Epistle of James*, 12 – 13, 21 – 22. Cf. also Pierre-Antoine Bernheim, *James, Brother of Jesus* (London: SCM, 1997), 227, 244.

particularly from Matthew and Luke, and frequently from the Sermon on the Mount/Plain.[46] The clearest comes in James 5:12 ("do not swear, either by heaven or by earth or by any other oath; but let your yes [be] yes and your no [be] no"; cf. Mt 5:34 – 37), but Davids provides a helpful chart of thirty-five other probable allusions.[47] Numerous additional theologically significant conceptual parallels appear as well.[48] The letter is thus heavily indebted to the Jesus tradition and is therefore fully Christian.

The very fact that many of James's injunctions do find non-Christian Jewish parallels, however, undermines the objection that it is not sufficiently *Jewish*-Christian. It is not distinctively Ebionite, but all that means in this instance is that it *is* orthodox![49] Later church traditions probably exaggerated the extent to which James promoted Torah-observant Christianity *in competition* with other branches of the faith. And the slower acceptance of James into the canon than the letters of Paul probably had to do more with questions about the relationship of the theologies of the two authors, particularly regarding faith and works, than with doubts about authorship.[50]

The recent dissertation of David Nienhuis moves in creative, new directions to argue not only for pseudonymity but also for a mid-second-century date for the letter. Dismissing the usually claimed allusions to James in 1 Clement and the Shepherd of Hermas as too ambiguous and inverting the normally assumed sequence of writing that accounts for the parallels between James and other early Christian literature, Nienhuis believes that James was penned by an emerging Catholic writer to complete the Catholic Epistles collection. This collection was then juxtaposed to the collection of Pauline letters to balance out Paul's potentially one-sided theology. Nienhaus makes much of the silence of second-century writings about James, the brother of Jesus, with respect to any letters that he might have penned. Nienhaus also notes how different this epistle's theology is from the consistent portrait of James as following the ritual as well as the moral law of Moses, traces of which one would have expected in an authentic first-century letter from that church leader.[51]

46. See esp. Patrick J. Hartin, *James and the Q Sayings of Jesus* (JSNTSup; Sheffield: SAP, 1991). John S. Kloppenborg ("The Emulation of the Jesus Tradition in the Letter of James," in *Reading James with New Eyes*, ed. R. L. Webb and J. S. Kloppenborg [London: T&T Clark, 2007], 121 – 50) finds James dependent on Q and deliberately rewording his source in keeping with the ancient tradition of making another's teaching, especially in the wisdom tradition, one's own. Others see James as purely utilizing the oral tradition of the sayings of Jesus even before Q took shape. The fullest analysis appears in Dean B. Deppe (*The Sayings of Jesus in the Epistle of James* [Chelsea, MI: Bookcrafters, 1989]), who does not rely on the Q-hypothesis.

47. Davids, *The Epistle of James*, 47 – 48.

48. See esp. Virgil V. Porter, Jr., "The Sermon on the Mount in the Book of James," *BSac* 162 (2005): 344 – 60, 470 – 82.

49. Cf. Richard Bauckham, "James and Jesus," in *The Brother of Jesus: James the Just and His Mission*, ed. Bruce Chilton and Jacob Neusner (Louisville: WJKP, 2001), 135: "We may now assert quite confidently that the self-consciously low Christology of the later Jewish Christian sect known as the Ebionites does not, as has sometimes been asserted, go back to James and his circle in the early Jerusalem church."

50. Ferdinand Hahn and Peter Müller, "Der Jakobusbrief," *TRu* 63 (1998): 70 – 73.

51. David R. Nienhuis, *Not by Paul Alone: The Formation of the Catholic Epistle Collection and the Christian Canon* (Waco, TX: Baylor Univ. Press, 2007).

However, surely a pseudepigrapher writing closer to the time of that later portrait of James would have had even more reason to make the theology of his letter match the traditions about James. The canonical epistle matches the portrait of James in Acts 15 without contradiction. As for expecting reference in the hagiographers to James's letter, early church tradition about the subsequent travels and teachings of the apostles and their associates rarely refers to their writings, even when we definitely know that such writings existed. This apparently was just not the place to include such information. Rather, references to the canonical writings usually appear instead in segments of documents devoted to the formation of the NT more generally.[52]

Conclusions and Significance

With this short letter, therefore, we have what is probably the first NT document written and the first existing Christian writing of any kind of which we know. James, the (half-)brother of the Lord Jesus and chief elder in Jerusalem during the first generation of Christianity (or at least from about AD 44 – 62), is writing to a group of primarily Jewish-Christian congregations, most likely in the mid-to-late forties, and probably somewhere in or around Syria. We have no indication as to where James himself resided at this time, but Jerusalem is obviously the best guess. James's letter thus joins the early chapters of Acts as a unique canonical witness, and the lone firsthand testimony, to very early Jewish Christianity. In short, these are our roots!

We will defer our summary of James's theology until after the commentary proper. Suffice it for now to say that faith in action, especially in *social* action, remains central for this author. Like the OT prophets and as with Jesus,[53] James sees no tension between (and indeed weds closely together) orthodoxy and orthopraxy — correct belief and correct behavior. A personal relationship with Jesus and the quest for social justice do not create the competing understandings of Christianity that church history has often made them appear. Both remain absolutely essential to the gospel.[54]

52. See esp. F. F. Bruce, *The Canon of Scripture* (Downers Grove, IL: IVP, 1988).

53. See further Craig L. Blomberg, "'Your Faith Has Made You Whole': The Evangelical Liberation Theology of Jesus," in *Jesus of Nazareth: Lord and Christ*, ed. Joel B. Green and Max Turner (Grand Rapids: Eerdmans, 1994), 75 – 93.

54. Cf. Pablo A. Deiros, *Santiago y Judas* (Miami: Editorial Caribe, 1992), 35 – 41.

Select Bibliography

Adamson, James B. *James: The Man and His Message*. Grand Rapids: Eerdmans, 1989.

———. *The Epistle of James*. NICNT. Grand Rapids: Eerdmans, 1976.

Andria, Solomon. "James." Pages 1509 – 16 in *Africa Bible Commentary*, ed. Tokunboh Adeyemo. Nairobi: Word Alive; Grand Rapids: Zondervan, 2006.

Baker, William R. "James." Pages 9 – 112 in *James-Jude: Unlocking the Scriptures for You*, ed. William R. Baker and Paul Carrier. Cincinnati: Standard, 1990.

———. *Personal Speech-Ethics in the Epistle of James*. Tübingen: Mohr, 1995.

Baker, William R., and Thomas D. Ellsworth. *Preaching James*. St. Louis: Chalice, 2004.

Barton, Bruce B., David R. Veerman, and Neil Wilson. *James*. Wheaton: Tyndale, 1992.

Bauckham, Richard. *James*. London: Routledge, 1999.

Bernheim, Pierre-Antoine. *James, Brother of Jesus*. London: SCM, 1997.

Blomberg, Craig L. *The Historical Reliability of the Gospels*. Rev. ed. Downers Grove, IL: IVP, 2007.

———. *Interpreting the Parables*. Downers Grove, IL: IVP, 1990.

———. *Jesus and the Gospels: An Introduction and Survey*. Nashville: Broadman & Holman, 1997.

———. *Matthew*. New American Commentary. Nashville: Broadman, 1992.

———. *From Pentecost to Patmos: An Introduction to Acts through Revelation*. Nashville: Broadman & Holman, 2006.

———. *Preaching the Parables: From Responsible Interpretation to Powerful Proclamation*. Grand Rapids: Baker, 2004.

Bray, Gerald, ed. *Ancient Christian Commentary on Scripture*. Vol. 11. *James, 1 – 2 Peter, 1 – 3 John, Jude*. Downers Grove, IL: IVP, 2000.

Brosend II, William F. *James and Jude*. NCBC Cambridge: CUP, 2004.

Burdick, Donald W. "James." Pages 159 – 205 in *The Expositor's Bible Commentary*. Vol. 12, ed. Frank E. Gaebelein. Grand Rapids: Zondervan, 1981.

Byrskog, Samuel. *Jesus the Only Teacher: Didactic Authority and Transmission in Ancient Israel, Ancient Judaism and the Matthean Community*. Stockholm: Almqvist and Wiksell, 1994.

Campbell, R. Alastair. *The Elders: Seniority within Earliest Christianity*. Edinburgh: T&T Clark, 1994.

Chester, Andrew, and Ralph P. Martin, eds. *The Theology of the Letters of James, Peter, and Jude*. Cambridge: CUP, 1994.

Cheung, Luke L. *The Genre, Composition and Hermeneutics of James*. Carlisle: Paternoster, 2003.

Chilton, Bruce D., and Craig A. Evans, eds. *James the Just and Christian Origins*. Leiden: Brill, 1999.

———, eds. *The Missions of James, Peter and Paul: Tensions in Early Christianity*. Boston: Brill, 2005.

Church, Christopher. "James." Pages 323–422 in *Hebrews-James*, ed. Edgar V. McKnight and Christopher Church. Macon, GA: Smyth & Helwys, 2004.

Davids, Peter H. *The Epistle of James*. NIGTC. Grand Rapids: Eerdmans, 1982.

Deiros, Pablo A. *Santiago y Judas*. Miami: Editorial Caribe, 1992.

Deppe, Dean B. *The Sayings of Jesus in the Epistle of James*. Chelsea, MI: Bookcrafters, 1989.

Dibelius, Martin. *James*. Rev. ed. Heinrich Greeven. Hermeneia. Philadelphia: Fortress, 1975 (Germ. orig. 1921).

Doriani, Daniel M. *James*. Reformed Expository Commentary. Phillipsburg, NJ: Presbyterian & Reformed, 2007.

Edgar, David H. *Has God Not Chosen the Poor? The Social Setting of the Epistle of James*. JSNTSup; Sheffield: SAP, 2001.

Eisenman, Robert. *James the Brother of Jesus*. New York: Viking, 1996.

Evans, Mary J. "James." Pages 776–79 in *The IVP Women's Bible Commentary*, ed. Catherine C. Kroeger and Mary J. Evans. Downers Grove, IL: IVP, 2000.

———. "The Law in James." *Vox Evangelica* 13 (1983): 29–40.

Felder, Cain H. "James." Pages 1786–1801 in *The International Bible Commentary*, ed. William R. Farmer. Collegeville: Liturgical, 1998.

France, R. T., David Wenham, and Craig Blomberg, eds. *Gospel Perspectives*, 6 vols. Eugene, OR: Wipf & Stock, repr. 2003–4.

Gench, Frances T. *Hebrews and James*. Westminster Bible Companion. Louisville: WJKP, 1996.

Guthrie, George H. "James." Pages 197–273 in *The Expositor's Bible Commentary, Revised Edition*, ed. Tremper Longman III and David E. Garland, vol. 13. Grand Rapids: Zondervan, 2006.

Hartin, Patrick J. *James*. SP. Collegeville: Liturgical, 2003.

———. *James of Jerusalem: Heir to Jesus of Nazareth*. SP; Collegeville: Liturgical, 2004.

———. *James and the Q Sayings of Jesus*. JSNTSup; Sheffield: JSOT, 1991.

———. *A Spirituality of Perfection: Faith in Action in the Letter of James*. Collegeville: Liturgical, 1999.

Hemer, Colin J. *The Book of Acts in the Setting of Hellenistic History*, ed. Conrad Gempf. Tübingen: Mohr, 1989.

Hiebert, D. Edmond. *The Epistle of James: Tests of a Living Faith*. Chicago: Moody, 1979.

Hodges, Zane C. *The Epistle of James: Proven Character through Testing*. Irving, TX: Grace Evangelical Society, 1994.

Hoppe, Rudolf. *Der theologische Hintergrund des Jakobusbriefes*. Wurzburg: Echter, 1977.

Hort, F. J. A. *The Epistle of St. James*. London: Macmillan, 1909.

Hubbard, David A. *The Book of James: Wisdom that Works*. Waco, TX: Word, 1980.

Hughes, R. Kent. *James: Faith That Works*. Wheaton: Crossway, 1991.

Huther, Johann E. *Critical and Exegetical Handbook to the General Epistles of James, Peter, John, and Jude*. New York: Funk & Wagnalls, 1887.

Isaacs, Marie E. *Reading Hebrews and James*. Macon, GA: Smyth & Helwys, 2002.

Jackson-McCabe, Matt A. *Logos and Law in the Letter of James*. Leiden: Brill, 1999.

Johnson, Luke T. *The Letter of James*. AB. New York: Doubleday, 1995.

———. *Brother of Jesus, Friend of God: Studies in the Letter of James*. Grand Rapids: Eerdmans, 2004.

Kaiser, Sigurd. *Krankenheilung: Untersuchungen zu Form, Sprache, traditionsgeschichtlichem Hintergrund und Aussage zu Jak 5,13 – 18*. Neukirchen-Vluyn: Neukirchener, 2006.

Kamell, Mariam J. "The Concept of 'Faith' in Hebrews and James." In *The Epistle to the Hebrews and Christian Theology*, ed. Richard Bauckham, Daniel Driver, Trevor Hart, and Nathan MacDonald. London: T&T Clark, forthcoming.

———. "James 2:12 – 13." St. Andrews, unpublished paper, 2007.

———. "Wisdom in James: An Examination and Comparison of the Roles of Wisdom and the Holy Spirit." M.A. Thesis: Denver Seminary, 2003.

———. "Word/Law in James and the Promised New Covenant." Washington, DC: Unpublished SBL Conference Paper, 2006.

Keenan, John P. *The Wisdom of James*. Mahwah, NJ: Paulist, 2005.

Keener, Craig S. *The IVP Bible Background Commentary: New Testament*. Downers Grove, IL: IVP, 1993.

Kistemaker, Simon J. *Exposition of the Epistle of James and the Epistles of John*. Grand Rapids: Baker, 1986.

Klein, Martin. *Ein volkommenes Werk: Vollkommenheit, Gesetz und Gericht als theologische Themen des Jakobusbriefes*. Stuttgart: Kohlhammer, 1995.

Klein, William W. *The New Chosen People: A Corporate View of Election*. Grand Rapids: Zondervan, 1990.

Kugelman, Richard. *James and Jude*. New Testament Message. Wilmington: Glazier, 1980.

Kühl, Ernst. *Die Stellung des Jakobusbriefes zum alttestamentlichen Gesetz und zur paulinischen Rechtfertigungslehre*. Königsberg, Prussia: Koch, 1905.

Lea, Thomas D. *Hebrews and James*. Holman New Testament Commentary. Nashville: Broadman & Holman, 1999.

Levine, Amy-Jill, ed. *A Feminist Companion to the Catholic Epistles and Hebrews*. Cleveland: Pilgrim, 2004.

Lockett, Darian R. *Purity and Worldview in the Epistle of James*. London: T&T Clark, 2008.

Louw, J. P., and Eugene A. Nida. *Greek-English Lexicon of the New Testament: Based on Semantic Domains*. 2 vols. New York: United Bible Societies, 1998.

Ludwig, Martina. *Wort als Gesetz*. Frankfurt am Main: Peter Lang, 1994.

MacArthur, John F., Jr. *The Gospel according to Jesus*. Rev. ed. Grand Rapids: Zondervan, 1994.

———. *The Gospel according to the Apostles*. Nashville: Word, 2000.

Maier, Gerhard. *Der Brief des Jakobus*. Wuppertal: Brockhaus, 2004.

Martin, Ralph P. *James*. WBC. Waco, TX: Word, 1988.

Martin, Raymond A. "James." Pages 7 – 51 in *James, I-II Peter, Jude*, ed. Raymond A. Martin and John H. Elliott. Augsburg Commentary on the New Testament. Minneapolis: Augsburg, 1982.

Maynard-Reid, Pedrito U. *Poverty and Wealth in James*. Maryknoll, NY: Orbis, 1987.

Mayor, Joseph B. *The Epistle of St. James*. 3rd ed. London: Macmillan, 1913.

McDonnell, Rea. *The Catholic Epistles and Hebrews*. Wilmington: Glazier, 1986.

Metzger, Bruce M. *A Textual Commentary on the Greek New Testament*. 2nd ed. New York: United Bible Societies, 1994.

Millet, Robert L. *Grace Works*. Salt Lake City: Deseret, 2003.

Moo, Douglas J. *The Letter of James*. Pillar New Testament Commentary. Grand Rapids: Eerdmans, 2000.

———. *The Letter of James: An Introduction and Commentary*. TNTC. Grand Rapids: Eerdmans, 1985.

Moore, Scott R. "Affinities of the Epistle of James with Synagogue Homily and Midrash." M.A. Thesis: Denver Seminary, 2007.

Motyer, Alec. *The Message of James: The Tests of Faith*. Bible Speaks Today. Leicester: IVP, 1985.

Mounce, William D., ed. *Mounce's Complete Expository Dictionary of Old and New Testament Words*. Grand Rapids: Zondervan, 2006.

Nienhuis, David R. *Not by Paul Alone: The Formation of the Catholic Epistle Collection and the Christian Canon*. Waco, TX: Baylor University Press, 2007.

Nystrom, David. *James*. NIVAC. Grand Rapids: Zondervan, 1997.

Ortlund, Raymond., Jr. *God's Unfaithful Wife: A Biblical Theology of Spiritual Adultery*. Downers Grove, IL: IVP, 2003 (= *Whoredom: God's Unfaithful Wife in Biblical Theology*. Leicester: IVP; Grand Rapids: Eerdmans, 1996).

Painter, John. *Just James: The Brother of Jesus in History and Tradition*. Rev. ed. Columbia: University of South Carolina Press, 2004.

Penner, Todd C. *The Epistle of James and Eschatology: Re-reading an Ancient Christian Letter*. JSNTSup. Sheffield: SAP, 1996.

Perkins, Pheme. *First and Second Peter, James, and Jude*. Louisville: John Knox, 1995.

Popkes, Wiard. *Der Brief des Jakobus*. Leipzig: Evangelische Verlagsanstalt, 2001.

———. "New Testament Principles of Wholeness." *Evangelical Quarterly* 64 (1992): 319–32.

Porter, Stanley E. *Verbal Aspect in the Greek of the New Testament, with Reference to Tense and Mood*. New York: Peter Lang, 1989.

Richardson, Kurt A. *James*. New American Commentary. Nashville: Broadman & Holman, 1997.

Robertson, A. T. *Grammar of the Greek New Testament*. Nashville: Broadman, 1934.

———. *Word Pictures in the New Testament*. Vol. 6. Nashville: Broadman, 1933.

Rodin, R. Scott. *Stewards in the Kingdom: A Theology of Life in All Its Fulness*. Downers Grove, IL: IVP, 2000.

Rogers, Cleon L. Jr., and Cleon L. Rogers III. *The New Linguistic and Exegetical Key to the Greek New Testament*. Grand Rapids: Zondervan, 1998.

Ropes, James H. *A Critical and Exegetical Commentary on the Epistle of St. James*. International Critical Commentary. Edinburgh: T&T Clark, 1916.

Ruckstuhl, Eugen. *Jakobusbrief, 1–3 Johannesbrief*. Rev. ed. Wurzburg: Echter, 1988.

Scaer, David P. *James: The Apostle of Faith*. St. Louis: Concordia, 1993.

Scherer, Nic. "The Unity of God and the Duplicity of Humanity in the Letter of James." M.A. Thesis: Denver Seminary, 2007.

Schlosser, J., ed. *The Catholic Epistles and the Tradition*. Leuven: Leuven University Press and Peeters, 2004.

Schneider, John R. *The Good of Affluence: Seeking God in a Culture of Wealth*. Grand Rapids: Eerdmans, 2002.

Shanks, Hershel, and Ben Witherington III. *The Brother of Jesus: The Dramatic Story and Meaning of the First Archaeological Link to Jesus and His Family*. San Francisco: HarperSanFrancisco, 2003.

Sider, Ronald J. *Just Generosity: A New Vision for Overcoming Poverty in America*. Grand Rapids: Baker, 1999.

———. *Rich Christians in an Age of Hunger*. 4th ed. Dallas: Word, 1997.

Sine, Tom. *Mustard Seed versus McWorld: Reinventing Life and Faith for the Future*. Grand Rapids: Baker, 1999.

Sleeper, C. Freeman. *James*. Abingdon New Testament Commentary. Nashville: Abingdon, 1998.

Songer, Harold S. "James." Pages 100–140 in *The Broadman Bible Commentary*. Vol. 12, ed. Clifton J. Allen. Nashville: Broadman, 1972.

Stassen, Glen H. *Just Peacemaking: Ten Practices for Abolishing War*. Cleveland: Pilgrim, 1998.

———. *Just Peacemaking: Transforming Initiatives for Justice and Peace*. Louisville: WJKP, 1992.

Stulac, George M. *James*. IVP New Testament Commentary. Downers Grove, IL: IVP, 1993.

———. "Who Are 'The Rich' in James?" *Presbyterion* 16 (1990): 89–102.

Tamez, Elsa. *The Scandalous Message of James: Faith Without Works Is Dead*. Rev. ed. New York: Crossroad, 2002.

Taylor, Mark E. *A Text-Linguistic Investigation into the Discourse Structure of James*. London: T&T Clark, 2006.

Taylor, Mark H. "The Voice of the Prophets in the Letter of James." M.A. thesis. Denver Seminary, 2008.

Thomas, John Christopher. *The Devil, Disease and Deliverance: Origins of Illness in New Testament Thought*. JSNTSup. Sheffield: SAP, 1998.

Tidball, Derek. *Wisdom from Heaven: The Message of the Letter of James for Today*. Fearn, Scotland: Christian Focus, 2003.

Townsend, Michael J. *The Epistle of James*. London: Epworth, 1994.

Tsuji, Manabu. *Glaube zwischen Vollkommenheit und Verweltlichung: Eine Untersuchung zur literarischen Gestalt und zur inhaltlichen Kohärenz des Jakobusbriefes*. Tübingen: Mohr, 1997.

Wachob, Wesley H. *The Voice of Jesus in the Social Rhetoric of James*. Cambridge: CUP, 2000.

Wall, Robert W. *Community of the Wise: The Letter of James*. New Testament in Context. Valley Forge, PA: Trinity Press International, 1997.

Wallace, Daniel B. *Greek Grammar beyond the Basics*. Grand Rapids: Zondervan, 1996.

Webb, Robert L, and John S. Kloppenborg, eds. *Reading James with New Eyes: Methodological Reassessments of the Letter of James*. London: T&T Clark, 2007.

Weiss, D. Bernhard. *Das Neue Testament Handausgabe*. Vol. 3. Rev. ed. Leipzig: J. C. Hinrichs, 1902.

Willmer, Wesley K., and Martyn Smith. *God and Your Stuff: The Vital Link between Possessions and Your Soul*. Colorado Springs, CO: NavPress, 2002.

Witherington, Ben III. *Jesus the Sage: The Pilgrimage of Wisdom*. Minneapolis: Fortress, 1994.

———. *Letters and Homilies for Jewish Christians*. Downers Grove, IL: IVP, 2007.

Zodhiates, Spiros. *The Epistle of James and the Life of Faith*. Vol. 2. Grand Rapids: Eerdmans, 1959.

CHAPTER 1

James 1:1 – 11

Literary Context

The first verse of James's epistle contains all of the expected elements in a first-century Greco-Roman letter: the sender, the recipients, and a greeting. The rest of the document, however, does not resemble conventional epistolary format nearly as much. James pens no thanksgiving, no standard letter body (comprising information and exhortation, in that order), and no discernible letter closing. Instead, he immediately launches into the three key themes of his correspondence. First, he introduces them briefly in 1:2 – 11, and then he repeats them with some variation in 1:12 – 27. The letter body can be seen as beginning in 2:1, even though exhortation permeates everything he writes. James 1:2 – 4 introduce the topic of "trials" or "temptations" (πειρασμοί), vv. 5 – 8 emphasize the need for "wisdom" (σοφία), while vv. 9 – 11 turn to issues of riches and poverty.

James 1:12 – 18 begins the second cycle with a slightly expanded treatment of "trials or temptations," but whereas James focused on the positive potential of these tests as character-building experiences in his first cycle, here he treats them primarily as seductions to sin. James 1:19 – 26 focuses more on speech than on wisdom, but the two concepts are intertwined throughout 3:1 – 4:12; James apparently views them as closely linked. James 1:19 – 26 also stresses the need for obedience to God's Word. Finally, 1:27 highlights the widow and orphan, paradigms of the dispossessed, in keeping with the theme of riches and poverty, while simultaneously forming the thesis statement of the letter, thus keeping personal piety and social action closely linked.

James 1:12 forms a hinge between 1:2 – 11 and 1:13 – 18. The "trial" (πειρασμός) here remains the positive kind — a test to be passed — as in vv. 2 – 4. But conceptually, this text introduces vv. 13 – 18, which go on to speak of the proper Christian response to temptation (using forms of the cognate verb "test" or "tempt" [πειράζω]), whereas vv. 5 – 11 at best indirectly treat trials or tests. Nevertheless, despite the three discrete topics detectable in vv. 2 – 11, a thread seems to run through all three subsections. It is the trials discussed in vv. 2 – 4 that form the most immediate need to pray for wisdom (vv. 5 – 8). These trials, likely involving the economic exploitation by rich non-Christian landlords of largely impoverished Jewish-Christian peasants, likewise lead naturally to James's comments about rich and poor in vv. 9 – 11.[1]

- ➡ **I. Greetings (1:1)**
- **II. Statement of Three Key Themes (1:2 – 11)**
  - **A. Trials in the Christian Life (1:2 – 4)**
  - **B. Wisdom (1:5 – 8)**
  - **C. Riches and Poverty (1:9 – 11)**
- III. Restatement of the Three Themes (1:12 – 27)
  - A. Trials/Temptations in Relation to God (1:12 – 18)
  - B. Wisdom in the Areas of Speech and Obedience (1:19 – 26)
  - C. The "Have-Nots" and the Responsibility of the "Haves": The Thesis of the Letter (1:27)

Main Idea

Christians should respond to trials by rejoicing at the maturity they can foster, by asking God for wisdom, and by viewing them as leveling experiences that often invert the roles of rich and poor.

Translation

(See next page.)

Structure

V. 1 forms the standard letter introduction. Following that, the three key themes of James appear briefly, in turn, without any additional introductory formalities. While the trials of vv. 2 – 4 produce the need to ask for wisdom (vv. 5 – 8) and can involve economic exploitation (vv. 9 – 11), the three subsections of this text can be treated somewhat separately. Each subsection contains two main commands.

The initial treatment of trials calls believers to view them as opportunities for rejoicing (v. 2a).[2] The two subordinate adverbial clauses define the time and basis

1. Cf. the similar collocation of themes and language in *Exod. Rab.* 31:3: "Happy the man who can withstand the test, for there is none whom God does not prove. He tries the rich man to see if his hand will be opened unto the poor, and the poor man He tries in order to see whether he will accept chastisement without repining."

2. The NLT brings this out more explicitly with its dynamically equivalent translation, "whenever trouble comes your way, let it be an *opportunity* for joy ... your endurance has a *chance* to grow" (italics ours).

James 1:1-11

1a	Sender	James, a slave of God and of the Lord Jesus Christ,
b	Recipients	to the twelve tribes in the dispersion,
c	Greetings	greetings!
2a	Exhortation	**Consider it pure joy**, my brothers and sisters,
b	time	whenever you fall into various trials,
3	basis (of 2a)	because you know that the testing of your faith produces endurance.
4a	Exhortation	And **let endurance have its complete effect**
b	purpose	in order that you might be complete and whole
c	apposition	lacking in nothing.
5a	condition	Now if any of you lacks wisdom,
b	Exhortation	**you should ask from the God**
c	description	who gives to all without hesitation or
d	alternative	mocking
e	Result (of 5b)	and **it will be given to you**.
6a	Expansion (of 5b)	But **ask in faith**,
b	restatement	in no way doubting;
c	illustration (of 8ab)	for the one who doubts is like a wave of the sea,
d	description	blown by the wind and
e	expansion	tossed about;
7	basis (of 6ab)	for that person must not suppose that they will receive anything from the Lord;
8a	expansion (of 6ab)	[for that] person is double-minded,
b	apposition	unstable in all their ways.
9	Exhortation	**Let the believer in humiliating circumstances boast in their exalted position.**
10a	Contrast	But **[let] the rich person [boast] in their humiliation**,
b	illustration (of 11c)	because like a flower of the grass they will pass away;
11a	expansion	for the sun rises with its scorching wind and
b	series	the grass withers and
		its flower falls and
		its beautiful appearance is destroyed;
c	basis (of 10a)	in the same way, **the rich will fade away** in the midst of their daily life.

for this command. Not just in some situations but "whenever" trials beset a person (v. 2b), one must rejoice, because the circumstances can build character — in this case most notably by fostering perseverance (v. 3a). The second imperative follows from this specific ethical observation: believers must allow perseverance to mold them into what God wants (v. 4a). The purpose for this command is stated positively and then restated negatively. As Christians grow, they come closer and closer to maturity or wholeness, that is, to a state in which they no longer remain significantly spiritually deficient (v. 4bc).

The first command in the subsection on wisdom enjoins believers to ask God for it (v. 5b). Subordinate to this imperative are a condition for asking and a description of the nature of the God who is addressed. In response to proper asking, God promises to bestow the wisdom requested. The condition for asking is if someone has a need (v. 5a). The description portrays God as eager to give and as not "criticizing" (HCSB) the petitioner (v. 5cd). The result of asking for wisdom is receiving it (v. 5e).

The second command repeats but also elaborates the first: asking should be done with faith or, phrased negatively, without doubting (vv. 6ab). Three parallel clauses begin explicitly or implicitly with a "for" (γάρ). The second of these supplies the actual basis for the elaborated command to ask with faith and without doubt; otherwise God will not grant the petitioner anything (v. 7). The third offers an expansion of this rationale: such petitioners do not clearly believe that God is the source of all wisdom; thus they waver between dual allegiance to God and some other "god" or "gods" (v. 8ab; cf. 4:4).[3] The first clause provides an illustration of the rationale: such wavering resembles the billowing of the waves in a wind-blown sea (v. 6c). The illustration actually precedes the rationale and its expansion, perhaps to help the listeners better understand and/or accept James's explanations when he presents them.

The third subsection pairs its two commands right at the outset. Materially poor believers are called to rejoice in their lofty spiritual position, with all of the privileges that God promises Christians (v. 9). In striking contrast, rich believers are called to rejoice in their abased spiritual position, acknowledging total dependence on God for everything good (v. 10a). Once again, an illustration precedes the principle being illustrated. Even rich people's lives are remarkably fragile and transient, like the short-lived wildflowers of the field (v. 10b). This comparison is expanded by the series of descriptions of how these flowers wither so rapidly (v. 11ab). James concludes with the point of the illustration: rich people likewise die all too quickly and even unexpectedly (v. 11c). This undeniable observation from life-experience thus forms the basis for James's implied exhortation for the rich not to trust in their possessions, a warning that forms the "flip side" of his explicit command for them to humble themselves before God (v. 10a).

3. It is possible that we are not meant to supply a "for" (γάρ) at the beginning of v. 8 but allow the sentence to stand asyndetically juxtaposed to v. 7 for emphasis, expanding the description of the person who doubts. Considerably less likely is the HCSB: "An indecisive man is unstable ..." — a rendering that leaves v. 8 conceptually almost unconnected to what precedes it.

Exegetical Outline

- **I. Greetings (1:1)**
- **II. Statement of Three Key Themes (1:2 – 11)**
  - **A. Christians Should Respond to Trials by Rejoicing at the Maturity They Can Foster (vv. 2 – 4).**
    1. They should count them as grounds for thorough joy (vv. 2 – 3).
    2. They should allow perseverance to lead them to maturity (v. 4).
  - **B. Christians Should Respond to Trials by Asking God for Wisdom (vv. 5 – 8).**
    1. They must ask, sometimes persistently, and they will receive (v. 5a-d).
    2. The assured result is that God will give wisdom (v. 5e).
    3. The manner of prayer must be with faith that does not doubt that God can give (vv. 6 – 8).
       - a. This is because the doubter is unstable, like turbulent sea waves (v. 6).
       - b. This is because the doubter will receive nothing from the Lord (v. 7).
       - c. [This is because] the doubter is torn between two allegiances (v. 8).
  - **C. Christians Should Respond to Trials by Viewing Them As Leveling Experiences That Often Invert the Roles of Rich and Poor (vv. 9 – 11).**
    1. Poor Christians must boast in their exalted position (v. 9).
    2. Rich Christians must boast in their humble position (vv. 10 – 11).

Explanation of Text

James 1:1 James, a slave of God and of the Lord Jesus Christ, to the twelve tribes in the dispersion, greetings! (Ἰάκωβος θεοῦ καὶ κυρίου Ἰησοῦ Χριστοῦ δοῦλος ταῖς δώδεκα φυλαῖς ταῖς ἐν τῇ διασπορᾷ χαίρειν). The Greek name for James might easily have come down to English as Jacob. But in Latin the alternate rendering *Jacomus* developed alongside *Jacobus*, so that a number of modern European languages now have two male names from the same linguistic root.[4] "Slave" preserves the sense of the Greek word here (δοῦλος) better than "servant." Christians committed themselves to Jesus as their absolute divine master just as actual slaves had to swear unconditional allegiance to their human masters.[5]

Because "slave" is anarthrous, "God" and "Lord" follow suit, which means that Granville Sharp's rule, in which two singular, personal, nonproper nouns joined by a coordinating conjunction and governed by a single article refer to the identical entity, does not come into play. But except for the article, all of the necessary elements are present, so this *could* be an early equation of Jesus with God.[6] He is, at the very least, Master and Messiah (Lord and Christ). "The Lord Jesus Christ" is the fullest of the many combinations of the name Jesus with various titles or appellations in the NT.[7]

4. *OED*, 5:549.
5. See esp. throughout Murray J. Harris, *Slave of Christ: A New Testament Metaphor for Total Devotion to Christ* (Leicester: Apollos, 1999).
6. Cf. Alec Motyer, *The Message of James: The Tests of Faith* (BTS; Leicester: IVP, 1985), 27.
7. See further Craig L. Blomberg, "Messiah in the New Testament," in *Israel's Messiah in the Bible and the Dead Sea Scrolls*, ed. Richard S. Hess and M. Daniel Carroll R. (Grand Rapids: Baker, 2003), 111 – 41.

Commentators have often marveled that James does not refer to himself either as an apostle (cf. Gal 1:19) or as Jesus' brother, and some have used these omissions as an argument for pseudonymity. Most likely, however, James is implying that his familial relationship to Jesus gives him no extra authority, while his addressees would have already known of his role as chief elder in Jerusalem. Instead, he wants to stress that he is a fellow slave to God in Christ, just like his readers.[8] Indeed, it seems less likely that a pseudepigrapher would have used so nonauthoritative a descriptor.[9]

As we discussed in our introduction (pp. 28 – 29), "the twelve tribes in the dispersion" most likely refer to a collection of Jewish-Christian congregations somewhere outside Israel toward the eastern end of the Mediterranean basin, perhaps in Syria. "Greetings" (χαίρειν) forms the rough equivalent of our English "hello" and appears as the most common form of salutation in letter introductions of the day.[10]

James 1:2 Consider it pure joy, my brothers and sisters, whenever you fall into various trials (Πᾶσαν χαρὰν ἡγήσασθε, ἀδελφοί μου, ὅταν πειρασμοῖς περιπέσητε ποικίλοις). James begins his preliminary discussion of trials in this verse, introducing the theme of joy in the midst of the trial. He addresses the "brothers and sisters" (ἀδελφοί), that is, fellow Christians. It is important to stress that this word remains gender inclusive when referring to coreligionists, unless context clearly dictates otherwise. In contemporary contexts in which "brothers" no longer automatically connotes both genders, faithfulness to the original meaning requires an inclusive language translation.[11]

This verse starts off with the command to "consider it all joy," an imperative that has been highly abused in interpretation. First, the word for "all" (πᾶσαν) does not mean "everything" in this context, but functions adjectivally here, implying "pure" or "entire." In other words, it does not form part of the direct object ("Consider *everything*") but identifies the type of joy one should have.[12] "Joy" (χαράν), in turn, speaks of a state of being rather than an emotion.[13] Joy proves quite different from happiness, so that this verse does *not* support the idea that a Christian must smile all the time! Joy may be defined as a settled contentment in every situation or "an unnatural reaction of deep, steady and unadulterated thankful trust in God."[14] Here appears our first example of James's use of a linking- or catch-word (recall p. 23), in this case with "greetings" (χαίρειν) in v. 1. This technique helps to tie together patterns of thought and ideas while moving the argument forward.[15]

8. "Thus the designation combines the softness of humility and the strength of authority in an integrated vision of leadership under the lordship of God" (Guthrie, "James," 210).

9. Hartin (*James*, 51) adds that by not further identifying himself, the author leads his readers to assume that he is the most well-known early Christian leader named James at that time.

10. Burchard, *Der Jakobusbrief*, 50. For examples, see John McRay, *Paul: His Life and Teaching* (Grand Rapids: Baker, 2003), 265 – 68.

11. A point acknowledged even by Vern S. Poythress and Wayne A. Grudem in *The Gender-Neutral Bible Controversy: Muting the Masculinity of God's Words* (Nashville: Broadman & Holman, 2000), 263 – 68, who severely criticize inclusive-language translations of the Bible at numerous other junctures.

12. Johnson (*The Letter of James*, 176) offers "consider it entirely as joy" as a translation of this line.

13. Patrick J. Hartin ("The Call to be Perfect through Suffering [James 1,2 – 4]: The Concept of Perfection in the Epistle of James and in the Sermon on the Mount," *Bib* 77 [1996]: 477) notes that in James, "joy emerges as the proper response in situations where one's faith is tested."

14. Derek Tidball, *Wisdom from Heaven: The Message of the Letter of James for Today* (Fearn, Scotland: Christian Focus, 2003), 22.

15. William F. Brosend II (*James and Jude* [NCBC; Cambridge: CUP, 2004], 34) calls this technique *gradatio*, which he describes as "literally a ladder leading the reader from one

The third key piece of this opening command is the verb "consider" (ἡγήσασθε). This is a verb of thought rather than emotion. James is not commanding how one should *feel*, but rather how one should *think* about one's circumstances.[16] Thus one is to "consider" or "reckon" any given difficult circumstance as "pure joy."[17]

We should have this settled attitude "whenever" (ὅταν) we "fall into" (from περιπίπτω[18]) trials (cf. NET). James is not instructing his readers to seek out hardships, but this is the attitude that he wants them to have *when* external testing arrives. The root of the word for "trials" (πειρασμοῖς) offers a range of meanings, denoting either "an outward trial or process of 'testing' or … the inner enticement to sin."[19] Here the former remains clearly in view. James highlights that Christianity does not shelter one from any adversity; Christians *will* face trials.[20] The concern here, however, is how each person will respond. Lastly, by describing them as "various" (ποικίλοις), James shows that he provides instruction not just for one specific kind of test but for many.

James 1:3 … because you know that the testing of your faith produces endurance (γινώσκοντες ὅτι τὸ δοκίμιον ὑμῶν τῆς πίστεως κατεργάζεται ὑπομονήν). This verse introduces the rationale behind the command of the previous verse: *why* we should count it all joy. James begins with the causal participle, "knowing" (γινώσκοντες). He explains how his audience can be joyful — "because you know. . . ." The content of what they know is the purpose of their trials. God allows them in order to test us, or even better, to "prove" us.[21] The noun "testing" (δοκίμιον)[22] has a different root than before (when it was πειρασμοῖς); the implication here is of testing that leads to approval, a proving of the worth of something (cf. ASV).

This approval produces "endurance" (ὑπομονήν), a key value for James.[23] The RSV captures the active nature of this patience, calling it "steadfastness," for this is not a passive virtue but a steady clinging to the truth within any situation. Tamez expresses it as "militant patience,"[24] embracing the idea that James does not advocate a downtrodden passivity, but rather an engaged waiting (cf. NEB, "fortitude"), a concept foreign to our culture in which patience is often considered letting others walk over us. In short, "endurance is faith stretched out."[25]

---

rung to the next." James also shows a remarkable use of alliteration in this verse, linking "trials" (πειρασμοῖς), "fall into" (περιπέσητε), and "various" (ποικίλοις) together.

16. D. Edmond Hiebert (*The Epistle of James: Tests of a Living Faith* [Chicago: Moody Press, 1979], 71) calls this a settled conviction because of the aorist tense of this command. While in many contexts, this may be to "abuse" the aorist, here it seems to work well.

17. William R. Baker ("James," in William R. Baker and Paul Carrier, *James-Jude* [Cincinnati: Standard, 1990], 18) notes that "problems are to be viewed with joy not because we actually enjoy them, but because they are part of God's plan for us."

18. BDAG (804) notes that this verb, as here, often takes a dative direct object.

19. Moo, *The Letter of James*, 53. We will see the latter meaning in 1:13 – 14.

20. David E. Garland, "Severe Trials, Good Gifts, and Pure Religion," *RevExp* 83 (1986): 384.

21. Philip Yancey (*Where Is God When It Hurts?* [Grand Rapids: Zondervan, 1977], 15) refers to an incident in which Helmut Thielicke responded to the question of what the greatest defect of American Christianity was with the reply that we have an "inadequate view of suffering."

22. Marie E. Isaacs ("Suffering in the Lives of Christians: James 1:2 – 19a," *RevExp* 97 [2000]: 185) explains that τὸ δοκίμιον is "that which has withstood the test and proved to be genuine." This textual variant is to be preferred to the minority reading of "genuineness" (δόκιμον); see Johnson (*The Letter of James*, 177) for further explanation.

23. Eugene H. Peterson captures this well with his book title, *A Long Obedience in the Same Direction*, rev. ed. (Downers Grove, IL: IVP, 2000), an expression borrowed from Friedrich Nietzsche!

24. Tamez, *The Scandalous Message of James*, 14.

25. Bruce B. Barton, David R. Veerman, and Neil Wilson, *James* (Wheaton: Tyndale, 1992), 7.

James 1:4 And let endurance have its complete effect, in order that you might be complete and whole, lacking in nothing (ἡ δὲ ὑπομονὴ ἔργον τέλειον ἐχέτω, ἵνα ἦτε τέλειοι καὶ ὁλόκληροι ἐν μηδενὶ λειπόμενοι). James continues his pattern of using catchwords to move an idea forward, here expanding on the concept of "endurance" (ὑπομονή). He insists that we let this tenacity accomplish all God intends for it. The present imperative "let have" (ἐχέτω) calls "for the continuation of an action in progress."[26] James describes this work as "perfect" or "complete" (τέλειον).[27] This expression can denote not only perfection but maturity, as frequently in the OT with the Hebrew equivalent *tāmîm*. Both meanings seem intended here: we can aspire to maturity in this lifetime, but we will ultimately attain perfection in the eschaton. As believers, we must constantly strive for perfection, even while knowing that we will never fully reach it until our resurrection and glorification.[28]

James moves on, expanding the purpose of the endurance. Perseverance itself is not the ultimate goal; James has something greater in mind. He repeats the idea of maturity or perfection, qualifying it with "whole" or "complete" (ὁλόκληρος). This word summarizes what a Christian should become, stressing "the incremental character of the process" in which "perfection is not just a maturing of character, but a rounding out as more and more 'parts' of the righteous character are added."[29] In case "complete and whole" are not clear enough, James also supplies the corresponding negative descriptor, "lacking in nothing" (ἐν μηδενὶ λειπόμενοι). This predicate participle describes the nature of a mature Christian who has successfully come through testing. Johnson adds that James's seeming redundancy "provides the moral edge to the exhortation," for in "moral or spiritual realities, 'lacking' means 'falling short.'"[30]

James 1:5 Now if any of you lacks wisdom, you should ask from the God who gives to all without hesitation or mocking and it will be given to you (Εἰ δέ τις ὑμῶν λείπεται σοφίας, αἰτείτω παρὰ τοῦ διδόντος θεοῦ πᾶσιν ἁπλῶς καὶ μὴ ὀνειδίζοντος καὶ δοθήσεται αὐτῷ). James next discusses a crucial attribute for spiritual maturity and wholeness. This verse begins with a first-class conditional statement, which assumes that people will lack wisdom. Vv. 5 – 8 tie in with vv. 2 – 4 by the catchword "lack" (from λείπω), but here the focus shifts slightly by highlighting a key attribute that Christians must not lack as they move toward maturity. The conceptual link with the previous section, however, appears when we understand that wisdom is often precisely that which enables us to stand in times of trials and which leads us to perfection.

"Wisdom" remains crucial throughout James, referring to "the endowment of heart and mind which is needed for the right conduct of life."[31] In the Bible in general, wisdom does not equate with mere knowledge or intelligence but adds the practical element of living out what one believes, and James holds true to that tradition.[32] Scholars

26. Cleon L. Rogers Jr. and Cleon L. Rogers III, *The New Linguistic and Exegetical Key to the Greek New Testament* (Grand Rapids: Zondervan, 1998), 552.

27. Johnson (*The Letter of James*, 178) observes that "it is the deed or effect of endurance that is 'perfect,'" not necessarily the person.

28. Cf. esp. Martin, *James*, 17.

29. Davids, *The Epistle of James*, 70. George M. Stulac (*James* [Downers Grove, IL: IVP, 1993], 38) describes the importance of this verse as showing that "perseverance turns out to be not the end in itself, but rather the lifestyle by which the servant of Jesus Christ attains maturity."

30. Johnson, *The Letter of James*, 179.

31. F. J. A. Hort, as quoted in Raymond B. Brown, "The Message of the Book of James for Today," *RevExp* 66 (1969): 418.

32. This sense is thoroughly Jewish, and there is a consistent tradition that it comes only from the Lord; cf. Pr 2:6;

debate the relationship between wisdom and the Holy Spirit in James, because the latter appears only in 4:5 (if even there), while the "wisdom from above" (3:17 – 18) closely resembles the fruit of the Spirit in Paul (Gal 5:22 – 23).[33] While there does seem to be a great deal of overlap in their roles (see below, pp. 178 – 79), this verse indicates that they cannot be entirely equated, because believers would not lack the Holy Spirit.[34]

James next tells the person lacking wisdom to "ask" (αἰτείτω) of God. This is one "lack that cannot be made up by human effort, for it is a gift of God and must therefore be asked of him."[35] No matter how hard we try to work toward perfection, we cannot fill the lack of wisdom without God's generosity. The injunction to ask is a third person imperative, a more rhetorically indirect form that still retains the force of a command.[36] The present tense of "ask" suggests possible ongoing action — repeated or continuous prayer — and combined with "it will be given" (δοθήσεται) likely reflects James's knowledge of the Jesus tradition behind Mt 7:7 already in Greek.[37] We are told to ask of the "giving God" (διδόντος θεοῦ). Here the present participle suggests that "giving" represents a continuous characteristic of God.[38] More surprising, perhaps, is the promise that God gives "to all" (πᾶσιν), showing his nature as the one who gives whether or not we deserve it.

James further describes God's giving with a term (ἁπλῶς) that can mean either "singly" or "generously." Moo opts for the idea of singleness of heart or "integrity," a "linguistic move [that] would make sense in light of James's tendency to portray Christian character as a reflection and outgrowth of God's." He argues that James is not trying to show God's generosity in giving but rather God's "single, undivided intent to give us those gifts we need to please him."[39] Johnson, however, believes that "in connection with the verb 'giving,' the adverb probably should be seen in the light of the use of *haplotēs* in such contexts to mean 'generosity/liberality.' "[40] Davids argues for a different take on the option of "single-mindedness," namely, that the combination of this word (ἁπλῶς) with "not mocking" (μὴ ὀνειδίζοντος) encourages the meaning of "without mental reservation," and sees God as one who "gives sincerely, without hesitation."[41] This last interpretation seems viable both from the word's derivation from "single, sincere, straightforward" (ἁπλοῦς), as well from the context. In any case, ἁπλῶς clearly contrasts with the double-mindedness depicted in the next verse, where the person's "lack of unity ... will undermine the request."[42]

8:22 – 31; 9:10; Sir 1:1; 24:23; 39:5 - 6; 51:17; Wis 8:21; 9:6. Martin (*James*, 17) points out that wisdom differs from intelligence in that it has both moral and experiential overtones. Proverbs 1:7 implies "devotion to Yahweh and a resolve to walk in the ways of his law" as the source and definition of wisdom.

33. For the equation, see esp. J. Andrew Kirk, "The Meaning of Wisdom in James: Examination of a Hypothesis," *NTS* 16 (1969): 24 – 38.

34. See esp. Mariam J. Kamell, "Wisdom in James: An Examination and Comparison of the Roles of Wisdom and the Holy Spirit" (M.A. thesis, Denver Seminary, 2003).

35. Sophie Laws, *The Epistle of James* (London: Black, 1980), 54.

36. While we will often render these as "*let* him/her [do something]," this translation could suggest that one is merely granting permission. It is important to recall that a sense of "should" or "ought" still attaches to the command.

37. Bauckham (*James*, 85 – 86) sees vv. 5 – 6 as an expansion of Mt 7:11/Lk 11:13 that is an important "creative re-expression of the wisdom of Jesus by his disciple the sage James."

38. James H. Ropes (*A Critical and Exegetical Commentary on the Epistle of St. James* [ICC; Edinburgh: T&T Clark, 1916], 139) points out that believing in this attribute of God forms a motivation for prayer.

39. Moo, *The Letter of James*, 59. Cf. Martin, *James*, 18.

40. Johnson, *The Letter of James*, 179. Cf. Laws, *The Epistle of James*, 55.

41. Davids, *The Epistle of James*, 72 – 73. Cf. Wall, *Community of the Wise*, 52; Maier, *Der Brief des Jakobus*, 62.

42. Brosend, *James and Jude*, 36.

Interestingly, James promises that God does not mock or reproach (μὴ ὀνειδίζοντος) us when we request wisdom, so there is no need to feel shame when coming to him. He will not belittle our stupidity. Instead, James insists that "[it] will be given" (δοθήσεται) to the one asking.[43] This promise begs the question of *what* will be given. Does God promise to give us the outline for our lives if we ask, or to give us complete clarity on every decision we might ever need to make? No, he promises wisdom, namely, the ability to discern *how* he would have us live. This is not an unqualified statement that everything we ask for will be given to us, but rather that we will receive the practical knowledge and understanding we need to endure our trials when we ask the God whom we know gives without hesitation. Because of the "you (pl.)" (ὑμῶν) earlier in the verse, it creates better English style, while preserving the gender-inclusiveness of the pronoun, to translate "to him or her" (αὐτῷ) at the end of the sentence with the corresponding second person plural (cf. TNIV).

James 1:6 But ask in faith in no way doubting; for the one who doubts is like a wave of the sea blown by the wind and tossed about (αἰτείτω δὲ ἐν πίστει μηδὲν διακρινόμενος· ὁ γὰρ διακρινόμενος ἔοικεν κλύδωνι θαλάσσης ἀνεμιζομένῳ καὶ ῥιπιζομένῳ). James now gives the condition required for receiving from the Lord: faith. He again begins with a linking word, here the command "ask" (αἰτείτω), repeating the more indirect third person form. He qualifies his command with respect to *how* to ask and *how not* to ask. Laws therefore suggests that James is turning to the idea of unanswered prayer.[44]

James describes the way we ought to ask as "in faith in no way doubting" (ἐν πίστει μηδὲν διακρινόμενος). Here "faith" refers not to initial belief, but to a continuing confidence in the identity and nature of our God.[45] We are also told not to doubt (cf. Mk 11:23 par.), another command that has often been misinterpreted in the history of the church. James does not demand that a believer never question what God gives them, lest their faith prove null and void. Rather, given the context, he maintains that we should not doubt the *character* of God as one who gives unflinchingly.[46] To doubt his character can also imply that a person is unwilling to trust God with their life or that they do not believe that he is who he claims to be.[47]

To this kind of doubt James strenuously objects. He describes the one who questions God's character as "a wave of the sea, blown by the wind and tossed about" (κλύδωνι θαλάσσης ἀνεμιζομένῳ καὶ ῥιπιζομένῳ). This image was used by classical writers to refer to the ordinary instability of the sea, not just to times of storm,[48] depicting the

43. This is an example of the divine passive, with God as the implied subject.

44. Laws, *The Epistle of James*, 56.

45. Ropes (*A Critical and Exegetical Commentary on the Epistle of St. James*, 140) observes that faith forms a "fundamental religious attitude" in all areas of life, far more than just the trust that one will receive what one asks for. Meanwhile, the one who doubts is a person "whose allegiance wavers, not one tormented by speculative intellectual questionings, which do not fall within James's horizons."

46. Kistemaker (*James and the Epistles of John*, 40) offers Ac 2:12 as an example of a place where doubt or perplexity was not sinful, but instead led to further faith. Cf. also the father's cry for faith in Mk 9:24. Baker ("James," 20) adds that "the primary problem is not the amount of confidence the petitioner has when he utters his prayer. Rather, the problem is that he does not have confidence in the nature of God generally," thus *contra* the "name-it-and-claim-it" heresy.

47. Abraham becomes the prime biblical example of faith (see esp. Ro 4:20; Heb 11:8 – 10), and he clearly at times doubted God's promises. Still, over the years he displayed far more trust than doubt in God. It is this sort of overall integrity of faith throughout life that God is looking for in his followers.

48. Ropes, *A Critical and Exegetical Commentary on the Epistle of St. James*, 142.

constant moving up and down of waves without consistency or pattern. Moo elaborates: "the picture here is not of a wave mounting in height and crashing to shore, but of the swell of the sea, never having the same texture and shape from moment to moment, but always changing with the variations in wind direction and strength."[49] This provides the perfect image of the doubting person who oscillates between faith and skepticism, unwilling to trust in Christ once for all and to stay the course in allegiance to him.

James 1:7 For that person must not suppose that they will receive anything from the Lord (μὴ γὰρ οἰέσθω ὁ ἄνθρωπος ἐκεῖνος ὅτι λήμψεταί τι παρὰ τοῦ κυρίου). James next draws out the consequences of doubting. The demonstrative pronoun "that" (ἐκεῖνος) makes crystal clear the identity of the person James is discussing — the doubter from v. 6. The pronoun also connotes a sense of disdain. The "man" or "person" (ὁ ἄνθρωπος) here is clearly gender inclusive, for doubting is not something that only men do! James declares that this kind of person must not expect anything (οἰέσθω ... ὅτι λήμψεταί τι) from God. Ropes finds a negative sense in "suppose" (οἰέσθω), conveying the idea of wrong judgment.[50] Martin expands the concept, convinced that the word "speaks of a person marked by irresolution where moral choices are concerned."[51] Thus, as Brosend explains, this expression is "easily analogous to situations of indecision or rapidly changing opinions,"[52] an attitude not congruent with God's unity of purpose.

James 1:8 For that person is double-minded, unstable in all their ways (ἀνὴρ δίψυχος, ἀκατάστατος ἐν πάσαις ταῖς ὁδοῖς αὐτοῦ). Here James concludes his discussion about the doubter. This is the first time he uses the term that normally carries the more specific meaning of "male" (ἀνήρ) as opposed to the more generic use of "man" or "person" (ἄνθρωπος). Here, however, ἀνήρ clearly refers back to the same person discussed in vv. 5 – 7 (the doubter). Moo and Carson both suspect that James's idiolect (his distinctive use of certain words and grammatical forms) have turned "male" (ἀνήρ) and "man" (ἄνθρωπος) into complete synonyms[53] (akin to "human" and "person"), a hypothesis worth testing as we proceed through the epistle.

James appears anomalous also in that his is the earliest known usage of the word "double-minded" (δίψυχος), having perhaps coined the term. Its only other scriptural use comes in 4:8, where it appears as parallel to "sinners," giving the word a negative moral taint.[54] It thus seems to mean "being uncertain about the truth of someth[ing], *doubting, hesitating*, lit. *double-minded*,"[55] depicting some-

49. Moo, *The Letter of James*, 61.

50. Ropes, *A Critical and Exegetical Commentary on the Epistle of St. James*, 142. BDAG (701, bold-face type omitted) defines the word (οἴομαι) as "to consider someth. to be true but with a component of tentativeness, *think, suppose, expect*." Thus the noncommittal element seems to form part of the word's meaning.

51. Martin, *James*, 20.

52. Brosend, *James and Jude*, 37.

53. Moo, *The Letter of James*, 62; D. A. Carson, *The Inclusive Language Debate: A Plea for Realism* (Grand Rapids: Baker, 1998), 162. Tellingly, Poythress and Grudem (*The Gender-Neutral Bible Controversy*) include no discussion of this verse.

54. Stanley E. Porter ("Is *dipsuchos* [James 1,8; 4,8] a 'Christian' Word?" *Bib* 71 [1990]: 469 – 98) concludes that "double-minded" (δίψυχος) is a "Christian" word in the sense that it appears solely in Christian literature through at least the second century. He also argues for this as an instance of a Christian writer not merely reacting to his culture, but also being creative in his writing. Laws (*The Epistle of James*, 58) points out the "idea of doubleness as the essence of sin, as found in the OT (e.g. Ps. xii.2; 1 Chron. xii.33; Ecclus. i.28)."

55. BDAG, 253 (bold-face type omitted). It lies clearly in opposition to the pure, single-minded nature of God shown in v. 5.

one Ropes describes as having their "soul divided between faith and the world."[56] This echoes Jesus' statements in Mt 6:24 (par. Lk 16:13) that no one can serve two masters. The theme is picked up just prior to James's second use of "double-minded" in 4:8 when he rephrases this theme of Jesus in 4:4, thus even more clearly supporting the link to Jesus' teaching. To be thus divided in one's soul renders one useless for the kingdom. This statement has its background in the OT theology of loving God with an undivided heart (cf. Dt 6:5; 18:13), here contrasting that with the person who is hypocritical, a faithless person "not wholly devoted to the fear of God."[57]

James calls this double-minded person "unstable" (ἀκατάστατος), a word that some argue has overtones of rebellion but probably has more to do with unsteadiness. A double-minded person is "unstable, restless, [or] vacillating."[58] Such people may not be willfully rebellious, but they are often unwilling to commit to anything and thus prove unreliable. One cannot necessarily depend on them.

The last phrase, "in all their ways" (ἐν πάσαις ταῖς ὁδοῖς αὐτοῦ), shows them to be consistently inconsistent throughout their lives.[59] This verse sheds further light on the original question of who is a doubter and what it means to be double-minded: these are people who are unwilling to let go of the world and truly follow Christ, torn between sin and obedience, reluctant to let go of the pleasures of the world for the sake of discipleship. This description hits close to home in an age of nominal Christians who attend church from time to time, perhaps even regularly, but who refuse to let God interfere with their daily lives and goals.

James 1:9 Let the believer in humiliating circumstances boast in their exalted position (καυχάσθω δὲ ὁ ἀδελφὸς ὁ ταπεινὸς ἐν τῷ ὕψει αὐτοῦ). Vv. 9 – 11 introduce the topic of wealth and poverty and unfold the startling reversal in roles between rich and poor.[60] James begins with the present tense imperative to "boast" (καυχάσθω), normally a negative concept referring to an inappropriate expression of pride or inflated sense of righteousness. Outside of this verse and 4:16, all the other appearances in the NT come in Paul, and many of them are negative. The verb, however, can also have the "positive meaning of rejoicing or glorying in God, which comes from the OT."[61] Given James's dependence on the thought world of the OT, it is not surprising that he uses it in this sense.

But whom does James tell to boast? It is the "poor brother" (ὁ ἀδελφὸς ὁ ταπεινός), or the "believer in humiliating circumstances."[62] The word "poor" (ταπεινός) has its background in the Hebrew *ʿānāw*, with its nuance of "humble" or "lowly."[63] The LXX uses this word "to depict a person who is of little significance in the world's

56. Ropes, *A Critical and Exegetical Commentary on the Epistle of St. James*, 143. Cf. Wallace I. Wolverton, "The Double-Minded Man in the Light of Essene Psychology," *AThR* 38 (1956): 166 – 75.

57. Davids, *The Epistle of James*, 74.

58. BDAG, 35.

59. Cf. Laws, *The Epistle of James*, 61.

60. Martin (*James*, 24) points out a conceptual link with the previous section: while riches often lead to temptations, poverty usually produces trials.

61. Davids, *The Epistle of James*, 76, citing Ps 32:11; 149:5. H. H. Drake Williams ("Of Rags and Riches: The Benefits of Hearing Jeremiah 9:23 – 24 within James 1:9 – 11," *TynBul* 53 [2002]: 273) sees Jer 9:23 – 24 as essential background for understanding the identity of the rich person as a believer in this passage.

62. Maynard-Reid (*Poverty and Wealth in James*, 38) notes that "the question of the poor person's situation is high on the agenda of James" because "it appears so early in the document." If this letter was written in the late 40s, then the poverty implied here could have been caused by the recent famine, depicted in Ac 11:27 – 30, in which Christians, ostracized by much of the populace, would have suffered particularly severely.

63. Edgar (*Has God Not Chosen the Poor?* 147 – 48) adds

evaluation, even one who is oppressed by the world."[64] Martin explains the various terms James uses for poor, showing that "poor" (ταπεινός) usually implies the social status of James's readers and "poor" (πτωχός) their economic state, and that the former refers to those who are poor because of their religious choice to follow Christ.[65] Hence the people under discussion in this paragraph are literally poor, but they are not the totally destitute described in 2:2, 5 – 6, 15 – 16, and James uses this term to highlight their spiritual state of humility as well.

James thus does contrast the physically rich and poor as literal opposites in this paragraph, but potentially alludes to their spiritual state as well. These poor are clearly Christians, however, since James calls this one a "brother" (ἀδελφός), a word primarily used in the Bible for fellow believers. This distinction is important to help clarify that James does not direct his command to boast as applicable to all poor people in general. Rather, he addresses the believing poor in the communities to which he writes.

James encourages his audience to glory in their "height" or "exalted position" (ὕψει). Is this elevated status some kind of *current* spiritual progress that is more advanced because of their poverty (see also on 2:5)? If scarcity of goods inherently improves one's spirituality, no biblical text would ever command help for the poor! Far more likely is the view that sees James as referring to our promised exaltation in the life to come. Focusing on our future destiny can, of course, begin to reframe our perspectives on the present as well, as we look beyond our socioeconomic status and begin to see the world through God's eyes.[66]

James 1:10 But [let] the rich person [boast] in their humiliation, because like a flower of the grass they will pass away (ὁ δὲ πλούσιος ἐν τῇ ταπεινώσει αὐτοῦ, ὅτι ὡς ἄνθος χόρτου παρελεύσεται). This verse turns to the opposite category, "the rich" (ὁ πλούσιος). These people must be seen as literally wealthy. They are not called "brothers" (ἀδελφοί), which raises the question of whether or not they refer to Christians. Because this debate involves information from all three verses in this subsection, we will treat the issue in an excursus after our discussion of v. 11. These rich people are told to boast[67] in their "humiliation" (ταπεινώσει), a noun derived from ταπεινός, the substantive used in v. 9 and thus a further example of word linking. It would make little sense to glory in physical destitution, so presumably James intends some kind of spiritual humbling.

James may also be reminding the rich that they will die like everyone else and thus forfeit all their material possessions (cf. Lk 12:16 – 21). In a sense James anticipates the modern slogan that "the person who dies with the most toys still dies!"[68] If James is referring to non-Christians, then his

that the "word means humble, of lowly standing, in a servile or subservient position," which would often indicate poverty, but the two do not necessarily equate. He states that "whether the term should be seen to mean 'subservience to God' or 'subservient in society' is not immediately clear, but the two nuances are not mutually exclusive." Craig L. Blomberg (*Neither Poverty nor Riches: A Biblical Theology of Possessions* [Leicester: IVP, 1999], 149) notes that in this context, contrasted with the materially rich, this word "becomes a virtual synonym for the financially impoverished."

64. Moo, *The Letter of James*, 64.

65. Martin, *James*, 23.

66. Cf. Douglas J. Moo, *The Letter of James: An Introduction and Commentary* (TNTC; Grand Rapids: Eerdmans, 1985), 67: "exaltation includes the believer's present enjoyment of his exalted spiritual status as well as his hope of participating in the glorious eternal kingdom inaugurated by Christ."

67. The verb is supplied from the previous verse due to the lack of a verb in this sentence.

68. As a response to the claim that "the person who dies with the most toys *wins*!"

pronouncement is dripping with irony, as he demands that the rich boast in what will damn them at the final judgment. In contrast to the poor who can rejoice in their future spiritual glory, these rich can anticipate only humiliation. If he has Christians in mind, however, then their humiliation comes in acknowledging their dependence on Christ rather than on "mammon."

To illustrate this humiliation, James turns to the world of vegetation: "like a flower of the grass they will pass away" (ὡς ἄνθος χόρτου παρελεύσεται). One translation for "flower of the grass" (ἄνθος χόρτου) is a "wildflower," which tends to last one or two days before drying out and dying and whose beauty lingers only as a memory. The imagery of a fading flower appears frequently in the OT (e.g., Job 14:2; Ps 103:15; Isa 40:6 – 7) to contrast humanity's frailty with God's immutability. At the very least, James is stressing that the wealth and status of the rich remain remarkably transient.[69]

James 1:11 For the sun rises with its scorching wind and the grass withers and its flower falls and its beautiful appearance is destroyed. In the same way, the rich will fade away in the midst of their daily life (ἀνέτειλεν γὰρ ὁ ἥλιος σὺν τῷ καύσωνι καὶ ἐξήρανεν τὸν χόρτον καὶ τὸ ἄνθος αὐτοῦ ἐξέπεσεν καὶ ἡ εὐπρέπεια τοῦ προσώπου αὐτοῦ ἀπώλετο· οὕτως καὶ ὁ πλούσιος ἐν ταῖς πορείαις αὐτοῦ μαρανθήσεται). This verse concludes the eschatological upheaval James presents by supplying a series of illustrations.

James uses four gnomic aorists, which portray timeless truths rather than past events. First, he depicts the sun rising with its "scorching heat" or "wind" (τῷ καύσωνι). This term can refer either to the oppressive heat or to the searing, sirocco wind that swept through the desert. Either can quickly produce drought, but the desiccating winds seem more likely in view (cf. NASB — "with a scorching wind"), because the heat of the day peaks not at the sun's rising but in early afternoon.[70] Moreover, the term need not refer to either the sun or the wind alone; a combination of the two would thoroughly destroy all but the hardiest of plants. Martin highlights two elements in this illustration: "the complete and swift destructiveness of the wind" and "the inevitability of its coming."[71]

Next, James points out three different ways in which the plant's life is completely ended: "the grass withers and its flower falls and [lit.,] the beauty of its face is destroyed." "Face" (προσώπου) is a Semitism for "appearance." The genitive appears to be attributed, hence, "beautiful appearance."[72] The final fate of a flower's beauty and glory turns out to be utter ruin, destroyed by the extremes of the elements and brought low by nature's cycles. In identical fashion, the rich will fade away even in the midst of their daily pursuits. As with the flowers, their destruction is inevitable and thorough. Some argue that "daily life" (ἡ πορεία) refers more specifically to business activities and that James is claiming that, in the midst of trying to make more money, the rich will pass away.[73] But the root of this word means simply "comings" or "goings." More probably, James implies just that, while "on the go" from place to place, the rich will die, regardless of the specific activity they are engaged in at that moment.[74]

69. Moo (*The Letter of James*, 67) argues that in the NT this verb for "pass away" is never used to denote eschatological judgment and thus must refer to current transience.

70. So also Hiebert, *The Epistle of James*, 95.

71. Martin, *James*, 27.

72. See Daniel B. Wallace, *Greek Grammar Beyond the Basics* (Grand Rapids: Zondervan, 1996), 89, on the difference between an "attributive genitive" and an "attributed genitive."

73. E.g., Maynard-Reid, *Poverty and Wealth in James*, 47.

74. Davids (*The Epistle of James*, 78) alerts us to this common Semitism for "way of life" and concludes that "it would be stretching it too far to refer it to the traveling merchants of 4:13ff."

In Depth: Are the Rich in 1:10 – 11 Christians?

James clearly labels the poor person in v. 9 as a "brother" or fellow "believer." But what about the "rich" person in vv. 10 – 11? In favor of seeing at least a few in James's community as the rich depicted here is the overall parallelism between the two parts of the paragraph and especially the fact that "let him or her boast" (καυχάσθω) has to carry over from v. 9 to v. 10. It would be natural, then, to supply "brother" (ἀδελφός) as well. This is the view that has dominated throughout most of church history.[75] James 4:13 – 17 indicates that the community does have some at least moderately well-to-do people within it who can travel and boast of their hopes to make more money (on their Christian identity, see below, 206 – 7). On this view, the humility in which the rich person should boast is not eschatological judgment but their present spiritual state as believers. One should not take pride in possessions but in Christ alone.[76]

On this interpretation, James is enjoining both the rich and the poor to evaluate themselves by spiritual rather than material standards. For James to command rich *non-Christians* to boast in their eternal damnation would require him to be using a kind of bitter irony or sarcasm that the rest of the context does not support.[77] The idea of "fading away" at the end of v. 11 could still be a general conclusion about all, Christian or not, who depend on their riches for their identity.[78] Regardless of people's spiritual condition, their economic state remains transitory. Realistically, "James may just as well be thinking of the death of the rich man as of his condemnation."[79] There is nothing in this text that forces it to refer to eternal judgment.[80]

Others, however, argue that v. 10 is less literal, that "brother" (ἀδελφός) goes only with the "poor" (ταπεινός), and that the call to "boast" (καυχάσθω) is indeed bitterly ironic. The rich have already had their day and judgment is coming.[81] Maynard-Reid argues that those interpretations that try to spiritualize poverty to allow some rich to be considered believers are created solely to

75. Ropes, *A Critical and Exegetical Commentary on the Epistle of St. James*, 145.

76. See, e.g., James B. Adamson, *The Epistle of James* (NICNT; Grand Rapids: Eerdmans, 1976), 61 – 62.

77. See, e.g., Ropes, *A Critical and Exegetical Commentary on the Epistle of James*, 146.

78. Williams ("Of Rags and Riches," 281) shows how Jer 9:23 – 24 is regularly used in Jewish texts to "cause God's people to re-evaluate their understanding of wisdom, strength, and riches.... Judgment will come in the future to those trusting in their own human wisdom, strength, and riches." This text as a background supports the traditional view of Jas 1:10.

79. Moo, *The Letter of James*, 68.

80. James's knowledge of the Sermon on the Mount could suggest that his illustration of withering like wildflowers alludes to the transient clothing of *believers*, like the lilies of the field in Mt 6:28 – 30.

81. See, e.g., Davids, *The Epistle of James*, 77; George M. Stulac, "Who Are 'The Rich' in James?" *Presb* 16 [1990]: 98 – 99; and, in most detail, René Krüger, "El vuelco irritante y definitivo: Santiago 1:9 – 11 y el anuncio de la inversión total de la situación," *Cuadernos de Teología* 23 (2004): esp. 55 – 59.

"placate the wealthy Christians within our own contemporary communities," and that the question of whether the rich can also be Christian is somewhat irrelevant. Rather, he decides that James uses an ironic twist regarding the economically wealthy to "underscore the humiliation in which the rich person lives."[82] Martin argues that James's one entirely unambiguous example of the non-Christian wealthy (2:7) helps tip the balance in favor of a non-Christian referent, given the ambiguity of 1:10.[83] James then uses "rich" (πλούσιος) with a polemical overtone here and holds out no future hope for them, implying that they are not Christians at all.[84] Tamez insists that the rich "will fail completely in their pursuits, namely, their business dealings, which are precisely the cause of their ruin since usually they are rooted in injustice and the desire for gain."[85]

Good arguments thus appear for both positions. On balance, we agree with William Baker, who argues that "in terms of logic, the irony of suggesting that a person should take pride in what amounts to his own eternal condemnation is too twisted to be taken seriously."[86] Drake Williams adds that the background of Jer 9:23 – 24 helps us to understand this boast not in terms of irony, but rather as a "heroic boast of believers," encouraging "God's people to look towards the future when riches will mean little and being in God's plan will mean a great deal."[87] James 5:1 – 6 offers a sharp denunciation of the non-Christian rich, but the words mean exactly what they say ("Weep and wail for the miseries coming upon you"). Nowhere else in this letter does James employ a kind of irony in which the actual meaning of a command is the exact opposite of its literal meaning. Combining this observation with the recognition of at least some diversity of socioeconomic status within the earliest church more generally, the Christian interpretation seems preferable.[88]

Theology in Application

Introduction (1:1)

Although James is no messiah, the title "servant of God" recalls the suffering "servant of the Lord" from Isaiah (esp. Isa 52:13 – 53:12). If Jesus' own brother and chief elder of the Jerusalem church refused to exploit his office and his relationships, how much more ought Christian leaders in other times and places view themselves

82. Maynard-Reid, *Poverty and Wealth in James*, 44.

83. Martin, *James*, 26. Basically, he argues that if James had wanted to identify this person as a believer, he could have done so clearly, as he shows the opposite in 2:7.

84. Davids, *The Epistle of James*, 77.

85. Tamez, *The Scandalous Message of James*, 34.

86. Baker, "James," 22.

87. Williams, "Of Rags and Riches," 282.

88. Cf. also Blomberg, *Neither Poverty nor Riches*, 149 – 50.

and behave as mere slaves. First Corinthians 4 offers important later reflection in more detail on this theme.

The Positive Potential of Trials (1:2 – 4)

The first of the three key themes in James demonstrates that tough times can be viewed positively. V. 12 will support this conviction. James 4:13 – 5:18 elaborates on the theme of testing, in the contexts of temptation to worship riches (4:13 – 17), experiencing economic exploitation (5:1 – 12), and suffering severe illness (5:13 – 18). By introducing all three of his themes here, at the beginning of his letter, in short compass, James implicitly applies his teaching on trials to the social circumstances of his audience. Despite the fact that the majority of them are afflicted by unjust discrimination and deprivation, they can nevertheless choose to view their situation as an opportunity for character building.

Jewish Christians would naturally recall the accounts of the Israelites' rebellious wandering in the wilderness for forty years between the exodus and the entry into the Promised Land. Instead of imitating their ancestors' failure, they should instead emulate the Maccabean martyrs, whose faith and joy under torture had become legendary (cf. 2Mc 7).[89] Jesus in his Beatitudes had pronounced those who were persecuted for his sake blessed (Mt 5:11 – 12; Lk 6:23) and had called on his followers to become mature (or perfect, Mt 5:48), as in Jas 1:4.[90] Ro 5:2 – 5 and 1Pe 1:6 – 7 (cf. 4:13) likewise describe the need to rejoice in various trials and sufferings because of the genuineness of faith that they can produce. The verbal parallels among these passages suggest that James, Paul, and Peter may have all drawn from a common early Christian ethical tradition in their directives.[91] If this is the case, then James's teaching proves all the more fundamental for Christian living.

But how can believers rejoice in tough times (v. 2), especially when they find themselves suffering intensely? Frankly, many of us would prefer that this passage were not in the Bible! But it may also be one of the most profound and crucial for truly mature Christian living.[92] To begin with, James does not command us to wear the artificial "happy faces" that so many seem to think are required in church or other Christian circles. Denying one's true emotions seldom accomplishes anything good. But while we cannot *will* ourselves to be jovial rather than depressed, we can choose how we *think* — hence the verbs about considering and knowing in vv. 2 – 3.[93] The joy James has in mind "is an eschatological catchword, not an emotion

89. For other intertestamental texts, see Rudolf Hoppe, *Der theologische Hintergrund des Jakobusbriefes* (Wurzburg: Echter, 1977), 19.

90. Just as the Beatitudes and antitheses in Mt 5 help explain the perfection or maturity enjoined in the Sermon on the Mount, so Jas 3:17 – 18 enumerates the attribute James has in mind by the same term here (*teleios*). See the excursus in Hartin, *James*, 75 – 80.

91. See the tables and discussion in Davids, *The Epistle of James*, 65 – 66.

92. Cf. the NLT rendering of v. 4: "for when your endurance is fully developed, you will be strong in character and ready for anything."

93. On these right and wrong ways to apply v. 2, see esp. R.

... a theological perception of trials, which considers their complete demise by a God who promises a new day."[94]

We must also stress that these verses do not claim to teach that everything that happens to us *is* somehow good and therefore a reason for rejoicing (as in the KJV mistranslation of Ro 8:28 — "all things work together for good to them that love God"), but that if we let God work through even evil events, he can produce good (cf. the NIV/TNIV of Ro 8:28 — "in all things God works for the good of those who love him").[95] Even if we do not understand those purposes in this life, we will do so in the life to come, the glory and infinity of which will far outweigh our "light and momentary troubles" (2Co 4:17).

Vv. 2 – 4 can be both "overapplied" and "underapplied." On the one hand, there is no automatic promise here, as if trials guaranteed blessings or maturity in this life. Even believers can choose to allow difficult circumstances to drive them away from the Lord through resentment, indifference, or disobedience.[96] Thus James commands them to "let endurance have its complete effect" (v. 4). At times, it seems that God allows his people to get perilously close to the brink of destruction, but he never pushes them over the edge (cf. 2Co 4:8 – 12). Indeed, when they rely on him to preserve them, they grow, mature, and come out the other side of the trials stronger and more whole, character traits our world desperately seeks but desires to gain without the suffering that is usually required to obtain them.[97]

In light of the full range of NT teaching, this "wholeness" is characterized by the absence of self-centeredness and division, the presence of the fruit of the Spirit, the ability to teach others, deeper insight into God's will and ways, greater trustworthiness — in short, growing in the likeness of Jesus Christ.[98] Trials do not necessarily demonstrate that one is carefully obeying God's will, though it is true that those in "front-line" kingdom work are often attacked by the enemy. But one may be going through hard times because of one's sin or tactlessness or simply because of the fallenness of this evil age. Scripture, moreover, never calls God's people to *seek* suffering or persecution; if we live long enough, plenty of it will come our way without us looking for it![99]

On the other hand, one dare not limit the application of this subsection just to the kind of trials of economic exploitation that James's audience was experiencing. The use of the adjective for "various" or "many kinds" (v. 2) highlights this point.

Kent Hughes, *James: Faith That Works* (Wheaton, IL: Crossway, 1991), 18 – 19.

94. Wall, *Community of the Wise*, 48. Cf. Kurt A. Richardson, *James* (NAC; Nashville: Broadman & Holman, 1997), 58.

95. Cf. further Carroll D. Osburn, "The Interpretation of Romans 8:28," *WTJ* 44 (1982): 99 – 109.

96. Cf. the "foolish responses" enumerated by Tidball, *Wisdom from Heaven*, 21 – 22.

97. Cf. esp. Bauckham, *James*, 183.

98. Wiard Popkes, "New Testament Principles of Wholeness," *EvQ* 64 (1992): 319 – 32, esp. 328 – 31.

99. Cf. Frances T. Gench, *Hebrews and James* (Westminister Bible Companion; Louisville: WJKP, 1996), 91: "Such experiences are not to be sought; nor are they to be avoided as foreign to the Christian faith."

Against those who think, for example, that God never wants people to be sick or poor, so that believers should "name and claim" health and wealth, v. 2 forms the first of several texts in James that confront and decry this heresy bluntly (see further under 4:13 – 17 and 5:13 – 16). Paul teaches plainly that God's power is perfected in human weakness and that his grace is sufficient to enable us to endure (2Co 12:9). Even when believers have largely themselves to blame for difficulties, God's sovereignty is not thwarted and he still works to bring something good out of the situation. Genesis 50:20 provides the classic demonstration of this precious theological truth: even as Joseph's brothers intended their mistreatment of him for evil, "God intended it for good"![100]

Praying Faithfully for Wisdom (vv. 5 – 8)

The second key theme in James explores the nature of true wisdom, especially in the area of speech. James 1:19 – 26 will introduce the focus on speech, while 3:1 – 4:12 will combine the two and unpack them in detail. Here, James's point is simply that we must ask God whenever we lack wisdom and ask in a spirit of confident trust that he (and he alone, among the entities that humans choose to worship) eagerly desires to supply it. The most pressing need for wisdom among James's original addressees would have involved knowing how to react to the most difficult of their trials just introduced, specifically the unjust treatment by their landlords (5:1 – 6). Because they were Christians, we must understand the "all" to whom God gives his wisdom to be limited to believers, at least in this context.[101]

Wisdom, more generally, embodies God's preeminent gift to believers to enable them to persevere during trials.[102] Wisdom in Scripture is inseparable from allegiance to God and moral living. "The fear of the Lord is the beginning of wisdom"; this assertion is best known from Pr 9:10, but it reappears in Ps 111:10 and Pr 1:7 as well. In Pr 8 – 9, Wisdom is personified as a lady who calls to the people of the village to come and learn from her and avoid her evil nemesis, Dame Folly, who can pose even as a prostitute. This personification of Wisdom intensified in the intertestamental period, just as the wisdom literature represented in the Hebrew Scriptures by Job, Ecclesiastes, Song of Songs, and especially Proverbs later proliferated with such influential apocryphal books as Sirach and the Wisdom of Solomon (see esp. Sir 24 and Wis 7). Both Matthew and John appear to portray Jesus as Wisdom at numerous junctures (see esp. Mt 11 – 12 and the *logos* Christology of Jn 1).[103]

100. For detailed theological reflection on this antinomy, see esp. D. A. Carson, *Divine Sovereignty and Human Responsibility: Biblical Perspectives in Tension* (Atlanta: John Knox, 1981).

101. C. Freeman Sleeper, *James* (Abingdon New Testament Commentary; Nashville: Abingdon, 1998), 51.

102. Patrick J. Hartin, *A Spirituality of Perfection: Faith in Action in the Letter of James* (Collegeville: Liturgical, 1999), 66.

103. For a full treatment of the theme throughout biblical history, see Ben Witherington III, *Jesus the Sage: The Pilgrimage of Wisdom* (Minneapolis: Fortress, 1994).

The most direct canonical parallel to Jas 1:5 – 8 appears in Mt 7:7 and Lk 11:9 with Jesus' invitation to his followers to ask and receive. But an echo of Lk 11:34 (cf. Mt 6:22) may be heard here, too, as Luke uses an adjective meaning "good," "generous," or "single-minded" (ἁπλοῦς) — cognate to the adverb "without hesitation" (ἁπλῶς) that appears in Jas 1:5. The simplicity or single-mindedness of God may be the thread that ties together the three key themes of James; thus, believers must behave with unswerving loyalty to the God who is wholeheartedly devoted to them.[104] The opposite of this loyalty is duplicity, which cannot be present when one truly asks in faith (cf. Mk 11:23 – 24; Mt 21:21).[105]

James's use of "wisdom" (v. 5) gives the lie to so many worldly definitions of the concept, both ancient and modern. Not a mere intelligence quotient, accumulation of knowledge, critical acumen, practical expertise, or life experience, wisdom from a biblical perspective begins with following the God who has now revealed himself in Jesus Christ. It then proceeds with godly living. A person who does these things is truly wise, whether any of the commonly held attributes of wisdom are present or not. Conversely, the smartest, most skillful and critically honed person who rejects the Lordship of Jesus cannot be said to be wise in the fullest sense of the word.

This contrast between worldly and godly wisdom leads to the proper application of vv. 6 – 8. James is *not* insisting we know *how* God wants to answer our prayers, so that we can ask for precisely what we already proclaim he wants to give us. There would be no need to ask for wisdom in the first place if this were the case. Moreover, "faith" that sees the entire future is no longer faith but sight. With Heb 11:1, "faith is the assurance of things hoped for, the conviction of things not seen" (NASB). We regularly cry out with the man who appealed to Jesus for healing for his demon-possessed son, "I do believe; help me overcome my unbelief" (Mk 9:24)! And the present tense imperatives in vv. 5 – 6 suggest that we may have to persist in our requests over a period of time rather than offering up glib, fleeting prayers that we trust will suffice.

Rather than pretending we know God's will in perplexing situations, therefore, James teaches us to be sure of *whom* we are trusting for the answers to our questions (cf. the NLT in v. 6: "be sure that you really expect him to answer"). We cannot be wavering between two masters; here this implies trusting God and not depending on our possessions to "get us through" (cf. Mt 6:24; Lk 16:13).[106] Most of us turn to

104. Cf. Laws, *The Epistle of James*, 29 – 32. Closely related is Hartin's emphasis on "perfection" as the integrating motif (*A Spirituality of Perfection*, esp. 1 – 15), because consistency in single-mindedness produces what James means by perfection.

105. It is this kind of doubt, not honest questioning, that prevents one from receiving anything from the Lord. See David Nystrom, *James* (NIVAC; Grand Rapids: Zondervan, 1997), 62.

106. Cf. Moo, *The Letter of James: An Introduction and Commentary*, 64. Stulac (*James*, 43) thinks that "the doubt then is a vacillation between self-reliance and God-reliance." Ironically, those who confidently believe that they can "name it and claim it" actually rely on themselves rather than God, because they have reduced prayer to a formula they think can enable humans to manipulate God and guarantee a certain outcome.

God only when we have exhausted every other option. The vacillation portrayed here recalls the ancient Jewish genre of "two-ways" literature (nicely represented in the NT in Mt 7:13 – 27) and its doctrine of each human having good and evil impulses that war against one another.[107] Of course, God graciously gives us many good things even when we do not ask him, fail to persist in asking, or ask with wrong motives; the world would be bleak indeed if this were not the case. But there may be many other good things we are missing out on because we do not take the time to pray even more (see further under 4:2 – 3).

The Great Reversal (vv. 9 – 11)

This third main theme in James will be repeated in 1:27 and elaborated in 2:1 – 26. Here James intends merely to introduce what has often been called "the great reversal." The theme of the unjust rich and the pious poor trading places when God judges the world has a long biblical history. But if we are right that James speaks of both poor and rich as Christians here, this is not an exact replica of that pattern. Still, as background to the exaltation of the poor and humiliated believer, one thinks of the exodus, the defeat of the Canaanites, psalms and proverbs that promise rewards for piety even among the impoverished, and the prophetic hopes for a coming day when exiled Israel's fortunes will be restored, both literally and figuratively.[108]

The Virgin Mary prophesied the lifting up of the humble and the throwing down of "rulers from their thrones" (Lk 1:52). In Jesus' teaching, Matthew's and Luke's versions of the first beatitude (Mt 5:3, Lk 6:20) combine to show that the "poor" who are blessed are both the economically marginalized and those who trust in God as their only hope.[109] Among Jesus' parables, the rich fool (Lk 12:13 – 21) and the rich man and Lazarus (Lk 16:19 – 31) stand out as illustrating the danger of thinking one is a part of God's covenant community only to find oneself worshiping riches instead of God. The latter passage also promises spiritual, eschatological compensation for abject poverty among God's people in this world.[110]

The illustration of vv. 10b – 11a endured as a proverb among Jews and Jewish Christians. If not directly quoting the prophet, James is clearly alluding to segments of Isa 40:6 – 8. The prophet is told to cry out that "all people are like grass, and all human faithfulness is like the flowers of the field. The grass withers and the flowers

107. Oscar J. F. Seitz, "Antecedent and Signification of the Term Δίψυχος," *JBL* 66 (1947): 211 – 19. Cf. idem, "Afterthoughts on the Term 'Dipsychos,'" *NTS* 4 (1957 – 58): 327 – 34.

108. For a detailed treatment of the most relevant texts, see Blomberg, *Neither Poverty nor Riches*, 33 – 85. See esp. Ex 11:2 – 3; 12:25 – 26; Jos 8:30 – 35; Ps 49:10 – 20; 73:1 – 28; Pr 1:4, 28; Isa 54 – 55; 60 – 66.

109. See, e.g., Craig L. Blomberg, *Matthew* (NAC; Nashville: Broadman, 1992), 98 – 99.

110. See, e.g., Craig L. Blomberg, *Interpreting the Parables* (Downers Grove, IL: IVP, 1990), 203 – 8, 266 – 68; idem, *Preaching the Parables: From Responsible Interpretation to Powerful Proclamation* (Grand Rapids: Baker, 2004), 45 – 55.

fall, because the breath of the LORD blows on them. Surely the people are grass. The grass withers and the flowers fall, but the word of our God endures forever." First Peter 1:24 – 25 quotes from these words, again suggesting that they may have been incorporated into basic, foundational Christian instruction before either James or Peter wrote their letters.[111]

At first glance, v. 9 could appear to promote passivity, as if teaching that, because God will one day right all wrongs, we must meanwhile just put up with injustice, including material deprivation. But the text never says anything like that here, and 5:7 – 11 will suggest a somewhat different approach (see below, pp. 229 – 30).[112] Yet despite our best efforts, many wrongs are not righted in this life, so that the beleaguered believer must have an eschatological perspective on affliction, as we saw in 1:2 – 4 (above, p 50).

Even in this life, Christians have access to immense spiritual privileges that can often help them rise above their humiliating[113] physical or social circumstances. The faith, joy, and selflessness of impoverished Two-Thirds World believers regularly put visiting First-World Christians to shame. Rich believers, which by global standards include almost everyone who has access to this book, must beware of taking pride in their possessions. How many of us have fallen so in love with this world that, if we knew we were to die tonight, we would experience genuine sorrow because of missed opportunities for various earthly pleasures?[114] James does not teach that a person cannot be both rich and Christian, but he does suggest here that one's attitude to possessions proves crucial. Unless we recognize the utter transience of this life and the potential suddenness of its end,[115] and unless we live each moment for Christ with a sense of urgency about redeeming the time (Eph 5:16), we risk tacitly worshiping the world.

111. Cf. Scaer, *James*, 50 – 51.

112. See esp. Christopher Church, "James," in Edgar V. McKnight and Christopher Church, *Hebrews-James* (Macon, GA: Smyth & Helwys, 2004), 337 – 42.

113. The TNIV and NASB each correctly use "humiliation" with reference to the rich person in v. 10. A similarly strong rendering belongs in v. 9 as well.

114. "Modern materialism and consumerism often quietly or cynically mock spirituality; material self-gratification when denied only serves to occasion further doubts about God. Religion in much of Western society has become 'big business.' This serves to blind Christians to the opportunity of embracing a spirituality that defines one's own interests through the needs of others who in some respects may be less fortunate" (Cain H. Felder, "James," in *The International Bible Commentary*, ed. William R. Farmer [Collegeville: Liturgical, 1998], 1789).

115. Cf. the following renderings of v. 11b: "wealthy people will fade away with all of their achievements" (NLT); "in the midst of a busy life, they will wither away" (NRSV).

CHAPTER 2

James 1:12 – 18

Literary Context

James 1:2 – 11 has introduced the three key themes of the epistle. Vv. 12 – 27 go back through all three but begin to expand the treatment of each. First, James explores further the topic of perseverance in trials (vv. 12 – 18). After reviewing the positive role of trials in v. 12 as tests to be passed (recall vv. 2 – 4), in vv. 13 – 18 he shifts to their negative potential when believers allow trials to turn into temptations. Vv. 19 – 26 return to the theme of wisdom (recall vv. 5 – 8), now particularly in the area of speech and in obedience to God's Word. More broadly, true wisdom leads to good works — doing rather than just listening. V. 27, finally, brings up the topic of the dispossessed, tying in with the concept of riches and poverty introduced in vv. 9 – 11 and introducing the thesis of the letter. One could, of course, keep all of vv. 12 – 27 together as a unit, as we did with vv. 2 – 11. But the additional length of the passage, coupled with the tightly-knit structure of vv. 19 – 27 (see below, pp. 83 – 84), makes it natural to treat vv. 12 – 18 by themselves.

V. 12 ties in loosely with vv. 9 – 11, given the economic trials that exacerbated the gap between the rich and poor.[1] V. 18 likewise subtly prepares for the theme of hearing and doing the word in vv. 19 – 27 by referring to the role of "the word of truth" in regenerating believers.[2] The perfect gifts in v. 17 set the stage for the perfect law of liberty in v. 25, just as the rebirth highlighted in v. 18 corresponds to the implanted word of v. 21. V. 19 even begins with the identical vocative as in v. 16 ("my beloved brothers and sisters"), suggesting to a few scholars that v. 19a should be taken as the conclusion to vv. 16 – 18, creating an inclusio around this short paragraph.[3] But it flows more naturally as the introduction to a new paragraph (vv. 19 – 21) and thus more likely forms a final link between the present text and the next one, again calling James's audience to attend carefully to his instruction.

1. Some scholars perceive a tighter connection; e.g., Martin Klein (*Ein volkommenes Werk: Vollkommenheit, Gesetz und Gericht als theologische Themen des Jakobusbriefes* [Stuttgart: Kohlhammer, 1995], 43) sees vv. 2 and 12 as forming an inclusio, marking off all of vv. 1 – 12 as dealing with the positive possibilities of trials, before vv. 13 – 15 turn to their negative counterparts. Cf. Johnson, *The Letter of James*, 184 – 91.

2. Aída B. Spencer ("The Function of the Miserific and Beatific Images in the Letter of James," *EvJ* 7 [1989]: 13) believes vv. 17 – 18 form a microcosm of the entire letter, centering on the theme of genuine faith needing to be humble faith in action.

3. E.g., Martin, *James*, 31; cf. NLT.

II. Statement of Three Key Themes (1:2 – 11)
 A. Trials in the Christian Life (1:2 – 4)
 B. Wisdom (1:5 – 8)
 C. Riches and Poverty (1:9 – 11)
➡ **III. Restatement of the Three Themes (1:12 – 27)**
 A. Trials/Temptations in Relation to God (1:12 – 18)
 1. God's Goodness in Testing (1:12)
 2. God's Non-Participation in Temptation (1:13 – 16)
 3. God's Creation of Everything Good (1:17 – 18)
 B. Wisdom in the Areas of Speech and Obedience (1:19 – 26)
 C. The "Have-Nots" and the Responsibility of the "Haves": The Thesis of the Letter (1:27)

Main Idea

Christians should not respond to trials or temptations by blaming God but by acknowledging him as the source of everything good. When Christians respond to external trials with proper perseverance, they will be blessed. When they allow such trials to turn into seductions to sin, they have only themselves to blame.

Translation

(See next page.)

Structure

This passage falls into three discrete sections, just as vv. 2 – 11 did, although the sections here are more closely tied together. V. 12 takes the form of a beatitude, pronouncing a blessing on anyone whom God views as responding to trials with appropriate perseverance. The basis for the blessing is the promise of eternal life that God has given to all believers, defined here as those who continually love him. The time for receiving this blessing, of course, is after the trial, in many cases after a considerable interval of time.

Vv. 13 – 15 shift from trials as tests to be passed to trials that may become temptations to sin. This short paragraph makes two fundamental, contrasting assertions. God tempts no one; rather, giving in to sin is entirely the responsibility of the human who makes the choice to do so. These two points are couched in the form of an exhortation not to blame God for making one sin (v. 13), followed by the assertion that each person is tempted by their own internal lusts (vv. 14 – 15).

James 1:12-18

12a	Assertion	**Blessed is the person**
b	identification	who endures a trial,
c	time (of 12d)	after having passed the test,
d	basis	because … they will receive the crown of life.
e	description	which [God] promised to those loving him.
13a	time (of 13b)	while being tempted,
b	Exhortation	**Let no one … say that "from God I am being tempted**,"
c	basis	for God cannot be tempted to do evil, and
d	general/specific	he himself tempts no one.
14a	Contrast	But **each person is tempted** by their own desires,
b	manner	being dragged away and
c	simultaneous	enticed [by them].
15a	Sequence	Then **that desire**, having conceived, **gives birth** to sin,
b	progression	and **that sin**, having matured, **gives birth** to death.
16	Warning	**Do not deceive yourselves**, my beloved brothers and sisters.
17a	Assertion	**Every good and perfect gift is coming down**
b	place	from above
c	restatement	from the Father of lights
d	description	in whom there is no variation or
e	restatement	shadow of turning.
18a	basis (of 18b)	Because he was willing,
b	assertion	**he gave birth to us**
c	means	by the word of truth,
d	purpose	in order that we might be a sort of firstfruit of his creation.

The exhortation of v. 13b is modified by three subordinate clauses: the time of the command (while being tempted — v. 13a),[4] the rationale (God cannot be tempted to do evil — v. 13c), and a restatement of the rationale, which also particularizes it (God does not tempt even one single person — v. 13d). Rather, people give in to their own inner desires to do wrong (v. 14). James vividly describes them as dragging and enticing a person. Though simultaneous actions, the former verb suggests a more forceful outside pull than the latter. Temptation can sneak up on us covertly; it can also attack overtly. While v. 15 is made up of two parallel independent clauses, they

4. This does not mean that one can blame God before or after the temptation! But it is usually during the struggle that we are most tempted to lash out against the One viewed as ultimately responsible for causing our problems. Cf. HCSB: "No one undergoing a trial should say, 'I am being tempted by God.'" This rendering also highlights the shift from the sense of "trial" to "temptation" better than many translations.

further the thought of v. 14, together describing the end result of temptation when left unchecked. A sequence of actions emerges as lust "begets" sin and sin produces death.[5]

The final subsection begins with a warning not to be deceived, which functions as a powerful command to pay close attention to what James is about to say (v. 16). Though a separate sentence, it does not add any content to vv. 17–18. It is simply a call to listen carefully to what follows. V. 17 transitions from what God does *not* supply (temptation—vv. 13–15) to what he *does* provide (every good and perfect gift). Good things come from above, that is, from God, who is the creator of the heavenly bodies and thus of the entire universe (v. 17ab).[6] James further describes this God as unchangeable, using two parallel expressions.[7] Because of his immutability, we can trust him *always* to supply every good thing and nothing but good things.

V. 18 rounds out this subsection and the entire passage by pointing to the preeminent example of God's good gifts—the regeneration of believers (v. 18b). The basis of this action is God's own sovereign will (v. 18a). He provides rebirth by means of "the word of truth"—that is, the gospel (v. 18c). And a key purpose of this regeneration is to offer a foretaste of his coming re-creation of the entire cosmos (v. 18d).

Exegetical Outline

➡ **III. Restatement of the Three Themes (1:12–27)**

A. Trials/Temptations in Relation to God (1:12–18)

1. Christians Can Acknowledge God's Goodness in Testing Because They Know They Will Be Blessed after Passing the Test (v. 12).
2. Christians Should Not Blame God for Temptation Because They and Not God Are the Problem (vv. 13–15).
   a. God is not the problem because he cannot be tempted to do evil and therefore cannot tempt others to do evil (v. 13).
   b. People are the problem because they succumb to temptation due to their own evil desires, which if unchecked lead to death (vv. 14–15).
3. Christians Should Instead Acknowledge God As the Source of Everything Good (vv. 16–18).
   a. Christians must guard against deception in this matter (v. 16).
   b. All good gifts come from God, as demonstrated ever since creation (v. 17).
   c. The best illustration of God's good gifts is his regeneration of Christians (v. 18).

5. Milton depicts these verses in *Paradise Lost* (Book II): Sin springs from the head of Satan when he plans his rebellion, and then Death is the result of his incestuous relationship with Sin. This picture and Shakespeare's depiction of Jas 2:13 throughout *Measure for Measure* may be the two most significant appropriations of James in English literature.

6. Cf. NLT: "from God above, who created all heaven's lights."

7. Cf. NET: "no variation or the slightest hint of change."

Explanation of Text

James 1:12 Blessed is the person who endures a trial, because, after having passed the test, they will receive the crown of life which [God] promised to those loving him (Μακάριος ἀνὴρ ὃς ὑπομένει πειρασμόν, ὅτι δόκιμος γενόμενος λήμψεται τὸν στέφανον τῆς ζωῆς ὃν ἐπηγγείλατο τοῖς ἀγαπῶσιν αὐτόν). This passage begins with a beatitude or blessing that can be entitled "the reward for obedience." We know beatitudes best from Jesus' teaching in Mt 5:3 – 12, but the form appears frequently in the OT and most prominently in Psalms, Proverbs, and the intertestamental book of Sirach.[8] Maynard-Reid argues that the person in view here is the same as the poor believer in v. 9,[9] but v. 12 seems to be a more general blessing on all who endure trials, not solely the poor person. Again it should be noted that James's use of his word for "person" (ἀνήρ) here is inclusive, not just referring to males.[10] The one pronounced blessed or "happy" is the one who "endures a trial" (ὑπομένει πειρασμόν). Here James links back with vv. 2 – 4 via both "trial" (πειρασμός) and "endure"/"endurance" (ὑπομένω/ὑπομονή) so that "trial" (πειρασμός) continues to refer to "tests" in this verse.[11]

Endurance will show people as "having passed the test" or "having been approved" (δόκιμος γενόμενος).[12] As in 1:3, the word for approval (δόκιμος) refers to the approval that comes from actually passing the test. Such people will receive "the crown of life" (τὸν στέφανον τῆς ζωῆς). This is not a royal crown but the laurel wreath that was given to winners in athletic competitions, including the Olympics. The genitive is best taken as appositional ("the crown *which is* life"),[13] rather than descriptive of the actual wreath ("the living crown"),[14] because the prize for which Christians strive *is* eternal life (cf. Rev 2:10).

James then further describes this crown as that which God promised "to those loving him" (τοῖς ἀγαπῶσιν αὐτόν). Thus we see the firm promise of God to his followers: they do not strive in futility with a vain, blind hope but instead endure purposefully with the goal of everlasting life with God in sight. The substantive participle "those loving" (ἀγαπῶσιν) functions as a synonym for all true believers, showing that God does not promise this crown of life to some elite few who strive harder or succeed better than the rest.[15] But

8. Matt A. Jackson-McCabe ("A Letter to the Twelve Tribes in the Diaspora: Wisdom and 'Apocalyptic' Eschatology in the Letter of James," *SBLSP* 35 [1996]: 504 – 17) shows how the beatitude form represents one part of the overlap between apocalyptic and wisdom literature in the book of James.

9. Maynard-Reid, *Poverty and Wealth in James*, 39.

10. Poythress and Grudem (*The Gender-Neutral Bible Controversy*, 329) argue that the verse envisions one particular man who exemplifies the blessing that applies to both men and women. But after James has used ἄνθρωπος and ἀνήρ interchangeably in vv. 7 – 8, this proves less likely. See above, p. 53; cf. also Sleeper (*James*, 60) and Maier (*Der Brief des Jakobus*, 70 – 71), who note that a number of late manuscripts change ἀνήρ to ἄνθρωπος to clarify this very point.

11. Martin (*James*, 33) points out the possibility that, in this transitional verse, the word πειρασμός could carry both meanings of "trials" and "temptations," an approach Johnson endorses (*The Letter of James*, 192). But there are no clues in the *preceding* context that would positively support this hypothesis, so it is better to wait until the clearly negative context of v. 13 before using a form of "tempt" in translation.

12. The aorist participle "having been" (γενόμενος) could also be rendered "having become," especially if "tested" (δόκιμος) is translated as "approved." The participle is more likely just temporal ("after having been/become") rather than also causal ("because he or she has been/become"), since the adjacent ὅτι-clause supplies the formal cause.

13. Likewise Davids, *The Epistle of James*, 80. Laws (*The Epistle of James*, 68) and Martin (*James*, 33) identify the construction with the virtually synonymous categories of epexegetic genitive or genitive of content, respectively.

14. As supported, e.g., by Hiebert, *The Epistle of James*, 99.

15. Laws (*The Epistle of James*, 67) observes that Ex 20:6; Dt 5:10; and Ro 8:28 all show "loving" as a consistent description

this also raises a serious question, whether those whose love for God does not permeate their lives ought casually to consider themselves Christians. Loving God should characterize a believer's entire life.[16] God's utter trustworthiness, in turn, guarantees his faithfulness to what he "promised" (ἐπηγγείλατο).[17]

James 1:13 Let no one say while being tempted that "from God I am being tempted," for God cannot be tempted to do evil, and he himself tempts no one (μηδεὶς πειραζόμενος λεγέτω ὅτι Ἀπὸ θεοῦ πειράζομαι· ὁ γὰρ θεὸς ἀπείραστός ἐστιν κακῶν, πειράζει δὲ αὐτὸς οὐδένα). This verse introduces the switch of topics from trials to temptations. James begins, "no one, while being tempted" (μηδεὶς πειραζόμενος). The verb, obviously cognate to "trial" (πειρασμός), here refers to something that entices one "to improper behavior."[18] Moo explains that what can change a trial into a temptation is the attitude with which we meet it, and we fail the trial when we turn to blaming God.[19] George Stulac draws out this idea by showing how vv. 2–4 along with vv. 13–15 present two parallel options to one and the same set of circumstances. In the first instance, we understand the trial in terms of testing, which leads us to perseverance and maturity.[20] In the second, we experience the same trial as a temptation, which leads us to sin and death. James warns against the second option here.[21] We need to learn to endure our trials in ways that bring glory to God.

V. 13 has important implications for Christian theodicy: no one should say that "from God I am being tempted" (ἀπὸ θεοῦ πειράζομαι). Often when we encounter trials or temptations, we instantly seek someone to blame. Possibly people in James's congregations are blaming God for their trials, making up an excuse for their own failures. This tactic produces a twisted picture of God, however, as one who purposely puts obstacles in his people's paths in order to tempt them to fall. Instead, James depicts God as the one who does *not* want his people to stumble and who gives them the strength to endure temptation. For God, James stresses, "cannot be tempted to do evil" (ἀπείραστος κακῶν).

Three main interpretations for the genitive of reference in this phrase compete for acceptance. First, "of evil" (κακῶν) could be a subjective genitive, leading to God as "unable to be tempted *by* evil."[22] Second, it could be an objective genitive, yielding "God cannot be tempted *to do* evil." The

of the faithful. We must also recognize that this crown is not promised to all the poor, irrespective of their faith commitments — as certain forms of liberation theology allege.

16. The present tense of the participle indicates ongoing action, so that James is not thinking of a momentary or superficial profession of faith, but rather a prolonged way of life.

17. Here appears the second textual variant in this letter that the UBS deems worthy of note. Given an A rating, the reading chosen has the vast majority of the textual support, but the Byz. tradition adds "the Lord," which explains why these words are present in the KJV. Given the strong textual support for omission and the fact that both variants (supplying either "God" or "the Lord") are natural scribal additions to clarify *who* promised these crowns, it seems the UBS is correct in preferring the shortest reading. Davids (*The Epistle of James*, 80) adds that "the suppression of the subject of the clause shows a typical Jewish reluctance to name God."

18. BDAG, 793.

19. Moo, *The Letter of James: An Introduction and Commentary*, 71.

20. Pheme Perkins (*First and Second Peter, James, and Jude* [Interpretation; Louisville: John Knox, 1995], 101) recognizes that "the value that James attributes to trials in generating the tested faith of those who receive salvation might easily give rise to the suspicion that God is responsible for the trials that believers undergo."

21. Stulac, *James*, 54. He also notes (p. 55) that "James would remember the Lord's teaching that it is not God's desire to tempt a person to live in any way displeasing to him, and that temptation should be resisted (Mt 6:13; 26:41)."

22. The primary supporter of this view was F. J. A. Hort (*The Epistle of St. James* [London: Macmillan, 1909], 23), who unpacked the expression by affirming that God is entirely inexperienced or has no contact with evil.

corollary of this second approach is that God cannot do evil by tempting us.[23] The third option suggests the translation, "God *ought* not to be tested by evil people."[24] Of these, the second makes the most sense, because contextually James is discussing why one should not blame God for the evil that occurs.

In the next statement, "and he himself tempts no one" (πειράζει δὲ αὐτὸς οὐδένα), "tempts" (πειράζει) reflects a gnomic present, by which James asserts that God never tempts his people at any time. James does not claim that God never *allows* temptation into our lives, nor does he imply that God never *tests* his people. He "is not denying that God does indeed subject men to testing, but he does deny the claim that God tests men with an evil intent, to lead them into sin."[25] The "himself" (αὐτός) serves to strengthen the contrast with the one who tempts us, as well as to emphasize the principle that God does not try to seduce his people to act wickedly. Our God can be turned to in times of temptation, for he does not cause it, James assures us. This principle accords with 1Co 10:13, where Paul promises that God will provide a way out for us to bear up under the pressures to cave in to sin.

James 1:14 But each person is tempted by their own desires, being dragged away and enticed [by them] (ἕκαστος δὲ πειράζεται ὑπὸ τῆς ἰδίας ἐπιθυμίας ἐξελκόμενος καὶ δελεαζόμενος). Having affirmed that God does not cause our temptations, James turns to the true source: temptation comes from within us. He refers to "each person" (ἕκαστος), pointing out that every single one of us experiences temptation from within. Each one "is tempted by their own desires" (πειράζεται ὑπὸ τῆς ἰδίας ἐπιθυμίας). Desire does not necessarily equate with lust, although that is one common translation for this word.[26] Rather, it refers here to any intense longing for an improper object, that is, anything that gets in the way of our pursuit of God.[27]

This proves crucial in pastoral ministry: what one person finds as intense temptation another person may never experience as even a faint enticement, and vice-versa. Temptations are tailored to the individual, and so we as believers must never belittle a person for struggling with something we think of as inane. Instead, we must realize that each of us has particular battles nuanced specifically for us, and we need to give both grace and exhortation to one another to stand firm in times of testing. Conversely, we must always flee temptation, regardless of how "little" it may seem to us. These inner longings, James says, busily work to pull us away from our Lord.

Even if we do not actively court temptations, we are "dragged away and enticed" (ἐξελκόμενος καὶ δελεαζόμενος) by them. These are most likely modal participles, describing the manner of the tempting. They also reflect well-known metaphors in the ancient world — the first from the occupation of fishing, the second from the practice of

23. E.g., Martin, *James*, 35; Moo, *The Letter of James*, 73; Laws, *The Epistle of James*, 71. This is the traditional interpretation.

24. See esp. Davids, *The Epistle of James*, 82 – 83. Cf. idem, "The Meaning of ἀπείραστος in James i. 13," *NTS* 24 (1978): 386 – 92. Davids finds support for this in Dt 6:16, where the people tested God by their complaints. But "ought not" is not the same thing as "cannot," which is what ἀπείραστος denotes, and blaming God (James's topic) is not the same as testing him (as the Israelites did in the OT).

25. Hiebert, *The Epistle of James*, 103.

26. Martin (*James*, 35) believes that "James identifies now the real origin of the πειρασμοί and the κακά of v 13." Johnson (*The Letter of James*, 193) clarifies that, while ἐπιθυμία in itself is neutral, it regularly contains the negative connotation of an immoral desire in both classical and biblical use.

27. Moo (*The Letter of James*, 74) describes it as "any human longing for what God has prohibited" and highlights the parallel uses of the word in 1Pe 2:11 and 1 Jn 2:17.

hunting. James forces us to take an honest look at the desires and thoughts that we foster and allow to grow within ourselves, tugging at us and alluring us. Many sinful actions begin as casual thoughts, but dwelling on them can turn minor temptations into major transgressions.

James 1:15 Then that desire, having conceived, gives birth to sin, and that sin, having matured, gives birth to death (εἶτα ἡ ἐπιθυμία συλλαβοῦσα τίκτει ἁμαρτίαν, ἡ δὲ ἁμαρτία ἀποτελεσθεῖσα ἀποκύει θάνατον). James now delineates the life cycle of sin.[28] The "then" (εἶτα), a comparatively rare word in the NT, consistently denotes sequence, showing that here we learn about the next step as the temptations within us start to drag us away. Having been enticed by our inner craving, the desire leads to sinful action. Meanwhile, sin, when we allow it free reign, results in (spiritual) death.[29] One thinks of Paul's classic statement about the wages of sin (Ro 6:23).[30] But here James uses a more vivid metaphor, showing the reproductive process as difficult to stop once it begins. Thus "the sexual connotation of *epithymia* ... is exploited by the vivid sexual imagery of the present verse."[31] One can almost envision three generations here: desire as a "parent," sin as a "child," and death as a "grandchild."

Centuries ago the Venerable Bede suggested that there were "three stages in temptation. The first is suggestion, the second is experiment, and the third is consent." Once we reach the consent stage, we have been carried away by sin, we have willingly left the path of righteousness, and we deserve to be separated from God.[32] The metaphors of growth and reproduction remind us that James is not thinking just of the major crises or blatant temptations that assault us but also of the countless little decisions we make on a daily basis, over a lifetime, that mold and shape us into the people we ultimately become.[33] As will become even clearer throughout the letter, James regularly judges a person "saved" only from the perspective of 20 – 20 hindsight, as one looks back on one's life as a whole.

James 1:16 Do not deceive yourselves, my beloved brothers and sisters (Μὴ πλανᾶσθε, ἀδελφοί μου ἀγαπητοί). Here we have another hinge verse that could fit with the preceding section as a final warning.[34] However, most commentators take it as the introduction to vv. 17 – 18. Vv. 16 – 18 are thus best seen as a further discussion of what does and

28. Again, see John Milton's *Paradise Lost* (Book 2, ll. 629 – 1055) for a literary picture of this relationship between Satan, Sin, and Death. Moo (*The Letter of James*, 75) explains that "James shifts metaphors to describe the havoc that *desire* can wreak in the spiritual life." This image of "desire" as a temptress who leads us astray is based heavily on Pr 5 – 9.

29. If one does not adopt the life-cycle imagery, the beginning of v. 15b can be translated as "when sin has run its course," thus still stressing the end results of sin. Perkins (*First and Second Peter, James, and Jude*, 101) observes that "those who persist in sin receive the antithesis of the crown of life. They experience death." Stulac (*James*, 56 – 57) warns that "we would be applying the verse in a way not intended by James if we derived a doctrinal statement that Christians can lose their salvation. James's concern is not for such a point of doctrine but for a life of genuine faith."

30. Johnson (*The Letter of James*, 194) points out further parallels to "the relationship between sin and death" in Jn 8:21; Ro 5:12, 21; 1Co 15:56.

31. Ibid., 194. Walter T. Wilson ("Sin as Sex and Sex with Sin: The Anthropology of James 1:12 – 15," *HTR* 95 [2002]: 147 – 68) reads these verses in the context of the larger social realities within which these Christians were living, so that "the self's courageous resistance to the temptations of its internal desire correlates with the community's resistance to the external testings associated with its socio-economic vulnerability" (168).

32. Gerald Bray, ed., *Ancient Christian Commentary on Scripture*, vol. 11: *James, 1 – 2 Peter, 1 – 3 John, Jude* (Downers Grove, IL: IVP, 2000), 12.

33. Cf. Patrice Rolin, "Les épreuves de la foi — Jacques 1,1 – 19a, analyse et interprétation," *FoiVie* 102.4 (2003): 59.

34. So, e.g., Martin, *James*, 37; Hiebert, *The Epistle of James*, 109.

does not come from God. If God does *not* send temptations, then the question naturally arises as to what he *does* give his people.[35] James begins with the warning, "do not deceive yourselves" (μὴ πλανᾶσθε). Martin labels this a "final call ... of vigilance."[36] The present imperative with μή could imply "stop" being deceived, although nothing in the context necessitates this. The word "deceive" suggests the sense of wandering (just as a "planet" was so named because it looked like a "wandering" star), going astray, or being mistaken.

James does not specify who is doing the deceiving, but in the Second Temple Judaism the agents of deception were often spirits or powers such as fallen angels. Thus, one could understand πλανᾶσθε as passive in voice and translate the warning, "do not be deceived." But it seems more likely that James intends a middle form, implying "do not allow yourselves to be deceived," or even "do not deceive yourselves," coming as it does on the heels of the conviction that people are tempted by their own evil desires. This warning echoes Jer 17:9 that "the heart is deceitful above all things."[37] We are prone to deceive even ourselves unless we constantly guard and preserve the truth. This verse is also the first time that James calls his audience "beloved" (ἀγαπητοί), a term of affection that helps to soften his blow. Indeed, he uses it three times in this letter to emphasize the fraternal nature of his appeal (cf. also 1:19 and 2:5).

James 1:17 Every good and perfect gift is coming down from above, from the Father of lights, in whom there is no variation or shadow of turning (πᾶσα δόσις ἀγαθὴ καὶ πᾶν δώρημα τέλειον ἄνωθέν ἐστιν, καταβαῖνον ἀπὸ τοῦ πατρὸς τῶν φώτων, παρ' ᾧ οὐκ ἔνι παραλλαγὴ ἢ τροπῆς ἀποσκίασμα). Here is what we should not be deceived about. James begins with the redundant combination, "all good giving and every perfect gift" (πᾶσα δόσις ἀγαθὴ καὶ πᾶν δώρημα τέλειον). The first phrase could emphasize the verbal sense of "giving," but more likely the terms are synonymous.[38] Most commentators agree that this phrase is perfectly well translated as "every good and perfect gift." The verse links verbally with 1:4 (on "perfection") and 1:5 (on a "giving" God). James may thus still have wisdom in mind here as God's preeminent gift.[39] Verbal and conceptual links with 3:17 – 18 (on "wisdom from above") further support this suggestion.[40] A key gift could also be the Holy Spirit, especially if James is thinking of Jesus' promise in Lk 11:13.[41]

James further affirms that each of these gifts "is coming down from above" (ἄνωθέν ἐστιν καταβαῖνον), that is, from God. The present tense of the participle "coming down" (καταβαῖνον), suggesting continuous or repeated action, indicates how God consistently lavishes his gifts on us. In classifying the participle, one could suggest an adverbial use of attendant circumstances ("every ... gift is from above, [and] *coming down* ..."), an

35. Davids, *The Epistle of James*, 85. Moo (*The Letter of James*, 77) adds how this passage also brings us "back to the theme of the singleness and integrity of God, especially in his giving," as well as contrasting his gifts with the trials that come our way.

36. Martin, *James*, 37.

37. Nystrom (*James*, 83) makes the observation that James "knows that we possess a tremendous capacity to fool ourselves and to believe certain things simply because we wish to believe them, even against overwhelming evidence."

38. Ropes (*A Critical and Exegetical Commentary on the Epistle of St. James*, 158) comments that this could be "either the act of giving or the thing given," but the "parallelism to δώρημα makes the latter sense probable."

39. Perkins (*First and Second Peter, James, and Jude*, 102) draws on Wis 7:11 – 12 to assert that "the primary referent of the perfect heavenly gift must be wisdom."

40. Martin (*James*, 38) itemizes the commonalities: "ἄνωθεν, verbs of downward motion, and also ... the way the character of the giver and the gift is set forth."

41. Cf. further Kamell, "Wisdom in James," 139.

attributive adjectival use ("every ... gift which *comes down* from above is ..."), or a periphrastic construction with the ἐστιν ("every gift *is coming down* from above"). The word order of the form of "to be" followed immediately by the participle tends to support the periphrastic construction (the predicate use of the adjectival participle), yielding the translation we have offered.[42]

The genitive "of lights" (φώτων) is objective, showing God as the Creator. The "Father of lights" appears in a context referring to God's activity—his showering good gifts on his people. So "Father" is likely to be a verbal noun in this context, which limits our options to two possible genitives: subjective (the Father produced by lights) or objective (the One who fathered the lights). Only the latter makes sense here. God is the one who created the lights of heaven—the sun, moon, and stars.[43]

The verse goes on to affirm that "to send good gifts belongs to God's unvarying nature."[44] James uses the qualifier, "in whom there is no variation or shadow of turning" (παρ' ᾧ οὐκ ἔνι παραλλαγὴ ἢ τροπῆς ἀποσκίασμα), to emphasize the complete lack of change in God's character.[45] The expression "shadow of turning" (τροπῆς ἀποσκίασμα) uses a descriptive genitive (equivalent to "turning shadow"). The pair of words probably once formed a technical, scientific expression, but that meaning has been lost in Koine Greek.[46] These words, nevertheless, "often refer to astronomical phenomena in the ancient world," and James almost certainly uses this expression with a similar referent here.[47]

There are two main interpretations. First, one can claim that "God neutralizes the astral powers and gives to man the freedom to decide his own destiny when faced with trials."[48] Given that he never changes, we are not bound by fate to the changes in the stars. The safer, less ambitious interpretation, which we prefer, reads this verse as declaring the "sovereignty of God over the stars."

42. So also Johnson, *The Letter of James*, 195; Davids, *The Epistle of James*, 87; Hiebert, *The Epistle of James*, 112.

43. Donald J. Verseput ("James 1:17 and the Jewish Morning Prayers," *NovT* 39 [1997]: 177–91) finds the background for this verse in the Jewish prayers that would be said at the start of each day, thanking God for the faithfulness that was "evidenced anew every morning," and shows that it functions to draw his readers in to "join in affirming the preserving mercy of God" (190–91). Christian-Bernard Amphoux ("A propos de Jacques 1,17," *RHPR* 50 [1970]: 127–36) dissents from the majority, taking "father of lights" to mean "creator of humans," following one Hellenistic meaning of the term, borrowed from the Iranians. But why look so far afield when there is a perfectly common and natural Jewish meaning available?

44. Ropes, *A Critical and Exegetical Commentary on the Epistle of St. James*, 161. James wants to make certain right from the beginning that his audience does not question God's character as generous to his people (cf. v. 5).

45. Here appears the third textual variant of this chapter that the UBS treats, granting the preferred reading only a {B} level of confidence. The reading chosen has the majority of the textual support, including the corrected א[2], A, and C as well as all of Byz. The reading "variation or of shadow of turning" (παραλλαγὴ ἢ τροπῆς ἀποσκιάσματος) has the original א and B, the two oldest relatively complete New Testaments. Grammatically, however, this reading makes no sense. Bruce M. Metzger (*A Textual Commentary on the Greek New Testament* [New York: UBS, 1994], 608) notes that it would be intelligible only if the "or" (ἢ) were understood as the relative pronoun "which" (ἥ) (i.e., "variation *which is* of shadow of turning"), a reading still "excessively turgid." The reading "variation or turning of shadow" (παραλλαγὴ ἢ τροπὴ ἀποσκιάσματος), reversing the nominative and genitive, has only a twelfth-century minuscule for support, making it not much of a contender. The reading "of variation or of shadow of turning" (παραλλαγῆς ἢ τροπῆς ἀποσκιάσματος) has the very early papyrus 𝔓[23] as its sole support. It turns all three nouns into genitives, probably by conflation, which Johnson (*The Letter of James*, 196) calls "virtually untranslatable." The remaining two options in the UBS add or substitute words for emphasis ("... nor even a foundation of any suspicion of a shadow") or to improve intelligibility ("variation or falling shadow"), but again with very little and very late support.

46. Davids (*The Epistle of James*, 87) observes that trying to pin down what precise astral phenomenon James has in mind creates more confusion than clarity.

47. Moo, *The Letter of James*, 78.

48. Martin, *James*, 39.

Moreover, "while they are always in motion he never changes whether in himself ... or in his dealings with his people."[49]

James 1:18 Because he was willing, he gave birth to us by the word of truth, in order that we might be a sort of firstfruit of his creation (βουληθεὶς ἀπεκύησεν ἡμᾶς λόγῳ ἀληθείας εἰς τὸ εἶναι ἡμᾶς ἀπαρχήν τινα τῶν αὐτοῦ κτισμάτων). James rounds out this section by giving the preeminent example of a good gift that God offers us. The verse begins with asyndeton for emphasis.[50] The participle "having willed" (βουληθείς) is probably causal. The word itself "emphasizes how God acted freely without external constraint in the creation of the universe and of humankind."[51] The main verb, "gave birth" or "bore" (ἀπεκύησεν), is the same one used in v. 15 with sin producing death. When not used metaphorically, as there, it requires a woman for its subject.[52] But here the subject is God, who was just described as "*father* of lights" in v. 17! Having already birthed (or created) the universe, he now adds saved human beings into his eternal family.[53]

This birthing occurred "by the word of truth" (λόγῳ ἀληθείας). "By the word" (λόγῳ) is an instrumental dative of means, showing the method God chose to bring us into the company of the redeemed. The genitive "of truth" (ἀληθείας) is descriptive, depicting the "word" by which we have been reborn as "true." This word of truth most likely equals the gospel message — the story of Christ's incarnation, death, and resurrection — and its significance.

Through this message we become "a sort of firstfruit" (ἀπαρχήν τινα).[54] Just as the first literal fruits to appear on a tree promise more to come, so also the first generation of Christians anticipated the rebirth or new creation of many more redeemed people in future ages. "'Firstfruit' might indicate something of the eschatological community's preferential status in the reign of God ... a point of considerable rhetorical importance if the readers are among society's least and last."[55] "A sort of" (τινα) clarifies the metaphorical nature of James's language; we are merely *like* a firstfruit, just as Paul would call Christ the firstfruit of all future resurrected beings (1Co 15:20). The partitive genitive, "of ... creatures" (κτισμάτων), confirms that believers form the first harvest that God is reaping from all that he fashioned, prior to the eventual re-creation of the entire cosmos. God's gifts thus ultimately lead to eternal life, the exact opposite of the results of temptation and sin in v. 15.

49. Ibid., noting that "James is offering a theodicy to vindicate the divine character in the face of those who doubted the goodness and reliability of God or who had given up hope in time of testing." Garland ("Severe Trials, Good Gifts, and Pure Religion," 392) adds that "God's goodness ... is not as periodic as the full moon or the morning sunrise. It does not fade into the west."

50. Hiebert, *The Epistle of James*, 110. It may also tie vv. 17 – 18 closely together, justifying James's lack of repetition of the subject (God) in the second verse (Burchard, *Der Jakobusbrief*, 77).

51. Martin, *James*, 39.

52. These two uses are the only NT uses of this verb. Translators have been reticent to render it with its most common, biological meaning here, lest God be viewed as taking on maternal attributes. But cf. Nu 11:12; Dt 32:18; and Isa 42:14. See further J. David Miller, "Can the 'Father of Lights' Give Birth?" *Priscilla Papers* 19 (2005): 5 – 7.

53. This birth could refer to all humans at their creation, in anticipation of the renewal of the entire cosmos (so, e.g., L. E. Elliott-Binns, "James i.18: Creation or Redemption?" *NTS* 3 [1956]: 148 – 61) or just to Christians at their redemption (so most authors). The latter of these is preferable, because the imagery suggests redemption, but all human beings are not redeemed.

54. James seems to be using this eschatological expression in the same way other NT writers do (cf. Ro 16:5; 1Co 16:15; Col 1:10; Eph 2:15; 2Th 2:13; 1Pe 1:23; Rev 14:4). Martin (*James*, 40 – 41) points out how the "firstfruit" metaphor fits well with the life-cycle imagery in v. 15.

55. Wall, *Community of the Wise*, 68.

Theology in Application

God's Goodness in Testing (1:12)

Even when believers perceive nothing good coming from affliction in this life, they can look forward to a magnificent eternal compensation for their suffering. If vv. 2 – 4 do not unambiguously refer to the eschaton, v. 12 does. As we saw with vv. 2 – 4, the most pressing trials James's community faces are elucidated in 4:13 – 5:18 (see above, pp. 49 – 50). It is quite possible that some of the poor, exploited Christians whom James addresses will never find justice within the fallen systems of this world. They *can*, however, count on the eternal, all-loving, and entirely just God of the universe to provide complete redress in the age to come (cf. 4:12). First, though, they must respond properly by continuing to trust him during the tough times of the present. The biblical texts and themes that informed our application of vv. 2 – 4 will likewise provide important background to v. 12 (see above, pp. 29, 43 – 44).

"Blessed" is sometimes translated as "happy," for the sake of using more contemporary English (e.g., GNB). But this can too easily suggest an emotion (recall comments on 1:2). Emotional happiness may be the last thing we can conjure up when we face trials! Rather, the word here means "fortunate" — because of the coming reward of eternal life.[56] But we may have to persevere for a prolonged period of time until we have passed whatever test God has for us and become "approved" (NASB) or shown to be "genuine" (NET). At the same, he always makes his power available to help us, through his indwelling Spirit, so that when we *do* respond properly, it is still by God's grace. When we *do not*, we cannot legitimately protest that we had no alternative (cf. 1Co 10:13).[57]

Our reward, however, makes perseverance the only logical response to trials. The "crown of life" represents one of five "crown" metaphors found in the epistles, all of which refer to unending, perfect paradise in the company of God, Christ, and all the redeemed. The other four speak of an incorruptible crown (1Co 9:25), a crown of rejoicing (1Th 2:19), a crown of righteousness (2Ti 4:8), and a crown of glory (1Pe 5:4). In each case, the context makes it clear that these are not rewards above and beyond eternal life itself, but vivid metaphors for the perfections of the life to come.[58] Indeed, it is arguable that this doctrine of rewards, popular as it is in some circles, comes more from the vestiges of the Roman Catholic concept of purgatory than from the Bible itself.[59] Every Christian may have a somewhat unique experience before Christ on the Judgment Day, with varying amounts of praise and

56. Or else, with David A. Hubbard (*The Book of James: Wisdom that Works* [Waco, TX: Word, 1980], 29), one redefines "true happiness" as being honored by God, which honor "comes to those who endure temptation."

57. Cf. Tidball, *Wisdom from Heaven*, 27.

58. Cf. the uses of "crown of righteousness" and "crown of glory" in the Pseudepigrapha (*T. Levi* 8:2, 9) as well.

59. Emma Disley, "Degrees of Glory: Protestant Doctrine and the Concept of Rewards Hereafter," *JTS* 42 (1991): 77 – 105.

censure, but after that we have complete perfection and happiness to which to look forward, which by definition excludes gradation.[60]

God's Non-Participation in Temptation (1:13 – 15)

Believers' responses determine whether suffering will ultimately prove a test to pass or a temptation to sin. Thus, when we do experience temptation, we dare not blame God but only ourselves. Intriguing is the absence of all mention of Satan or his minions here. James knows of the devil's role in temptation (note the "demonic wisdom" in 3:15) and will later call Christians to resist him (4:7). But here James's emphasis remains on people owning their own responsibility.

In the OT, God sometimes appears to be more directly involved with evil than in the NT (see the classic examples of his sending of the evil spirit on Saul [1Sa 16:14, 23] or inciting David to rebel against him by calling for a census [2Sa 24:1]). Yet even in the OT, various writers understood the intermediate role of Satan, under God's permissive will, as the more direct agent of evil (cf. esp. 1Ch 21:1 and Job 1 – 2).[61] Of course, this explanation works only when one understands that Satan is a created being who does not partake of God's uniquely incommunicable attributes such as omnipotence, omnipresence, and omniscience, and that he does nothing apart from what God's sovereign will allows him to do.[62] He is *not* God's equal but opposite, as in the "Star Wars theology" of light and dark sides of the Force. In that model, no one knows which side will ultimately prevail, whereas Christians rest assured that Jesus has already sealed Satan's doom. In fact, Sir 15:11 – 20, already in the second century B.C., contains material strikingly parallel in wording and concept to Jas 1:13.

In the NT, Jesus will teach his disciples to pray, "lead us not into temptation" (Mt 6:13; Lk 11:4), in the sense of "do not allow us to give into temptation" (cf. the parallel request, "but deliver us from evil").[63] But God may lead believers into the *place* in which the devil and/or their own natural desires will tempt them, just as the Holy Spirit led Christ into the wilderness where Satan tempted him (Mt 4:1 – 11; Lk 4:1 – 13). These temptation narratives should not be viewed as contradicting Jas 1:13, neither on this issue nor on the question of how Jesus could be tempted if he was fully God and God cannot be tempted to do wrong. The standard, orthodox

60. Interestingly, Martin Luther vehemently opposed the notion of eternally differing degrees of reward in heaven as antithetical to the NT emphasis on salvation by grace alone. See further Craig L. Blomberg, "Degrees of Reward in the Kingdom of Heaven?" *JETS* 35 (1992): 159 – 72.

61. The same kind of explanation may account for God's testing (tempting?) Abraham to sacrifice his son, Isaac (Gen.22:1). *Jubilees* 17:15 – 18 reflects a recurring Jewish tradition that it was Prince Mastema (another name for the devil) who challenged God to test/tempt Abraham and who was more immediately responsible. See Peter H. Davids, "The Pseudepigrapha in the Catholic Epistles," in *The Pseudepigrapha and Early Biblical Interpretation*, ed. James H. Charlesworth and Craig A. Evans (Sheffield: SAP, 1993), 229 – 30.

62. Cf. Richardson, *James*, 80, n. 68.

63. Hughes, *James*, 46.

answer throughout church history has been to point out simply that it must have been Jesus' human nature, not his divine nature, that was tempted.

All this, of course, goes beyond Jas 1:13 – 15, yet these are precisely the kinds of questions that people often raise when studying these verses. The more direct applications of this little paragraph revolve around James's emphasis in vv. 14 – 15 on Christians' owning up to their role in giving in to temptation. "The devil made me do it" may remain a popular slogan, but it represents deeply flawed theology. Satan never has the power to *make* a person do anything.[64] True, in the extreme case of demon-possession, it appears from the descriptions in the Gospels and Acts that diabolical powers can exercise a significant measure of control over an individual. But this control leads to such unnatural behaviors as changed speech, superhuman strength, revulsion at the name or presence of Christ, separation from society, and the like. Nowhere in Scripture are demons held responsible for "ordinary" sins such as lust, greed, theft, hatred, and so on.[65] To disavow personal responsibility for these kinds of sins and/or to seek exorcism for them is to credit the demonic world with more power than the Bible does and to fail to admit one's own freely chosen agreement with temptation's lure in choosing to sin (v. 14).

The ancient rabbis regularly attributed such behavior to the "evil impulse" (*yēṣer hā-rā*) that resided in every human, fighting against the "good impulse" (*yēṣer hā-ṭôv*).[66] Repentance and changed behavior form the appropriate Christian response to sin — not blaming God, seeking exorcism, or (esp. in our therapeutic society) blaming one's upbringing or one's friends or the government, and so forth.[67] And the stakes are high: if unchecked, a person can become so immersed in sin that their ultimate end is spiritual death (v. 15; see further under 2:14 – 26).[68]

God's Role in Giving Only Good Gifts (1:16 – 18)

If God is not directly responsible for producing anything evil, then it logically follows that what he *is* directly responsible for creating or giving can be only good. The most fundamental biblical background for this concept is Genesis 1 – 3. Everything that God fashioned on the six days of creation he observed to be "good" (1:4,

64. "Where so much present-day Christian preaching and conversation would have introduced 'the devil' or 'Satan,' James has no reference to this arch-enemy" (Motyer, *The Message of James*, 54).

65. Cf. Tidball, *Wisdom from Heaven*, 30.

66. Cf. further Joel Marcus, "The Evil Inclination in the Epistle of James," *CBQ* 44 (1982): 606 – 21.

67. "How, in an age when people sue the restaurant for serving fattening food and the teacher for their poor grades, but excuse themselves for not choosing salads over French fries or for not studying for the test, can we help but not finally blame God for any and every circumstance not of our liking? And if we do, how shall we understand true evil and develop the endurance to handle real temptation?" (Brosend, *James and Jude*, 47).

68. This warning does not foreclose the Calvinist-Arminian debate over "eternal security" or the "perseverance of the saints." Calvinists simply argue that such prolonged sinful activity, from which one never turns, belies the genuineness of any profession of salvation, while Arminians more readily speak of a true Christian having committed apostasy and forfeited salvation.

10, 12, etc.). Their corruption came only later, as the result of human sin (ch. 3). But God's plans will not be thwarted; human history will end with the re-creation of a new heavens and a new *earth* (Rev 21–22).

Of course, many events in this life that seem to come from God also seem undesirable. At such times, Christians must remember the two main principles of vv. 17–18. First, God does not change in the way that heavenly bodies or earthly shadows do (cf. esp. Mal 3:6–7). Therefore, he who created the heavens and earth can be trusted to continue to provide only good things for his children (cf. esp. Mt 7:11). Second, the preeminent example of his wonderful provisions is our rebirth (for firstfruits applied already to Israel, see Ex. 23:19), which, as James has already highlighted, more than compensates for anything we experience that seems to us far less than perfect (cf. esp. Ro 8:18; 2Co 4:17).[69]

Of course, we should not lose sight of what we have already learned from this passage. Because we live in a fallen world, much of what happens to us is not a direct gift from God, but the result of our own sin, someone else's transgression (going all the way back at times to the fall), or the devil's treachery. But if certain circumstances do come directly from God, then one day we will understand how they were indeed for our benefit. Frustratingly, it is often impossible to determine whether suffering in a given situation comes directly from God or not. Fortunately, our response ought not change either way, so we need not have the answer to that question. We are obliged never to sin, but always to turn to God in dependence on him and respond in a way that we know will please him, in keeping with his revealed Word. And because he remains sovereign, every set of circumstances may be said to come at least indirectly from him. We owe our very salvation to his sovereign will (v. 18),[70] so we can surely entrust all lesser items to it as well.[71] Because God is single-minded in giving only good gifts, we can be single-minded in following him and his will.[72]

69. Sooner or later most Christians can relate to the following: "I have recently felt very beaten over the head with the fallenness of the world.... During the past few weeks I have watched illnesses of various forms derail many people's lives, and I find myself very tired, with an intensifying heaven longing.... I find in me the settled realization that this world, with all the beautiful things in it and all the joyous experiences in it, is a fallen place and it is not my final home.... I cannot imagine how to make sense of the events of my life and the lives of those around me without the peace that comes from knowing that there is a God who will vindicate and comfort us, and also that this world is NOT the way it was intended to be" (Mariam J. Kamell, "Scum of the Earth Church Newsletter" [April 2005], 1).

70. The solitary causal participle, "because he was willing"—lit., "having willed [it]" (βουληθείς)—can be clarified by various translations: "in the exercise of his will" (NASB), "by his sovereign plan" (NET), "by His own choice" (HCSB), or "in fulfillment of his own purpose" (NRSV).

71. Cf. Rea McDonnell, *The Catholic Epistles and Hebrews* (Wilmington: Glazier, 1986), 43.

72. Cf. Timothy B. Cargal, *Restoring the Diaspora: Discursive Structure and Purpose in the Epistle of James* (Atlanta: Scholars, 1993), 77–78.

CHAPTER 3

James 1:19 – 27

Literary Context

The opening sections of James's letter introduce his three most important themes (1:2 – 11). The rest of ch. 1 goes back through these themes again, adding a distinctive but related emphasis to each. Previously, we saw the topic of trials expanded by the addition of a discussion of temptations (vv. 12 – 18). Here, the subject of wisdom is applied particularly to the area of speech ethics, reminding the readers that wisdom necessitates obedience (vv. 19 – 26). As in vv. 5 – 8, James employs a simile, again using the rare verb for "is like" (ἔοικεν; vv. 6, 23), strengthening the wisdom tie. Finally, the issue of remedying the problems caused by class divisions between rich and poor is addressed in the context of "true religion" and the responsibility of the "haves" for the "have-nots" (v. 27). This verse also appears to form the thesis for the entire letter.

The actual word for "wisdom" (σοφία) does not appear in vv. 19 – 26, so one might argue that these verses are unrelated to 1:5 – 8, in which wisdom first appeared. Some begin the body of James's letter here and see a brand new topic introduced, such as "hearing and doing the word," (recall above, p. 24). One counterargument highlights the central role of obedience to the gospel in a wise life, the Christian equivalent of the "fear of the Lord" (recall Pr 1:7). One thinks especially of the end of Jesus' Sermon on the Mount on hearing *and doing* Christ's words (Mt 7:24 – 27 par.).

A more significant argument notes the link between speech and wisdom in 3:1 – 4:12. There, 3:1 – 12 clearly highlights the power of the tongue (i.e., speech) for good and bad; 3:13 – 18 contrasts the "wisdom" that is from below with that which comes from above; and 4:1 – 12 returns to the issue of speech ethics, rebuking the verbal fights occurring within the community (vv. 1 – 10) and calling on believers not to slander one another (vv. 11 – 12). A specific verbal repetition occurs with the metaphor of the "bridle" applied to the tongue (1:26) as the instrument enabling control of one's whole body (3:2). Finally, 3:13 epitomizes the summary of wisdom from above as good "works" done "in humility," using the identical word and phrase as in 1:25 and 1:21, respectively.

At the same time, 1:19 – 27 ties in with its immediate context. "My beloved brothers and sisters" (v. 19) repeats verbatim the address of 1:16.[1] The "implanted word" (v. 21) refers to the new covenant message, just as "the word of truth" did in v. 18. James pronounces a blessing (in beatitude form) on the one doing Christian works in v. 25, just as he had blessed the one enduring trials (v. 12). In fact, all of vv. 19 – 27 can be seen as explaining how to avoid turning trials into temptations, as in vv. 13 – 18.[2] Looking ahead, the theme of the right behavior of rich toward poor (1:27) clearly anticipates the detailed elaboration of this theme in 2:1 – 26.

- II. Statement of Three Key Themes (1:2 – 11)
  - A. Trials in the Christian Life (1:2 – 4)
  - B. Wisdom (1:5 – 8)
  - C. Riches and Poverty (1:9 – 11)
- III. Restatement of the Three Themes (1:12 – 27)
  - A. Trials/Temptations in Relation to God (1:12 – 18)
  - ➦ **B. Wisdom in the Areas of Speech and Obedience (1:19 – 26)**
    - **1. The Three Commands (1:19)**
    - **2. Slow to Anger (1:20 – 21)**
    - **3. Quick to Listen (1:22 – 25)**
    - **4. Slow to Speak (1:26)**
  - **C. The "Have-Nots" and the Responsibility of the "Haves": The Thesis of the Letter (1:27)**
- IV. The Three Themes Expanded (2:1 – 5:18)
  - A. Riches and Poverty (2:1 – 26)
    - 1. Favoritism Condemned (2:1 – 13)
    - 2. The Problem of Faith without Works (2:14 – 26)

Main Idea

Christians should respond to God's Word with obedient listening, careful speech, and a humble demeanor. Or, in the words of v. 19, they should be quick to listen, slow to speak, and slow to anger. A key application of obedience and humble conduct involves care for the dispossessed even while maintaining personal purity.

1. Again, some would put this call (v. 19a) as the conclusion to the preceding paragraph (e.g., Johnson, *The Letter of James*, 199), but such appeals function far more commonly as introductions to new paragraphs.

2. Tsuji, *Glaube zwischen Vollkommenheit und Verweltlichung*, 67 – 72.

Translation

James 1:19-27

19a	Entreaty	**Know [this]**, my beloved brothers and sisters:
19b	Exhortation	**Let every person be quick to listen**,
	in a series	**slow to speak**,
		slow to anger.
20	Assertion	For **a person's wrath does not produce the righteousness of God**.
21a	time	having put off all dirtiness and
21b	restatement	excess of wickedness,
21c	manner	in humility
21d	exhortation	Therefore … **receive the implanted word**
21e	description	which is able to save your souls.
22a	Exhortation	**Become doers of the word and**
22b	contrast	**not hearers only**
22c	description	who deceive themselves.
23a	condition (of 23c)	For if someone is a hearer of the word and
23b	contrast	not a doer,
23c	inference	**this one is like a person**
23d	description	who considers their natural face
23e	place	in a mirror.
24	Explanation	For **they consider themselves intently and**
	in a series	**depart and**
		immediately forget what sort [of person] they are.
25a	Contrast	But the one who looks closely into the perfect law of liberty and
25b	expansion	remains [in it] and
		is not a forgetful hearer but a doer who acts
25c	result (of 25a and b)	**this one is blessed in their doing**.
26a	Condition	If anyone seems to be religious,
26b	simultaneous	while not bridling their tongue but
26c	contrast	deceiving their heart,
26d	inference	**the religion of this one [is] worthless**.
27a	Assertion	**This is religion [that is] pure and undefiled before [our] God and Father**:
27b	apposition	to visit orphans and widows in their distress and
27c	simultaneous	to keep oneself unstained from the world.

Structure

The internal structure of 1:19 – 27 is the least clear of the passages so far surveyed. There is a reasonable consensus that this passage can be broken into three subsections: vv. 19 – 21, 22 – 25, and 26 – 27. But how are these parts related to each other and to the whole pericope? A promising suggestion is that of William Baker, who sees v. 19 introducing the thesis statement of the section, with its three commands to be quick to listen, slow to speak, and slow to anger. Vv. 20 – 21 then unpack the theme of being slow to anger. Vv. 22 – 25 develop the idea of being quick to listen, with its emphasis that true listening to God's Word leads to obedience.[3] V. 26 then treats the topic of being slow to speak.[4]

At one level, v. 27 seems separate from vv. 19 – 26, as it returns to James's third key theme, introduced in vv. 9 – 11, on wealth and poverty. Its twin emphases (see below) could easily merit an entire sermon or lesson in and of itself.[5] Yet Hellenistic moralists elsewhere linked brevity in speech with religious or philosophical maturity, so the pairing of vv. 26 – 27 need not jar us.[6] On another level, v. 27 probably functions as James's conclusion to all of vv. 19 – 27.[7] The three commands of v. 19 encapsulate a surprisingly large part of Christian obedience, but v. 27 epitomizes the whole "package" of God's will for believers.[8] This verse thus forms an apt conclusion to the two-part introduction to James's letter, with its double treatment of his three key themes (vv. 2 – 11, 12 – 27).[9] As such, we may also consider it the thesis statement of the letter, tucked between the introduction and the letter body where such theses often appear (cf., e.g., Ro 1:16 – 17; 2Th 2:2; Col 1:15 – 20; 2Ti 2:2).[10]

One may subdivide the four parts of vv. 19 – 27 further. The tripartite thesis of v. 19b is preceded by an entreaty to "know" what James is about to stress (v. 19a). It resembles the warning of v. 16 in form but without the ominous overture not to be "deceived." It appears as an exhortation (i.e., a command) but is not as marked,

3. Cf. the REB for v. 22a: "Only be sure you act on the message."

4. Baker, "James," 29 – 43. Cf. William R. Baker and Thomas D. Ellsworth, *Preaching James* (St. Louis: Chalice, 2004), 32; Hartin, *James*, 105 – 10.

5. See Mariam Kamell, "The Emergent Need for James," unpublished paper presented at the Evangelical Theological Society convention (Washington, DC, November 2006).

6. Luke T. Johnson, "Taciturnity and True Religion: James 1:26 – 27," in *Greeks, Romans, and Christians*, ed. David L. Balch, Everett Ferguson, and Wayne A. Meeks (Minneapolis: Fortress, 1990), 329 – 39.

7. Brosend (*James and Jude*, 48) sees the unifying theme as "actions speak louder than words."

8. It also contrasts nicely with what is proscribed in vv. 19 – 26 (Hubbard, *The Book of James*, 40).

9. For a complementary explanation of the relationship among the three parts, we may consider C. John Collins, "Coherence in James 1:19 – 27," *JOTT* 10 (1998): 80 – 87. Collins observes that "receiving the word" elsewhere in the New Testament regularly refers to a proper response to the public ministry of God's Word. Thus v. 21 prepares for this theme by depicting church preaching or teaching. The threefold elaboration of v. 19 then reflects the warning not to become angry when one's sins are pointed out by that teaching (v. 20), to respond with humble obedience instead (vv. 22 – 25), and to remember that our behavior outside of church must match our response inside (vv. 26 – 27).

10. See further the outlines and their explanations in Craig L. Blomberg, *From Pentecost to Patmos: An Introduction to Acts through Revelation* (Nashville: Broadman & Holman, 2006), 235 – 38, 288 – 91, 376 – 78.

content-wise, as the exhortations that actually unpack the main ethical injunctions of the epistle. Vv. 20 – 21 flesh out the skeleton of an assertion (v. 20: human anger does not produce divine righteousness) and an exhortation (v. 21: receive the implanted word). The latter is modified by a temporal reference (after putting off moral filth), a restatement of the nature of the filth (an excess of evil), the manner of reception (in humility), and a description of the word (able to save souls).

Vv. 22 – 25 likewise begin with a topic sentence that governs the entire section (v. 22), this time made up of an exhortation and a contrast (be doers of the word and not just hearers). James further describes the hearers as self-deceiving. Vv. 23 – 24 employ an illustration in the form of a condition and inference (if anyone hears but does not do, they are like people who look in the mirror but do not attend to whatever problems they might see there). V. 25 then moves from the metaphorical level to the spiritual truth being illustrated, but does so by contrast (the person looking into the perfect law of liberty is the one to emulate, not the one looking in the mirror).[11] James expands this truth (one must also *remain* in it), again contrasted with what not to do (forgetting), and with the results of looking and remaining then identified (the blessing that comes in the very act of obedience).[12]

V. 26 subdivides into the main assertion (the one who only seems to be religious displays worthless faith) and the simultaneous, contrasting actions that lead to this conclusion (not bridling one's tongue but deceiving one's heart).[13] V. 27, finally, subdivides into a two-part description of a contrasting form of religion (pure and undefiled) and into the twofold content of that religion (social action and personal piety).[14] As already noted, v. 27 can be somewhat separated off from the surrounding verses or linked more tightly together with them, depending on one's perspective.

Exegetical Outline

III. Restatement of the Three Themes (1:12 – 27)

➦ **B. Wisdom in the Areas of Speech and Obedience (1:19 – 26)**

1. The Thesis Statement: Be Quick to Listen, Slow to Speak, Slow to Anger (v. 19).
2. Christians Should Respond to God's Word with Humility Rather Than Wrath (vv. 20 – 21).
   a. Christians should not be easily angered because anger does not usually enable them to live by God's standards (v. 20).
   b. Christians should respond to God's Word humbly as they recognize how it has worked in their lives in the past (v. 21).

11. A pattern found frequently in James and in wisdom literature more generally, with opposing virtues and vices. See further Luís Alonso Schökel, "Culto y justicia en Sant 1,26 – 27," *Bib* 56 (1975): 537 – 44.

12. But with what not to do mentioned first rather than second this time, highlighting the contrast between negative and positive models all the more. See Gilberto Marconi, "Una nota sullo specchio di Gc 1,23," *Bib* 70 (1989): 399.

13. Alternately, one could take the ἀλλά in v. 26 as emphatic rather than adversative, stressing the results of not bridling one's tongue. Cf. NET: "*and so* deceives his heart."

3. Christians Should Respond to God's Word by Not Merely Listening to It but by Also Obeying It (vv. 22–25).
   a. The topic sentence: Do not just hear the Word but do it, too (v. 22).
   b. People who only listen but do not obey are as ridiculous as those who fail to groom themselves even after careful self-observation in a mirror (vv. 23–24).
   c. People who do carefully study God's Word and obey it are truly blessed (v. 25).
4. Christians Should Respond to God's Word with Careful Rather Than Rash Speech (v. 26).

C. The "Have-Nots" and the Responsibility of the "Haves" as the Thesis of the Letter (v. 27).

1. Social Action Is Epitomized by Helping the Most Helpless of This World (27a).
2. Personal Morality Is Epitomized by Separation from the Sin of This World (v. 27b).

Explanation of Text

James 1:19 Know [this], my beloved brothers and sisters, let every person be quick to listen, slow to speak, slow to anger (Ἴστε, ἀδελφοί μου ἀγαπητοί· ἔστω δὲ πᾶς ἄνθρωπος ταχὺς εἰς τὸ ἀκοῦσαι, βραδὺς εἰς τὸ λαλῆσαι, βραδὺς εἰς ὀργήν). James commences this next section with a proverb that he then explains in the following verses. He begins with the imperative "know"[15] (ἴστε)[16] and again addresses his audience as "beloved brothers and sisters," both softening the abruptness of his command and disclosing familial concern and authority. The second imperative, "let ... be" (ἔστω), focuses on their character, that is, who they ought to be, both individually and as a church.

The proverb begins by telling people to be "quick to hear" (ταχὺς εἰς τὸ ἀκοῦσαι). The prepositional phrase (lit., "for to hear") functions idiomatically as the virtual equivalent to a dative of respect ("quick with respect to hearing"). We are told to "hurry up and listen," with the word for hurry or quickness (ταχύς) implying the idea of rapid pursuit.

In contrast, however, James adds "slow to speak" (βραδὺς εἰς τὸ λαλῆσαι).[17] Here "slow" (βραδύς) indicates a sense of hesitation or delay. Most people behave as if the proverb were reversed — quick to speak and slow to listen! Credible Christian relationships require careful attention to others' perspectives. However, "slow to speak" scarcely

14. The NLT puts it nicely: "Pure and lasting religion in the sight of God our Father means that we must care for orphans and widows in their troubles, and refuse to let the world corrupt us."

15. This form could also be an indicative, but given James's pattern of beginning new sections with imperatives, especially when following them with vocatives, it is best to read it as an imperative.

16. This textual decision was granted only a {B} rating in the UBS, because of the wide variety of options. These variants are caused largely by James's abrupt shift from v. 18 and scribes' desire to create some sort of transition. The numerous readings can be grouped together into two main options, one of which employs the imperative "know" (ἴστε), from "I know" (οἶδα), while the other adopts "therefore" (ὥστε). The former is the much better attested reading, with the corrected ℵ (the original merely has an alternate reading, "let him know" (ἴστω), B and C. The *Byz* tradition, like other later texts, opts for the reading with the transitional "therefore" (ὥστε), which can be understood as trying to smooth out a rough text. In all, the former is the better attested as well as the harder reading. Davids (*The Epistle of James*, 91) points out the parallel between vv. 16–18 and 19–21: both begin with an imperative and a vocative, and both end with a reference to "the word" (λόγος).

17. Sleeper (*James*, 61) notes the parallel with Jesus' teaching in Mt 5:21–22, adding that "for Jesus, the loss of verbal self-control deserves the most serious punishment."

means "never speak," for we must proclaim truth in many contexts.

The final part of James's proverb gives one last challenge, that of being "slow to anger" (βραδὺς εἰς ὀργήν).[18] Here anger refers not so much to general outbursts of frustration as to deeply-seated wrath or rage. We should be hesitant as believers to allow our anger to settle into something that we nurse and that can control us. These last two activities that we are to "be slow" to undertake obviously reflect the greater of the three problems in James's community (see 3:1 – 4:12), but all three are interconnected. Speaking and wrath link together whenever anger provokes hasty speech, and often both of these problems stem from inadequate listening.[19]

James 1:20 For a person's wrath does not produce the righteousness of God (ὀργὴ γὰρ ἀνδρὸς δικαιοσύνην θεοῦ οὐκ ἐργάζεται). James goes on to explain *why* we should be so wary of anger.[20] It is important to remember that this is not Paul writing, so that when James talks about the "righteousness of God" (δικαιοσύνην θεοῦ), he may mean something quite different than Paul's characteristic subjective genitive ("the righteousness produced by God"; cf. Ro 1:17; 3:5, 21, 22, 25, 26; 10:3; 2Co 5:21; Php 3:9). Here the genitive "of God" (θεοῦ) seems objective, because James is insisting that human wrath does not create the righteousness that can be offered or directed to God, the righteousness that we are called to live out on earth and that he demands from his followers.[21]

The verb used in this short verse is "work out" or "produce" (ἐργάζεται), a vivid expression for the activity that should lead to proper righteousness in our lives. If one accepts a later date for the epistle within the lifetime of James, he could have written this verse in opposition to the Zealot movement. In this situation, the righteousness of God, now understood as employing a subjective genitive, would refer to his saving activity and rule, which cannot be ushered in by violence or anger. This would then be "James's response to those who sought to bring in God's kingdom on earth" through violence.[22] On either reading of the genitive, Moo cautions that James does not forbid every kind of anger, including righteous anger, because wisdom sayings were "notorious for the use of apparently absolute assertions in order to make a general, 'proverbial' point."[23] But Johnson adds that "human anger is not a legitimate instrument for effecting those right relationships God desires for creatures," a conclusion that meshes well with the use of "righteousness" (δικαιοσύνη) in 3:18.[24]

18. Marie E. Isaacs (*Reading Hebrews and James* [Macon, GA: Smyth & Helwys, 2002], 192) observes that "in early Christian tradition, however, anger was not only perceived as dangerous (*1 Clem.* 39.7; *Did.* 3.2), but also as inimical to a Christian way of life (Ro 12:17 – 21; Eph 4:31 – 32; *1 Clem.* 13)."

19. This proverb is clearly dependent on "widespread Jewish wisdom teaching about speech and anger" (Moo, *The Letter of James*, 82); cf. Pr 10:19; 11:12 – 13; 13:3; 15:1; 17:27 – 28; 29:20; Ecc 7:9; Sir 1:22; 5:11 – 13. Stulac (*James*, 66) points out that "listening is most difficult when we are angry." Meanwhile, William R. Baker (*Personal Speech-Ethics in the Epistle of James* [Tübingen: Mohr, 1995], 87) brings out the variety of applications of this proverb: "popular, spiritual, and ecclesial," all of which appear somewhere in James and thus demand special application within his communities.

20. We must again stress that the "man" or "person" (ἄνθρωπος) in v. 19 precedes the "male" or "human" (ἀνήρ) here, demonstrating the generic or inclusive nature of the latter (cf. Maier, *Der Brief des Jakobus*, 90 – 91). It would, after all, be silly to argue that the anger of a *man* cannot produce God's righteousness while the anger of a *woman* could! Brosend (*James and Jude*, 49) notes that "research demonstrating that males are more prone to anger because of testosterone levels comes some 1,900 years after the writing of the letter."

21. Wall (*Community of the Wise*, 71), explains: "Because the phrase is used in James to qualify the importance of a wise response to trials, I suspect the [objective] use is primary here: wise conduct marks out God's people."

22. Martin, *James*, 48.

23. Moo, *The Letter of James*, 84.

24. Johnson, *The Letter of James*, 200. Davids (*The Epistle of James*, 93) expands, declaring that "the human outburst of

James 1:21 Therefore, having put off all dirtiness and excess of wickedness, in humility receive the implanted word which is able to save your souls (διὸ ἀποθέμενοι πᾶσαν ῥυπαρίαν καὶ περισσείαν κακίας ἐν πραΰτητι δέξασθε τὸν ἔμφυτον λόγον τὸν δυνάμενον σῶσαι τὰς ψυχὰς ὑμῶν). Because anger is not the right reaction to God, James concludes his thought on this topic with what *is* the proper response. This verse begins with the conjunction, "therefore" (διό), to connect this conclusion with the previous verse about anger. The aorist temporal participle, "having put off" (ἀποθέμενοι), implies that James's hearers will have, or ought to have, set aside their previous lifestyles.[25] This verb in Peter's and Paul's writings often conveys the image of conversion or baptism — "stripping off" the pre-Christian "clothing" — imagery that James may be drawing on here (cf. esp. Eph 4:22–24; Col 3:8; 1Pe 2:1). He wants them to have removed "all dirtiness and excess of wickedness" (πᾶσαν ῥυπαρίαν καὶ περισσείαν κακίας).

The first noun, "dirtiness" (ῥυπαρία), is a New Testament *hapax* and refers to external grime, as with filthy clothes, stained and muddy. But it also conveys the deeper meaning of moral defilement, of spiritual stains on our souls.[26] "Excess" (περισσεία) specifies a surplus or overabundance of this filth with which we have covered ourselves.[27] "Wickedness" (κακίας), a partitive genitive, meanwhile, denotes evil in character or sin that springs from bad attitudes within one's spirit.[28] These moral failures and taints of evil in our character are the grime and muck that we need to remove from ourselves as readily as taking off filthy clothes after a long day working or playing outside in the mud.[29]

Next appears an important punctuation variant. "In humility" (ἐν πραΰτητι) could be taken either with the previous clause or with the following, meaning either "take off … in humility" or "in humility receive. …" Either way, the prepositional phrase employs an instrumental dative of manner, describing here the way in which one should act. A case could be made that James intentionally places this phrase in a hinge position to refer to the attitude one should have both while divesting oneself of sinfulness and while receiving our new selves from God.[30] But if we must choose, the case seems stronger for taking it with the second clause, because receiving this transformed nature is impossible unless one displays an attitude of humility, and the verb that would be modified is much closer in the sentence.[31]

anger does not produce the type of righteousness that reflects God's standard."

25. All temporal participles that modify a main verb in the imperative mood take on some derivative imperatival force themselves. But it is technically incorrect to label this participle as imperatival per se, because it remains subordinate to a main verb later in the sentence; it is not a completely independent thought as with truly imperatival participles. See Wallace, *Greek Grammar Beyond the Basics*, 650–52.

26. Moo, *The Letter of James*, 86. "The NIV 'moral,' therefore, is an attempt to capture the ethical nuance of a word that basically means 'filth.'"

27. Johnson (*The Letter of James*, 201) argues that "there is no need to tease out more subtle significance" than that this admonition applies to every form of wickedness, and that περισσεία refers to "morally bad behavior, not the abstract sense of 'evil.'"

28. Davids (*The Epistle of James*, 94), in view of the parallel to 1Pe 2:1, reads κακία as "malice" rather than "wickedness" or "vice," more generally. In other words, it focuses more on a hatred of people.

29. Perkins (*First and Second Peter, James, and Jude*, 104) notes that while the implanted word is "another heavenly gift from God that brings salvation … there is a catch. The soul must be prepared.… The imagery suggests cleansing and clearing away evil so that the *emphytos logos* can bear fruit."

30. Baker ("James," 35) explains that "a humble attitude … is not only mandatory when we make God the Lord of our lives; it is also required in the preliminary step of cleaning the evil out of our houses. That's what repentance is." Thus, humility is as crucial for removing the filthy clothes as for receiving the implanted word.

31. Cf. Donald J. Verseput, "Plutarch of Chaeronea and the Epistle of James on Communal Behaviour," *NTS* 47 (2001): 513.

"Humility" (πραΰτης) is another key expression for James. By it, he is not commanding us to become doormats, enjoining a wimpy submissiveness to whatever might come one's way. Rather, he calls for a patient self-effacement free of any malice, anger, repressed frustration, or even arrogant assertiveness. In the Greco-Roman world, humility was not typically viewed as a virtue; many then saw it as an outright weakness.[32] In Judaism and Christianity, however, humility before God remains essential, as demonstrated by Christ's example of humble submission to the will of the Father even unto death.

In this state of humility, then, we ought to receive "the implanted word" (τὸν ἔμφυτον λόγον). While this may sound simply like language of a later addition congruent with salvation, this expression is actually more complex. In Greek thought, "implanted" (ἔμφυτος) meant something "innate," inherent from birth, as part of one's nature.[33] But if this word truly is innate, then we already have it and need not receive it.[34] The implication, however, could be that the "word" is innate to humanity, but as Christians we need to let God activate it within us.[35] A much better solution results from understanding "implanted" as implying the word of the gospel that has "taken up residence within believers," planted there by God.[36] Johnson argues for interpreting "the 'implanted word' as that 'word of truth' by which God gave them birth." Thus for Christians, "that word is now already *emphytos* ('implanted')."[37] This view makes sense of the "word" as presently inherent in Christians, but not before it was implanted at their new birth. Here "word" (λόγος) probably means the same thing as in v. 18—the message of salvation. To "receive" this word will, then, mean to so take it to heart that it replaces the earlier evil desires of vv. 14–15. As promised in Jeremiah's new covenant, it is fully internalized and written on our hearts (Jer 31:33).[38]

James qualifies the "word" as "being able to save your souls" (δυνάμενον σῶσαι τὰς ψυχὰς ὑμῶν). Here we have an interesting contrast between the aspectually undefined aorists "having put off" (ἀποθέμενοι) and "receive" (δέξασθε) and the ongoing aspect of the present participle "being able" (δυνάμενον). One simply puts off the old and receives the new, but the implanted word is continually able to save. The aorist infinitive "to save" (σῶσαι) is global or constative, viewing the entire process of salvation from start to fin-

32. Aristotle does use it, however, in direct opposition to anger (ὀργή) in *Nichomachean Ethics* 1125b, and *Rhetoric* 1380a (Johnson, *The Letter of James*, 201).

33. Cf. Matt Jackson-McCabe (*Logos and Law in the Letter of James: The Law of Nature, the Law of Moses, and the Law of Freedom* [Leiden: Brill, 2001], 27, 196), who sees this as a reference to Stoic philosophy, wherein Reason (the *logos spermatikos*) was implanted at the time of creation, innate to each person (see also Laws, *James*, 83–84). The only appearance of this term in pre-NT Jewish literature is Wis 12:10, where it clearly means "inborn" or "innate" and refers to the wickedness of the Canaanites. Based on this, others (e.g., Hort, *Epistle of St James*, 37) views James as referring to an "innate" word "always sounding there ... the voice of the word within is original and goes back to creation," in contrast with sin ("moral filth"), which entered after the fall and ought to be "removed."

34. Collins ("Coherence," 80–88) sees this expression of "receiving" as the key to understanding 1:19–27, for he argues that James wants to promote "a positive response to the public ministry of the word" in churches (81–82), and he concludes that "vv. 19–27 are about the manner, the frame of soul, in which James wanted his audience to listen to their leader/teacher when he spoke in their worship service" (84).

35. Laws (*The Epistle of James*, 83) offers the nuance that "the call to accept the word of the gospel is a call to man to be what he properly is, what he was created to be," thus "a call to receive this word, already 'natural' to man, would not then be a meaningless one."

36. Moo, *The Letter of James*, 87.

37. Johnson, *The Letter of James*, 202. Wall (*Community of the Wise*, 73) argues that the "'word' of wisdom is 'implanted' by the instruction of teachers," given James's later "concerns about the community's teachers (3:1–18)."

38. Cargal, *Restoring the Diaspora*, 89; Eugen Ruckstuhl, *Jakobusbrief, 1–3 Johannesbrief* (Wurzburg: Echter, rev. 1988), 14.

ish as an undifferentiated whole. The "word" of the gospel, therefore, is fully able to sustain and mature us, from the beginning of our relationship with Christ to the culmination of salvation in the eschaton.[39] "Soul" (ψυχή), finally, does not refer in this context merely to one's "spirit" as separated from the body, but rather to one's whole being or "life." Davids aptly summarizes that "the gospel, if obeyed, is able to save the person's *self*."[40]

James 1:22 Become doers of the word and not hearers only, who deceive themselves (Γίνεσθε δὲ ποιηταὶ λόγου καὶ μὴ μόνον ἀκροαταὶ παραλογιζόμενοι ἑαυτούς). James introduces his second command, this time unpacking the idea of what it means to be "quick to listen." This verse begins with the imperative γίνεσθε ("be, become"). Again we have a command about character. The present tense should probably be understood in an iterative sense, since James wishes to encourage repeated action that becomes a habit.[41] The next phrase, "doers of the word and not hearers only" (ποιηταὶ λόγου καὶ μὴ μόνον ἀκροαταί), contrasts two important components of Jewish life.[42] Hearing the Scripture read formed an essential element of religious ritual, but James here commands an aspect that was assumed but not always realized — putting the spoken word into action. He asks his audience to be *doers* who live out the Word to which they have listened, people who do not merely hear the message of salvation but actually practice their faith.

At first glance, v. 19 seems to contradict vv. 22–25. In the former James commends listening in contrast to speaking and anger. Here, however, James criticizes *mere* attentiveness, requiring it to lead to correct action.[43] But, of course, this is implicit already in v. 19, where James is not commending listening without action but condemning action without listening.

"Doers of the word" (ποιηταὶ λόγου) employs an objective genitive, denoting God's commands that we should obey. With the Sermon on the Mount as key background for James's instruction, the parallel with Mt 7:24–27 again comes readily to mind, especially with Jesus' words in the parable of the two builders: "Therefore everyone who hears these words of mine and puts them into practice is like a wise man who built his house on the rock" versus "everyone who hears these words of mine and does not put them into practice is like a foolish man who built his house on sand" (vv. 24, 26; cf. also Lk 11:28). James is fully aware of people's ability to hear words without letting them affect their lives. Meanwhile, he wants to challenge them to live out Jesus' teachings, especially the ethical core represented by his great Sermon.

The accompanying participle "deceiving" (παραλογιζόμενοι) can be either attributive, further describing the hearers as ones "who deceive themselves," or consecutive, showing that the result of *only* hearing is that they are "thereby deceiving themselves" (cf. NIV "and so deceive"). Either way, religious self-deception occurs in which people can be mistaken in thinking "that they are truly right with God when they really are not."[44] Such sham religion has devastating consequences for one's eternal destiny.

39. Stulac, *James*, 72.

40. Davids, *The Epistle of James*, 95 (italics ours).

41. Wall (*Community of the Wise*, 79) introduces this section with the statement that "true religion is a religion of results, not ritual, so that obedience to God's will measures devotion for God."

42. Martin (*James*, 49) explains that "the use of ποιεῖν ... in the ethical sense is typically Semitic."

43. Ibid., 47. Martin comments that "'hearing and doing' God's will, with the corollary that believers should not be quick to follow their own desires and designs, is a common theme in the Wisdom literature: see Pr 10:9; 13:3; 15:1; 29:20; Eccl 7:9; 9:18; Sir 4:29; 5:11; 6:33; 21:15."

44. Moo, *The Letter of James*, 90. Baker ("James," 36)

James 1:23 For if someone is a hearer of the word and not a doer, this one is like a person who considers their natural face in a mirror (ὅτι εἴ τις ἀκροατὴς λόγου ἐστὶν καὶ οὐ ποιητής, οὗτος ἔοικεν ἀνδρὶ κατανοοῦντι τὸ πρόσωπον τῆς γενέσεως αὐτοῦ ἐν ἐσόπτρῳ). This verse begins to elaborate the problem with mere listeners. James opens with a first-class condition, making an assertion assumed to be true for the sake of argument. In this case, it seems reasonable to assume that some in James's audience *would* have been hearers only and not doers, but "if" remains a better translation than "since," which removes the aspect of conditionality. Introducing a further discussion about the "hearer,"[45] James declares that such a person[46] "is like" (see comments on v. 6 above) someone "considering the face of their nature," where "nature" means either "genesis" (i.e., birth) or "existence" (κατανοοῦντι τὸ πρόσωπον τῆς γενέσεως αὐτοῦ). The root word for "consider" (κατανοέω) often implies intense or studied attention, not merely a passing glance.[47] Meanwhile the odd expression "face of genesis" (πρόσωπον τῆς γενέσεως) is simply a Semitism for "natural face."[48] This is the face they would have seen in any reflective surface since they were children.

The illustration unfolds as the person studies their face closely "in a mirror" (ἐν ἐσόπτρῳ).[49] Mirrors were typically used for toiletry, and as such "they formed useful items for illustrations for all teachers."[50] Mirrors in the ancient world were very different from our modern crystalline inventions. Generally made of polished bronze or copper, they produced dim and warped reflections. While one could gain a good impression of oneself, one could not simply glance at such a mirror and learn much. So one would have to "consider" carefully what one saw in a mirror. Martin adds that "what is seen in a mirror is meant to lead to action, usually regarded as remedial,"[51] for example, a dirty face that needs washing. Yet here this person goes away and fails to deal with the flaws that the mirror revealed.

James 1:24 For they consider themselves intently and depart and immediately forget what sort [of person] they are (κατενόησεν γὰρ ἑαυτὸν καὶ ἀπελήλυθεν καὶ εὐθέως ἐπελάθετο ὁποῖος ἦν). James continues to develop the analogy by adding that after the hearers "consider intently" (κατενόησεν), they "depart" (ἀπελήλυθεν) and "forget" (ἐπελάθετο). The three (aorist, perfect,

agrees that the deception relates to a person's salvation, "which is referred to in the final clause of v. 21. Although he should know better, he thinks he is saved."

45. James repeats himself at the beginning of this verse for emphasis.

46. This time "person" (ἀνήρ) parallels the generic "someone" (τις). Of course, men and women alike used mirrors in the ancient Mediterranean world, just like today. Maier (*Der Brief des Jakobus*, 96) again rightly insists on a gender-inclusive translation.

47. Cf. the semantic range given in BDAG, 522 (bold-face type omitted): "*notice, observe*," "to look at in a reflective manner, *consider, contemplate*," "to think about carefully, *envisage, think about* ..."

48. Laws (*The Epistle of James*, 86) wonders if "natural face" suggests a contrast with Torah, which was believed to present a fuller image of a person than they could discover on their own.

49. Nicholas Denyer ("Mirrors in James 1:22–25 and Plato, *Alcibiades* 132C–133C," *TynBul* 50 [1999]: 237–40) sees the dialogue of Socrates and Alcibiades as the background for this analogy in James, reading the argument here in James in Platonic terms. He argues that the contrast is between the ones who look merely at the external "simulacrum," and those who look at that which is spiritual, including God, and thus comes to "know themselves." This dualistic reading of the text is neither easily supportable nor necessary.

50. Davids, *The Epistle of James*, 98. Moo (*The Letter of James*, 92) points out that "by far the most common metaphorical application of looking into a mirror, in a natural extension from its normal use, was to the process of moral self-reflection." Sleeper (*James*, 64) adds that in wisdom literature, "ordinarily, as it does here, [the mirror] implies some kind of moral failure."

51. Martin, *James*, 50.

and aorist) verbs in this sentence are best understood as gnomic, thus here translated with the present tense (recall the four gnomic aorists in v. 11). James repeats the idea that such people have actually seemed to pay close attention to their reflection, examining it carefully, before they leave. Some, therefore, see James depicting these people as starting well by closely examining their face, but then emphasizing the fact that they depart without doing anything. The second verb is in the perfect tense and thus the most heavily marked, so it is possible that James does seek to emphasize the departure. Compounding the problem, they "immediately" (εὐθέως) forget. "The point is that the impression is only momentary."[52]

But at this point we begin to wonder if perhaps this illustration is not better understood as a deliberately ridiculous analogy, for no one in their right mind who examines their image that closely would then utterly neglect the flaws they discover and instantly forget whatever they had seen. Likewise, James seeks to stress how ludicrous it is for people so rapidly to ignore and forget what they have heard. Baker highlights the absurdity of this picture of a person who "examines intently his very own face in the mirror, but within seconds he cannot even pick himself out of a police lineup."[53] To treat God's Word in such cavalier fashion remains equally absurd.

James 1:25: But the one who looks closely into the perfect law of liberty and remains [in it] and is not a forgetful hearer but a doer who acts, this one is blessed in their doing (ὁ δὲ παρακύψας εἰς νόμον τέλειον τὸν τῆς ἐλευθερίας καὶ παραμείνας, οὐκ ἀκροατὴς ἐπιλησμονῆς γενόμενος ἀλλὰ ποιητὴς ἔργου, οὗτος μακάριος ἐν τῇ ποιήσει αὐτοῦ ἔσται). This verse returns to the example of the "doer," now portrayed as the one who "looks closely into the perfect law of liberty" (παρακύψας εἰς νόμον τέλειον τὸν τῆς ἐλευθερίας) and then obeys. The aorist participle "having looked" (παρακύψας) probably represents another gnomic use (thus our present-tense translation, "looks"), though it could reflect a true temporal and past-referring form ("having looked," "after looking"). In either case, the sequence between looking and remaining (in the next clause) is clear. Like the "hearer," the doer also looks carefully. The verb παρακύπτω has the sense of to "stoop down and look into closely," much like the image of a child who bends over to get nearer to a bug they wish to examine.[54] But unlike the person peering into the mirror, this one acts on what they see.

The "perfect law" (νόμον τέλειον)[55] could have several referents.[56] James could be discussing the Torah, the Torah plus Christ, the basic gospel message, or any combination of the three. He adds a further modifier, though, which aids in the identification — the descriptive genitive "of liberty" (τῆς ἐλευθερίας) — demonstrating that this law does not trap, bind, or weigh one down but is characterized by freedom. We would argue that this most likely refers to the gospel message, particularly in its role as fulfilling the OT prophecies about a new or renewed covenant (see esp. Jer 31:31 – 34).[57] All

52. Davids, *The Epistle of James*, 98.

53. Baker, "James," 37.

54. To read too much into the changing verbs for "to look," as if one referred to more intense scrutiny, strains one side of the analogy or the other. Cf. Moo, *The Letter of James*, 93.

55. Here τέλειον is best understood as "perfect," not "mature," because James is referring to both the completeness of the law for our salvation and the flawlessness of the law in all its aspects.

56. Wall (*Community of the Wise*, 83 – 98) offers an extensive excursus regarding this "perfect law of liberty" in James and in Scripture more generally, pointing out that "perfect" "in this context reminds the reader that the law is God's perfect gift (cf. 1:17) for those undergoing testing" (81).

57. Mariam J. Kamell, "Word/Law in James and the Promised New Covenant," unpublished SBL conference paper (Washington, DC, 2006). Cf. Cargal, *Restoring the Diaspora*, 104.

of the qualifications given in this verse make it unlikely that just the Mosaic law is in view, but rather something that contrasts with or at least adds to it. It is true that similar qualifiers can be found in Jewish literature describing Torah pure and simple (see esp. *Aboth* 6:2; *b. B. Metz.* 85b),[58] but when Jas 2:12 refers again to the law of liberty, it is in clear contrast to Old Testament laws (2:11).[59] Even here, v. 25 functions as the concluding positive model to vv. 22–25, just as v. 21b did for vv. 20–21, so it seems likely that the law of liberty must correspond to the implanted word.[60] Additionally, the transition from "word" to "law" occurs *within* this small pericope that is clearly one section, thus strengthening the correspondence.

At the same time, James would not likely have retained the term "law" if the Hebrew Scriptures did not also feature in his thinking. Thus Davids defines the law of liberty as "the OT ethic as explained and altered by Jesus."[61] Moo concurs, explaining that "the addition of the word 'perfect' connotes the law in its eschatological, 'perfected' form, while the qualification 'that gives freedom' refers to the new covenant promise of the law written on the heart" and "accompanied by a work of the Spirit enabling obedience to that law for the first time."[62] The earlier this letter is and the more Jewish James's communities are, the more likely the Hebrew Scriptures form an integral part of "the perfect law of liberty," even if they must be interpreted in light of the coming of the Messiah and his revelation.[63]

The person looking into this law also "remains" (παραμείνας). The same two options carry over from the last clause for explaining the aorist tense of this participle—gnomic or purely temporal. Though it comes from the meaning of the verb itself rather than from its tense, the emphasis rests on the continuance or perseverance. Because of this characteristic of remaining, the person who looks so closely into this law can be described not as "a hearer of forgetfulness" (ἀκροατὴς ἐπιλησμονῆς), with the descriptive genitive meaning "a forgetful hearer," but as "a doer of work" (ποιητὴς ἔργου), utilizing an objective genitive. Pointing forward, the collective singular "work" anticipates the plural "deeds" that must flow from faith in 2:14–26.

Those who display such deeds will be "blessed in their doing" (μακάριος ἐν τῇ ποιήσει αὐτοῦ). Here the blessing actually validates the inherent worth of good works, for the reward comes "in" or "by" the doing itself (a locative dative of sphere

58. Phillip Sigal, "The Halakah of James," in *Intergerini Parietis Septum (Eph. 2:14)*, ed. Dikran Y. Hadidian (Pittsburgh: Pickwick, 1981), 337–48.

59. A key point missed by Benedict T. Viviano ("La loi parfaite de liberté: Jacques 1,25 et la loi," in *The Catholic Epistles and the Tradition*, ed. J. Schlosser [Leuven: LUP and Peeters, 2004], 213–24), as he argues for the "law of liberty" as Torah pure and simple, based on the five uses of νομός in this passage including examples from the Decalogue.

60. Hiebert, *The Epistle of James*, 136. Martin (*James*, 51) adds that "in this context 'law' is for James a norm of conduct, and he can write of the equivalence of the obedient and the faithful ποιητὴς ἔργου and the ποιητὴς λόγου. So νόμος and λόγος seem to be equal terms."

61. Davids, *The Epistle of James*, 100. Isaacs (*Hebrews and James*, 193–94) points to this as one of the times when one needs to be sure to separate James from Paul, since there is nothing in James to suggest a need to claim "freedom for Christians from the injunctions of the Mosaic *Torah*," but rather a concern that "the law/word of God, articulated in Jesus, should be positively acted upon and not merely passively received." Stulac (*James*, 80) reminds us of Jesus' claim in Mt 5:17 to fulfill the law, as well as to give freedom in Jn 8:36.

62. Moo, *The Letter of James*, 94. Cf. Guthrie, "James," 227.

63. Corrado Marucci ("Das Gesetz der Freiheit im Jakobusbrief," *ZKT* 117 [1995]: 321–28), discusses a whole spate of partially parallel concepts and expressions in Second Temple and early rabbinic Jewish literature. But he also notes the consistent patristic witness to the distinctively Christian nature of this law (328–30). Whether or not James also intends an emphasis on human free will, as Marucci argues from these parallels, is less clear.

or an instrumental dative of means, respectively). This is not an eschatological blessing, but the promise of personal fulfillment in the very process of doing what believers know to be right.[64]

James 1:26 If anyone seems to be religious, while not bridling their tongue but deceiving their heart, the religion of this one is worthless (Εἴ τις δοκεῖ θρησκὸς εἶναι μὴ χαλιναγωγῶν γλῶσσαν αὐτοῦ ἀλλὰ ἀπατῶν καρδίαν αὐτοῦ, τούτου μάταιος ἡ θρησκεία). V. 26 unpacks the remaining command from v. 19 — that we must be "slow to speak." James begins with the conditional statement, "if anyone seems to be religious" (εἴ τις δοκεῖ θρησκὸς εἶναι). Again the first-class condition is assumed true for the sake of argument. It is also probably true in reality that some in James's congregations would merely have *seemed* to be religious. The verb "seem" (δοκέω) implies something subjective, based on opinion and not necessarily on fact. James describes this person's "religion" as based on external appearances rather than inward realities. The semantic domain of "religious" (θρησκός) and its cognates is not as broad as their English equivalents but focuses on devotion to God or the gods, especially "as it expresses itself in cultic rites" or "worship."[65] While in our culture to call someone "religious" can imply that his or her beliefs are shallow and fake, θρησκός on its own in Greek did not have those connotations. Combined with "seems" (δοκεῖ), however, shallowness is exactly what James wants to depict here.[66]

James further describes this seemingly religious person as "not bridling their tongue" (μὴ χαλιναγωγῶν γλῶσσαν αὐτοῦ). The image of a bridle, normally used with horses, will recur in 3:2, again in relation to the tongue. As a verb, "bridle" (χαλιναγωγέω) usually carries the active sense of putting a bit into an animal's mouth in order to direct it.[67] Thus James begins his characterization of the tongue as a separate entity that can and will destroy a person if it is not restrained and controlled.[68] "The ancient world agreed that the wise person was also taciturn. Silence was generally better, and always safer, than speech" (cf. esp. Pr 10:19 or 29:20).[69]

Wrongful speech can come in the form of angry words or maligning another's character,

64. Stulac (*James*, 80) points to the OT emphasis on "the blessing inherent in obeying God's laws."

65. BDAG, 459 (bold-face type omitted). J. P. Louw and E. A. Nida (*Greek-English Lexicon of the New Testament: Based on Semantic Domains* [New York: United Bible Societies, 1998], 532) offer the following definition: "pertaining to being devoted to a proper expression of religious beliefs" and note that in a number of languages translators would have to use a phrase such as "to live as God would have one live," or "to live like one should who believes in God" or "to always do what God requires."

66. Davids (*The Epistle of James*, 101) notes that the "specific practices James has in mind are unclear," whether fasting, prayer, or community worship, but he agrees that "the person has the outward practice of religious activity and so considers himself pious."

67. The participle is naturally understood as concessive — "even though" or "in spite of not bridling their tongue" — although nothing in the context necessitates it being anything more than temporal ("while not bridling ..."). The present tenses of "bridling" (χαλιναγωγῶν) and of "deceiving" (ἀπατῶν) suggest that these are consistent, ongoing problems, not merely occasional lapses.

68. "Tongue" (γλῶσσα) could well be synecdoche, a part for the whole, with the tongue as one key part of the physiology of producing "speech" more generally.

69. Johnson, "Taciturnity and True Religion," 329. Johnson goes on to ask why and how speech should be connected to authentic religion and shows in Hellenistic culture as well as wisdom literature that control of speech was seen as a sign of character. Cf. the identical conceptual cluster at the end of *Abot. Rab. Nath.* 22: "All my life I grew up among the sages and have found nothing better for anybody than silence. If for the wise silence is becoming, how much more for the foolish! Wisdom does not lead to words, nor is it words that lead to wisdom — only works. He who is verbose brings on sin, as it is said, in the multitude of words there wanteth not transgression (Pr 10:19); and it says, even as a fool, when he holdeth his peace, is counted wise (Pr 17:28)." A large number of rabbinic traditions praise silence.

something sadly prevalent in church life in every era. Gossip, for example, does not merely annoy those who are maligned; it threatens the gossiper's spiritual health. James supplements his description by observing that such people are "deceiving their heart" (ἀπατῶν καρδίαν αὐτοῦ). This principle resembles Jesus' teaching in Mk 7:20–23 or Mt 12:32–37, that it is what comes out of people's mouths that reveals the states of their hearts.[70] Thus, those who gossip are not merely slipping into a bad habit, but rather are betraying their inner selves (paralleling James's teaching about hearers in v. 22). James pronounces the religious worship of such people "worthless" (μάταιος). This word has a range of meanings that "pertain to being of no use": "idle, empty, fruitless, useless, powerless, lacking truth."[71] James insists that their religion proves so futile that it might as well be nonexistent or lifeless.

James 1:27: This is religion [that is] pure and undefiled before [our] God and Father: to visit orphans and widows in their distress and to keep oneself unstained from the world (θρησκεία καθαρὰ καὶ ἀμίαντος παρὰ τῷ θεῷ καὶ πατρὶ αὕτη ἐστίν, ἐπισκέπτεσθαι ὀρφανοὺς καὶ χήρας ἐν τῇ θλίψει αὐτῶν, ἄσπιλον ἑαυτὸν τηρεῖν ἀπὸ τοῦ κόσμου). In contrast to this worthless religion, James proceeds to describe religion that is "pure and undefiled before our God and Father" (καθαρὰ καὶ ἀμίαντος παρὰ τῷ θεῷ καὶ πατρί). He uses vocabulary that derives from ritual worship but here applies it to moral purity. We recall the psalmist's declaration in Ps 24:4 that those who please God are people with clean hands and a pure heart—where ritual and moral metaphors also overlap. James indicates that the one who watches and judges our worship is the God whom he further describes as our (loving) Father,[72] echoing Jesus' prayer in Mt 6:9. Using "is this" (αὕτη ἐστίν) as a virtual colon, James launches into a description of religion that balances social justice and personal piety.[73]

The first requirement of pure religion is "to visit orphans and widows in their distress" (ἐπισκέπτεσθαι ὀρφανοὺς καὶ χήρας ἐν τῇ θλίψει αὐτῶν). Here is a classic example "of what the doers of the [perfect] law do."[74] This verb appears often in conjunction with visiting the sick or imprisoned, thus hinting at what the word "distress" (θλίψις) confirms, namely, that Christ's followers must attend to the most helpless of society.

"Visit" (ἐπισκέπτεσθαι) implies not only going to see these people but also caring for them.[75] Orphans and widows, lacking fathers and husbands, respectively, formed two paradigms of the needy and dispossessed in patriarchal societies. The OT consistently refers to God's concern for this group, as seen especially in Dt 10:18; 24:19; Ps 146:9; Jer

70. Baker ("James," 39) affirms that "James is right on the mark when he asserts ... that the tongue is a reliable gauge of true spirituality." He adds that "James's point ... is not so much to help us evaluate religions as to examine religious devotees, mainly ourselves" (40). The witness we give by our casual speech speaks volumes about the value of our belief.

71. BDAG, 621.

72. These two titles may be in apposition, with the latter further explaining the former (i.e., the God who is also our Father). Recall vv. 17–18. Granville Sharp's rule also applies in that God and Father are nontitular, personal, singular nouns, joined by a καί and governed by a singular article, thus referencing the same person. The article probably functions as at least partially equivalent to a possessive pronoun.

73. Moo (*The Letter of James*, 95) shows how James has been consistently growing "more practical and specific" throughout this chapter "in his call to respond appropriately to the word of God." He goes on to warn, however, that "we would badly misunderstand these verses were we to think that James is intending to summarize here all that true worship of God should involve." Still, James warns his readers that faith *without* these elements is nothing (96).

74. Garland, "Severe Trials, Good Gifts, and Pure Religion," 388.

75. Burchard, *Der Jakobusbrief*, 94.

7:6; and Zec 7:10. God often promises to judge his people based on how well they care for the husbandless and fatherless.[76] Meanwhile, "distress" (θλίψις) implies that these people are in tribulation or pain, possibly experiencing pressure from society to somehow fit its mold.[77] Our concern for the helpless of society, including the ones who make us uncomfortable, demonstrates that our religion is pure. James asks, in essence, "Did you in fact realize that the meeting of needs is not peripheral, nor optional, but central and obligatory to your faith?"[78]

Conversely, James clarifies that social justice is necessary but not sufficient for true religion. The second crucial condition is "to keep oneself unstained from the world" (ἄσπιλον ἑαυτὸν τηρεῖν ἀπὸ τοῦ κόσμου).[79] The first adjective refers here to "untainted character, *pure, without fault*,"[80] yet another ritual term used for moral description. "World" (κοσμός) appears elsewhere three times in James (2:5; 3:6; 4:4), in each case referring to the fallen world system within which believers must somehow navigate God-honoring lives. Here emerges a perfect example of being "in the world but not of it," where we must function as salt and light to the needy, but not lose our ability to arrest corruption and illuminate the darkness in the midst of ministry.[81]

The two tasks must be held in balance so that we do not lose social justice in our quest for personal piety or sacrifice moral purity in trying to reach the physically needy. James insists that the two go hand-in-hand; neither may supplant the other. And separation from sin includes the renunciation of social and structural as well as personal sin.[82] The two halves of the verse thus form a fitting summary of the three main points James will next unpack in more detail in the body of the letter. The right use of wealth, the implementation of God's speech ethics, and a godly response to trials and temptations all involve a personal dimension and societal element.

76. Laws (*The Epistle of James*, 89) adds that "inasmuch as God is known to have an especial care for orphans and widows, a worship of him should naturally be expressed in a similar concern." See esp. Mt 25:31–46.

77. Martin (*James*, 53) suspects that "the 'affliction' spoken of in the term θλίψις may anticipate the eschatological woes preceding the end time."

78. Motyer, *The Message of James*, 16.

79. David J. Roberts ("The Definition of 'Pure Religion' in James 1[27]," *ExpTim* 83 [1972]: 215–16) argues for the reading supported only by 𝔓[74] ("protect the needy in their affliction from the world"), because he feels that the idea of keeping *oneself* from the world does not fit James's teaching about striving for social justice. Bruce C. Johanson ("The Definition of 'Pure Religion' in James 1[27] Reconsidered," *ExpTim* 84 [1973]: 118–19) contests Roberts' premise, showing that James uses "world" (κόσμος) to refer not just to external outward social involvement but also to moral contamination. Roberts' oversight likewise dooms Paul Trudinger's recent resuscitation of his position in "The Epistle of James: Down-to-Earth *and* Otherworldly?" *DRev* 122 (2004): 61–63.

80. BDAG, 144.

81. Martin (*James*, 53) cautions one that "to guard oneself from (ἀπό) worldly influence may seem to be an ethical call to asceticism and the practice of a recluse. But James's stress is very much on life *in* society where he detects corrupting influences at work." Cf. Sleeper, *James*, 67.

82. See esp. René Krüger, "Una definición muy peculiar de religión según Santiago 1:27," *Cuadernos de teología* 22 (2003): 79–91.

Theology in Application

The Three Commands (1:19)

The three injunctions that comprise the heart of this pericope hardly prove unique to the New Testament. Deeply embedded in biblical and extrabiblical Jewish teaching, especially in wisdom literature, they prove basic to a life of love for one's neighbor (cf. 2:8). A particularly close parallel to two of James's commands appears in Sir 5:11 — "Be quick to hear but deliberate in answering" — while Pr 16:32 and Ecc 7:9 both enjoin believers to be slow to anger. Already in his self-revelation to Moses in Ex 34:6 – 7, a programmatic text for much later biblical theology,[83] God stressed how he was "slow to anger, abounding in love and faithfulness, maintaining love to thousands, and forgiving wickedness, rebellion and sin. Yet he does not leave the guilty unpunished." In Jesus' teaching, compare especially Mt 5:21 – 26, which deals with hatred as a kind of mental murder. Together, the three mandates form a central part of the climactic Pauline fruit of the Spirit — "self-control" (Gal 5:23).

For James's community, these mandates prepare the way for his more explicit teaching on careful speech as a corrective to the problem of too many wanting to teach (3:1 – 12) and too many wrangling with each other and speaking half-truths about one another because of improper personal ambition and desire (4:1 – 12).[84] For Christians in every age, it is not "any reluctance to confess Christ that is meant, or any slackness in the work of mission, but rather patience to listen to God attentively before trying to speak in his name, and such a sense of the majesty and mystery of God and of the reverence due to His Word as kills cocksureness and glibness and makes men humble both in their theological activity and in their witness."[85]

Slow to Anger (1:20 – 21)

Controlling one's temper remains a challenging task for many Christians. Anger must be dealt with in a constructive fashion that addresses the causes for someone becoming upset. V. 19, in fact, suggests one crucial way for people to become slow to anger — by first being quick to listen and slow to speak. In other words, try first to understand a situation from the perspective of those who are upsetting you and let your speech be based on that understanding.[86] At the same time, being "slow to anger" is not the same as simply suppressing or stifling one's rage. The OT prophets regularly denounced the sins of their contemporaries in harsh, even sarcastic lan-

83. See W. Ward Wilson and Craig L. Blomberg, "The Image of God in Humanity: A Biblical-Psychological Perspective," *Them* 18.3 (1993): 8 – 15.

84. Or "perhaps they were trying to get even with their oppressors by heaping words of revenge upon them" (Hubbard, *The Book of James*, 36).

85. C. E. B. Cranfield, "The Message of James," *SJT* 18 (1965): 186.

86. This form of empathy proves crucial to forgiveness as well, as the literature on the topic regularly stresses. See Craig L. Blomberg, "On Building and Breaking Barriers: Forgiveness, Salvation and Christian Counseling with Special

guage (e.g., Isa 44:6–20; Jer 7:1–8:3; Am 4 and 6). Christ cleared the moneychangers from the temple in righteous indignation over the misuse of a place of worship (Mk 11:15–19 pars.). Jesus and Paul both regularly ranted against the hypocrisy of the conservative religious insiders who failed to demonstrate love and justice for others in their zeal to uphold the law (see esp. Mt 23; Gal 1:6–9; Php 3:2–6).[87] Indeed, most all the biblical woes about future judgment against sin reflect some anger. The key difference is that in each of these cases, it is *God's* perfectly holy wrath that is unleashed against injustice, not merely *human* rage (v. 20). Still, believers can properly reflect a measure of this anger, especially when protesting the mistreatment of others.[88]

Too often, however, we appeal erroneously to the concept of righteous indignation to justify what are self-centered attempts to get our own way, disguised in pious language.[89] Minimizing this tendency requires reminding ourselves that we have already been transformed by Christ's love, as we return again and again to the spiritual resources available to us by the indwelling Spirit working through the truths of the gospel (cf. v. 21). One is reminded here of other apostolic teachings about putting off the old nature and putting on the new (cf. esp. Col 3:8–10, in which sins of speech are highlighted) or trading malice, deceit, slander, and the like for the "pure spiritual milk," which helps one grow in salvation (1Pe 2:1–2).

For the gospel as the "implanted word," one may consult a wide array of ancient Jewish references to the law, or to faith or truth as planted in God's people.[90] To receive this word in humility does not imply self-deprecation, but the acknowledgment that the power at work for good within us is from Christ's Spirit and not ourselves.[91] Still, our goal is to be peacemakers (3:18), so we should not turn personal grievance or vengeance into a virtue, nor make it our issue to carry out God's wrath.

Quick to Listen (1:22–25)

In v. 19, being quick to listen is a good thing. Now James clarifies that listening to God's Word must be accompanied by application of it. This subparagraph,

Reference to Matthew 18:15–35," *Journal of Psychology and Christianity* 25 (2006): 137–54.

87. Cf. further Craig L. Blomberg, "The New Testament Definition of Heresy (or When Do Jesus and the Apostles Really Get Mad?)," *JETS* 45 (2002): 59–72.

88. See the excellent treatment in Nystrom, *James* (104–8), of when righteous anger is justified.

89. Oecumenius captured the correct balance already in the sixth century: "We must be careful when we get angry not to let it develop into an uncontrollable fury. This is where those who are slow come into their own. It may be wrong to be slow in other things, but when it comes to anger, tardiness is the right policy, because by the time we get round to it the reasons for it may have dissipated" (Bray, *James, 1–2 Peter, 1–3 John, Jude*, 17).

90. For a list of texts, see F. Manns, "Une tradition liturgique juive sous-jacente à Jacques 1,21b," *RSR* 62 (1988): 85–89.

91. Mary J. Evans, "James," in *The IVP Women's Bible Commentary*, ed. Catherine C. Kroeger and Mary J. Evans (Downers Grove, IL: IVP, 2000), 776. Evans believes that historically women have been particularly susceptible to this misapplication.

therefore, presents hearing *and doing* the Word as the most fundamental Christian outgrowth of good listening. Not to allow what one learns in the gospel to drive one to obedience proves self-deceptive (v. 22). In the biblical world, most people would only *hear* the Scriptures read aloud; they would not own copies to read for themselves, so James's phraseology would have proved natural.

Even when understood as the right response to God's redeeming grace, Torah-obedience still centered around the need to carry out numerous discrete commandments (see classically Ps 119). But for James the "perfect law of liberty" forms the Christian's guide (v. 25) — not Torah per se, but the Old Testament as fulfilled in Christ and interpreted through the grid of the gospel — in short, the new covenant.[92] This "law" frees human beings from their inability to live up to the demands of Torah and, after Christ's coming, from any attempt to receive forgiveness of sins except by trusting in Christ's once-for-all sacrifice. These latter two concepts, so central to Paul and Hebrews (see esp. Gal 3–4; Ro 6–8; Heb 7–10), while not explicitly presented in James, dovetail perfectly with the language of the letter here. Far from driving a wedge between James and other New Testament authors with respect to the issue of law-keeping,[93] this passage demonstrates James's harmony with additional apostolic testimony on the topic.

The very people reading this book may be among those most prone to deceive themselves into thinking they are obeying the gospel, precisely because they are studying detailed reference works like this one! They are probably scholars, pastors, teachers, or serious and committed laypeople if they go into this much depth in their analysis of Scripture.[94] But countless Christians with access to and interest in such resources often fool themselves into thinking that new insights, proclaiming God's Word in their spheres of influence, or the good feelings that come from communing with God and others in the process of studying the Bible can substitute for

92. Kamell, "Word/Law in James and the Promised New Covenant." Cf. Bauckham, *James*, 146–47; Baker and Ellsworth, *Preaching James*, 36.

93. As, e.g., throughout Martina Ludwig (*Wort als Gesetz* [Frankfurt am Main: Peter Lang, 1994]), who sees James endorsing a positive view of law-keeping little different from the non-Christian Judaism of his day. Cf. Hartin, *A Spirituality of Perfection*, 78–82.

94. "No contemporary reading of James can afford to ignore the insights of liberation theology, not least its hermeneutic of suspicion applied to exegesis of biblical treatments of wealth and poverty. In such matters, it is vital to ask ourselves, not only, 'Is it I/we about whom this text is speaking?', but also, 'In whose interests is my/our reading of this text?' Those of us who enjoy even very moderate affluence in a western context must forget neither how considerable is our wealth by the standards of the world's poorest nor how grossly inequitable is the global economic system to which we owe that wealth. Especially for those of us who write books like this from such a context — but to some degree also for those who read them — there is a particularly seductive temptation. It is that of aligning oneself with liberation theology — or even, purportedly, with the poor — in a merely rhetorical way, as though mere talk of the poor as a theological locus (cf., e.g., Araya 1987: 20) or of theology from the underside of history (cf., e.g., Gutierrez 1983: 169) could be a means of adopting their perspective. Nowhere does interpretation of James more easily rebound, as it were, upon itself, falling foul of James' own strictures against saying or hearing without doing (2:15–16; 1:22–25). This is why James himself warns that 'we who teach will be judged with greater strictness' (3:1). All the same, there can be no praxis without the kind of transformation of attitude that serious engagement with the text of James can enable" (Bauckham, *James*, 185).

actual obedience to Scripture's commands.[95] By contrast, those whose devotion to God's Word leads to greater obedience to his will not only demonstrate the reality of their faith, but find blessing in the very process of honoring God through their behavior. Whereas the first beatitude in James promised "the crown of life" in the age to come, here the blessing explicitly occurs as one does what God requires. Frederick Buechner phrases it nicely: vocation is the place God calls you to be "where your deep gladness and the world's deep hunger meet."[96]

Slow to Speak (1:26)

Care in speaking coincides with empathy in listening and will help us be slow to anger as well. Here is a caution for Christian *leaders* to take particularly to heart. Because so much of their ministry involves speaking, it would be unrealistic to be commanded to speak *little*. But they can always try to think first, hear other people's perspectives, and have their tempers under control before they speak. The child's taunt that "sticks and stones may break my bones but words will never hurt me" is a bald-faced lie. Hurtful words can pack quite a wallop![97]

The punch that this verse provides involves James's assertion about "religion" that consistently[98] cannot keep its speech within proper constraints as worthless or futile. Almost all Christians struggle with gossip or badmouthing others — talking about them behind their backs with inaccurate information or without any constructive purpose (even when disguised as prayer requests!). And in this age of quasi-illiterate text-messaging, out-of-control email, overused cell phones, endless personal websites, blogsites and "facebook," and the inanity of most of what is posted on myspace.com, it is easy to spend large amounts of time producing or imbibing just vain drivel![99] As Toby Ziglar nicely summarizes, this is "when words get in the way of true religion."[100]

The "Have-Nots" and the Responsibility of the "Haves" as the Thesis of the Letter (1:27)

As James rounds out what we now call his first chapter, he offers a striking two-part definition of the external manifestations of true belief. Injunctions to ritual

95. Cf. Charles R. Swindoll, *Improving Your Serve* (Waco, TX: Word, 1983), 170 – 71.

96. Frederick Buechner, *Wishful Thinking: A Theological ABC* (New York: Harper & Row, 1973), 95.

97. For a wonderful collection of applications and corrective models, see William R. Baker, *Sticks and Stones: The Discipleship of Our Speech* (Downers Grove, IL: IVP, 1996).

98. The probable force of the present tense with the participle "bridling," since we all fail in this area from time to time.

99. "A popular aphorism holds, 'It is better to keep silent and be thought a fool than to speak and remove all doubt.' Wisdom traditions, Scripture, the rabbis, and the desert ammas and abbas concurred. Many people in our day, however, are convinced that every person's every thought is worthy of being voiced or at least of being 'blogged' to the world on the Internet" (Brosend, *James and Jude*, 98).

100. See his article so entitled in *RevExp* 100 (2003): 269 – 77.

purity and ministry to the dispossessed deeply permeated the Hebrew Scriptures (see esp. Leviticus and Amos, respectively; cf. above, pp. 94–95). Yet one could virtually write an entire history of both Israel and the church in terms of the movements and periods in which *either* social action *or* personal holiness seemed to triumph over the other. The true outworking of a life of faith, personally and ecclesiastically, clearly requires both. Doing good, even in the name of Jesus, will bring few to Christ when others see no inward transformation in those reaching out to them.[101] Conversely, the most pious, moral believers who refuse to help the needy of the world will find their attempts to convince others of Jesus' love often falling on deaf ears.[102] Of course, "true religion has more features than James has mentioned. The emphasis here is that for God to accept our worship it must be accompanied by loving ministry and a holy life."[103] Neither orthodoxy nor orthopraxy may be subordinated in favor of the other.[104]

101. Cf. Solomon Andria, "James," in *Africa Bible Commentary*, ed. Tokunboh Adeyemo (Nairobi: Word Alive; Grand Rapids: Zondervan, 2006), 1511: "pure religion is not just a non-governmental organization, an NGO doing social work. The work done by believers is the product of their faith and the religion is characterized by the holy lives of its members."

102. Cf. further Tidball, *Wisdom from Heaven*, 90–94.

103. Thomas D. Lea, *Hebrews and James* (Nashville: Broadman & Holman, 1999), 267.

104. Cf. esp. Deiros, *Santiago y Judas*, 103, 111–16.

CHAPTER 4

James 2:1 – 13

Literary Context

After introducing his three key themes in 1:2 – 11 and nuancing them in 1:12 – 27, James is now ready to unpack them in greater detail in reverse order. Chapter 2 thus presents his elaboration of the third theme — riches and poverty. This chapter clearly divides into vv. 1 – 13 and vv. 14 – 26. The first segment is unified by the theme of not showing favoritism, the second by the principle that true faith demonstrates itself by good works. But the dominant illustrations of each of these points involve the contrasts between rich and poor. In vv. 2 – 4, preferential treatment favoring the rich over the poor is condemned; in vv. 14 – 17, maintaining the status quo when the poor are in dire need proves the absence of saving faith. Moreover, the contrast between the wealthy and the impoverished reappears in vv. 5 – 7 as the rich non-Christians exploit the poor believers, while in vv. 23 – 25 the two illustrations of saving faith show that both rich and poor can be saved.

We would therefore expect additional thematic links between one or both of these halves of ch. 2 with the two texts in ch. 1 that introduced the rich-poor contrast (1:9 – 11 and 1:27), and we are not disappointed. With respect to 2:1 – 13, mercy literally "boasts" (κατακαυχᾶται) over judgment (v. 13), just as in 1:9 poor believers were told to boast in their exalted position (their forgiven state that allows them to escape judgment). Contrary to the example of 2:1 – 4, in which the poor person is disgraced, James has already made clear that special concern should be shown to the dispossessed (1:27).

But there are key verbal links with other parts of James as well. Although διεκρίθητε in 2:4 should be translated "discriminated," the same root verb has already appeared in 1:6 (διακρινόμενος) with the concept of "doubting." The common concept behind both uses is that of making a distinction.[1] In the one case people doubt because they waver between two options, trying to discern what is best. In the other case people discriminate, because they make the wrong choice entirely as to how to react to two different situations. Jas 2:5 repeats verbatim the expression "he

1. BDAG, 231.

promised to those who love him" from 1:12, further demonstrating the interchangeability in these contexts of "kingdom" and "eternal life," which are the two things James declares God has promised. Jas 2:6 – 7 anticipates the oppression that 5:1 – 6 will denounce even more severely. The "royal law" of 2:8 and the "law of liberty" of 2:12 hark back to the "perfect law of liberty" in 1:25. The words of praise in 2:8, "you do well," reappear in identical form in 2:19 with probable irony (the demons do well to believe in God but that does not save them!). One wonders, therefore, if there is just a tinge of similar irony in 2:8, as if James is hinting that no one can adequately obey the law of neighbor love.[2]

- III. Restatement of the Three Themes (1:12 – 27)
  - A. Trials/Temptations in Relation to God (1:12 – 18)
  - B. Wisdom in the Areas of Speech and Obedience (1:19 – 26)
  - C. The "Have-Nots" and the Responsibility of the "Haves": The Thesis of the Letter (1:27)
- IV. The Three Themes Expanded (2:1 – 5:18)
  - A. Riches and Poverty (2:1 – 26)
    - ➦ **1. Favoritism Condemned (2:1 – 13)**
      - **a. Faith and Favoritism Are Incompatible (2:1)**
      - **b. Rich and Poor in a Christian Assembly (2:2 – 4)**
      - **c. Reasons for Rejecting Favoritism (2:5 – 11)**
      - **d. Living by the Law of Liberty (2:12 – 13)**
    - 2. The Problem of Faith without Works (2:14 – 26)

Main Idea

Christians must not discriminate either in favor of or against anyone because such behavior is inconsistent with God's choice of the poor, the conduct of the rich, and the law of love. Instead, they must live in ways that anticipate the Judgment Day, demonstrating God's fairness to all and his grace to believers.

Translation

(See next page.)

2. Cf. the story of the scribe who questions Jesus about the greatest commandment in Mk 12:28 – 34. After the scribe reiterates and praises Jesus' reply, which climaxes with this very command to love one's neighbor, Jesus declares, "You are not *far* from the kingdom of God." But he does not declare him to have attained it.

James 2:1-13

1	Exhortation	My brothers and sisters, **do not … hold the faith of our Lord Jesus Christ, the Glory**.
	manner	in favoritism
2a	Illustration (of 4)	For if a person … comes into your assembly
	description	gold-ringed in shining clothing but also
b	contrast	a [person] … comes in
	description	poor in filthy clothing and
3a	expansion	you show special regard for the one wearing the shining clothing and
b	content	you say, "You sit here well," and
c	contrast	to the poor one you say, "You stand there or sit under my footstool,"
4a	rhetorical quest.	**have you not discriminated among yourselves and**
b	restatement	**become judges with evil thoughts?**
5a	Exclamation	**Listen**, my beloved brothers and sisters!
b	Rhetorical quest.	**Did not God choose the poor …**
c	reference	in the eyes of the world
		… to be rich
		in faith, and
d	restatement	heirs of the kingdom,
e	identification	which he promised to those loving him?
6a	Contrast	**But you dishonored the poor.**
b	Rhetorical quest.	**Do not the rich oppress you and**
c	general/specific	**drag you into courts?**
7a	Expansion	**Do they not blaspheme the good name**
b	identification	by which you were called?
8a	Condition (of 8c)	If, however, you fulfill the royal law
b	manner	according to the Scripture, "You shall love your neighbor as yourself," (Lev 19:18)
c	result	**you do well.**
9a	Contrast	if you show favoritism
b	result	But … **you commit sin**
c	sequence	being convicted by the law as violators.
10a	Basis	For **whoever keeps the whole law, but**
b	contrast	**stumbles in one, has become answerable for the whole.**
11a	General/specific	For **he who said "do not commit adultery" also said "do not murder."** (Ex 20:14, 13)
b	illustration (of 10)	if you do not commit adultery but do murder
		Now … **you have become a violator of the law.**

Continued on next page.

Continued from previous page.

12a	Inference	**In such a way speak**
b	parallel	and **in such a way act**
c	manner	as ones about to be judged
d	means	by the law of liberty.
13a	Explanation	For **judgment is merciless to the one not showing mercy.**
b	Contrast	[But] **mercy triumphs over judgment.**

Structure

V. 1 introduces the thesis for this segment of James's letter in the form of a command: Don't show favoritism. Vv. 2 – 4 proceed immediately to give an example, admittedly extreme, but perhaps similar to what had at some point actually occurred in James's churches. A giant compound conditional clause in vv. 2 – 3, which illustrates preferential seating for a rich visitor and shameful prejudice against a poor one, prepares for the apodosis in the form of a rhetorical question in v. 4 that demands an affirmative reply: "Yes, we have discriminated." Vv. 1 and 4 create an inclusio around this paragraph with the command not to show favoritism and the criticism that they indeed have shown it.[3]

Vv. 5 – 11 give three reasons for James's conclusion after an exclamation calls on his listeners to pay close attention (v. 5a). Again James employs rhetorical questions. Rephrased as statements, they affirm that (1) the poor, rather than the rich, more often become believers (v. 5b); (2) the rich are the very class currently persecuting James's churches (v. 6b – 7); and (3) their claims to love one's neighbor ring hollow if they discriminate so egregiously (vv. 8 – 9).[4] Reason (1) is followed immediately by the contrasting observation that these Christians are shaming the poor (v. 6a). V. 10 spells out the basis for the charge leveled under (3) by asserting that breaking one law constitutes a violation of the whole. V. 11 then illustrates this principle with two fundamental commandments from the Decalogue. Without suggesting that the categories are mutually exclusive, we may follow Davids in labeling the first two arguments as "rational" and the third one as "biblical."[5]

3. Gilberto Marconi, "La struttura di Giacomo 2," *Bib* 68 (1987): 251.

4. Many commentators make a major break between vv. 1 – 7 and 8 – 13, because no further reference to the rich appears after the former section and the theme of the law emerges only in the latter. But this overlooks the formal features of the passage and unnecessarily breaks up the series of three illustrations. See further Duane F. Watson, "James 2 in Light of Greco-Roman Schemes of Argumentation," *NTS* 39 (1993): 94 – 121.

5. Davids, *The Epistle of James*, 111.

The final two verses sum up what James's readers should conclude. They cannot hope for a favorable judgment from the Mosaic law if they have ever broken one of its laws; they must rather entrust themselves to God's mercy in the "liberating law" of the gospel. The sequence of thought here is harder to follow than in the rest of this section because v. 13a appears to explain vv. 10 – 11 even better than it does v. 12, and because the two halves of v. 13 are juxtaposed by asyndeton (without any connecting conjunction where one would have been expected). But v. 13a may well function as a kind of summary of the whole passage as well, accounting for its reference back to earlier portions of the pericope.[6]

Exegetical Outline

- **IV. The Three Themes Expanded (2:1 – 5:18)**
  - **A. Riches and Poverty (2:1 – 26)**
    - ➡ **1. Favoritism Condemned (2:1 – 13)**
      - a. The warning and central thesis: Christians must not discriminate against others (v. 1).
      - b. The illustration of the problem: Christians must not discriminate against the poor in favor of the rich (vv. 2 – 4).
      - c. The rationale for the warning: Discrimination is wrong for at least three reasons (vv. 5 – 11).
        - i. It is inconsistent with God's choice of the poor (vv. 5 – 6a).
        - ii. It is inconsistent with the conduct of the rich (vv. 6b – 7).
        - iii. It is inconsistent with the law of love (vv. 8 – 11).
      - d. Conclusion (the warning restated positively as an exhortation): Christians must act in ways which are consistent with God's coming judgment (vv. 12 – 13).
        - i. Remember God's coming liberation of those who do his will (v. 12).
        - ii. Remember God's coming condemnation of lawbreakers (v. 13a).
        - iii. Remember that God's mercy (liberation) triumphs over his judgment (condemnation) for those who are believers (v. 13b).

6. Cf. also Stulac, *James*, 105; Church, "James," 359. It is possible that 2:1 – 13 is structured along the lines of the rabbinic form known as a *proem midrash*, in which an initial text of Scripture is introduced and briefly expounded (in this case Lev 19:15 on favoritism), which triggers a second, related text unpacked in greater detail (here Lev 19:18 on neighbor love). In each case, as here, illustrations, analogies, and stories appear frequently. Finally, the "sermon" returns to the initial text or theme, which would account for the ending of our text. See Scott R. Moore, "Affinities of the Epistle of James with Synagogue Homily and Midrash" (Denver Seminary: M.A. Thesis, 2007).

Explanation of Text

James 2:1 My brothers and sisters, do not in favoritism hold the faith in our Lord Jesus Christ, the Glory (Ἀδελφοί μου, μὴ ἐν προσωπολημψίαις ἔχετε τὴν πίστιν τοῦ κυρίου ἡμῶν Ἰησοῦ Χριστοῦ τῆς δόξης). James begins his unpacking of the theme of riches and poverty by warning against combining faith with favoritism. This verse sets the stage for his subsequent illustration by giving a command not to "show prejudice" (NET) to others. The word for "not" (μή) with the present imperative "hold" (ἔχετε) could imply that discriminatory actions were already occurring, which means we could translate it as "stop holding!" But given the universal nature of the problem, a general prohibition seems more likely here.[7]

"Favoritism" (προσωπολημψία) is a descriptive word for showing partiality; it literally means to receive someone according to their face. It is most likely a Semitism[8] and describes the essence of judging based on external appearances. "True faith has no place for the social distinctions of the world."[9] "The faith" (τὴν πίστιν) is qualified by "of our Lord Jesus Christ, the Glory" (τοῦ κυρίου ἡμῶν Ἰησοῦ Χριστοῦ τῆς δόξης). The first genitive, "of the Lord" (τοῦ κυρίου), most likely is objective. This fits James's general pattern of discussing those who have faith *in* the Lord.[10] On the whole in James, God's or Christ's faithfulness (what the subjective genitive would denote) is assumed, while people's responses are held in question.[11]

It is interesting to note that this is the second and last mention of Jesus Christ in this entire epistle, which has led to speculation that these references (1:1; 2:1) were added later in an effort to make an otherwise entirely Jewish epistle somewhat "Christian." As we have observed, however, James was well versed in Jesus' teachings; indeed, the entire epistle is heavily dependent on them, so such theories fail to convince (see pp. 33 – 34).

The last genitive, "of glory" (τῆς δόξης), can be taken in two different ways. The first, and by far the most common, is as a descriptive or qualitative genitive, that is, "our glorious Lord Jesus Christ" (cf. Jas 1:25; 1Co 2:8). The second, appropriate in such a strongly Christological context, is appositional, so that Christ is equated with the *shekinah* glory of God, the "localized presence of Yahweh."[12] If this reading is accepted, James's letter displays a high Christology very early in the development of the church.[13]

Moo argues against this second interpretation

7. Cf. Johnson, *The Letter of James*, 220.

8. The parallel Hebrew term *nāśāʾ pānîm* appears in the OT in both a positive (1Sa 25:35; Mal 1:8) and a negative sense (Lev 19:15; Ps 82:2), the latter especially in judicial contexts (see Davids, *The Epistle of James*, 105). See also 1Sa 16:6 – 13 for God's rejection of this kind of judgment. Johnson (*The Letter of James*, 221) adds that "the prepositional phrase sharpens the dative of accompanying circumstances" and that the plural "suggests not simply a general attitude but specific and repeated acts" (cf. NRSV: "your acts of favoritism").

9. Davids, *The Epistle of James*, 105.

10. Kistemaker, *James and the Epistles of John*, 75.

11. Contra, e.g., Hartin, *James*, 117.

12. John B. Polhill, "Prejudice, Partiality, and Faith: James 2," *RevExp* 83 (1986): 396. Laws (*The Epistle of James*, 95 – 97) examines the OT evidence that shows how the "eschatological hope of the future enjoyment of the presence of God may be expressed as a hope for the return of glory." Likewise in the NT, "Jesus is frequently associated with, or described in terms of, glory" (96). She argues against reading in the full idea of a hypostasis of Yahweh into this passage; rather, but she sees the absolute noun "glory" as standing in apposition to Lord.

13. Jack Freeborn ("Lord of Glory: A Study of James 2 and 1 Corinthians 2," *ExpTim* 111 [2000]: 185 – 89) offers another reading, in which he asks whether it is "possible that the glory ascribed to the Lord Jesus Christ in James 2:1 includes this sense of honour for the poor wise man" (186). James would then be using "glory" in the sense of "honoring" a wise but poor teacher, Jesus being the prime example. But unless James's readers were well-versed in Paul, this linkage seems remote.

by claiming that "never in the OT or in the NT is the word 'glory' used by itself as a title of God or of Christ."[14] But, as Robert Sloan observes, the term "has a long pre-history in Jewish history and theology as a euphemism for Yahweh," building on the light in the tabernacle (Ex 40:34) and temple (1Ki 8:11) and Ezekiel's vision of the heavenly throne (Eze 1:28). It is widely used throughout the NT in close association with God and Christ to refer to their presence,[15] and in this context it is not occurring "by itself," but with a triad of related titles. Furthermore, a simple descriptive genitive seldom puts the noun functioning as a modifier so far from the word modified; the unique syntax must be stressing the role of "glory" in some fashion. Baker observes:

> Such a deft reference to Christ as the manifestation of God's presence seems more compatible with the emphasis here on impartiality. This interpretation is reinforced by the reference to Christ as Lord and Judge upon his return in 5:7–9. "Glory" is best recognized, then, as signifying the presence of God as judge.[16]

James 2:2 For if a person, gold-ringed in shining clothing, comes into your assembly, but also a [person], poor in filthy clothing, comes in (ἐὰν γὰρ εἰσέλθῃ εἰς συναγωγὴν ὑμῶν ἀνὴρ χρυσοδακτύλιος ἐν ἐσθῆτι λαμπρᾷ, εἰσέλθῃ δὲ καὶ πτωχὸς ἐν ῥυπαρᾷ ἐσθῆτι). This verse begins with a third-class condition, introduced by "if" (ἐάν), offering a hypothetical situation that illustrates James's point. Even though some doubt is introduced as to whether such a scenario has actually occurred, the actions are unfortunately realistic enough that they most likely resemble events that have taken place in James's churches.[17] Debate surrounds the term "assembly" or "synagogue" (συναγωγή), with the discussion focused on whether this term refers to a church setting (the more traditional view) or to a judicial setting (an increasingly popular option). Because the debate appeals to data throughout vv. 1–4, for the moment we will leave it to one side (but see below, pp. 110–11). The use of the word συναγωγή, however, at the very least demonstrates the early and Jewish context of this letter.

The first of two characters whom James introduces is a person "gold-ringed in shining clothing." James vividly depicts this person's wealth without using the term "rich" (πλούσιος). The term "gold-ringed" (χρυσοδακτύλιος) is a *hapax*, and some suggest that James created it.[18] It colorfully describes a person as having, literally, "gold fingers." Someone with gold rings would be showing off both status and wealth, so James presents a person who has both rank and money.[19] The second part of the description, "in shining clothing"

14. Moo, *The Letter of James*, 101. But a parallel might exist in Jn 14:17 with "the Spirit of truth," meaning "the Spirit who is the Truth."

15. For both of these points and numerous additional Scriptural references, see Robert B. Sloan, "The Christology of James," *CTR* 1 (1986): 20–21.

16. Baker and Ellsworth, *Preaching James*, 48. For further support for the appositional genitive, see William R. Baker, "The Christology in the Epistle of James," *EvQ* 74 (2002): 55; John Reumann, "The Christology of James," in *"Who Do You Say That I Am?" Essays on Christology*, ed. Mark A. Powell and David R. Bauer (Louisville: WJKP, 1999), 132; Maier, *Der Brief des Jakobus*, 105–6.

17. Martin (*James*, 60) adds that "it is better ... to understand vv 2–3 as depicting a familiar scene, which is implied by the use of the indicative mood in what follows (especially vv 4, 6, 7)." Likewise, Wall, *Community of the Wise*, 103.

18. E.g., Hartin, *James*, 117.

19. In the mid-first century, the Roman philosopher Seneca mocked the fashions of rich Roman men: "We go on stifling whatever is left of morality. By the smoothness and polish of our bodies we men have surpassed a woman's refinements. We men have taken over the cosmetics of whores, which would not indeed be worn by decent women. With a delicate soft gait we swing our steps high—we do not walk, we strut. We adorn our fingers with rings; a gem is arranged on every joint" (*Natural Questions* 7.31.2).

(ἐν ἐσθῆτι λαμπρᾷ), implies resplendent, luxurious clothing. This person enters the gathering in a way guaranteed to bring attention to him- or herself,[20] flaunting wealth before a largely poor congregation. Commentators debate whether this rich person is a Christian, but because the issue is bound up with whether this is a church or a judicial gathering, we will again defer addressing this question for now.

James next introduces a person who is "poor, in filthy clothing" (πτωχὸς ἐν ῥυπαρᾷ ἐσθῆτι).[21] The word for poor (πτωχός) is the Greek term for the most severe forms of poverty, implying "destitute," someone without virtually any resources. This person's clothes are described as "filthy" (ῥυπαρᾷ), a cognate to the word James used in 1:21 for moral uncleanness, but here is used for literal dirt. This person may well own only one set of clothing, and those clothes are disgustingly unclean.

James 2:3 ... and you show special regard for the one wearing the shining clothing, and you say, "You sit here well," and to the poor one you say, "You stand there or sit under my footstool" (ἐπιβλέψητε δὲ ἐπὶ τὸν φοροῦντα τὴν ἐσθῆτα τὴν λαμπρὰν καὶ εἴπητε, Σὺ κάθου ὧδε καλῶς, καὶ τῷ πτωχῷ εἴπητε, Σὺ στῆθι ἐκεῖ ἢ κάθου ὑπὸ τὸ ὑποπόδιόν μου). Continuing his illustration, James indicts his congregation: "you show special regard" (ἐπιβλέψητε) to the rich person. This continues the idea of looking only at the external appearance and making a judgment, exactly what James has prohibited in v. 1.[22] This favoritism emerges in the preferential treatment they give to the wealthy individual.

James continues, "[If] you say: 'you sit here well'" (εἴπητε, Σὺ κάθου ὧδε καλῶς). It is interesting to note that the problem begins with speaking. Back in 1:19, James has told his audience to be "slow to speak," while here we can see hasty judgment leading to sinful speech. The "you" (σύ) is emphatic, showing the desire of the speaker to impress and single out this wealthy person. The "here" (ὧδε) suggests privileged position, near the speaker and the front of the room, where all can see the honored visitor. The adverb "well" (καλῶς) is awkward, translated by some as "please,"[23] but by most as "well," perhaps suggesting that the honored individual is ushered to a chair (rather than the customary bench).

The usher orders the poor man, however, to, "stand there or sit under my footstool."[24] The treatment remains far from complimentary, and again the sin appears in speech that is based on an external judgment. "The emphasis of the author in James 2 ... is on the fact that his readers

20. Here, because this is an illustration involving specific individuals, James could have had a man in mind, but rich women were perhaps even more likely to dress ostentatiously with gaudy jewelry (cf. Peter's warning in 1Pe 3:3).

21. Wachob (*The Voice of Jesus in the Social Rhetoric of James*, 75) comments that although there are certain similarities between the two individuals — "both are litigants expecting justice at the hands of a judicial assembly, and like those who judge their case, they are members of the elect community — it is their differences rather than their similarities that are emphasized."

22. Johnson (*The Letter of James*, 222) explains that "although literally [ἐπιβλέψητε] means simply to 'look upon,' it is used in the LXX in the sense of 'look upon with favor,'" a favor here based entirely on external appearances. Cf. NASB: "pay special attention to." BDAG (368) includes this usage under its definition, "to pay close attention to, with implications of obsequiousness" (bold-face type omitted).

23. E.g., Ropes, *A Critical and Exegetical Commentary on the Epistle of St. James*, 190 (cf. NAB).

24. This verse contains the first textual variant the UBS supplies for ch. 2, and it is given a {B} rating. While there is some good textual support for the variant readings (B *et al* reverse the word order, while 𝔓74vid, ℵ, C2, *Byz*, *et al.* add a "here" [ὧδε] after the second "sit" [κάθου]), both variants increase the parallelism of the commands. Thus the reading that the UBS has chosen is the harder and shorter reading, and is thus preferable despite the lack of an overwhelming "winner" within the external evidence.

have conceded superiority to the rich, vis-à-vis the poor."[25] The poor person is offered the choice of standing in a corner of the room or being seated under or by a footstool. One should probably not make too much of the change of tenses from the aorist "stand" (στῆθι) to the present "sit" (κάθου), because James contrasts the two locations, not the idea of one position as a "one-time" event versus the other as "ongoing."[26] Offering someone a seat right by the speaker's footstool invokes the metaphor of subjection, implying the dominance of the speaker over the poor person, just as Psalm 110:1 describes God putting Messiah's enemies under his footstool after their conquest.

James 2:4 ... have you not discriminated among yourselves and become judges with evil thoughts? (οὐ διεκρίθητε ἐν ἑαυτοῖς καὶ ἐγένεσθε κριταὶ διαλογισμῶν πονηρῶν;). James finally poses the question that forms the main clause of this long compound, conditional sentence. The "not" (οὐ) implies that the question demands a positive answer: "Yes, you *have* discriminated." While in 1:6 this verb (διακρίνω) means to doubt, that meaning does not fit this context. Rather, here James appears to employ the more active sense of "discriminate" or "make a distinction."[27] "The passive of *diakrinō* demands being taken as internal dividedness ... they are trying to live by two measures at once and are 'divided in consciousness.'"[28] The plural "among yourselves" (ἐν ἑαυτοῖς) probably refers to the fact that the two visitors within the larger meeting have been treated differently.[29]

James then levels a second indictment that they "have become judges with evil thoughts." This clause anticipates his later assertion in 4:12 that "there is one lawgiver and judge." When we attempt to discern people's value based on external features, we not only try to usurp God's role as judge, but we fail miserably in the process. The term "thoughts" (διαλογισμῶν) can imply either internal intentions or external conversations. In this context, it may refer to both, as some speak audibly in support of their distinctions between rich and poor, while others mentally concur. Either way, people are condemned if their reasoning process leads them to discriminate for or against others.

The adjective "evil" (πονηρῶν) shows that James views this way of thinking and acting as wicked. The congregation has turned from worshiping God to becoming evil-intentioned judges (taking the genitives as descriptive).[30] "The problem of discrimination is a perennial one for Christians because it is a tendency of basic human nature to favor those we serve to profit from the most."[31]

25. Maynard-Reid, *Poverty and Wealth in James*, 60.

26. Since both the rich and the poor persons are told to "sit" (κάθου), using the present tense, James cannot be referring here to any unique, ongoing attention to the rich person. In fact, "to sit" (κάθημαι) appears only in the present tense in its imperative forms in the NT, so this may simply have been standard usage.

27. Moo (*The Letter of James*, 104) argues for "make distinctions," seeing discrimination as "another manifestation of a wavering, divided attitude toward God" that was first seen in 1:5 – 7. Cf. Martin's "become divided" (*James*, 63).

28. Johnson, *The Letter of James*, 223.

29. See Davids (*The Epistle of James*, 110), who observes that this term suggests that both visitors are Christian.

30. Cf., e.g., Ropes, *A Critical and Exegetical Commentary on the Epistle of St. James*, 193.

31. Polhill, "Prejudice, Partiality, and Faith," 398. In James's day, "Roman laws explicitly favored the rich. Persons of lower class, who were thought to act from economic self-interest, could not bring accusations against persons of higher class, and the laws prescribed harsher penalties for lower-class persons convicted of offenses than for offenders from the higher class" (see Craig S. Keener, *The IVP Bible Background Commentary: New Testament* [Downers Grove, IL: IVP, 1993], 694).

In Depth: Is This a Worship Service or Christian Court?

Some have proposed a courtroom setting for the example of Jas 2:2 – 4.[32] For support, they point to the legal language in vv. 1 ("favoritism" [προσωπολημψία]) and 4 ("you have discriminated" [διεκρίθητε] and "judges" [κριταί]). V. 2 offers the only use in the entire NT of "assembly" (συναγωγή) for a *Christian* gathering (otherwise it means a purely Jewish "synagogue"). If James had wanted to portray a worship service, it is argued, he would have spoken of a "church" (ἐκκλησία), as he does in 5:14. Moreover, he probably has Lev 19:15 in mind — "Do not pervert justice; do not show partiality to the poor or favoritism to the great, but judge your neighbor fairly" — which would again support a legal setting.[33] Later rabbinic texts that condemn partiality toward the rich in court prove remarkably parallel (*Deut. Rab.* 5.6; *b. Sheb.* 30b – 31a). Finally, v. 6 introduces the comparison with rich persons dragging the poor Christians into court. Given that Paul urged the Corinthian believers to replicate Jewish practice and deal with lawsuits between Christians "in-house" (1Co 6:1 – 6), the forensic context for Jas 2:1 – 4 then seems likely.[34]

If one assumes a courtroom setting, the rich person is most likely a Christian. True, a few have seen the wealthy visitor as a non-Christian landholder who is suing his impoverished tenant and is thus coming to where his tenants gather. According to Maynard-Reid, in James "the rich are outside the sphere of salvation and faith," and therefore this wealthy person *necessarily* is a non-Christian.[35] But Martin retorts that "how to treat pagans would hardly cause division,"[36] and it seems highly unlikely that a powerful non-Christian landlord would even bother to submit to a gathering moderated by poor Christians. An in-house dispute would much more naturally involve fellow believers. It is also interesting to note that James does everything *but* call this person "rich" (πλούσιος); thus, if James does draw a sharp salvific line between the "rich" (πλούσιος) and the "poor" (πτωχός), that line has not been crossed here.[37]

Many, however, argue that this is a church service, with rich and poor entering into worship. This side takes the more natural interpretation of

32. Roy B. Ward ("Partiality in the Assembly: James 2:2 – 4," *HTR* 62 [1969]: 87 – 97) was one of the first in over a century to argue for this interpretation, and a slight majority of more recent studies have followed him. But Dale C. Allison Jr. ("Exegetical Amnesia in James," *ETL* 76 [2000]: 162 – 65) shows that this was a frequent approach in Protestant literature from the 1600s to the 1800s that was somehow forgotten.

33. Johnson (*The Letter of James*, 221) argues this position partially from the use of "favoritism" (προσωπολημψία): "the usage in Lev 19:15 makes it clear that the original context of the language was that of judging cases in the community: unjust judgment was that based on appearances rather than on the merits of the case." Sir 7:6 – 7 harshly condemns favoritism in judging.

34. Laws, *The Epistle of James*, 101 – 2; recall above on "thoughts" (διαλογισμῶν).

35. Maynard-Reid, *Poverty and Wealth in James*, 63.

36. Martin, *James*, 61.

37. Ward, "Partiality," 96.

"assembly"/"synagogue" (συναγωγή) as a place for religious gathering and instruction. Given the probable early date for the writing of this letter and its Semitic roots, it is reasonable for James to use the Jewish term for such a gathering. But "if these are Christians entering a service of worship, would they need to be told where to go?"[38] This objection is then best countered if the rich and poor here are not Christians but interested visitors. If one assumes a worship context, the question of whether this rich person could be a believer becomes more difficult. As we have seen, some argue that James consistently excludes the rich from the saved, including here. Perhaps this rich person came to the assembly to gain honor and more clients within the patron-client structure of Greco-Roman society. Perhaps he came to investigate what some of his clients or tenants were involved in. Perhaps he was a genuine seeker. In any way, he receives effusive deference from the congregants. But if one admits the possibility that rich people can be Christians, then there is nothing here that requires this person to be an unbeliever. This person may be simply a Christian visitor.[39]

Of the various combinations of options, the strongest seems to be the judicial gathering with rich and poor Christians as the two main persons of note.[40] The Jewish parallels, legal language, and background in Lev 19:15 prove most decisive. A wealthy believer, who may not be familiar with this particular congregational gathering, is willing to submit to the ruling of a Christian court, as Paul will later enjoin in 1Co 6. How much more, James implies, if the wealthy are willing to submit themselves to this court, should the poor in the congregation not defer to the rich merely on the basis of their class!

James 2:5 Listen, my beloved brothers and sisters! Did not God choose the poor in the eyes of the world to be rich in faith and heirs of the kingdom which he promised to those loving him? (Ἀκούσατε, ἀδελφοί μου ἀγαπητοί· οὐχ ὁ θεὸς ἐξελέξατο τοὺς πτωχοὺς τῷ κόσμῳ πλουσίους ἐν πίστει καὶ κληρονόμους τῆς βασιλείας ἧς ἐπηγγείλατο τοῖς ἀγαπῶσιν αὐτόν;). To support his commands, James appeals to God's election of the poor. He begins with an aorist imperative, comparable to our "listen up" (ἀκούσατε)! Along with the vocative address to his spiritual siblings, he shows that he is introducing an emphatic point. His first main reason for not discriminating in favor of the rich may be called a "rational argument."[41] James here lays out the "spiritual vantage-point" from which "Christians should judge others."[42]

38. Davids, *The Epistle of James*, 109.

39. For a vigorous, recent defense of the worship context, see Brosend, *James and Jude*, 61 – 64.

40. So also Guthrie, "James," 230; Hartin, *James*, 117 – 18; John P. Keenan, *The Wisdom of James* (New York and Mahwah, NJ: Paulist, 2005), 67 – 68.

41. Davids, *The Epistle of James*, 111.

42. Moo, *The Letter of James*, 106. Edgar (*Has God Not Chosen the Poor?* 168) points out concerning 2:2 – 4 that "the consequences of this example are drawn out in 2.4 – 7, where

He then asks if God did not "choose the poor ... of the world to be rich in faith." The aorist verb may well carry almost a gnomic or timeless sense ("Does not God [perennially] choose the poor?").[43] Again, the "not" (οὐχ) introduces a question that expects a positive answer, a rhetorical device that James uses consistently in the next few verses. While Paul uses the idea of "chosen" (ἐξελέξατο) as a key theological term, almost equivalent to "predestined" (cf. Ro 8:29), it is important to read James's message in its own right. Here election may have something of a salvific sense, but for James Christians have also been chosen as the new community of God's people here on earth. If one wants a parallel in Paul, 1Co 1:26 – 29 on the socioeconomic position of the majority of the Corinthians when they were "called" proves much closer.[44]

The objects of God's choice are "the poor in the eyes of the world" (τοὺς πτωχοὺς τῷ κόσμῳ). As in v. 2, James continues to refer to the destitute, those without material resources.[45] On the whole, the church was made up of the poor, a situation true across the empire at the time with a small number of important exceptions.[46] This election of "the poor" is based on OT passages that affirm God's care for them "and the resulting fact that 'poor' became a term for the pious ... not only in the OT, but also in the intertestamental and rabbinic literature."[47] Thus the poor in view here turn to God as their only hope.[48] They are neither the materially poor but religiously indifferent, nor the materially rich but pious Christians. "God is on the side of the poor, not because they are poor but because they are responsive to him and are near the Kingdom."[49]

The dative τῷ κόσμῳ, however, is more controversial. There are three main options: a locative dative of place ("in the world"), a dative of respect or reference ("with respect to worldly goods"), or an ethical dative ("in the eyes of the world").[50] Of these three, the last seems the clearest, coming directly after a passage in which judgment was passed on the poor because of their looks. Maynard-Reid and Tamez argue strongly for the first, that these are only the literal poor.[51] One problem with this view is that it can assume that God elects *all* poor

the real status of the πτωχοί, who are dependent on God and honoured by God, and the πλουσιοί, who live in opposition to God, is made clear."

43. Stanley E. Porter, *Verbal Aspect in the Greek of the New Testament, with Reference to Tense and Mood* (New York: Peter Lang, 1989), 237.

44. Wiard Popkes, *Der Brief des Jakobus* (Leipzig: Evangelische Verlagsanstalt, 2001), 166.

45. Martin (*James*, 65) argues that James "uses the definite article with πτωχός" to suggest "that he did not mean to imply that God chose all the poor because they were poor but simply that God chose poor people." Presumably this would be a generic use of the article to refer to a category in general rather than every single element within it.

46. Rodney Stark (*The Rise of Christianity* [San Francisco: HarperSanFrancisco, 1997], 29 – 47) has argued that first-century Christianity was not nearly as monolithically poor as has usually been affirmed. He references biblical scholarship from the last half century that has indeed stressed the important role played by a tiny minority of well-to-do Christians in its earliest phase, but his sources do not support the extent to which he tries to turn the early Jesus society into a socially and economically diverse movement.

47. Davids, *The Epistle of James*, 111. Moo (*The Letter of James*, 108) evocatively elaborates that, according to the NT, God "delights especially to shower his grace on those whom the world has discarded and on those who are most keenly aware of their own inadequacy. James calls on the church to embody a similar ethic of special concern for the poor and the helpless."

48. That is, "those without financial security, who have come to depend upon God with their future" (Wall, *Community of the Wise*, 115).

49. Andria, "James," 1512.

50. The first two categories are common in all major intermediate Greek grammars. The third appears in several older advanced grammars, identified as a Semitism, but often without definition. G. B. Winer (*A Treatise on the Grammar of New Testament Greek Regarded as the Basis of New Testament Exegesis* [Edinburgh: T&T Clark, 1870], 265) more helpfully calls it a dative of opinion or judgment and notes classical Greek parallels as well.

people, merely on the basis of their socioeconomic status. By this logic, we should never help anyone escape poverty, lest they lose their salvation! If poverty were inherently salvific, Scripture would never have commanded us to help alleviate it, an observation that calls into question the second view as well.[52]

Arguing for the third reading, Isaacs insists that James is not trying to "draw attention to the economic poverty of its constituents, but to their low esteem in the eyes of the world, brought about as a consequence of their religious faith."[53] Bauckham appears to combine the second and third options, paraphrasing the term as "poor with respect to those material goods which the world considers wealth."[54] Given the invariable material connotations of "the poor" and the pervasiveness of cultures of honor and shame in the ancient Mediterranean world, this interpretation seems best.

The poor, James continues, have been chosen to be "rich in faith" (πλουσίους ἐν πίστει). Here the idea of "rich" cannot denote physical wealth but must mean a surplus or overabundance. This excess occurs "in the sphere of faith,"[55] which in James implies not only belief but also the practical ability to live out one's relationship with God. Martin adds that they are "rich" in the sense that "they have a place in the kingdom of God."[56] The poor have also been chosen to be "heirs of the kingdom which he promised to those loving him." The term "heirs" (κληρονόμους) makes its sole appearance in James here. "The language of inheritance is rooted in the biblical tradition," beginning first with God promising the land to Abraham.[57] Laws points out the present and future nature of the promises for the poor: a wealth of faith in the present and heirs of the kingdom in the future.[58] Given James's dependence on Christ's teaching, it seems logical that he would have been influenced by Jesus' discussions about the kingdom of heaven, which is breaking into our world (through Christ), as well as remaining eschatological and eternal. Here the future aspect appears to be more in view.

The verb "promised" (ἐπηγγείλατο) with its indirect object clause repeats the end of 1:12 verbatim. This object clause proves crucial for understanding the identity of these "poor": they are the poor who are also "loving him" (ἀγαπῶσιν αὐτόν). The present participle suggests an ongoing nature to the action: love for God characterizes their lives. This answers the question of whether James identifies all the poor as rich in faith. He does not. Those inheriting the kingdom are those poor who choose to love God.[59] Nevertheless, it is true that the poor are often more inclined to depend on God than the rich. "In the spiritual long run, poverty is a distinct advantage despite the present misery it may inflict."[60] Thus, James inverts the standard value system of the Greco-

51. Maynard-Reid, *Poverty and Wealth in James*, 62 – 63; Tamez, *The Scandalous Message of James*, 25.

52. Cf. Cranfield, "The Message of James," 191; Bauckham, *James*, 194.

53. Isaacs, *Hebrews and James*, 198. Cf. Ruckstuhl, *Jakobusbrief, 1 – 3 Johannesbrief*, 16.

54. Bauckham, *James*, 87.

55. Ropes, *A Critical and Exegetical Commentary on the Epistle of St. James*, 194.

56. Martin, *James*, 65.

57. Johnson, *The Letter of James*, 225.

58. Laws, *The Epistle of James*, 103. This seems to echo Jesus' teaching in Mt 5:3 or Lk 6:20.

59. Davids (*The Epistle of James*, 112) summarizes all the elements of this verse well: "The world sees only their poverty; God sees their exalted state because of his election of them to eschatological exaltation, for they are those who love him and thus receive his promise.... The term 'the poor,' then, has ... picked up a religious quality, for it is virtually a name for the true believers (the Matthean version of the beatitude in Mt 5:3 is an accurate interpretation in part). But it does so without losing the quality of material poverty, for it is a materially poor person who has been discriminated against."

60. Baker, "James," 50.

Roman world's culture of bestowing honor on the rich and shame on the poor.

This verse well exemplifies the Bible's frequent juxtaposition of divine sovereignty and human responsibility. Without the closing three words about "those loving him" (τοῖς ἀγαπῶσιν αὐτόν), one might imagine that God's election of the poor occurred unilaterally, apart from human involvement. Without the verb about God's choice (ἐξελέξατο), one could envision salvation as something merited by a person's love of God. Together, it becomes clear that both God's designation of an individual and that person's faith must be present.[61]

James 2:6 But you dishonored the poor. Do not the rich oppress you and drag you into courts? (ὑμεῖς δὲ ἠτιμάσατε τὸν πτωχόν. οὐχ οἱ πλούσιοι καταδυναστεύουσιν ὑμῶν καὶ αὐτοὶ ἕλκουσιν ὑμᾶς εἰς κριτήρια;). This verse begins with the emphatic pronoun "you" (ὑμεῖς). Thus James contrasts the discriminatory actions of a predominantly poor congregation with those of God, who has chosen the poor in order to bless them. "You," James says, "dishonored the poor." This was a strong charge in a culture of honor and shame; we might reword it as "humiliated" (cf. Goodspeed's NT). "The poor" (τὸν πτωχόν) could refer to a specific person, as in the example of vv. 2 – 4, or the article could be generic, denoting poor people in general. If v. 6a reflects an actual situation, as depicted in vv. 2 – 4, then this congregation "dishonored" (ἠτιμάσατε) the poor person who came into their meeting (perhaps better accounting for the simple aorist verb). But even if James earlier depicted an exaggerated hypothetical situation, he now affirms that his listeners have indeed dishonored the poor in seeking to curry favor with the rich in general. God has chosen these poor, but the church shows deference to the rich who do not respond in kind.[62] In the words of the African proverb, "thin cows are not licked by their friends"![63]

James continues, again with a "not" (οὐχ) that introduces a question expecting a positive answer,[64] inquiring, "Do not the rich oppress [καταδυναστεύουσιν][65] you?" Clearly, *these* are not Christian rich people; rather, James is referring to the non-Christian rich as a class and thus he uses the term πλούσιος (recall above, p. 110). The present tense of the verb "oppress" could indicate ongoing action, but at the very least it implies current action (i.e., "are not the rich oppressing ... ?"). This congregation is undergoing persecution by the rich, a group to whom they still defer, while the rich may not be distinguishing between persecution of the poor and persecution of the Christians. The additional mistreatment the poor might receive for being Christians, however, would compound their economic exploitation.

James goes on to highlight at least one type of oppression that was occurring: "they drag you into courts." The "they" (αὐτοί) appears for emphasis; the rich individuals the congregations attempt to please are the same people who perse-

61. Cf. further William W. Klein, *The New Chosen People: A Corporate View of Election* (Grand Rapids: Zondervan, 1990), 226 – 28. Cf. Maier, *Der Brief des Jakobus*, 110: "With ἐξελέξατο comes the free gift of the mercy of God into view. But the chosen person is similarly the one 'who loves him,' and therefore the one who accepts God's mercy and who will live for him" (translation ours).

62. Polhill, "Prejudice, Partiality, and Faith," 397.

63. Andria, "James," 1512.

64. This is one aspect of the deliberative rhetoric used by James in this chapter, asking questions not to receive an answer but to emphasize a point. Other elements in this chapter are the use of examples and the overall intention to dissuade the audience from their pattern of action. See Watson, "James 2 in Light of Greco-Roman Schemes of Argumentation."

65. The only other use of this verb in the NT is in Ac 10:38, referring to those under the devil's power. Maynard-Reid (*Poverty and Wealth in James*, 63) adds that "the term is very strong and has violent, physical overtones, with the emphasis on exploitation and domination."

cute them. The verb "drag" (ἕλκουσιν) "denotes violence, whether physical or legal."[66] James does not explain why the rich press charges against the poor, but one common motive was to gain more land in property disputes. Another option envisions the rich as attempting to collect debts the poor owed, an action that would likely result in the poor being thrown into debtors' prison unless they could repay (cf. Mt 18:23 – 35).[67] James points out the ridiculous nature of kowtowing to people who treat the poor in this manner. He does not, however, condemn the rich for *being* rich; his invective condemns their *actions*.

James 2:7 Do they not blaspheme the good name by which you were called? (οὐκ αὐτοὶ βλασφημοῦσιν τὸ καλὸν ὄνομα τὸ ἐπικληθὲν ἐφ' ὑμᾶς;). James introduces one more rhetorical question concerning the rich. He again includes the "they" (αὐτοί) to emphasize *their* actions. He uses the strong word "blaspheme" (βλασφημοῦσιν) to depict their behavior.[68] "In the New Testament, words from the root βλασφημία all carry the basic concept of violating the power and majesty of God."[69] By siding with these rich, the church aligns itself with blasphemers! "The good name" (τὸ καλὸν ὄνομα) most likely refers to Jesus (with or without "Lord" or "Christ").[70]

Various commentators have suspected a baptismal allusion here, a context in which the name of Christ was invoked or called upon the believer,[71] but it is hard to be sure that James is alluding to any setting so specific.[72] Depending on how early the events in Ac 11:26 happened, in which those in Antioch started calling followers of "the Way" Christians, and how quickly and widely that name might have caught on, James could also be referring to the term "Christian" here. The awkward phrasing of the clause "by which you were called" (lit., "the having been called upon you [name]") may help support this. Believers were first called Christians before they began to call themselves by that title, and James could be affirming that what began as an insult is actually a holy title. In sum, "James's first reason for not showing favoritism, especially to the rich, is that the rich perennially have been against God and his people and have demonstrated themselves to be against Christ and His church."[73]

James 2:8 If, however, you fulfill the royal law according to the Scripture, "You shall love your neighbor as yourself," you do well (εἰ μέντοι νόμον τελεῖτε βασιλικὸν κατὰ τὴν γραφήν, Ἀγαπήσεις τὸν πλησίον σου ὡς σεαυτόν, καλῶς ποιεῖτε). James now turns from his "rational"

66. Johnson, *The Letter of James*, 226.

67. For a good treatment of the socioeconomic assumptions and behaviors of the day, see Brosend, *James and Jude*, 62 – 66. Cf. Dibelius, *James*, 139; Laws, *The Epistle of James*, 105. A classic biblical example of this is Jezebel conniving to get Naboth's vineyard for Ahab in 1Ki 21.

68. "Blaspheming the name" need not imply a persecution of Christians as such. Rather ridicule of "the name" may have been no more than a mocking reference to the individual's beliefs in order to undermine the reliability of someone's character (Perkins, *First and Second Peter, James, and Jude*, 110).

69. Nancy J. Vyhmeister, "The Rich Man in James 2: Does Ancient Patronage Illuminate the Text?" *AUSS* 33 (1995): 281 – 82. Martin (*James*, 66) argues that this term, when used in reference to people, means only slander, not blasphemy. But this use is directed against the Lord's name, so "slander" seems too mild a translation. "What seems to be in view here is verbal abuse hurled at believers, which disparages their religion and the Lord they claim to follow" (Guthrie, "James," 235).

70. Johnson (*The Letter of James*, 226) proposes that the full reference to the Lord Jesus Christ of glory in 2:1 forms the most logical antecedent.

71. This is a Septuagintalism indicating "possession or relationship, particularly relationship to God" (Davids, *The Epistle of James*, 113).

72. It is interesting to note the similarity of this phrasing with that of the middle line of Ac 15:17, also uttered by James.

73. Baker, "James," 51.

argument(s) to his biblical support. Perhaps this section responds to a potential objection that deference to the rich does show love to *them*.[74] He begins with a first-class condition, assuming the truth of the protasis for the sake of argument. He thus considers the outcome of fulfilling the royal law. Μέντοι can be taken as either affirmative ("really") or adversative ("however"). The latter fits better here, because this sentence contrasts with the previous one about those who blaspheme. The verb "fulfill" (τελέω) continues James's pattern of using this root that refers not just to completing a requirement, but also to attaining maturity or even perfection. Thus the nuance is not that this law is obeyed in some minimal sense, but rather that it is substantially or even perfectly followed. We might suspect that James is setting us up for a Pauline contrast — of course, no one *does* actually obey the law this well — but we dare not yet presuppose this approach.

Most discussion on this verse centers on the understanding of "royal law" (νόμον βασιλικόν).[75] Is this (1) the Torah as a whole; (2) the Torah as fulfilled and expanded by Christ; (3) a new law given by Christ; or (4) the specific love commandment highlighted here as the supreme law or summary of God's will for his people in any era? While option (1) fits a Jewish author writing early in the history of Christianity, the qualification of "law" with "royal" makes it unlikely that this is merely Torah by itself.[76] "Royal" (βασιλικόν) comes from the same root as "kingdom" (βασιλεία). This is kingdom law, in which Jesus' kingdom teaching must play a central part.[77]

Nevertheless, without reading in Paul's concept of "the law of Christ" (1Co 9:21; Gal 6:2), an early *Jewish*-Christian writer is not likely to have entirely jettisoned the Torah, so (3) seems equally unlikely. Option (4) at first glance appears attractive because the commandment quoted comes from the Torah, specifically Lev 19:18 — a verse Jesus, Paul, and the rabbis all affirmed as summarizing many of the interpersonal laws.[78] Jesus, in fact, affirmed it as the second half of his summation of the entire Torah, with the first half being to love the Lord wholeheartedly (see Mt 22:34 – 40; Mk 12:28 – 34; cf. Lk 10:25 – 37). Here it makes sense for James to use only the second half, because his discussion focuses on our relationships with others. Nevertheless, one wonders if βασιλικόν would have been understood as "supreme" or "highest," since its only standard usages were "royal" or "kingly."[79]

This leaves (2) as the most likely option. The royal law is described as "according to the Scripture" (κατὰ τὴν γραφήν). Almost always, NT writers use this expression to introduce passages from the OT. But the phrase would prove redundant if "the royal law" by itself referred to all of and nothing but the Hebrew Bible. Davids, therefore, asks if it is not "most natural to see a reference to the whole law as interpreted and handed over to the church in the teaching of Jesus, i.e., the sovereign rule of God's kingdom (cf. Matthew 5)?"[80] Option (2) thus emerges as best not just by the process of elimination but also because it best fits James's Jewish milieu combined with his dependence on Christ's teaching. It becomes natural, therefore, to assume that this royal law matches "the perfect

74. Richard Kugelman, *James and Jude* (Wilmington: Glazier, 1980), 26.

75. The term "royal" (βασιλικόν) is shifted toward the end of the clause for emphasis. See esp. Hiebert, *The Epistle of James*, 163.

76. But see Pierre Keith ("La citation de Lv 19, 18b en Jc 2, 13," in *The Catholic Epistles and the Tradition*, ed. Schlosser, 227), who thinks the contrast is between the *whole* law and the love command.

77. See esp. Motyer, *The Message of James*, 97.

78. See esp. Laws, *James*, 108.

79. Louw and Nida, *Greek-English Lexicon*, 481.

80. Davids, *The Epistle of James*, 114. Cf. Maurice Hogan, "The Law in the Epistle of James," *SNTSU* 22 (1997): 88.

law of liberty" of 1:25 as another way of referring to the (re)new(ed) covenant of Jer 31:31 – 34 now inaugurated by Jesus. "According to the Scripture," then, specifies which part of this royal law James's listeners need to apply here.[81] They *must*[82] love their neighbor as themselves, including the poorest people, who can offer them nothing material in return.

"Neighbor" (πλησίον) thus embraces everyone, even enemies, just as Jesus taught (Lk 10:25 – 37), not merely those close to us relationally, financially, or religiously. James's use of "yourself" (σεαυτόν) does *not* promote modern psychologies (before they were invented!) that intentionally enjoin "self-love" before we can love others. Rather, the love commands throughout Scripture *assume* that people have a healthy, balanced view of self, rather than taking pathologies into account.[83] Otherwise, we can become so wrapped up in trying to love ourselves and always feeling inadequate in doing so that we never turn to loving others.

Finally, James concludes, if you do keep this law, "you do well." This provides an interesting parallel with the climax of his letter disseminating the Apostolic Decree (Ac 15:29), the only other writing by James that we have, even secondhand. While the Greek words are different (εὖ πράξετε),[84] the meaning and structure are identical. For James, faith reveals itself in how it is lived.

James 2:9 But if you show favoritism you commit sin, being convicted by the law as violators (εἰ δὲ προσωπολημπτεῖτε, ἁμαρτίαν ἐργάζεσθε ἐλεγχόμενοι ὑπὸ τοῦ νόμου ὡς παραβάται). James is now ready to contrast showing favoritism with loving all of one's neighbors. Discrimination is sin and breaks the law. The word here for "show favoritism" (προσωπολημπτεῖτε) is the verb from the same root as the noun in 2:1, again with the connotation of viewing people's external appearances only instead of seeing them as whole persons. Leviticus 19:15 explicitly forbade such partiality in favor of either rich or poor. The word "sin" (ἁμαρτίαν) originally meant to "miss the mark" (as in an archer's arrows failing to hit their target), but here the failure is moral. "Commit" (ἐργάζεσθε) implies the active, willful out*working* of a choice.

Those who show favoritism are "being convicted by the law as violators." The present passive participle "being convicted" (ἐλεγχόμενοι) conveys the ongoing sense of God's response. The sinners have willingly removed themselves from the yoke of heaven by transgressing God's law, and thus they stand under his judgment. The participle may best be categorized as one of attendant circumstances, with "being convicted" as conceptually coordinate (though grammatically subordinate) with "committing sin."[85] The term "violators" (παραβάται) refers to people who are conscious transgressors of a law, people who have no excuse for being where they are or for doing what they are doing.[86] Therefore this participial phrase forces the hearer to realize that favoritism *is* willful sin. One wonders if the unqualified reference to "the law" (τοῦ νόμου) now encompasses merely the Hebrew Scriptures, because vv. 10 – 11 will most naturally be interpreted as referring to

81. Cf. the NAB: "You are acting rightly, however, if you fulfill the law of the kingdom. Scripture has it, 'You shall love your neighbor as yourself.' "

82. The future tense, "you shall love" (ἀγαπήσεις), found already in the LXX, is imperatival and represents a common Semitic construction.

83. Motyer (*The Message of James*, 97) comments on how the Bible envisions that we love ourselves: "never (it is to be hoped!) with an emotional thrill; rarely, as a matter of fact, with much sense of satisfaction; mostly with pretty wholesale disapproval; often with complete loathing — but always with concern, care and attention."

84. After all, Acts is *Luke's* rendering of what James, in the original context, would most likely have spoken in Aramaic.

85. Cf. Johnson, *The Letter of James*, 231.

86. Moo, *The Letter of James*, 113.

Torah, while the "law of liberty" in v. 12 resumes discussion of a broader law.[87] At any rate, by showing favoritism, we fail to treat all neighbors equally as ourselves, and thus we fail to keep God's law.

James 2:10 For whoever keeps the whole law, but stumbles in one, has become answerable for the whole (ὅστις γὰρ ὅλον τὸν νόμον τηρήσῃ πταίσῃ δὲ ἐν ἑνί, γέγονεν πάντων ἔνοχος). James continues his discussion of the law by stressing its seamless unity. Because of the negative function of this law in vv. 10 – 11, contrasted with the positive function of liberty in vv. 12 – 13, it would seem that just the Torah is in view here. The specific laws cited in v. 11 clearly come from the Decalogue, as the heart of the OT's legal material. This hypothetical person may "guard" or "keep" (τηρήσῃ) the entire law. Thus they attempt to guide their life by the regulations spelled out for them in the Hebrew Scripture.

However, they may "stumble in one" (πταίσῃ ἐν ἑνί), with stumbling implying lawbreaking.[88] By juxtaposing the keeping of the *whole* law with stumbling in *one* [law], we can see that Torah-obedience is the guideline for how this person lives their life.[89] If they stumble when thus guided by the law, James says that they have "become answerable for the whole" (γέγονεν πάντων ἔνοχος). Laws points out the primarily legal meaning of "answerable" (ἔνοχος), which with the genitive, as here, "has three possible meanings: liable for punishment; guilty of crime; or liable in respect of a person or thing against which an offence has been committed." She supports the third option.[90] As people try to direct their lives by the law, they find themselves bound to keep all.[91] This insistence resembles Jesus' discussion of the law in Mt 5:17 – 20 and Paul's in Gal 5:1 – 15.

James 2:11 For he who said "do not commit adultery" also said "do not murder." Now if you do not commit adultery but do murder you have become a violator of the law (ὁ γὰρ εἰπών, Μὴ μοιχεύσῃς, εἶπεν καί, Μὴ φονεύσῃς· εἰ δὲ οὐ μοιχεύεις φονεύεις δέ, γέγονας παραβάτης νόμου). James illustrates the principle of v. 10 by giving an example. The substantival participle "he who said" (ὁ εἰπών) represents God, the one who gave the law to Moses and inspired the OT.[92] Both Johnson and Moo point out the critical nature of this emphasis on the one who spoke, inasmuch as "the individual commandments are part and parcel of one indivisible whole, because they reflect the will of the one Lawgiver."[93]

87. Cf. Martin, *James*, 67.

88. Normally one would expect "whenever" (ὅταν) with the subjunctive verb rather than the less uncertain "whoever" (ὅστις). James thus shows that he does not view the scenario as improbable, "but as a real possibility" (Hiebert, *The Epistle of James*, 166).

89. Davids (*The Epistle of James*, 116) comments that "the statement itself is more or less a truism, even if the form is Jewish. Although penalties may vary, one is counted a criminal no matter which particular section of the code one may have broken." Cf., e.g., Philo, *Allegorical Interpretation*, 3.241; *4 Macc.* 5:20.

90. Laws, *The Epistle of James*, 112.

91. Marjorie O. Boyle ("The Stoic Paradox of James 2.10," *NTS* 31 [1985]: 611 – 17) argues that we ought to return to understanding this statement in light of the Stoic paradox that "all virtues and vices are equal, and its corollary that he who has one virtue has all while he who lacks one has none" (611) — an interpretation of this verse supported by Augustine and Erasmus, but generally ignored in the twentieth century. She argues that "a Judaic derivation for this verse does not nullify its expression of a Stoic paradox" (616). It is certainly possible that diaspora Jewish-Christians would recognize the parallels in multiple religious contexts, but unlikely that this one would be the major parallel envisioned.

92. Davids (*The Epistle of James*, 117) points out that "the use of εἰπών ... εἶπεν καί [is] a circumlocution in Jewish style to avoid naming God, the choice of verb pointing to the law as the orally pronounced personal command of God." He adds that "the examples James selects show he is not at all concerned with ritual commands or minutiae."

93. Moo, *The Letter of James*, 115; see also Johnson, *The Letter of James*, 232.

But why these two examples? One answer looks ahead in James, where in 4:2–4 these ideas return, as people "murder" out of envy and are "adulterous" in their relationship with God. Another option is to look at the Sermon on the Mount in Mt 5:21–30, where these are the two laws out of the Ten Commandments that Jesus picks out to expand. Davids adds that murder was "frequently associated with discrimination against the poor and failure to love the neighbor,"[94] which would fit James's context well. In any event, his point in vv. 10–11 is to show that neglecting the poor transgresses a central tenet of God's will. Nevertheless, it goes beyond what can be legitimately inferred from the text to argue that no sin is any worse than any other. All sins may separate us from God, but we would still far prefer someone else to tell a "white lie" than to initiate a nuclear holocaust![95]

James 2:12 In such a way speak and in such a way act as ones about to be judged by the law of liberty (οὕτως λαλεῖτε καὶ οὕτως ποιεῖτε ὡς διὰ νόμου ἐλευθερίας μέλλοντες κρίνεσθαι). Here appears the clearest evidence in vv. 8–13 that there are two different laws under discussion in this passage.[96] James returns to the "law of liberty," first introduced in 1:25, as a positive contrast to the law of vv. 10–11, which served only to condemn. Thus, this passage suddenly sounds remarkably Pauline: If one attempts to live according to Torah, one is doomed to failure because one can never keep all of it. Rather, one ought to live according to the new law or covenant that Christ creates by fulfilling and supplementing Torah and according to the freedom it brings.[97] But lest we think this a license to sin, Moo explains that "God's gracious acceptance of us does not end our obligation to obey him; it sets it on a new footing. For the will of God now confronts us as a *law of liberty*—an obligation we discharge" with joy because we stand both forgiven and empowered by the Holy Spirit.[98] The genitive "of liberty" (ἐλευθερίας) remains descriptive, depicting a "liberating" law.

Next James uses two imperatives to touch on the two key pieces of right living: how we speak and how we act. "For the first time, James warns about eschatological judgment and suggests that conformity to the demands of the law will be the criterion of that judgment," anticipating his teaching in 2:14–16.[99] That this judgment is described as "about to" (μέλλοντες) happen indicates the certainty of this future event more than its exact timing. The complementary infinitive "to be judged" (κρίνεσθαι), meanwhile, links back to 2:1 and 4, where forms of discrimination (from διακρίνω), or incorrect judgment, appeared. Even Christians must undergo judgment, but our judgment will take place before Christ, who has already offered us freedom through his grace and mercy. This, in turn, should lead us to help liberate rather than oppress others (again, recall Mt 18:23–35).[100]

James 2:13 For judgment is merciless to the one not showing mercy. [But] mercy triumphs over judgment (ἡ γὰρ κρίσις ἀνέλεος τῷ μὴ ποιήσαντι ἔλεος· κατακαυχᾶται ἔλεος κρίσεως). Finally,

94. Davids, *The Epistle of James*, 117. He adds a list of key texts: Jer 7:6; 22:3; Sir 34:26; *Test. Gad* 4:6–7; 1Jn 3:15; Am 8:4.

95. Cf. Jesus' distinctions concerning the "weightier matters of the law" in Mt 23:23 par. Barton, Veerman, and Wilson (*James*, 53) put it well: "James's point here is not that showing favoritism is as 'bad' as murder, but that no matter what commandment someone breaks, that person is guilty of an offense against God. He or she has violated the will of God. We cannot excuse the sin of favoritism by pointing to the rest of the good we do. Sin is not simply balanced against good—it must be confessed and forgiven."

96. Cf. Perkins, *First and Second Peter, James, and Jude*, 107.

97. Adamson (*The Epistle of James*, 118–19) is one of the strongest supporters of this view.

98. Moo, *The Letter of James*, 117.

99. Ibid., 116.

100. Stulac, *James*, 104.

James contrasts the nature of judgment for the unbeliever with the believer's experience. Here the key verb ποιέω (underlying "showing") appears again, indicating an active, "doing" aspect to showing mercy. "The one who does not show mercy would be the person failing to care for any creature or other person ... especially the failure to help the poor."[101] Martin warns against diminishing "the severity of this verse," because "those who fail to demonstrate a living and consistent faith are in danger of facing harsh judgment at the end, for they live as though ethical issues were of no consequence."[102]

The asyndeton introducing the next clause, along with the brevity of the entire statement, places extra emphasis on James's last assertion: "mercy triumphs over judgment" (κατακαυχᾶται ἔλεος κρίσεως). The related verb καυχάομαι is a common Pauline term for boasting, but the compound form used here (κατακαυχάομαι) appears only here and twice in Ro 11:18. With this verb, a sense of victory emerges, of conquering and being able to boast about something. While it can denote arrogance, that Pauline sense does not transfer into this passage.[103]

James's assertion can sound universalist if taken out of context, as if one day all would be saved. Here, however, he is discussing how mercy triumphs over judgment for the Christian. Those who never show any mercy cannot have internalized and accepted God's mercy. "Once faith understands the salvation God works, that the divine mercy has overcome the divine justice, faith must include a stance of mercy toward others."[104] God's judgment is inexorable, "but where there is evidence of merciful deeds, God's attribute of mercy triumphs over the dictates of his justice, and the balance is tipped in man's favour."[105] True believers (the ones showing mercy to others) will find God's mercy in Christ annuls the condemnation they otherwise would have received. The mercy in view in this verse is thus both human and divine.[106] But unbelievers (the ones not showing mercy at all) can look forward only to their just condemnation. Vv. 14 – 17 will proceed to give a pointed example of precisely such mercilessness.

101. Davids, *The Epistle of James*, 119; he adds that "the connection must be that in humiliating the poor (whom God honors) and in transgressing the law of love (thus breaking the law) they are also failing to show mercy. As such they could expect no mercy in the final judgment."

102. Martin, *James*, 72. He does, however, see v. 13b as hope in contrast to the threat of v. 13a, and an echo of the promise of Mt 5:7.

103. William Dyrness ("Mercy Triumphs over Justice: James 2:13 and the Theology of Faith and Works," *Them* 6 no. 3 [1981]: 13) observes that "mercy does not merely vindicate itself, it is able to triumph"; he ties in the "two major theological streams in James which are interrelated: Christians are to reflect God's merciful call to the poor and to realize his wisdom in their lives" (15). In relation to Paul's different uses of the same vocabulary, Dyrness comments that "James interprets Judaism in the light of Jesus' teaching. Paul develops Christian truth against the backdrop of Judaism" (16).

104. Richardson, *James*, 126.

105. Laws, *The Epistle of James*, 117.

106. Mariam Kamell, "James 2:12 – 13" (unpublished paper, St. Andrews, 2007), 20 – 22. Cf. esp. Hort, *The Epistle of St. James*, 57.

Theology in Application

Warning against Discrimination (2:1 – 4)

The key biblical precedent behind this paragraph is the command in Lev 19:15 not to show partiality toward *either* rich *or* poor. Clear reiterations of this principle come in Elihu's speech in Job 34:19 and in Peter's discourse with Cornelius in Ac 10:34. Partiality in *judgment* is explicitly proscribed in Dt 1:17 and Jn 7:24. Of course, the larger theme of warning against the dangers of riches and of displaying concern for the poor pervades almost every part of the Bible;[107] one thinks particularly of the reversals depicted in the parables of Lk 14:7 – 24 and 18:1 – 14. And Christ's glory (Jas 2:1), whether taken as an attribute or a title, reflects a key characteristic of Yahweh himself, which he does not give to another (Isa 42:8). One cannot help but suspect at least a subtle reference to the deity of Christ here, but it may in fact be overt (see above, pp. 106 – 7). The TCNT captures both the ethical and Christological themes of this paragraph with its paraphrastic rendering of v. 1: "Are you really trying to combine faith in Jesus Christ, our glorified Lord, with the worship of rank?"[108]

One hardly knows where to start or stop in applying these anti-discrimination mandates. Even as Western culture has seemingly made some progress in curbing the extremes of past racism and sexism, abuse of the unborn and the elderly continues at epidemic rates. Many conservative Christians vote against equal rights for gays and lesbians without any balancing, positive actions to show them Christ's love, making the legislation merely judgmental rather than fully scriptural. The poor, even in America, seem hardly to matter, as the neglect of the thousands trapped on the Gulf Coast in the wake of Hurricane Katrina demonstrated on a terrifying scale. The movie *Hotel Rwanda* expresses the feelings of many caught in countless famines or civil wars on the so-called "dark continent," when one of the white expatriate military leaders explains to the native black hotel owner why the Americans and Europeans are abandoning the besieged Rwandans: "You're worse than a nigger; you're an African!"

Meanwhile, Americans go on spending record amounts of borrowed money that they cannot realistically expect to pay back and succumb to daily barrages of advertising that make them think they first "want" and then "need" so much that they do not. Christian expenditures on beauty products, clothes, cars, entertainment, sports and recreation, technology, and church facilities suggest not only that much

107. See throughout Blomberg, *Neither Poverty nor Riches*.

108. Michael J. Townsend (*The Epistle of James* [London: Epworth, 1994], 34) explains the progression of thought from the Christological to the ethical theme: part of the Christian task "is to live as those amongst whom the reign of Christ is a reality, so pointing forward to the ultimate hope for humankind. This is why James can move from an exalted Christological statement to a very practical demand."

of the fallen world system has gotten into the church but that this world *is* at times the church's own god.[109] At least in James's churches, the possibility of destitute people entering was real; in many middle- or upper-class suburban congregations they would never dare![110]

Rationale: Experience and Scripture (2:5 – 11)

God's choice of the poor (v. 5) closely resembles Paul's matter-of-fact observations about how few in Corinth were wise, influential, or well-born (1Co 1:26 – 28). Of course, "not many" implies that a few did fall into these categories, a reminder that neither Paul nor James is countenancing salvation by socioeconomic bracket. What, then, do we do with the common slogan, made famous by liberation theology and Mother Teresa, about "God's preferential option for the poor"? How should we react to affirmative action, a euphemism for what some would call "reverse discrimination"? God loves everyone equally. But for that very reason he wants all to have equal access to at least a modicum of his good gifts in creation (cf. 2Co 8:13 – 15; 1Ti 6:17 – 19). If one tire on a car is low in air pressure, we give extra attention to that tire until it is as inflated as the rest. To redress prolonged and systemic discrimination may require a temporary imbalance in the opposite direction, but if such "bias" likewise lingers too long, we have merely replaced one prejudice with another.[111]

The exploitation of the poor by the rich is another recurring scriptural theme. Proverbs 17:5 reminds us that those who mock the poor demonstrate "contempt for their Maker," while those who gloat over others' misfortune "will not go unpunished." The prophet Amos unleashes as harsh an invective against such people as any writer of Scripture. Amos 6:1 – 6 berates the wealthy of Judah who enjoy all their luxuries without grieving the destruction and exile of Israel. Amos 8:4 – 6 lambastes those who constantly cheat the poor, while wanting nothing more fervently than for Sabbaths to end so that they can return to their commercial enterprises.

Today, many Christians do not even take any holidays or Sabbaths from making as much money as they can, nor do they dare to challenge their employers about their companies' unjust treatment of overseas workers, false advertising, or less than full and accurate financial disclosure. Instead, like those whom James rebukes, we kowtow to the rich, especially when they might give to our Christian causes, and we line their pockets by buying *their* goods even when they do us *no* good. Kent Hughes minces no words: "materialism perverts the human soul.... How else do we account

109. For poignant illustrations, see Nystrom, *James*, 128, 134 – 35.

110. Cf. Richardson, *James*, 112 – 13. Bauckham (*James*, 190) profoundly proclaims: "The propensity of the rich to ignore the poor is not only an ethical but also a religious matter. To truly confront the plight of the poor would disturb the rich in their comfortable cocooning of themselves against the realities of life." Again, "the illusions of affluence are virtually the religion of contemporary western society. Its spiritual malaise cannot be cured without profound and practical attention to the destitute."

111. Cf. the very balanced remarks on this topic in Tidball, *Wisdom from Heaven*, 65 – 67; Deiros, *Santiago y Judas*, 129 – 39.

for the adulation we give to selfish celebrities who spend their lives exploiting us? The answer can only be that a materialistic focus fosters spiritual derangement."[112] And some of these high-profile public superstars are explicit in their ridicule of all things Christian (cf. Jas 2:6 – 7). It is even harder for many American Christians to acknowledge complicity in our nation's and our business community's intentional and unintentional exploitation of the poor at home and abroad.[113] Clearly the topic is complex, but disavowing all responsibility or hiding our heads in the sand only perpetuates the injustice.[114]

The antidote is true love for neighbor and self that recognizes what is genuinely best for both them and us (vv. 8 – 11). The "royal" or "kingdom" law of v. 8 draws on all the rich background of Jesus' teaching in the Gospels on the present and future arrival of God's kingly reign in power.[115] Clearly, it continues the repeated biblical insistence on the centrality of the command to love others, especially those hardest for us to love, including God as well (cf. Lev 19:18; Mt 19:19; 22:39; Mk 12:31; Lk 10:27; Jn 15:12; Ro 13:9; Gal 5:14; 1Jn 3:11).[116] James reminds us that we cannot drive a wedge between law and love. Unlike the "situation ethics" of relativism, love does involve certain absolute standards of right and wrong. Unlike the inflexible legalism of those who multiply countless, unbiblical absolutes, law is regularly recontextualized to reflect what truly proves loving.[117]

The Laws of Justice and Mercy (2:12 – 13)

Jesus' beatitude on showing mercy (Mt 5:7) may be in James's mind here, but the closest biblical parallels to the contrast in these two verses are found in the parable of the unforgiving servant (Mt 18:32 – 35) and in the Lord's Prayer (Mt 6:12, 14 – 15). If we absolutely refuse to show mercy to others, we demonstrate that we have never truly received God's mercy ourselves (cf. also Sir 27:30 – 28:7). When we pray for God's forgiveness, we declare that we are simultaneously forgiving those who have

112. Hughes, *James*, 94. Cf. Brian S. Rosner, *Greed as Idolatry: The Origin and Meaning of a Pauline Metaphor* (Grand Rapids: Eerdmans, 2007).

113. But see Ronald J. Sider, *Rich Christians in an Age of Hunger*, 4th ed. (Dallas: Word, 1997). Missing the mark in much of his critique of Sider in precisely this area is John R. Schneider, *The Good of Affluence: Seeking God in a Culture of Wealth* (Grand Rapids: Eerdmans, 2002).

114. For a plethora of practical ideas of how individuals and churches can become part of the solution rather than part of the problem, see Tom Sine, *Mustard Seed versus McWorld: Reinventing Life and Faith for the Future* (Grand Rapids: Baker, 1999). Addressing more systemic issues well is Ronald J. Sider, *Just Generosity: A New Vision for Overcoming Poverty in America* (Grand Rapids: Baker, 1999).

115. See esp. George R. Beasley-Murray, *Jesus and the Kingdom of God* (Grand Rapids: Eerdmans, 1986); Bruce D. Chilton, *Pure Kingdom: Jesus' Vision of God* (Grand Rapids: Eerdmans, 1996).

116. In a unique and significant merger of biblical scholarship and spiritual formation, Scot McKnight (*The Jesus Creed: Loving God, Loving Others* [Brewster, MA: Paraclete, 2004]) shows how the double love command permeates every major topic and phase of Christ's life and thus should equally characterize his disciples' lives. On the striking combination of equality *and* universality in James's love ethic, see Gerd Theissen, "Amour du prochain et égalité — Jc 2/1 – 13: un moment fort de l'éthique chrétienne primitive," *ETR* 76 (2001): 325 – 46.

117. Cf. Tidball, *Wisdom from Heaven*, 118.

sinned against us.[118] Proverbs 21:13 more specifically insists that those who close their ears to the cries of the poor will have their cries ignored by God.

A lot of political and religious rhetoric in recent years at home and abroad has insisted that forgiveness of heinous personal and institutional offenses or reconciliation between estranged parties can occur only after justice has been dispensed. But this will never come close to happening in a world as fallen as ours, so the order of events must be reversed. As Miroslav Volf has so powerfully demonstrated, forgiveness and reconciliation can *lead to* a more just system, particularly when offenders fully own the crimes they have committed and tell the truth in public contexts.[119] The remarkable successes of Truth and Reconciliation commissions in war-torn parts of the world, beginning with South Africa, particularly when accompanied by Christian faith, prove to what extent mercy can triumph over justice even prior to Judgment Day.[120] Victor Hugo's classic novel, *Les Miserables*, like the musical and film made from it, constitutes a powerful narrative presentation of this truth. One of the most effective sermons one of us has heard preached involved little more than the dramatic retelling of the plot of this story; these verses comprise an excellent springboard for such a message.

118. Arland J. Hultgren, "Forgive Us, As We Forgive (Matthew 6:12)," *WW* 16 (1996): 284 – 90.

119. Miroslav Volf, "The Social Meaning of Reconciliation," *Int* 54 (2000): 159 – 72.

120. Desmond M. Tutu, *No Future without Forgiveness* (New York: Doubleday, 1999). For other applications in the realm of public ethics, see Church, "James," 368 – 69.

5 CHAPTER

James 2:14 – 26

Literary Context

The second half of Jas 2 continues to unpack the theme of riches and poverty, a point often missed because of the inordinate attention given to the apparent contradiction between vv. 20 – 26 and Paul's principle of justification by faith alone. But James's insistence that faith without works is dead follows as a corollary from the theme of vv. 1 – 13, further illustrated by the shocking refusal of some so-called Christians to offer even the slightest help to the most destitute in their midst (vv. 14 – 17).

The two exemplars of James's principle of works completing or vindicating one's faith — Abraham and Rahab — contrast with each other in several respects, creating a powerful merismus, a figure of speech "which makes equal the most extreme members of a whole and therefore all the other members who fall in between."[1] Ralph Martin points out the numerous verbal links between vv. 1 – 13 and 14 – 26: "my brothers" and "faith" (vv. 1, 14), a poor person inadequately clothed (vv. 2, 15), "faith" showing itself in "love" or "works" (v. 5 and ten times in vv. 14 – 26), "you do well" (vv. 8, 19), and the name one of God's people has been "called" (vv. 7, 23).[2] More immediately linking vv. 12 – 13 with what follows is the motif of acts of mercy, acts that are lacking in vv. 14 – 17 but which Rahab and Abraham exhibited on various occasions.[3]

We do not find similar links between 2:14 – 26 and 3:1 – 12, because there James has moved on to unpacking his second key theme — wisdom and speech. But we do hear resonances of 2:14 – 26 elsewhere in the epistle, especially where the theme of rich and poor is prominent. Workless faith resembles the vain religion of 1:26 – 27. On the one hand, the person claiming to be a believer but displaying no works cannot be saved, just as the rich oppressors will be eternally judged (5:3 – 4). Those who demonstrate true faith through their good works, on the other hand, will be exalted, at least in the life to come, however humiliating their circumstances in this world may have been (1:9). That Abraham was called God's friend (2:23) also anticipates the fundamental contrast of 4:4 between friendship with God and friendship with the world.[4]

1. Wall, *Community of the Wise*, 143 – 44.
2. Martin, *James*, 78 – 79.
3. Roy B. Ward, "The Works of Abraham: James 2:14 – 26," *HTR* 61 (1968): 283 – 90.
4. Hartin, *James*, 160.

Main Idea

Those who claim to be believers but offer not the slightest aid to Christians in dire need, whom they are in a position to help, demonstrate the emptiness of their claims. True saving faith will by nature produce good works, as illustrated by examples as diverse as Abraham and Rahab.

Translation

(See next page.)

Structure

The structure of 2:14–17 proves remarkably similar to that of 2:1–4. An initial thesis (v. 14) gives way to an illustration in the form of a compound conditional sentence (vv. 15–16), and then a rephrasing of the thesis (v. 17). Instead of a command, followed by one long rhetorical question (vv. 1, 2–4), James creates an ABB'A' chiasm in vv. 14–16 beginning and ending with the short question, "What does it profit?" In between the two halves of the illustration, he then draws a formal conclusion with an indicative statement in v. 17.[5]

V. 18a poses a potential objection that someone might raise to James's logic. All the rest of this passage makes sense as James's multifaceted reply (vv. 18b–26). The first part asks yet another rhetorical question, which assumes the continuing monotheism of the Jewish Christian audience (v. 19a). But an exclamation tinged with sarcasm meets the implied affirmative response—even demons know there is only one God who is sovereign but that does not make them believers (v. 19b)!

5. Marconi, "La struttura di Giacomo 2," 254.

James 2:14-26

14a	Rhetorical Q.	**What is the profit**, my brothers and sisters
b	condition	if someone should claim to have faith but
c	contrast	does not have works?
d	Restatement	**Is such faith able to save them?**
15	Illustration (of 16c)	If a brother or sister should be naked and lacking in daily food, and
16a	expansion	someone of you should say to them, 'Go in peace, be warmed and filled," but
b	contrast	you do not give them anything for their bodily needs
c	parallel (to 14a)	**what is the profit?**
17a	Conclusion	Likewise, also, **faith by itself ... is dead**
b	condition	if it does not have works.
18a	Problem	But **someone might say you have faith and I have works.**
b	Resolution	**Show me your faith without works**
c	contrast	and **I will show you my faith**
d	means	by my works.
19a	Rhetorical Q.	**Do you believe that God is one?**
b	Exclamation	**You do well;**
	Expansion	**even the demons believe and tremble!**
20	Rhetorical Q.	**Do you want to know, O empty person, that faith without works is workless?**
21a	Example	**Was not Abraham our father justified by works**
b	means	having offered up his son Isaac
c	place	on the altar?
22a	Inference	**You see that faith was working with his works** and
b	sequence	**faith was brought to maturity by his works.**
23a	Verification	And **the Scripture was fulfilled** which says,
		"Abraham believed God and
b	simultaneous	it was accounted to him as righteousness," (Ge 15:6)
c	expansion	and he was called a friend of God.
24	Conclusion	**You see** therefore **that a person is justified by works and not by faith alone.**
25a	Parallel (to 21a)	Likewise, **was not Rahab the prostitute also justified by works**
b	means	having welcomed the messengers and
c	sequence	having sent them out by another road?
26a	Illus. (of 26b)	For just as the body without a spirit is dead, so also
b	conclusion	**faith without works is dead.**

The second part uses a rhetorical question with the vocative to address the hypothetical objector directly, in classic diatribe form (v. 20).[6] A decisive illustration for James is the example of Abraham, whose willingness to sacrifice his son Isaac formed the epitome of demonstrating one's justification (v. 21). V. 22 draws the appropriate conclusion: faith and works were working together in him to complete the entire process of salvation. For further verification, James appeals to the wording of Scripture that later calls Abraham God's friend (v. 23). Once again, the conclusion follows inexorably: faith by itself is inadequate (v. 24).

The third part turns to the closely parallel example of Rahab — note the syntactical similarities between vv. 21 and 25. An analogy about the relationship between body and spirit permits James to repeat his main idea one final time: faith without works is dead (v. 26).[7]

Exegetical Outline

- IV. The Three Themes Expanded (2:1–5:18)
  - A. Riches and Poverty (2:1–26)
    - 1. Favoritism Condemned (2:1–13)
    - ➡ **2. Workless "Faith" Exposed (2:14–26)**
      - a. An illustration of workless faith: People who claim to be Christians but fail to help poverty-stricken fellow believers are in fact not saved (vv. 14–17).
        - i. The thesis stated as a rhetorical question: Can workless faith save? (v. 14).
        - ii. The illustration unfolded: James considers the example of Christians who refuse to help their fellow-believers in time of need (vv. 15–16).
        - iii. The thesis restated as a declaration: Workless faith cannot save (v. 17).
      - b. An objection considered: Despite allegations to the contrary, faith and works are inseparable (vv. 18–26).
        - i. The objection posed: Some may allege that faith and works are separable (v. 18a).
        - ii. The objection refuted: Faith and works are inseparable (vv. 18b–26).
          - (a) The refutation in a nutshell: Without works it is impossible to demonstrate the presence of a living faith (v. 18b).
          - (b) The refutation illustrated negatively: Demons have faith without works but are not saved (v. 19).
          - (c) The refutation illustrated positively: Abraham and Rahab demonstrated their faith by their works (vv. 20–25).
          - (d) The initial thesis again restated: Faith without works is dead (v. 26).[8]

6. Church, "James," 361.

7. For a plausible rhetorical outline according to Greco-Roman forms, see J. D. N. van der Westhuizen, "Stylistic Techniques and Their Functions in James 2:14–26," *Neot* 25 (1991): 95.

8. For a detailed analysis of the structure of this text, particularly in light of its many parallelisms, see Gary M. Burge, "'And Threw Them Thus on Paper': Recovering the Poetic Form of James 2:14–26," *SBT* 7 (1977): 31–45.

Explanation of Text

James 2:14 What is the profit, my brothers and sisters, if someone should claim to have faith but does not have works? Is such faith able to save them? (Τί τὸ ὄφελος, ἀδελφοί μου, ἐὰν πίστιν λέγῃ τις ἔχειν ἔργα δὲ μὴ ἔχῃ; μὴ δύναται ἡ πίστις σῶσαι αὐτόν;). The futility of faith without works forms the main idea and recurring assertion of this section. The idiomatic question with which James begins means "what good is it?" This was a common way for writers of the time to introduce rhetorical dialogue, presenting an argument with which the author disagreed.[9] The introduction opens the question in which James lays out the specific issue. His thesis question queries whether faith without works is any good.[10] The third-class condition introduced by "if" (ἐάν) again implies some doubt. James could be presenting a hypothetical objection for the sake of his argument, but it seems likely that some in his congregation were making precisely this inquiry. Why else would vv. 14 – 26 rebut the viability of a lifeless orthodoxy so strenuously?

The word πίστις is moved forward for emphasis, showing that "faith" (πίστις) is the key concept to be explored in this passage.[11] Thus far we have seen it in 1:3, 6 and in 2:1, 5; in each case it means full-orbed trust in Christ. But obviously someone can "claim" to have faith even when they do not. "Work" (ἔργον) has appeared as the final effect of endurance (1:4) and a correct response to the law (1:25), and its plural counterpart here fits this pattern nicely. More specifically, as 2:15 – 16 show, James uses the term to refer to deeds of grace or mercy, such as caring for the poor and not showing partiality. As in 2:1 – 13, vv. 14 – 26 elaborate on the proper way to "hold the faith of our Lord Jesus." Perhaps "works" (ἔργα) might be better translated as "action" in this context to "avoid confusion with Paul's teaching [against] nomistic religion, i.e., 'works of the law.'"[12]

Continuing his rhetorical dialogue, James inquires whether such "faith" can prove salvific. The inquiry begins with an untranslated μή, introducing a question that expects a negative answer. Perhaps the clearest translation would be, "such faith is not able to save them, is it?" The article here with "faith" (ἡ πίστις) is resumptive, showing that James is referring specifically to the faith of the previous clause, the "faith" that does not lead to works. The verb "save" (σῶσαι) in James refers to the entire process that begins with initial faith in Christ and climaxes in heavenly glorification.[13] "The thrust of James's argument is that indeed there is no profit (i.e., salvation-bringing efficacy) for anyone exhibiting the type of faith described in vv 15 – 16a."[14]

9. Davids (*The Epistle of James*, 120) observes that this expression always expects a negative answer.

10. Here begin James's bold statements that so many read as contradicting Paul. Sharyn Dowd ("Faith That Works: James 2:14 – 26," *RevExp* 97 [2000]: 195 – 205) observes a confidence, at least within evangelical scholarship, that "if Paul and James had sat down together and clarified their terms, they would have found nothing substantive about which they disagreed" (196), and proceeds to show how Paul supports the idea that true faith reveals itself in love (1Co 13:3; Eph 2:8; Gal 2:15; 5:6). See further throughout our exegesis of vv. 14 – 26.

11. Robert H. Stein ("'Saved by Faith [Alone]' in Paul Versus 'Not Saved by Faith Alone' in James," *SBJT* 4 [2000]: 4 – 19) points out that James uses πίστις sixteen times, eleven of which are in this passage alone, and he shows how James's opponent in the 'dialogue' here understands faith quite differently than James does, so that one must distinguish between the faith of the interlocutor and the faith of James himself.

12. Martin, *James*, 81. Cf. NJB: "How does it help ... when someone who has never done a single good act claims to have faith?"

13. Given the clearly eschatological use in 1:21, here "save" should also be understood to refer to eternal life and not merely to earthly rescue (cf. Moo, *The Letter of James*, 124).

14. Martin, *James*, 80. Donald J. Verseput ("Reworking the Puzzle of Faith and Deeds in James 2:14 – 26," *NTS* 43 [1997]:

James 2:15 If a brother or sister should be naked and lacking in daily food (ἐὰν ἀδελφὸς ἢ ἀδελφὴ γυμνοὶ ὑπάρχωσιν καὶ λειπόμενοι τῆς ἐφημέρου τροφῆς). Vv. 15–16 provide an incisive illustration of James's point and also exemplify his social concern for the poor. Tellingly, James does not use his standard gender-inclusive "brother" but intentionally includes the words for both "brother" (ἀδελφός) and "sister" (ἀδελφή).[15] Probably he highlighted the "sister" because women often comprised the more desperately needy and were the more easily overlooked in his society, especially when they lacked provision and protection by a father or husband. James may also have wanted to be sure that no one mistook this example for anything less than wholly inclusive.[16]

The term "naked" (γυμνός) frequently implies having no clothes on at all, but it can refer to someone who is poorly clad, having perhaps only an undergarment or one set of clothes that is threadbare and useless against any bad weather.[17] The present participle "lacking" (λειπόμενοι) may be the sign that this believer suffers consistently in this respect. In the expression "daily food" (τῆς ἐφημέρου τροφῆς), we hear an echo of the Lord's Prayer, "give us this day our *daily bread*" (Mt 6:11).[18] God's normal way of fulfilling this petition is through his people as they share with those in need, so the scandal of this example proves even more shocking.[19]

James 2:16 ... and someone of you should say to them, "Go in peace, be warmed and filled," but you do not give them anything for their bodily needs, what is the profit? (εἴπῃ δέ τις αὐτοῖς ἐξ ὑμῶν, Ὑπάγετε ἐν εἰρήνῃ, θερμαίνεσθε καὶ χορτάζεσθε, μὴ δῶτε δὲ αὐτοῖς τὰ ἐπιτήδεια τοῦ σώματος, τί τὸ ὄφελος;). James now completes his example of the destitute fellow Christian. Rhetorically, he returns to his original question in v. 14, showing this inadequate response to a person's need to be an illustration of faith without works. The "faith" part is incorporated by the fact that the main character of this verse is "someone of you" (τις ... ἐξ ὑμῶν), a member of the congregations to whom the letter was written. James pictures this person giving a pat answer to the destitute individual of v. 15—recognizing and verbally acknowledging the desperate need, but then not doing anything to help alleviate the situation.

115) adds that "James is not seeking to downgrade the importance of 'faith' in 2.14–26. On the contrary, faith retains its role as the primary distinguishing feature of the community. But as the prophets of old had denied the efficacy of sacrifice without obedience, so faith without works is dead."

15. Consistent gender-inclusive translations, while generally to be preferred, will lose James's distinction here, because the English translation will read just as it does for a simple "brother" (ἀδελφός). Nevertheless, even noninclusive translations usually render the plural verb as "are" and the plural pronoun in v. 16 as "them" (αὐτοῖς), even though correct English requires "if a brother or sister *is* ... and you say to her (or him)...." If an inspired writer, drawing on an occasional Greek practice (see Ropes, *A Critical and Exegetical Commentary on the Epistle of St. James*, 206), can use plural verbs or pronouns with singular antecedents, to impugn gender-inclusive translations that do the same thing unwittingly impugns a practice that God condoned in inspiring Scripture! See further Craig L. Blomberg, "*Today's New International Version*: The Untold Story of a Good Translation," *BT* 56 (2005): 206.

16. There is an interesting parallel here with the gender-inclusive τις and the responsibility to care for aging relatives in one's own family in 1Ti 5:8, and both are within the context of believers' communities.

17. Ropes, *A Critical and Exegetical Commentary on the Epistle of St. James*, 106. The use of "be" (ὑπάρχω), often also implying "possess," may show that the poverty mentioned here was a permanent or at least an enduring state for these people (Martin, *James*, 84).

18. Indeed, Klaus Haacker ("Justification, salut et foi: Étude sur les rapports entre Paul, Jacques et Pierre," *ETR* 73 [1998]: 177–88) highlights James's continuity with the Synoptic tradition throughout this pericope, making conscious interaction with Paul or Paulinism even less likely.

19. See Hartin, *James*, 158. Edgar (*Has God Not Chosen the Poor?* 169–70) suggests, though, that if these Christians were imitating the itinerant ministries of the twelve and the seventy/seventy-two (cf. Lk 9:1–6 pars.; 10:1–20), they might not have found anyone to provide food and clothing for them.

The expression "go in peace" (ὑπάγετε ἐν εἰρήνῃ) was a common way of saying "good-bye" (lit., "fare well") and depicts the conversation's end (cf. NAB: "Good-bye and good luck"). In effect, the believer confronted with the needy brother or sister pronounces a blessing on the poor person. They clearly show they understand the needs by declaring, "be warm and filled" (θερμαίνεσθε καὶ χορτάζεσθε), but there appears an extreme contrast between their words and their inaction. These two verbs are either middle ("warm yourselves and fill yourselves") or passive ("be warmed and be filled"). If middle, the insult to the poor person merely becomes even more outrageous.[20] If passive, then how did the person in a position to help think the poor person would receive aid? Laws suggests that "this use of the passive to express hope should further be understood as a reverential periphrasis: the hope is not simply that somehow or other these wants will be supplied, but that *God* will supply them."[21] Johnson replies, "It is not the form of the statement that is reprehensible, but its functioning as a religious cover for the failure to act."[22] And this is what angers James: the more well-to-do believer does *not* take care of the physical needs of the other despite all their spoken good wishes.

The neuter plural for "needs" (τὰ ἐπιτήδεια) refers to "the necessary things," the things a person needs in order to survive. They are further qualified by "of the body" (τοῦ σώματος), a genitive that can be understood in three ways. It can be partitive, implying that this person did not offer help for even the essential requirements of the body. It can be objective, referring to things necessary for the body rather than, say, for the spirit. Most likely, it is a simple descriptive genitive, referring to any "bodily" needs that we have.

James closes with the inclusio of "what is the profit?" (τί τὸ ὄφελος;), showing that he believes his original question in v. 14 has been answered by his illustration. The one who refuses to help another cannot be saved (v. 14), in the same way that well-wishing by itself affords the needy person no aid (v. 16).[23] "The example was crass and would have shocked many pagans" with the insensitivity shown, "let alone people accustomed to the OT prophets and the application of the laws of charity in late Judaism."[24] Just as words without action profited the poor person nothing, so faith without works profits the "believer" nothing.

James 2:17 Likewise, also, faith by itself, if it does not have works, is dead (οὕτως καὶ ἡ πίστις, ἐὰν μὴ ἔχῃ ἔργα, νεκρά ἐστιν καθ' ἑαυτήν). This verse summarizes vv. 14 – 16.[25] The two clauses repeat language from v. 14, lengthening the inclusio begun at the end of v. 16. We can finally begin to compose definitions of what James means by "faith" and "works." James assumes that "faith" includes works. This faith is the saving faith of a life lived in sanctification.[26] Thus when he wants

20. Hiebert, *The Epistle of James*, 180. Martin (*James*, 85) supports the middle voice reading, but stresses that "either voice points to the fact that some professed believers are failing to meet the needs of other church members."

21. Laws, *The Epistle of James*, 121. She adds that this "is probably intended as a caricature of what to his supposed man [*sic*] of faith would seem a wholly appropriate response. Confronted with a case of need, he commits it with prayer to God, who clothes the naked and feeds the hungry ... and sends away his fellow-believers with expressions of confidence. To James such a response is wholly inadequate."

22. Johnson, *The Letter of James*, 239. Wallace (*Greek Grammar Beyond the Basics*, 437) believes that "the suppression of the agent serves as an indictment."

23. Moo, *The Letter of James: An Introduction and Commentary*, 103.

24. Davids, *The Epistle of James*, 122.

25. "By itself" (καθ' ἑαυτήν) comes at the end for emphasis, but it refers back to "faith" (i.e., faith without any action), not to "dead."

26. Motyer (*The Message of James*, 109) comments that "we must say ... not 'faith and works', but faith productive of works."

to talk about less than genuine faith, he has to qualify it, as throughout this whole passage, as not having works.

"Works" here are not the Pauline "works of the law,"s such as circumcision, but rather the works of love, such as caring for those who are in need, not showing favoritism, being humble, or being slow to speak. In essence, works are the sum total of a changed life brought about by faith. Where "Paul denies the need for 'pre-conversion works,'"[27] James emphasizes the absolute necessity of post-conversion works.[28] James calls a "faith" that does not bring about a changed life dead, lifeless, and useless. It does not work to save a person, for it cannot, lacking life itself. As Davids summarizes, "a 'faith' which is purely doctrinal and does not result in pious action (i.e., charity) is a dead sham, totally useless for salvation."[29]

James 2:18 But someone might say you have faith and I have works. Show me your faith without works and I will show you my faith by my works (Ἀλλ' ἐρεῖ τις, Σὺ πίστιν ἔχεις, κἀγὼ ἔργα ἔχω. δεῖξόν μοι τὴν πίστιν σου χωρὶς τῶν ἔργων, κἀγώ σοι δείξω ἐκ τῶν ἔργων μου τὴν πίστιν). The debate continues regarding faith with and without works, again by means of an interlocutor. James seems to be introducing someone opposing his statement in v. 17 regarding faith being dead in itself, because v. 18 begins with the adversative, "but someone might say" (ἀλλ' ἐρεῖ τις).[30] But the rest of v. 18 spawns a great deal of confusion over who is speaking and for how long.[31]

If one reads this verse as a whole, then this speaker seems to support James's argument, agreeing that "you" (James's churches) have faith and "I" (James) have works. This speaker's words could then end mid-verse or they could continue to the end of v. 18 or even to the end of 19. Thus the argument of the passage would start with an objector in v. 14a claiming to have faith without works. James would then reply with his example and summary in vv. 14b–17, and then another voice would respond in vv. 18–19 to the original speaker in v. 14a. This interlocutor, an *ally* of James, challenges the original objector to prove their faith without any tangible evidence, while maintaining the need for works to demonstrate the reality of true, saving faith.[32]

However, while it was common in diatribes to use an imaginary opponent to further one's argument, it was not common to use imaginary supporters.[33] Moreover, this rendering is not the normal way to take the introduction, "but someone will say" (ἀλλ' ἐρεῖ τις),[34] in which the τις

27. Martin, *James*, 81.

28. Moo, *The Letter of James: An Introduction and Commentary*, 100–101.

29. Davids, *The Epistle of James*, 119.

30. The future indicative in a hypothetical statement approximates the force of the subjunctive. The frequency of such hypothetical objections in the diatribe form discourages us from trying to identify the interlocutor with a specific person or movement. It is certainly false to claim that "James is counting on his readers'/listeners' ability to make the easy identification of τις with Paul" (Vasiliki Limberis, "The Provenance of the Caliphate Church: James 2.17–26 and Galatians 3 Reconsidered," in *Early Christian Interpretation of the Scriptures of Israel: Investigations and Proposals*, ed. Craig A. Evans and James A. Sanders [Sheffield: SAP, 1997], 414)!

31. Dibelius (*James*, 154) calls this "one of the most difficult New Testament passages in general" for a reason!

32. Cf. Joseph B. Mayor, *The Epistle of St. James*, 2nd ed. (London: Macmillan, 1897), 99–100; Spiros Zodhiates, *The Epistle of James and the Life of Faith*, vol. 2 (Grand Rapids: Eerdmans, 1959), 22; Adamson, *The Epistle of James*, 124–25. Martin (*James*, 87) finds some support for this view, but rejects it in the end because "the sudden appearance of an 'ally'—since his unheralded appearance is uncalled for—speaks against" this position.

33. Moo, *The Letter of James*, 127.

34. To make sense of this first interpretation, ἀλλά must be translated as "indeed," which is an attested NT use of the conjunction (e.g., Jn 16:2; 1Co 3:2; 2Co 7:11; 11:1; Php 1:18), but usually in contexts where a contrast between clauses makes little sense.

would seem to refer back to the one claiming to have faith without deeds in v. 14, not least because v. 18 reads naturally as an objection to James's response to this person in v. 17, the conclusion to James's last paragraph. In other words the "someone" (τις) in v. 18 seems to reflect either the same or another imaginary *opponent* of James.[35]

McKnight comments that "the τις of 2:18a introduces an interlocutor and therefore states the position of an opponent," an opponent who "argues no necessary connection between faith and works," seeing them as two separate pieces of the Christian religion.[36] He goes on to suggest reading this person's declaration as "*one* has faith and *one* has works," "not in the sense that they are two possible avenues to salvation (Ropes) but in the sense that they are unconnected items pertaining to one's faith."[37] This position has commanded the consensus support of the most recent round of scholarship on these verses. However, it devalues the pronouns in a way that does not naturally fit the grammar. Since the pronouns would already be assumed in the verbs, they must be placed here for emphasis. To dismiss them so perfunctorily is to ignore a seemingly purposeful distinction between "you" (σύ) and "I" (ἐγώ).[38] As Davids, who holds this view, concedes, "if this ['you' and 'I' meaning just 'someone' and 'someone else'] is what James means, he has expressed it very awkwardly."[39]

A third approach limits the quotation to the first three words of v. 18, phrased as a question: "Do you really have faith?" (σὺ πίστιν ἔχεις). This makes the pronouns "you" and "I" both refer to James, exactly what one would expect. The questioner addresses James, "Do you [even] have faith [at all since you stress works so much]?" James's suppressed reply would then be "yes," and he continues explicitly, "*and* I have works. Show me your faith...."[40] But this view switches speakers at an unusual point. "And I" reads far more naturally as the second half of the objector's words rather than as a follow-up to a suppressed answer to a clause that does not even clearly form a question.

A fourth option, only rarely defended, takes all of vv. 18–19 as the objection with v. 20 beginning James's reply. But vv. 18–19 do not naturally contrast with vv. 20–26. Advocates of this view, as a result, have to assume that the point of the supposed objection is that it is possible to hold to good works by themselves, entirely apart from faith.[41]

35. Verseput ("Reworking the Puzzle of Faith and Deeds in James 2.14–26," 107) contends that while "but someone might [will] say" (ἀλλ' ἐρεῖ τις) *could* be used to introduce an ally, "it would not naturally be read in this manner following the trenchant statement of the author's thesis in vv. 14–17."

36. Scot McKnight, "James 2:18a: The Unidentifiable Interlocutor," *WTJ* 52 (1990): 360, 362.

37. McKnight, "James 2:18a," 363. Baker ("James," 60) states the argument well: "the hypothetical objector views both 'faith' and 'deeds' as equally satisfactory expressions of Christian faith, and it doesn't even matter to him who is assigned what," possibly akin to Paul's understanding of spiritual gifts. Ropes (*A Critical and Exegetical Commentary on the Epistle of St. James*, 209, 211) points to a few parallels to this use of personal pronouns or their equivalent in secular Greek, but BDF §281 notes that the construction is comparatively rare. Hiebert (*The Epistle of James*, 184) thinks that the use of "you" and "I" reflects the least likely way a Greek writer would normally express the concept of "someone" and "someone else."

38. McKnight ("James 2:18a," 364) does acknowledge the difficulty with pronouns in his proposed reading. While Moo (*The Letter of James*, 129) also acknowledges the problem, he correctly perceives that "this view is clearly becoming the majority view among scholars."

39. Davids, *The Epistle of James*, 123. Martin (*James*, 87) comments that the typical construction for this type of statement would be ἄλλος ... ἄλλος ("another ... another").

40. Edgar, *Has God Not Chosen the Poor?* 170–71; Cargal, *Restoring the Diaspora*, 125–26. For a detailed defense, see Heinz Neitzel, "Eine alte *crux interpretum* im Jakobusbrief 2, 18," *ZNW* 73 (1982): 286–93.

41. Christian E. Donker, "Der Verfasser des Jak und sein Gegner: Zum Problem des Einwändes im Jak 2, 18–19," *ZNW* 72 (1981): 227–40. Cf. Ricardo Pietrantonio, "¿Está la justicia enraizada en el NT?" *RivBib* 48 (1986): 114–18; Timo Laato, "Justification according to James: A Comparison with Paul," *TJ* 18 (1997): 81.

That view makes sense of v. 18a but not of v. 18b, where the two remain combined in the objector's mind. And it would presuppose that the objector thought that James was supporting faith without works, exactly the opposite of what the larger context of vv. 18–19 shows to be James's view.

The best option, barely ever considered, may be that the entire clause, "you have faith and I have works," is the opponent's statement rephrased by James from his own side. On this view the "you" (σύ) could refer to the opponent/speaker, while the "I" (ἐγώ) refers to James himself, thus making all of v. 18a the opponent's statement but taking the pronouns literally rather than as referring merely to "someone" and "another person."[42] On this reading, the "someone" (τις) stays consistent between v. 14 and v. 18. Likewise, this approach accepts the idea that the objector sees both faith and works as two separate but equally valid methods of showing genuine Christianity, while remaining truer to the grammar than the current consensus view. Martin presents this perspective clearly, but then speculates, less convincingly, that vv. 18b–19 continue the objector's complaint. But this requires inverting the meaning of the pronouns from v. 18a to v. 18b, which creates an entirely convoluted hypothesis.[43]

Still, Martin's original instincts were sound. If the interlocutor has ended his retort at the same point as the "consensus" view posits, with v. 18a, then v. 18b begins James's answer: "Show me your faith without works, and I will show you my faith by my works." On this perspective, exactly as on the one that takes the "you" and "I" of v. 18a as equivalent to the indefinite pronoun, James challenges his opponent to demonstrate his faith, leading up to his test in v. 19. The difference is that v. 18a is now understood as indirect discourse. Even better than taking the "you" to be the opponent directly is the view that sees it as a representative member of James's congregations. Thus James posits that "someone will say [that] you [someone in James's audience] have faith and I [James] have works."[44] The main weakness with this view is that indirect discourse regularly included the "that" (ὅτι), bracketed in this translation. But in Koine Greek, the sharp, classical boundaries between direct and indirect discourse were often blurred, and writers might shift suddenly from one to the other without any contextual indicators.[45] It could also be objected that, on this view, we might have expected a second person *plural* form for "you," but v. 16 has already referred to "some*one* ... of you (pl.)" (τις ... ἐξ ὑμῶν), while v. 14 has likewise introduced a "someone" (τις) who has faith without works, so such particularizing should cause no surprise.[46]

James 2:19 Do you believe that God is one? You do well; even the demons believe and tremble! (σὺ πιστεύεις ὅτι εἷς ἐστιν ὁ θεός, καλῶς ποιεῖς· καὶ τὰ δαιμόνια πιστεύουσιν καὶ φρίσσουσιν).[47]

42. Martin, *James*, 87.

43. Ibid., 88–89.

44. See esp. Johann E. Huther, *Critical and Exegetical Handbook to the General Epistles of James, Peter, John, and Jude* (New York: Funk & Wagnalls, 1887), 91–92. Cf. also D. Bernhard Weiss, *Das Neue Testament Handausgabe*, vol. 3 (Leipzig: J. C. Hinrichs, rev. 1902), 275; Ernst Kühl, *Die Stellung des Jakobusbriefes zum alttestamentlichen Gesetz und zur paulinischen Rechtfertigungslehre* (Königsberg, Prussia: Koch, 1905), 29–31; Verseput, "Reworking the Puzzle of Faith and Deeds in James 2.14–26," 108, n. 22.

45. See BDF §470; cf. Jn 20:18; this addresses the objection of Dibelius (*James*, 157), that "this peculiar mixture of direct and indirect address is much too improbable."

46. Similar explanations for the singular form have been used with other solutions as well; see esp. Burchard, *Der Jakobusbrief*, 118–21.

47. Here appear several textual variants, with the chosen reading rated a {B} by the UBS. None of the variants dramatically changes the meaning of the theological affirmation. Two readings smooth out stylistic problems, but both still mean "God is one" (εἷς ὁ θεός ἐστιν and ὁ θεὸς εἷς ἐστιν). Two other variants solve the conceptual problem of affirming "God is one" (the doctrine of the simplicity of God), thinking that what

James now expands his rebuttal to the interlocutor of v. 18a. It is as though his opponent spoke up in his own defense by affirming a central theological truth about God, boldly declaring the doctrine that comes from the OT Shema, "Hear, O Israel: The LORD our God, the LORD is one" (Dt 6:4 [TNIV]).[48] James may have viewed this person's appeal to the Shema as reflecting a lifeless orthodoxy, offering by rote a memorized theological truth. Or the person could be sincerely highlighting a central doctrine of belief for both Judaism and Christianity.

But James insists that correct doctrine by itself is insufficient. With biting sarcasm he praises the objector's theology: "You do well" (καλῶς ποιεῖς). Unlike the earlier use of this expression in 2:8, where it may have been genuinely positive or at worst mild irony, here he bitterly mocks the hollowness of their faith.[49] "Such belief is indeed necessary, but not enough for salvation."[50]

To show that correct doctrine is not enough, James appeals to demonic "faith." Satan and all his evil hordes are monotheists; even *they* know there is only one God and that his loyalties remain undivided. The demons *do* something about their belief: they tremble violently when faced with the one true God of the universe. The word "tremble" (φρίσσουσιν) means more than just slight shuddering; it refers to uncontainable, uncontrollable, violent shaking from extreme fear.[51] James asserts that the demons can match the original challenger's theology point for point, and they are overwhelmed by the truth of these doctrines, but they remain condemned.[52] Thus one cannot have "workless" doctrine, because that leaves one salvifically in the same position as the demons! The comparison, however, should not be pressed to say that the objector is actually demonized. Rather, James uses an extreme example to make his point that the demons are so certain of the existence of the one God that they are horrified, but even that does not bring them to salvation (because their knowledge does not change their behavior?).

James 2:20 Do you want to know, O empty person, that faith without works is workless? (θέλεις δὲ γνῶναι, ὦ ἄνθρωπε κενέ, ὅτι ἡ πίστις χωρὶς τῶν ἔργων ἀργή ἐστιν;). At this point James is ready to begin a new stage in his argument, inserting OT examples to prove his point.[53] To introduce

is actually at stake is only the issue of monotheism. This solution thus affirms, through the lack of an article, that "there is one God" (εἷς ἐστιν θεός and ἐστιν θεός), an understandable inference of later scribes. The second of these two readings could also mean "God exists," a thought almost entirely irrelevant to the context, but this is also the least attested reading.

48. This crucial belief for both Jews and Christians formed the distinction between these two groups of people and almost all Greco-Roman peoples of that day. Cf. the helpful survey by Antonía Tripolitis, *Religions of the Hellenistic-Roman Age* (Grand Rapids: Eerdmans, 2002).

49. Moo (*The Letter of James*, 130) argues that James could actually be commending this person for their correct theology, while at the same time pointing out its inadequacy, but Stulac (*James*, 114) labels it "devastating irony."

50. Davids, *The Epistle of James*, 125.

51. Moo (*The Letter of James*, 131) points out that this verb "refers to the reaction of fear provoked by contact with God or the supernatural. It occurs particularly frequently in the papyri to describe the effect that a sorcerer aims to produce in his hearers." It is a NT *hapax*. Dibelius (*James*, 159 – 60) provides a good sampling of extrabiblical texts to demonstrate the force of the verb. Recall the reactions of the demons to Christ in Mk 1:23 – 28; 5:1 – 20; and similar texts.

52. The fate of the people of Jericho makes a fascinating parallel here: "It was her [Rahab's] faith that acted for Yahweh that distinguished her from her townspeople. In Joshua 2:9 – 11 Rahab described the fear that fell upon all the people because they heard of the works of Israel's God and knew they were doomed. In a manner parallel to the demons in James 2:19, they *knew of* and *feared* Yahweh, but their knowledge did not save them" (Mariam J. Kamell, "The Concept of 'Faith' in Hebrews and James," in *The Epistle to the Hebrews and Christian Theology*, ed. Richard Bauckham et al. (London: T&T Clark, forthcoming).

53. Davids (*The Epistle of James*, 126) takes this verse as rounding off the rational argument of vv. 18 – 19, while vv. 21 – 26 then offer the biblical argument.

them, he asks if his opponent is really "willing to recognize" (NASB) the truth on this topic. He then insults this interlocutor with the label "empty" (κενός) or hollow. The word can denote both "deficient understanding" and "moral error." Given the letter's background in wisdom literature, the moral sense seems dominant. Any opponent is a "fool" in the Hebrew sense of a sinner or rebel against God.[54] Generally speaking, NT authors likewise treat foolishness in this fashion, including "the implication that the intellectual failure has moral bases or implications."[55]

Finally, James incorporates a pun on the word "work" (ἔργον), using the negative adjective from the same root — "workless" (ἀργή).[56] The term can also mean idle or useless. Faith that lacks works does not work! In other words, it is entirely ineffective to save.[57] The play on words does not work as easily in English, but it should be retained if at all possible. Baker highlights the warning contained within the pun: James is "trying to shake us out of our delusion that we are saved if we are not," if our faith is work-less to save us.[58]

James 2:21 Was not Abraham our father justified by works, having offered up his son Isaac on the altar? (Ἀβραὰμ ὁ πατὴρ ἡμῶν οὐκ ἐξ ἔργων ἐδικαιώθη ἀνενέγκας Ἰσαὰκ τὸν υἱὸν αὐτοῦ ἐπὶ τὸ θυσιαστήριον;). Here James begins his proof, moving from hypothetical examples (vv. 15 – 17) to historical ones (vv. 21 – 25). The first example he gives involves Abraham. The negative οὐκ implies that James expects a "yes" answer to this question. According to James, it was Abraham's action of willingness to sacrifice his son (Ge 22:1 – 18) that justified him in God's eyes. This seems to contradict texts like Ro 4:2 – 4 and Gal 3:6, until we realize that Paul used Abraham as an example of faith providing initial justification, while James uses this example to refer to final, eschatological justification. Thus James shows that Abraham was able to prove his faith as real because he was willing to act on it, so that he was brought to salvation at the end.[59]

James 2:21, 24, and 25 are the only verses in James that contain forms of the verb "justify" (δικαιόω); in each case, the term means to "show to be righteous."[60] Thus both Abraham and Rahab (see below, pp. 140 – 41) were shown, in history, to be righteous by their actions, giving proof of their prior spiritual state (cf. Ge 22:12, with its "now I know"). The adverbial participle "having offered up" (ἀνενέγκας) could be causal ("because he had

54. Martin, *James*, 90. Formally, James appears to contradict Jesus' teaching in Mt 5:22b against calling someone foolish or empty-headed, but it may be that there Jesus was implying "without just cause" (cf. the textual variant in v. 22a).

55. Moo, *The Letter of James*, 132.

56. Here the reading "workless" (ἀργή) is preferable to the variant "dead" (νεκρά), since the latter represents a harmonization with 2:17, and the former is the sort of wordplay of which James is fond (recall all the catchwords in 1:2 – 8 alone).

57. Jesus uses this term in Mt 20:3, 6, referring to the idle workers in the parable of the laborers in the vineyard.

58. Baker, "James," 62 – 63. Cf. Richardson, *James*, 136 – 37: "For Paul the goal was justification; for James the goal was usefulness. In the context of [Romans] faith must not be allowed to boast in its own works in the judgment.... In the context of James's letter faith must not be allowed to boast in self-sufficiency (cf. 2:7; 3:14)."

59. Cf. R. E. Glaze Jr. ("The Relationship of Faith to Works in James 1:22 – 25 and 2:14 – 26," *TTE* 34 [1986]: 41): "James dealt with an experience of Abraham long after God had declared him righteous because of his faith. He was showing, therefore, not that Abraham gained a right relationship with God through works, but that his willingness to express his faith through obedience justified his claim to faith."

60. Martin (*James*, 91 – 92) suggests that "in vv 21 – 24 Abraham's works ... are the evidence that God declares Abraham as 'righteous,'" which then indicates "that a mainly demonstrative sense lies behind δικαιοῦν." "This line of interpretation takes up the Jewish understanding of 'justification' because righteousness is there seen as the covenant fidelity or obedience expected of those who are to survive the judgment."

offered up"), thus making the sacrifice the reason Abraham was shown to be justified; or instrumental ("by having offered up"), identifying the sacrifice as the means by which Abraham was shown justified. The prepositional phrase "by works" (ἐξ ἔργων), itself instrumental, could make the participle instrumental as well, specifying the works by which Abraham was justified. In fact, however, James may intentionally have *not* qualified the participle in order to leave both causal and instrumental options open.[61]

James 2:22 You see that faith was working with his works and faith was brought to maturity by his works (βλέπεις ὅτι ἡ πίστις συνήργει τοῖς ἔργοις αὐτοῦ καὶ ἐκ τῶν ἔργων ἡ πίστις ἐτελειώθη). This verse explains James's example, drawing out what the reader is to take from it. The verb "was working with" (συνήργει) comes from a root that means to "work together with, assist, help."[62] The imperfect form here emphasizes the ongoing nature of the "working together" (cf. HCSB: "faith was active together with his works"; and ESV: "faith was active along with his works"). This tense choice adds to James's argument that faith must work itself out in daily life, clearly an example of what Paul would call sanctification, the lifetime of growing obedience to God.[63]

The other key verb here is the aorist passive "was brought to maturity" (ἐτελειώθη), recalling the τελέω vocabulary of completion and fulfillment first introduced in 1:4. Abraham's willingness to sacrifice his son not only showed his faith to be real, but also through his obedience his faith actually "grew up." Abraham's faith was not mature until he acted upon it. In the process he learned more about God's character, further bolstering his faith.[64] His confidence in God's trustworthiness was "brought to the goal for which it was intended."[65]

James 2:23 And the Scripture was fulfilled which says, "Abraham believed God, and it was accounted to him as righteousness," and he was called a friend of God (καὶ ἐπληρώθη ἡ γραφὴ ἡ λέγουσα, Ἐπίστευσεν δὲ Ἀβραὰμ τῷ θεῷ, καὶ ἐλογίσθη αὐτῷ εἰς δικαιοσύνην καὶ φίλος θεοῦ ἐκλήθη). James summarizes his example of Abraham by appealing to Genesis 15:6 and other biblical texts. The verb "was fulfilled" (ἐπληρώθη) is the standard verb for the fulfillment of Scripture in the NT, both when events previously predicted take place and when later occurrences flesh out or "fill full" the meaning of earlier ones, as here. Abraham's willingness to sacrifice his son richly filled his earlier profession of faith with fuller meaning.[66]

The Scripture on which James draws stands out because Paul uses the identical passage to argue for

61. Paul makes no mention of the binding of Isaac (known as the ʿ*Aqedah*), and Martin (*James*, 92) observes that "for James, whose polemic interest is not that of Paul, the faith of Abraham led to his works of obedience."

62. BDAG, 969.

63. Johnson (*The Letter of James*, 243) notes that above all, "it is *faith* that is the subject of both clauses. Faith makes possible (co-works) the deeds, and the deeds bring the faith to its mature expression."

64. Davids (*The Epistle of James*, 128) adds that Abraham's faith is here "perfected," "doubtless meaning 'is brought to maturity' and thus indicating the unfinished state of faith without works." Johnson (*The Letter of James*, 243) explains that James finds "the *graphē* declaring Abraham righteous in Gen 15:6 was fulfilled by the *deed* that Abraham performed by offering his son Isaac."

65. Scaer, *James*, 92.

66. Cf. Edgar, *Has Not God Chosen the Poor?* 174. Davids (*The Epistle of James*, 129) sees this verb functioning in a midrashic method of adding a second OT text to the discussion. Thus while Ge 22:1 – 12 is under discussion, Ge 15:6 is added to say "the same thing James has been arguing." Irving Jacobs ("The Midrashic Background for James II.21 – 3," *NTS* 22 [1976]: 461) argues that James "reflects a complex of ideas widely current in early times, relating to Abraham's love for God as characterized by his faith-obedience, his total submission to the Divine will." Jacobs highlights esp. Philo, *De Abr.* 32, 170 and *b. Sot.* 31a.

work-free faith in Ro 4:3, 9, 22 and Gal 3:6.[67] But Paul is promoting faith apart from the *law*, while James argues that Abraham's willingness to sacrifice Isaac shows that he really did believe God and the promise of descendants for him. This active faith is what was "reckoned to him" or "accounted to him." The expression "as righteousness" (εἰς δικαιοσύνην) forms a Septuagintalism, employing the preposition "for" (cf. the Hebrew *l*-prefix) with an accusative object to depict what was credited to Abraham. This choice of the word "righteousness" recalls Pauline language, where it regularly referred to the imputation of right standing before God through faith in Christ. James, however, is closer to the OT use of righteousness as equivalent to *ḥesed* or "covenant faithfulness."[68] First Maccabees 2:52 likewise alludes to Ge 22 in the language of Ge 15:6 and in the form of a rhetorical question: "Was not Abraham found faithful when tested (ἐν πειρασμῷ εὑρέθη πιστός), and it was reckoned to him as righteousness?"[69]

Because of his acts of faith, Abraham was also given the distinct honor of being called "a friend of God" (φίλος θεοῦ). This part of the verse is not a direct quotation from the OT, although the idea clearly appears in 2Ch 20:7 and Isa 41:8, which in turn may have been based on Genesis 18:17 – 18. Because God could not hide from Abraham what he was about to do (in blessing Abraham's seed but judging Sodom and Gomorrah), he was treating him like an intimate confidant.[70] Here, too, we see that God not only dealt with him legally, in terms of justifying him for his active faith, but he also dealt with him interpersonally. Abraham's faith in God helped to build a relationship between them, and God reciprocated by calling him his friend.[71]

James 2:24 You see therefore that a person is justified by works and not by faith alone (ὁρᾶτε ὅτι ἐξ ἔργων δικαιοῦται ἄνθρωπος καὶ οὐκ ἐκ πίστεως μόνον). James returns to his main point in vv. 14 – 26 for a fourth time (recall vv. 14, 17, and 20). In this sentence, he wants to ensure that his audience has reached the proper conclusion from the example of Abraham. The plural "you see" (ὁρᾶτε) shows that he is addressing everyone in his congregations again, not merely the imaginary disputant. He pulls "by works" (ἐξ ἔργων) to the front of the sentence for emphasis, underscoring his argument. James again uses the verb for a demonstration of justification, so that his statement connotes that "*by works* a person is shown to be justified." It is by people's actions that they prove the reality of their professions of faith, both to others and to God.

It is interesting to note that this is the only time

67. John G. Lodge ("James and Paul at Cross-Purposes? James 2,22" *Bib* 62 [1981]: 195 – 213) sees in an elaborate layering of chiasms the answer to the conflict between James and Paul: 2:22, on faith working, forms the climactic center. Lodge concludes that "to say that the faith of Abraham, the friend of God, worked along with these works and was perfected by them is to say no more and no less than that his faith was 'working through love' (Gal 5,6; 1Cor 13,4 – 7)" (213).

68. Cf. Ben Witherington III, *Letters and Homilies for Jewish Christians* (Downers Grove, IL: IVP, 2007), 477.

69. Cf. *Jub* 19:9: "This (is) the tenth trial with which Abraham was tried. And he was found faithful, controlled of spirit."

70. Cf. Hiebert, *The Epistle of James*, 196. Cf. also Lea (*Hebrews and James*, 288 – 89), who notes that Scripture stresses how God took the initiative in this process. By contrast, Jewish tradition increasingly highlighted Abraham's meritorious hospitality. See Andrew E. Arterbury, "Abraham's Hospitality among Jewish and Early Christian Writers," *PRSt* 30 (2003): 359 – 76.

71. This is in stark contrast with James 4:4 and the person who is an enemy of God. In *Apoc. Abr.* 9:6 – 7, God declares to the patriarch, "I will announce to you guarded things and you will see great things which you have not seen, because you desired to search for me, and I called you my beloved," while in the *T. Abraham* 15:14 – 15 an archangel declares to God about Abraham: "from the beginning he has been your friend and he did everything which is pleasing before you. And there is no man like unto him on earth, not even Job, the wondrous man." Cf. also *Apoc. Zeph.* 9:4 – 5.

in the NT that the three words "by faith alone" (ἐκ πίστεως μόνον) appear without intervening material. That expression is the best Greek translation of the Reformation rallying call, *sola fide*, "by faith alone," but this is exactly the opposite of what James is arguing for![72] Augustine perhaps best resolves this tension between Paul and James on the issue of faith and works: "Paul said that a man is justified through faith without the works of the law, but not without those works of which James speaks."[73]

This verse does stand in stark contrast to Ro 3:28, even without the word "alone" explicitly in Paul's Greek. But again it is essential to remember the distinction between James's and Paul's use of the words "faith," "works," and "justify" in these two contexts (above, pp. 131–32, 136), so that no insoluble contradiction emerges. As Joachim Jeremias famously epitomized it, Paul speaks of Christian faith (trust in Jesus) and Jewish works (obeying the law so as to justify oneself), whereas James refers to Jewish faith (pure monotheism) and Christian works (good deeds that flow from salvation).[74] Or, as Frances Gench nicely phrases it, "Paul is dealing with obstetrics, with how new life begins; James, however, is dealing with pediatrics and geriatrics, with how Christian life grows and matures and ages."[75] What James describes as the *end result* of justification bringing a person to maturity or "completion" (using the verb τελειόω), Paul acknowledges in Philippians 1:6 when he expresses his confidence that "he who began a good work in you will carry it on to 'completion' [from the related verb ἐπιτελέω] until the day of Christ Jesus."[76]

Ronald Fung differentiates between what he calls "forensic justification by faith" and "probative justification by works."[77] The first is a legal declaration made by God at the time one commits one's life to Christ. The second is the demonstration by a transformed life that such a commitment was genuine. Or, to use Ben Witherington's words, James 2:24 is

> a statement that Paul would never have made. If, however, we take—and we should—the vindication in James 2:24 as referring to that final verdict of God on one's deeds and life work, then even Paul can be said to have agreed. Even he speaks of a final justification/vindication that is dependent on what believers do in the interim (Gal 5:5–6). This final vindication or acquittal is in view here. Paul would agree that one cannot be righteous on that last day without having done some good deeds between the new birth and that last day in the spiritual pilgrimage.[78]

72. The Reformation slogan came in part from Luther's German translation of the Bible, which added "alone" (*allein*) as an interpretive gloss in Ro 3:28. Martin (*James*, 96) actually sees James's use of μόνον as support for Paul's view of faith, for neither Paul nor James would have supported a faith that did nothing. Johnson (*The Letter of James*, 244) draws out the parallel use of μόνον in 1:22, with the contrast there of "hearing only" vs. "doing the word."

73. Bray, *James, 1–2 Peter, 1–3 John, Jude*, 31. Or, with Calvin, "salvation is by faith alone," but "by a faith that is not alone" (Hughes, *James*, 122, 123). For a fascinating, detailed study, from a reasonably traditional Roman Catholic viewpoint, that essentially agrees with this perspective, while recognizing the problems caused by Luther's introduction of "alone" into the text of Paul (cf. previous note), see Rolf Walker, "Allein aus Werken: Zur Auslegung von Jakobus 2, 14–26," *ZKT* 61 (1964): 155–92.

74. Joachim Jeremias, "Paul and James," *ExpTim* 66 (1955): 568–71. Cf. Christine Renouard, "La maturité de la foi selon Jc 2,14–26," *FoiVie* 102.4 (2003): 61–71; and Robert V. Rakestraw, "James 2:14–26: Does James Contradict the Pauline Soteriology?" *CTR* 1 (1986): 31–50.

75. Gench, *Hebrews and James*, 106.

76. Romano Penna, "La giustificazione in Paolo e in Giacomo," *RivBib* 30 (1982): 362.

77. Ronald Y. K. Fung, "'Justification' in the Epistle of James," in *Right with God: Justification in the Bible and the World*, ed. D. A. Carson (Grand Rapids: Baker, 1992), 162.

78. Witherington, *Letters and Homilies for Jewish Christians*, 478.

It is also important to remember that James was most likely writing earlier than Paul and thus not intentionally using the same vocabulary with contrasting meanings. Had James known how Paul would later phrase things, he might have altered his language here.[79] Meanwhile, James's point is "quite simply that God will recognize the devotion of those whose public professions of monotheistic faith are embodied in public works of mercy toward one's neighbor."[80]

James 2:25 Likewise, was not Rahab the prostitute justified by works, having welcomed the messengers and having sent them out by another road? (ὁμοίως δὲ καὶ Ῥαὰβ ἡ πόρνη οὐκ ἐξ ἔργων ἐδικαιώθη, ὑποδεξαμένη τοὺς ἀγγέλους καὶ ἑτέρᾳ ὁδῷ ἐκβαλοῦσα;). In case the example of Israel's great patriarch was not enough to convince his listeners, James brings forth a second example, this time from Jos 2. While the "likewise" (ὁμοίως) leads one to expect a parallel illustration, Rahab differs in almost every way from Abraham. Whereas Abraham was a wealthy, moral male, the father of the Jewish nation, and a major figure in his society, Rahab was probably poor, definitely immoral, a female, an outcast of the Canaanite nation, and a minor figure in her society.[81] By adding "the prostitute" (ἡ πόρνη), James emphasizes her status as a classic sinner.

As noted above (p. 136), Abraham and Rahab thus form a merismus, so that everyone in between them is included as needing to exhibit transformed living in order to demonstrate the genuineness of faith.[82] Just as with Abraham, James stresses that Rahab was also "justified by works" (ἐξ ἔργων ἐδικαιώθη).[83] Both of these OT characters became exemplars of faith *because of* their deeds. The participle "having welcomed"[84] (ὑποδεξαμένη) parallels "having offered" (ἀνενέγκας) in v. 21, again with the possibility of being either causal or instrumental. Since it further expands "by works" (ἐξ ἔργων), the instrumental reading may again be the best, but the participle legitimately suggests both ideas.

The example of Rahab proves more controversial, raising questions such as: What were the Israelite spies[85] doing in the house of a prostitute? And what are the moral implications of her lying to the

79. For a thorough survey and analysis of the options, with this conclusion, see D. Ryan Jenkins, "Faith and Works in Paul and James," *BSac* 159 (2002): 62 – 78.

80. Wall, *Community of the Wise*, 152.

81. Cf. Motyer, *The Message of James*, 115.

82. Martin (*James*, 97) adds two further similarities: both were noted for their hospitality and both were proselytes.

83. "Rahab's actions, however, set her apart as truly believing and knowing the God who is 'God in heaven above and on the earth below.' Her faith led her to act, and her actions brought about the salvation of herself and her whole family, and she was considered justified before God because her faith worked" (Kamell, "The Concept of 'Faith' in Hebrews and James," forthcoming). In her story, literal, physical salvation as well as spiritual salvation (being counted among the people of God) resulted from her faithful actions.

84. Wall (*Community of the Wise*, 153) muses that the role of this verb is to identify both Abraham and Rahab as "prophetic exemplars" whose hospitality toward imperiled neighbors — "entertaining angels unaware" — results in divine blessing. For elaboration, see Robert W. Wall, "The Intertextuality of Scripture: The Example of Rahab (James 2:25)," in *The Bible at Qumran: Text, Shape, and Interpretation*, ed. Peter W. Flint with Tae Hun Kim (Grand Rapids: Eerdmans, 2001), 217 – 36. Ward ("The Works of Abraham," 283 – 90) finds further support for this in the plural "works" in both verses, so that James must have had more than the single act of offering Isaac in mind. But the plural could just be generalizing.

85. The textual variant here seeks to deal with the oddity of calling the Israelite spies "messengers." The UBS committee's choice, granted an {A} level of confidence, is both the shortest and the hardest reading. The reading "messengers *of Israel*" (ἀγγέλους τοῦ Ἰσραήλ) clarifies the identity of the spies. The reading "spies" (κατασκόπους) addresses the problem that these men were not really messengers at all. Finally, the longest reading, "messengers, the spies" (ἀγγέλους τοὺς κατασκόπους) is a harmonizing variant, most likely created by a scribe who knew of both options and refused to exclude either.

guards who came searching for the spies? Regarding the former, perhaps it is best to see this as an example of God directing the spies to the house of the one person in Jericho whom he knew would be sympathetic to their cause. Richard Hess observes that "this house was more likely a tavern, hostel or way station, which could be used by visitors, than a brothel."[86]

Concerning the latter question, the example of Rahab may offer support for the hierarchical approach to ethics, in which at times a more fundamental moral principle must be kept even if it requires disobedience to a more subsidiary one. In this case, defending God's cause was a higher call than responding faithfully to an already doomed regime. Regardless, God saw her as justified through her actions of receiving and sending the spies, actions that flowed from her belief in the God of the Israelites.[87] Rahab is consistently applauded throughout Scripture, as well as in Jewish and Christian tradition, as a model of faith,[88] and she even appears in the lineage of Jesus (Mt 1:5), despite her shady background. If God accepted her rebellion against her nation's authorities, then it is not for us to condemn it.

James 2:26 For just as the body without a spirit is dead, so also faith without works is dead (ὥσπερ γὰρ τὸ σῶμα χωρὶς πνεύματος νεκρόν ἐστιν, οὕτως καὶ ἡ πίστις χωρὶς ἔργων νεκρά ἐστιν).[89] To conclude, James introduces one last analogy, that of the body and spirit, comparing the tangible and intangible dimensions of a person. Without an immaterial life-force animating the material body, the person is just a corpse. Likewise, James says, faith is dead without works to fill it with life.

Here is the final answer to the question first raised in 2:14, "is such faith able to save a person?" The answer, throughout all the arguments and examples of 2:14–26, has been a resounding "no." Faith that does not reveal itself in works—in a changed lifestyle that glorifies God and seeks his heart for the world—is dead, lifeless, workless, and worthless. In reality, it is not faith at all; it is only the shell or the corpse of faith. As Davids declares, "dead orthodoxy has absolutely no power to save and may in fact even hinder the person from coming to living faith, a faith enlivened by works of charity."[90]

86. Richard S. Hess, *Joshua* (Leicester: IVP, 1996), 83. This, of course, does not exclude the possibility of Rahab "plying her wares" there on the side.

87. Cf. Martin, *James*, 28: Glaze ("Relationship," 41) adds that "her works did not substitute for faith; they did, however, validate or justify her claim of belief in God."

88. See the list of references in Johnson, *The Letter of James*, 245. For full details, see A. T. Hanson, "Rahab the Harlot in Early Christian Tradition," *JSNT* 1 (1978): 53–60. The greatest number of references emerge in the rabbinic literature in which Rahab appears "as a profligate, as a proselyte, as the wife of Joshua and ancestress of prophets, and as herself a prophetess" (58).

89. Davids (*The Epistle of James*, 133) notes that "likewise" (οὕτως) forms an *inclusio* with 2:17, "neatly tying [James's] midrashic exegesis together as support for the main argument of 2:14–17," while Johnson (*The Letter of James*, 245) adds "dead" (νεκρόν) to the *inclusio*.

90. Davids, *The Epistle of James*, 134.

Theology in Application

A Contemporary Illustration (2:14 – 17)

Works as the necessary outgrowth of true, saving faith characterize the biblical witness from beginning to end. The law was never given as a means to salvation but as God's provision for the Israelites to live out their days as his covenant people *after* he had rescued them from Egypt. Although some Jews perverted this into a merit theology of judgment according to whether or not one's good works outweighed one's evil deeds, many others preserved this covenantal understanding of the law.[91] Galatians 5:6 likewise epitomizes Paul's understanding of "faith expressing itself through love," just as Php 2:12 – 13 and Eph 2:8 – 10 both balance classic texts on God's gracious initiative in salvation with the insistence on good deeds as a believer's response.

Gench shows keen insight when she observes that James's question is *not* "what good is faith without works?" but "what good is it to *say* you have faith but do not have works."[92] Nothing in this passage suggests that James believes in two kinds of faith — one that is mature and one that is nominal. One either has saving faith or one does not. It is likewise crucial to insist that, while this text applies incisively to a "dead orthodoxy," nothing in James's original situation demonstrates that this is the heart of his congregation's problem. Entire churches of believers from Jewish backgrounds would more likely have been overly consumed by certain *kinds* of works, not least the "badges of national righteousness" of circumcision, the dietary laws, Sabbath observance, set liturgical prayers, and so on.[93] But James probably fears that they lack the deeds of mercy that those truly in the process of spiritual transformation inevitably demonstrate.[94]

Vv. 15 – 16 offer a test case for merciful works. James assumes that the believers confronted with these desperately needy fellow Christians are less destitute and thus in a position to offer at least a little help. He provides no treatise on the most effective ways to help the poor. Christians will probably always debate that issue, but true believers will take *some* kind of action.[95] At the very least, they must cultivate

91. The fullest and most nuanced survey of Judaism's soteriology prior to and during the emergence of Christianity, demonstrating this diversity, is D. A. Carson, Peter T. O'Brien, and Mark A. Seifrid, eds., *Justification and Variegated Nomism*, vol. 1: *The Complexities of Second Temple Judaism* (Grand Rapids: Baker, 2001).

92. Gench, *Hebrews and James*, 106.

93. To use the term popularized by James D. G. Dunn. The extent of this preoccupation, however, can be exaggerated, as stressed by Friedrich Avemarie, "Die Werke des Gesetzes im Spiegel des Jakobusbriefes," *ZKT* 98 (2001): 282 – 309.

94. Cf. Laws, *The Epistle of James*, 121.

95. Keenan, *The Wisdom of James*, 83. This contrasts with those who have "studiously learned the art of dismissing socioeconomic disparities that may at times be glaring but remain unseen due to class blinders well in place. The poor, the homeless, the ex-convict, or the street beggar merely receives a perfunctory 'greeting' as the Sunday-only comfortable Christian hurries by, scarcely seeing the needy 'neighbor.' While it is true that one can get killed trying to be the good Samaritan today, this possibility is no warrant for distancing oneself from virtually every opportunity to extend Christian mercy" (Felder, "James," 1795).

generous, even sacrificial giving to help the poor as part of their ongoing personal and corporate stewardship of their possessions.[96] But in light of systemic injustice, we probably need to do much more. As Alec Motyer writes:

> We should be relentless in pushing governments — and pushing church leaders who have the opportunity to address world-governments in a significant way — to throw both economic and military caution to the winds in the face of the prior claims of human need. Meat mountains, butter mountains and powdered milk mountains are an offence to God and man if there is a hungry mouth in the world that can be filled through them. The pre-empting of the world's wealth for weapons of mass-destruction (whether "conventional" or nuclear) is blasphemy against the living God while those to whom he has given life die for want of food or medical care. Even the millions of money that go out through voluntary relief organizations pale into insignificance beside what governments could do.[97]

V. 16 makes James's example that much more frightening because "Go in peace" takes the form of a prayer and benediction. These "Christians" are actually praying that God *will* meet the needs of his people, disclosing their correct trust in God as provider, but they refuse to recognize that their involvement in the process is the way God wants to meet those needs.[98]

V. 17 rounds out the paragraph by insisting that professions of faith without *any* deeds to back them up ring hollow. So difficult has this teaching proved to some "grace only" Christians that they have turned exegetical cartwheels to make the text speak of Christians who may receive no rewards in heaven but still make it in, even if as through fire (cf. 1Co 3:15). Zane Hodges defines dead faith as "sterile, ineffective or unproductive," but stresses that this casts no doubt "on the truth of the unprofitable believer's profession." Later Hodges adds that "whenever a Christian ceases to act on his faith, that faith atrophies and becomes little more than a creedal corpse."[99] But there is no "little more" in the inspired text! James's language is much stronger. These people are already lifeless in the *present*; apart from a change of heart that leads to redemption, they can hardly count on *eternal* life as things currently stand.[100]

James's language does, however, support a properly qualified liberation theology and lordship salvation. While not necessarily justifying violence or Marxism in pursuit of one's cause, James certainly would share the concern of liberation

96. Richardson, *James*, 131.

97. Motyer, *The Message of James*, 110 – 11.

98. Keenan, *The Wisdom of James*, 82.

99. Zane C. Hodges, *The Epistle of James: Proven Character through Testing* (Irving, TX: Grace Evangelical Society, 1994), 63, 72. Theological presuppositions have dangerously preempted the actual teaching of Scripture here. People believing Hodges at this point could easily fool themselves into thinking they (or others) were saved when in fact they were not.

100. See esp. Gale Z. Heide, "The Soteriology of James 2:14," *GTJ* 12 (1992): 69 – 97. Heide responds in detail here to earlier presentations of Hodges' thesis, to which Hodges' later work offers no response.

theologians to do far more for the poor, individually and systemically, than many branches of recent Christianity have attempted.[101] So, too, while not claiming to know everything that Christ will require of a believer throughout life, James would most assuredly insist that it counts for nothing to claim to accept a free gift of salvation without transferring one's allegiance to Jesus as the Ultimate Master of one's life and possessions.[102] It is precisely those people who *do* make this claim who incur the scorn of devotees of other religions that recognize the need to do good in the world, thereby making it *harder* for such people to discern and accept authentic Christianity![103]

An Objection Rebutted (2:18–19)

Vv. 18–19 disclose additional hints of the spiritual malaise afflicting James's churches. The relationship between faith and works in v. 18 (on just about any of the diverse interpretations) rebuts an attitude of some who may have believed that "no one should act unmercifully; but some of us do the deeds of mercy, and others among us encourage them."[104] Here are the seeds of the clergy-laity division that later intruded into Christian circles, leading many churchgoers to think they were absolved of the responsibility of ministering to the needy as long as their leaders remained active in so doing.

The appeal to the "creed" of Dt 6:4, which faithful Jews recited on a daily basis, supports our earlier suggestions. While few Jews were guilty of a lifeless orthodoxy, their succumbing to a lifeless *ritual* was at least as old as Jer 7, triggering that prophet's infamous "temple sermon" that berated the people for thinking that right worship substituted for merciful behavior.[105] Moreover, given James's dependence on the sayings of Jesus, one wonders if he had in mind Jesus' repeated use of the prophet Hosea's warning that God desires mercy above sacrifice (Hos 6:6; cf. Mt 9:13; 12:7). Of course, this principle goes back substantially further (see esp. 1Sa 15:22). These days, how many so-called Christians have become consumed by the modern "worship wars" that at root are about wanting *my* preferred form of music or liturgy (or any other aspect of the church service) rather than recognizing that a

101. See throughout Tamez, *The Scandalous Message of James*; and Maynard-Reid, *Poverty and Wealth in James*.

102. See throughout John F. MacArthur Jr., *The Gospel according to Jesus* (Grand Rapids: Zondervan, rev. 1994); idem, *The Gospel according to the Apostles* (Nashville: Word, 2000). Keener (*The IVP Bible Background Commentary*, 696) contrasts James's approach with the "common modern conception that faith is a once-for-all prayer involving no commitment of life or purpose and is efficacious even if quickly forgotten"!

103. For just one of many possible examples, cf. the common Latter-day Saint attitude reflected in Richard R. Hopkins, *Biblical Mormonism: Responding to Evangelical Criticism of LDS Theology* (Bountiful, UT: Horizon, 1994), 130–36.

104. Richardson, *James*, 133. Cf. Mark Proctor ("Faith, Works, and the Christian Religion in James 2:14–26," *EvQ* 69 [1997]: 307–31), who thinks the objector believes it is adequate for any given congregation that some in their midst exhibit deeds of mercy, whereas James insists it is the responsibility of every single member.

105. Cf. Hubbard, *The Book of James*, 64; Scaer, *James*, 89–90.

vast diversity of forms is needed to reach and minister best to our incredibly diverse population?

The appeal to demonic monotheism in v. 19 intensely intrigues us. Of course, James's point may be merely that demons know all too well that only one God exists and that he is so powerful as to make them recoil in his presence, yet they are not saved thereby. But James could have made his point that dead orthodoxy fails to save, because unsaved demons share it, without the addition of "and they tremble." Perhaps he wants to warn against an emotionalism substituting for true faith as well. How much of contemporary Christianity judges authentic religion on the basis of the emotional experiences it produces, not by the practical fruit of faithful living (cf. esp. Mt 7:21 – 23)?[106] This passage also speaks to our culture's endemic religious laziness:

> Our churches today contain many people who agree with the imaginary challenger in James. Not only does "faith" not require any relationships or obligations to others, but any suggestion that it does is met with resistance. Twice as many Americans explicitly claim to be members of churches or synagogues as actually participate in the activities of those groups. Attempts to form bonds between wealthy suburban churches and inner-city congregations often meet great resistance.[107]

When such "nominalism" afflicts close friends and family members, we desperately want to believe that they are nevertheless right with God (and fortunately God, the only Judge, knows unerringly), but we take the dangerously easy way out when we fail to challenge them to levels of involvement that more clearly suggest true faith if in fact they are not true Christians at all.

Two Biblical Examples (2:20 – 26)

James realizes his listeners may not yet be convinced, so he turns to two excellent models from the Hebrew Scriptures, sandwiched in between three reaffirmations of his main point. V. 20 highlights one of the reasons for his repetition: people are frequently un*willing* to be convinced. The example of Abraham's willingness to sacrifice his only son (vv. 21 – 23), through whose descendants God had promised innumerable seed to occupy the Promised Land and through whom the world would be blessed, has taxed the imagination of history's greatest minds. It was this biblical account that led the famous Danish philosopher Søren Kierkegaard to develop his notion of faith as absurd, that is, as defying logical explanation.[108] Of course, God saved Abraham from the horrible deed, and Heb 11:17 – 19 avers that

106. James may well be "caricaturing unengaged faith not as intellectual but as worthless, no matter what emotional content it might have" (Keenan, *The Wisdom of James*, 86). Or, with William Barclay (*The Letters of James and Peter* [Philadelphia: Westminster, rev. 1976], 76), "there is nothing more dangerous than the repeated experience of a fine emotion with no attempt to put it into action."

107. Perkins, *First and Second Peter, James, and Jude*, 113.

108. See esp. the discussion in Bauckham, *James*, 159 – 74.

Abraham believed God could raise Isaac back to life after his death, if necessary. But whether one goes as far as Kierkegaard or not, it is surely the case that "the *actions* that James ascribes to Abraham are not ... keeping the law (Torah), nor even 'works of mercy,' but the radical obedience of faith itself," so that "James's great contribution to the Christian life is not on the doctrine of justification, but in helping us to see that true faith is radical obedience."[109]

The example of Rahab (v. 25), at the opposite end of almost every spectrum from Abraham, reminds us that even the least and the lost must exhibit their faith by good works, too. Sacrificial giving is not just for the rich, as the story of the widow's coins reminds us (Mk 12:41–44). This is another important caveat that much liberation theology fails to acknowledge. But what about those who seemingly have no opportunity to demonstrate good works at all, such as deathbed converts? It is hard to know for sure, but one can easily imagine their very professions of faith inspiring others who hear (or hear of) their words, as with the classic example of the criminal on the cross with Jesus (Lk 23:40–42). Thus they have exhibited at least one, highly significant good deed (wisdom literature regularly viewed repentance as such—see, e.g., Pr 28:13; Sir 17:23–24, 29; 18:21; 21:6; 44:16; Wis. 12:10), to say nothing of whatever other changed attitudes have occurred, whether or not they have the opportunity to express them to anyone else.

V. 26 completes this section of James by reiterating his main point once more. Faith and works must be as interrelated as a person's body and spirit. It is far too easy to jettison either side of the faith-works equation. "On one side are people who project confidence in their standing before God and yet show no evidence that their faith affects any of their actions." "On the other side are people whose lives demonstrate such a frantic flurry of activity that they literally have no time to think or talk about their faith."[110] True, saving faith by definition means that the Spirit enters a person's life to begin conforming them to the likeness of Christ. This transformation cannot be quantified, may be different for every person in detail, and regularly involves many fits and starts or forward and backward steps; but, over time, it does result in changed living. And one of the key areas affected will be concern for the poor and corollary actions to help them.

109. Townsend, *The Epistle of James*, 52, 53.

110. Barton, Veerman and Wilson, *James*, 60, 61.

CHAPTER 6

James 3:1 – 12

Literary Context

A major break occurs at the end of Jas 2. The apostle turns from unpacking the theme of riches and poverty to his elaboration of the theme of wisdom and obedience, particularly in the area of speech. This section will span 3:1 – 4:12. As a result, there are not many direct links between 3:1 – 12 and the immediately preceding passage, 2:14 – 26, although the references to the body in 3:2 – 3 recall 2:26.

Jas 3:1 – 12 does, however, hark back to numerous passages earlier in the epistle. That not many should become teachers (v. 1) conceptually parallels the command of 1:19 to be slow to speak.[1] The judgment that teachers must face (3:1) reminds us of James's discussion of judgment without mercy for those who show no mercy in 2:13a, but also of the liberating judgment for believers (2:12, 13b). The reference to "perfection" or "maturity" in 3:2 echoes the language of 1:4 with some of the same debates over the meaning of the term. Keeping one's tongue in check in 3:2 employs the same root as the word for the "bit" in the horse's mouth in 3:3 and the identical verb translated "bridle" in 1:26, where the tongue was also its object. The analogy of the boat kept under control during strong winds (3:4) contrasts favorably with the "double-souled" person in 1:6, who is simply blown and tossed about. The "uncontrollable" evil of 3:8 employs the same term that in 1:8 meant "unstable." The curses that duplicitous believers call down on their opponents (3:9 – 10), finally, sound too close for comfort like the blasphemy the Christians' oppressors uttered in 2:7.[2]

A much tighter connection links 3:1 – 12 with 3:13 – 18. As with 1:5 – 8 and 19 – 26, a passage on wisdom is paired with one on speech, though this time in the reverse order (appropriate for an extended chiasm). Proper control of one's tongue (3:1 – 12) proves central to exhibiting good conduct and a gentle wisdom (v. 13). The bitter water that resembles the destructive use of the tongue (v. 11) prepares the reader for the bitterness that characterizes "wisdom from below," a pseudo-wisdom that often involves the evil speech of boasting, lying, and verbal strife (vv. 14 – 15). The same root word, noted above, for unstable or uncontrollable (or even rebellious)

1. Tsuji, *Glaube zwischen Volkommenheit und Verweltlichung*, 80.

2. For a partially overlapping list of connections with earlier texts in James, see Church, "James," 371.

entities occurs again in v. 16. Lastly, the good fruit of vv. 17 – 18 recalls the agricultural metaphors of figs, olives, and grapevines in vv. 11 – 12a.

James's teaching on the tongue further anticipates teaching later in his letter, particularly in 4:1 – 12, still on the broader topic of wisdom and speech. The misuse of the tongue leads particularly to the verbal quarrels censured in 4:1 – 6 and the slander proscribed in 4:11 – 12. Because we must face God's judgment (3:1), we should not implicitly reverse roles with him by speaking against others in violation and thus rejection of his law (4:11 – 12). Finally, there are several links with the last main section of James's letter. The boasting of 3:5 recurs in 4:16. The fire metaphor reappears in 5:3. Judgment for believers, warned of in 3:1, looms again in 5:9, while one final example of evil talk occupies 5:12.

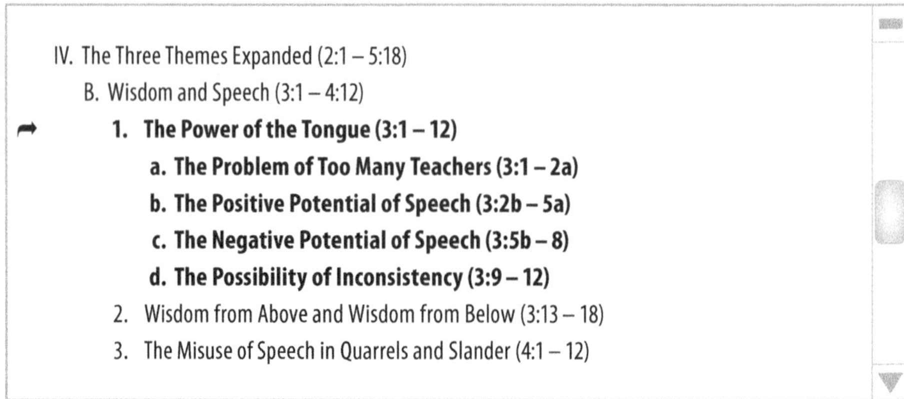
IV. The Three Themes Expanded (2:1 – 5:18)
- B. Wisdom and Speech (3:1 – 4:12)
  - **1. The Power of the Tongue (3:1 – 12)**
    - **a. The Problem of Too Many Teachers (3:1 – 2a)**
    - **b. The Positive Potential of Speech (3:2b – 5a)**
    - **c. The Negative Potential of Speech (3:5b – 8)**
    - **d. The Possibility of Inconsistency (3:9 – 12)**
  - 2. Wisdom from Above and Wisdom from Below (3:13 – 18)
  - 3. The Misuse of Speech in Quarrels and Slander (4:1 – 12)

Main Idea

Believers must control their speech because the tongue has an influence on life for good and bad that is all out of proportion to its size. This is particularly true for teachers, but it applies to everyone. Unique among creation is the human propensity for duplicitous speech.

Translation

(See next page.)

James 3:1-12

1a	Warning	**Not many should become teachers**, my brothers and sisters,
b	basis	because you know that we will receive a greater judgment.
2a	Explanation	For **we all stumble in many ways**.
b	condition (of 2c)	If anyone does not stumble in their words,
c	Assertion	**that one is a perfect person**,
d	apposition	able to hold the whole body in check.
3a	condition (of 3c)	Now if we put bits into the mouths of horses
b	purpose	in order that they be obedient to us,
c	Illustr. (of 2b-d)	**we guide even their whole body**.
4a	Parallel	**Behold also the ships ... are guided**
b	concession	although they are so large and
c	expansion	driven by harsh winds,
d	means	by a very small rudder
e	place	wherever the impulse of the pilot wishes.
5a	Comparison	So also **the tongue is a small member**,
b	contrast	yet **it boasts of great things**.
5c	Illustration	**Behold how small a fire [spark] ignites how great a wood [forest]**.
6a	Comparison	And **the tongue is a fire**.
b	General/partic.	**The tongue appoints itself as a world of unrighteousness** among our members.
c	description	that which stains the whole body and
d	expansion	sets on fire the course of existence and
e	source	is set on fire by Gehenna.
7a	Basis (of 10b)	**For every kind of animal and bird, reptile and sea creature is tamed and**
b	expansion	**has been tamed**
c	agency (of a and b)	by humankind.
8a	Contrast	But **no one of humans is able to tame the tongue**;
b	restatement	**it is an uncontrollable evil**,
c	contents	full of deadly poison.
9a	Basis (of 8b)	**By it we bless the Lord and Father**
b	contrast	and **by it we curse humans made in the image of God**.
10a	Restmnt. (of 9)	**From the same mouth come blessing and cursing**.
10b	Exclamation	**My brothers and sisters, these things ought not to be so!**
11	Rhetorical Q.	**Does a spring from the same opening pour forth both sweet and bitter [water]?**
12a	Alternatives	**Is it possible**, my brothers and sisters, **for the fig tree to produce olives or the grapevine figs?**
12b	Parallel	**Neither does a salty [spring] make sweet water**.

Structure

This segment of James has spawned more distinct proposals for its structure than any other comparably sized unit in the letter.[3] The first debate to confront us involves whether the entire passage is about teachers. Clearly everything in these twelve verses can apply directly to them but, after v. 1, James never mentions them explicitly again. The "we all" in v. 2a begins to generalize already, and the "anyone" in v. 2b may suggest that James is now thinking of all people. But the "for" at the beginning of v. 2 links it closely with v. 1, whereas v. 2b starts a completely independent thought. So the explicit warning against too many teachers should be identified as encompassing vv. 1 – 2a.[4]

The issue of speech, with the tongue as the obvious synecdoche for all forms of communication, now unites the rest of the passage. Vv. 3 – 4 clearly provide illustrations of the power of a very small object over a large domain, analogous to the tongue's control of the whole body (v. 2b). But how far does this section continue? After v. 8, no further reference to the tongue recurs, and while James is still talking about speech, it is humanity's potential for duplicity rather than the overall issue of power that takes center stage. So vv. 9 – 12 should probably be considered another subsection.

There is another shift, however, not always noticed, in the middle of v. 5. V. 2b introduces the positive potential of the tongue: perfect speech could lead to perfect control over the whole person. The analogies of the horse's bit and the ship's rudder (vv. 3 – 4) are at the very least neutral, but in this context more likely to be positive as well. The tongue can do great good![5] While the tongue's boasting in v. 5a begins to transition to the negative use of the tongue, some kinds of boasting can be appropriate (recall 2:13).[6]

From vv. 5b – 8, however, the imagery turns unrelentingly negative. Here the terrible potential for destructive speech surfaces in dark detail. The tongue is a fire (v. 5b), an unrighteous world (v. 6a), spoiling and burning creation (v. 6b), and inflamed by hell (v. 6c). It is compared and contrasted with the animal kingdom, which can be tamed in ways the tongue cannot, thus always remaining potentially

3. Duane F. Watson, "The Rhetoric of James 3:1 – 12 and a Classical Pattern of Argumentation," *NovT* 35 (1993): 48 – 64.

4. Wall (*Community of the Wise*, 162) well represents those who take the entire passage as referring solely to teachers, but contrast Moo (*The Letter of James*, 148): "while James has obvious concern about the application of his teaching to Christian leaders (cf. also v. 13), we doubt that he writes as directly as this to those leaders throughout the paragraph. V. 1, after all, is directed not to Christian leaders, but to any Christian who might want to become a teacher. The general address to the readers in 4:1 and 4:11 certainly demonstrates that the problem of sinful, critical speech involved more than the leaders." Moo supports the view that "a concern about people wanting to teach leads James into a general warning about the tongue."

5. Cf. Scaer, *James*, 100.

6. Ropes (*A Critical and Exegetical Commentary on the Epistle of St. James*, 232) points out that this is no empty boast but a justified one, in light of the genuine power the tongue has. Townsend (*The Epistle of James*, 60) speaks of James's "slight unease with his material" beginning to show.

murderous in its power (vv. 7 – 8). The four main sections represented in our translation and exegetical outline are thus best identified as vv. 1 – 2a, 2b – 5a, 5b – 8, and 9 – 12.

Exegetical Outline

- IV. The Three Themes Expanded (2:1 – 5:18)
  - B. Wisdom and Speech (3:1 – 4:12)
    - ➦ **1. The Power of the Tongue (3:1 – 12)**
      - a. Believers must not aspire to becoming teachers too hastily (vv. 1 – 2a).
        - i. This is because teachers (who depend so heavily on their tongues) will be judged more strictly when they sin (because of their more widespread influence) (v. 1).
        - ii. And teachers can sin just as often as do other people (v. 2a).
      - b. The tongue is a powerful influence for good, out of proportion to its size (vv. 2b – 5a).
        - i. Right speech is the preeminent sign of Christian maturity (v. 2b).
        - ii. The tongue is to the individual what a bridle is to a horse (v. 3).
        - iii. The tongue is to the individual what a rudder is to a ship (v. 4).
        - iv. In each case, a little object controls a big one, accomplishing great things (v. 5a).
      - c. The tongue is a powerful influence for bad, out of proportion to its size (vv. 5b – 8).
        - i. The tongue is like a small spark setting a large forest on fire (vv. 5b – 6).
        - ii. The tongue is like an untamable creature (vv. 7 – 8).
      - d. These simultaneous possibilities for good and evil create a unique inconsistency, contrary to God's creation (vv. 9 – 12).
        - i. It is deplorable that humans can simultaneously bless God and curse humans made in God's image (vv. 9 – 10).
        - ii. This kind of inconsistency does not occur in the rest of creation (vv. 11 – 12).

Explanation of Text

James 3:1 Not many should become teachers, my brothers and sisters, because you know that we will receive a greater judgment (Μὴ πολλοὶ διδάσκαλοι γίνεσθε, ἀδελφοί μου, εἰδότες ὅτι μεῖζον κρίμα λημψόμεθα). In returning to the theme of wisdom and speech, James begins by considering the tongue. However, he chooses to introduce it in relation to teachers, warning that only a small percentage of the people in his churches should aspire to this leadership role. The negative imperative, "not … should become" (μὴ … γίνεσθε) could imply "stop becoming [teachers]." In the ancient Mediterranean world teachers were held in high respect, so perhaps many in James's congregations were trying to attain that status, possibly as a way to overcome other social oppressions.[7] However, the proverbial conclusion to the sentence suggests a more timeless warning, akin to

7. Martin (*James*, 107) believes that "the negative μή is placed at the beginning of this verse for emphasis … the imperative is directed at the immediate situation of the church. If one is presently desirous of a teaching position then it is

"let not many become...."[8] In the Christian world, teaching is not so much a privilege as a responsibility for which we will be held accountable. Religious teachers in James's world were those who passed on sacred tradition. Their key task was to learn it accurately and transmit it exactly.[9] Only after written texts or oral traditions were correctly memorized were disciples of a rabbi ready to discuss them, lest they misrepresent them unwittingly.[10]

The participle "knowing" (εἰδότες) is causal, for here James gives the reason why not many should become teachers. The content of the knowledge and the reason for his warning involve this stricter judgment that teachers must face. The choice of verb and of the tense in "will receive" (λημψόμεθα) implies that judgment is something that God metes out, ultimately at the final judgment, although "anyone who has ever taught knows that evaluation and criticism are daily occurrences."[11]

The "judgment" (κρίμα), meanwhile, refers to a judicial verdict, implying potential censure (but scarcely *guaranteeing* eternal "condemnation," as the KJV might suggest).[12] Most likely, James is focusing on sins of speech, since he introduces that topic with v. 2. Because teaching in his world was almost exclusively oral, it seems reasonable to view James as arguing that the accountability is for verbal blunders in teaching others (cf. Jesus in Mt 23:13; Mk 12:38 – 40; Lk 12:48b; 20:47). As Moo explains, teachers "expose themselves to greater *danger* of judgment. Their constant use of the tongue means they can sin very easily, leading others astray at the same time."[13] Those who consistently and repeatedly fail in this area at the very least call into question whether they have what Paul would later call the gift of teaching (see below) and at worst call into question whether or not they really know Christ.

James 3:2a For we all stumble in many ways (πολλὰ γὰρ πταίομεν ἅπαντες). James reinforces his warning by insisting that everyone commits a diversity of sins. The "for" (γάρ) links this clause more closely with v. 1 than with v. 2b, while also beginning the transition to the broader audience. The verb "stumble" (πταίω) means either literally to "trip" or metaphorically to "make a mistake." Here James uses it in a theological sense for committing sins. He may be thinking especially of inadvertent, "minor" errors in judgment, as with many sins of speech. Because "to stumble" is an intransitive verb, "many" (πολλά) cannot be a direct

best that such a notion be seriously reconsidered." Cf. Cargal, *Restoring the Diaspora*, 143: the people's desires reflect "another indication of their preoccupation with achieving signs of status."

8. The second-person imperative occasionally functions slightly more permissively (or indirectly), more like third-person forms. See Richard A. Young, *Intermediate New Testament Greek: A Linguistic and Exegetical Approach* (Nashville: Broadman & Holman, 1994), 145.

9. Isaacs (*Hebrews and James*, 212) explains that "the teacher was regarded principally as the guardian and interpreter of tradition (cf. CD 13.7; 1QS 9:12 – 20). As such, in Jewish society he was highly regarded. The high status afforded the teacher, however, was in direct proportion to the weight of responsibility he carried to be faithful to the traditions with which he was entrusted." Greco-Roman contexts often presented the same ideals, even if more erratically applied.

10. For comprehensive detail on the teaching process in James's Jewish world, see Samuel Byrskog, *Jesus the Only Teacher: Didactic Authority and Transmission in Ancient Israel, Ancient Judaism and the Matthean Community* (Stockholm: Almqvist and Wiksell, 1994).

11. Sleeper, *James*, 88.

12. Baker (*Personal Speech-Ethics in the Epistle of James*, 123) sees 2:12 as background for the use of κρίμα here, arguing that "since judgment involves deeds and words, those such as teachers who deal principally with words in their vocation should expect a more difficult time (μεῖζον) in eschatological judgment." He also points out that the first person plural of λημψόμεθα shows James as including himself among those in the more precarious situation of judgment. Moo (*The Letter of James*, 149) argues that "James's shift to the first person plural — 'we' — reveals that he considers himself a teacher. And by identifying himself with those whom he warns, James also creates a more effective platform for his warning."

13. Moo, *The Letter of James*, 150.

object but must be an adverbial accusative. The most natural meaning in this context would be "in many ways," though James might have something slightly more specific in mind.[14] His use of "all" (ἅπαντες) provides a plural subject for the verb and makes his statement refer to everyone.[15]

James 3:2b If anyone does not stumble in their words, that one is a perfect person, able to hold the whole body in check. (εἴ τις ἐν λόγῳ οὐ πταίει, οὗτος τέλειος ἀνήρ δυνατὸς χαλιναγωγῆσαι καὶ ὅλον τὸ σῶμα). James goes on to qualify himself, however, with a condition that could provide an exception to his last statement. If people could remain sinless in speech, they could attain perfection.[16] In this first-class condition, the "if" (εἰ) clearly cannot be translated as "since," because, in fact, no mere human fits into this category. No one can reach the ideal of sinless speech, given the assertion in v. 2a.[17] Thus we should be doubly wary of teaching: the damage from bad instruction can be quite grave, and sooner or later every teacher *will* do damage.

V. 2b broadens the scope of this passage from focusing just on teachers to considering everyone. James ascribes sins of speech to every person in the world, continuing to add support for his caution to teachers.[18] Here again the word "perfect" (τέλειος) appears, this time more likely implying sinless and not merely "complete" or "mature."[19] Control of the tongue, even more than wisdom (cf. 1:4 – 5), proves essential for perfection.

Being able to control one's speech is indeed a prominent theme of wisdom literature (see, e.g., Pr 10:8, 11, 21; 11:9; 12:18, 25; 13:13; etc.), and thus to demonstrate this control shows one to be truly wise. However, perfection, or *full* maturity, is attained only in the life to come. The term "hold in check" (χαλιναγωγέω) first appeared in 1:26 (where we noted it could also mean "to bridle"), likewise in relation to sins of speech versus true religious maturity.

Here we are introduced to the concept that the tongue controls the rest of the body. To be able to keep one's tongue in check shows that one is also able to keep one's whole body in check — both physical movement and moral action. James is doubtless implying "that since speech sins are the most difficult to stop, if we could stop them, then we surely could stop all the rest."[20] But he may also be thinking of how evil proceeds from thought (cf. Jas 1:13 – 15; see also Mt 15:10 – 20), which is formulated into speech in our minds, whether or not we ever utter it, so that the tongue, as a synecdoche for speech and metonymy for thought more generally, is the key to all behavior as well as attitudes.[21]

14. Davids (*The Epistle of James*, 137) argues that "many" (πολλά) "probably refers to all types of times as well as sheer frequency."

15. Both the end-stress of the location of ἅπαντες and the compounded form (as opposed to the more common πάντες) make "everyone" emphatic (cf. Hiebert, *The Epistle of James*, 206).

16. Motyer (*The Message of James*, 119) points out that "according to Genesis 3:12 the first actual sin following the fall was a sin of speech," and he shows how biblical authors consistently use sins of speech as exemplary of sin as a whole (see Pss 5:9; 10:7; 140:3; Isa 6:5; Ro 3:13 – 14; and, supporting healthy speech, see 1Pe 3:10).

17. Hiebert, *The Epistle of James*, 207. This, then, is a classic example of a first-class condition assumed to be true for the sake of argument. Burchard (*Der Jakobusbrief*, 137) calls it "either an unreal condition or ironic" (translation ours).

18. Johnson (*The Letter of James*, 263) argues that "teachers particularly are vulnerable to failures in speech," because the teaching setting "provides temptations to virtually every form of evil speech: arrogance and domination over students; anger and pettiness at contradiction or inattention; slander and meanness towards absent opponents; flattery of students for the sake of vainglory."

19. Motyer (*The Message of James*, 120) adds that "it is not that a person strong enough to control the tongue is therefore also strong enough for every other battle," but rather that "winning this battle is in itself a winning of all battles."

20. Baker and Ellsworth, *Preaching James*, 83.

21. Cf. Motyer, *The Message of James*, 121.

A secondary level of meaning can also be seen if one understands "body" (σῶμα) in an ecclesial sense, so that the tongue of a teacher guides and controls the entire body of the church. On this reading, James highlights the responsibility of teachers for the health of their congregations.[22]

In Depth: Were the Teachers Only Men?

Some balk at translating "brothers" (ἀδελφοί) in v. 1 generically or inclusively, as "believers" or "brothers and sisters," even though they allow for it elsewhere.[23] Typically, they argue that teachers in the church according to the NT were only male. This view usually stems from a misunderstanding of 1Ti 2:12, which is often translated as if Paul had prohibited women from all teaching roles over men, at least with respect to Christian doctrine. But the most careful grammatical and contextual analyses of this verse suggest that Paul is not prohibiting two separate activities; rather, "teaching" and "exercising authority" are mutually defining and refer to the role of elder, just as 1Ti 3:2 assigns the distinctive function of teaching to elders/overseers and 5:17 speaks of them directing the affairs of the church.

The argument that prohibits women from all teaching over men also pays inadequate attention to the biblical distinctions between gifts and offices. "Teaching" can be a spiritual gift (Eph 4:11; Ro 12:7; 1Co 12:28), all spiritual gifts are given to men and women alike as the Holy Spirit determines (Ac 2:17 – 18; 1Co 12:11), and all spiritual gifts are to be used for the edification of the entire congregation (Eph 4:12 – 13). Nothing anywhere in Scripture even remotely suggests that if a woman has a particular gift she must restrict her exercise of that gift to interaction with other women (or perhaps also children), while Acts 18:26 portrays a Christian woman (Priscilla) in a positive light as she corrects some aspect of the public preaching of a Christian man (Apollos).

On the other hand, "teachers" is also one way of referring to "pastors" (Eph 4:11). "Pastors/shepherds," "elders," and "overseers" can all be synonyms (Ac 20:17, 28), and 1Ti 2:12 makes good contextual sense as restricting the *office* of elder (the "authoritative" teacher — understanding "to teach" and "to exercise authority" as mutually defining one another) to men. (Of course, "pastoring" can also refer just to the spiritual gift and be open to men and women alike.)

22. According to Martin (*James*, 104, 110 – 11), the tongue controls the church body more than the physical body. Wall (*Community of the Wise*, 164 – 5) agrees that this entire passage is to be read as directed to the leaders of the congregation and in light of the body as the church. Moo (*The Letter of James*, 152), however, argues against this interpretation, because "James gives no evidence that he, or his readers, would be familiar with the application of 'body' language to the church," and also because "all James's uses of the word 'body' ... are sufficiently explained without any hint of this ecclesiological application."

23. See esp. Poythress and Grudem, *The Gender-Neutral Bible Controversy*, 266.

In churches where there is a leadership body of individuals all recognized as holding equal authority and all involved in the regular, public teaching of the assembled congregation, one has true functional equivalents to NT elders.

In most contemporary evangelical churches, the senior pastor (or sole pastor) is the only person who is the true equivalent of an elder.[24] Of course, egalitarians would argue either (1) that even this "top" office need not be restricted to men today, because the first-century prohibitions were based on culture-specific rationales that no longer appear, at least in most of the Western world, or (2) that 1Ti 2:12 itself prohibited women from only a domineering or authoritarian (rather than authoritative) teaching over men. But even on the standard complementarian view of restricting the *office* of pastor-teacher-elder to men, there is nothing in James to suggest he uses the term "teacher" in this official capacity.[25] Neither, then, is there any reason to take "man" (ἀνήρ) in v. 2 in any narrower way than as a synonym for "person" (ἄνθρωπος), as in all previous occurrences in James thus far.

James 3:3 Now if we put bits into the mouths of horses in order that they be obedient to us, we guide even their whole body (εἰ δὲ[26] τῶν ἵππων τοὺς χαλινοὺς εἰς τὰ στόματα βάλλομεν εἰς τὸ πείθεσθαι αὐτοὺς ἡμῖν, καὶ ὅλον τὸ σῶμα αὐτῶν μετάγομεν). James proceeds to give us illustrations of the control that something very small can have over something very large, beginning with the common example of the horse[27] and bridle. Here a device as tiny as a bit or bridle can guide an animal that weighs far more than a person. Of course, the significance of this illustration is that the bit goes into the horse's mouth, so that, by controlling the animal's mouth, the rider is able to maneuver the whole horse. How much more can the human tongue empower the entire person!

24. On all these texts, and for documentation of the various points made in this excursus, see further Craig L. Blomberg, "Women in Ministry: A Complementarian Approach," in *Two Views on Women in Ministry*, ed. James R. Beck (Grand Rapids: Zondervan, rev. 2005), 121 – 84. Cf. idem, "Neither Hierarchicalist nor Egalitarian: Gender Roles in Paul," in *Paul and His Theology*, ed. Stanley E. Porter (Boston: Brill, 2006), 283 – 326.

25. Ruckstuhl (*Jakobusbrief, 1 – 3 Johannesbrief*, 22) reminds us of the numerous itinerant teachers in early Christianity, employing the spiritual gifts as described in 1Co 12, who held no office in any local congregation. Popkes (*Der Brief des Jakobus*, 220) speaks of both "hierarchical-sacramental" and "charismatic or prophetic" teachers (translations ours). He links the former (but not the latter) with the elders mentioned in 1Ti 5:17.

26. There is a difficult textual variant here; the reading the UBS chose rated only a {C}. Nevertheless, this reading, "but if" (εἰ δέ), is the hardest, creating an awkward conditional clause that does not contrast with what precedes it, and it is reasonably well supported externally (ℵ[2], B[*,2], K, L, Ψ, along with a number of minuscules and other old Latin, Coptic and Georgian translations). Other readings are "see" (ἰδέ), "for if" (εἰ δὲ γάρ) or "behold" (ἰδού), none of which find much external support but which all offer smoother readings or readings more parallel with v. 4. As for the first-class condition, there is no doubt that it is true, but James's point is still "argumentative" (Hiebert, *The Epistle of James*, 209).

27. The more classical Greek syntax of this verse also places the genitive noun "of horses" (ἵππων) into a highly emphatic position. See A. T. Robertson, *Grammar of the Greek New Testament* (Nashville: Broadman, 1934), 418. In other words, if the principle in view works with *horses*, how much more with humans!

James 3:4 Behold also the ships, although they are so large and driven by harsh winds, are guided by a very small rudder wherever the impulse of the pilot wishes (ἰδοὺ καὶ τὰ πλοῖα τηλικαῦτα ὄντα καὶ ὑπὸ ἀνέμων σκληρῶν ἐλαυνόμενα, μετάγεται ὑπὸ ἐλαχίστου πηδαλίου ὅπου ἡ ὁρμὴ τοῦ εὐθύνοντος βούλεται). James offers a second, parallel illustration, this time of a boat. Even more so than with the horse, he stresses the size and power of the great ships, which are likewise controlled and guided[28] by something a miniscule fraction of their size. The two concessive participles, "being" (ὄντα) and "being driven" (ἐλαυνόμενα), provide the idea that "although" ships can be huge and buffeted by severe storms, a tiny mechanism at one end of each boat can steer it.[29] Meanwhile, the term "smallest" (ἐλαχίστου) emphasizes how tiny the rudder is, probably exemplifying the elative use (meaning "very, very small," though not literally "the smallest," as in the superlative). Pilots retain their power over ships because they control the rudders. If, however, a rudder does not work properly, the ship can veer wholly out of control. In the same way, if the tongue is not harnessed, the entire person can become uncontrollable.[30] When functioning as it was designed, the tongue, like a rudder, enables those who steer wisely to set the course they desire.[31]

James 3:5a So also the tongue is a small member, yet it boasts of great things (οὕτως καὶ ἡ γλῶσσα μικρὸν μέλος ἐστὶν καὶ μεγάλα αὐχεῖ). James concludes this subsection by making the comparison with the tongue explicit, again by contrasting the small size of the tongue with the deeds of which it boasts. Like the horse, guided by a small bit in its mouth, and the ship, controlled by a tiny rudder at its stern, the little tongue maneuvers the whole person.[32] James's point is that people can either control their tongues or let their tongues control them.

"Great" (μεγάλα) can be taken either as a direct object (i.e., "boasts of great things") or as an adverb ("boasts greatly"). While there is no big difference between the two, the former might be preferred as a better lead-in to the following section that highlights the tongue's evil *actions*.[33] Here the term for boasting (αὐχέω) is probably used neutrally. It is the content of the boast that determines whether it is good or evil. The tongue legitimately claims substantial power. But, as Davids remarks, "it is not that the tongue steers the ship, but that the proper helmsman is often not in control."[34]

James 3:5b Behold how small a fire [spark] ignites how great a wood [forest] (ἰδοὺ ἡλίκον πῦρ ἡλίκην ὕλην ἀνάπτει). James moves into a new section of analogies, by which he will illustrate

28. Μετάγεται is a singular verb, even though its subject, "the boats," is plural, because neuter plural subjects in the NT regularly take singular verbs.

29. Johnson (*The Letter of James*, 257) adds that "the emphasis is on the difficulties for control posed by the combination of mass and force."

30. Baker (*Personal Speech-Ethics in the Epistle of James*, 125) sees in this illustration "three critical facets to the general point." First, the "tongue is not powerful in itself," but rather "is the focal point through which power is channeled into purposeful action." Second, "the accentuation of the smallness of the rudder (ἐλαχίστου) in contrast to the great size of the ship (τηλικαῦτα) draws attention to the value, or importance, of the tongue to the body which is vastly out of proportion to its relative size." And third, the "tongue does not control itself. It should be controlled by the person."

31. "Impulse" (ὁρμή) refers here more to "the moral will of the pilot" than to "the guiding of his hand" (Hartin, *James*, 175; Dibelius, *James*, 190). The NASB translates it as "inclination," while the REB renders the last clause of v. 4 as "whatever course the helmsman chooses."

32. The "and" (καί) takes on an adversative sense here. Cf. NET: "yet it has great pretensions." But "boasts" (αὐχεῖ) is not yet overly negative (cf. NRSV: "boasts of great exploits").

33. So also BDAG, 154; Louw and Nida, *Greek-English Lexicon*, 431.

34. Davids, *The Epistle of James*, 140.

the uncontrollable and destructive tendencies of the tongue. His initial illustration at first sounds unrelated to the topic at hand as he recalls the tiny[35] spark of fire needed to set a forest[36] ablaze. But even though James has shifted to a negative illustration, he continues to employ an analogy in which huge effects result, far out of proportion to the instigating force.

James 3:6 And the tongue is a fire. The tongue appoints itself as a world of unrighteousness among our members, that which stains the whole body and sets on fire the course of existence and is set on fire by Gehenna (καὶ ἡ γλῶσσα πῦρ· ὁ κόσμος τῆς ἀδικίας ἡ γλῶσσα καθίσταται ἐν τοῖς μέλεσιν ἡμῶν, ἡ σπιλοῦσα ὅλον τὸ σῶμα καὶ φλογίζουσα τὸν τροχὸν τῆς γενέσεως καὶ φλογιζομένη ὑπὸ τῆς γεέννης). Again James explains his illustration.[37] Obviously the tongue is not a literal fire.[38] His analogy underscores the widespread effects that fire can have when it burns out of control. In Colorado, where both of this book's authors have lived and taught, careless campers who leave one ember burning in a campfire can start wildfires that destroy tens and even hundreds of thousands of acres. James's point is that the tongue can have the same effect: one careless statement can ruin careers and destroy lives.

James utilizes four highly uncomplimentary clauses/phrases to highlight this horror. First, the tongue establishes itself as "a world of unrighteousness" (ὁ κόσμος τῆς ἀδικίας). Martin introduces the interesting option of taking this clause in apposition to the initial statement, thus rendering "the tongue is a fire, a world of unrighteousness placed among our members."[39] This seems a reasonable option, and in fact previous editions of the UBS set this phrase off with commas rather than putting a semicolon after "the tongue is a fire," as in UBS[4]. However, the translation and punctuation that we have chosen remains, with the majority view, the most natural rendering of the Greek text, given the emphatic repetition of "the tongue" (ἡ γλῶσσα) (which the TNIV has to omit, along with verb, in order to make the minority view work).[40]

The genitive "of unrighteousness" (τῆς ἀδικίας) is either partitive (yielding "the sum total of unrighteousness")[41] or descriptive (i.e., "an unrighteous world"). A few have tried to translate "world" (κοσμός) here as "adornment" (as in 1Pe 3:3). But Moo points out that "the most common meaning of *kosmos* in the NT is ... the fallen, sinful world-system," as in the other three uses in James, and thus he supports the descriptive genitive with the translation "world."[42] Davids offers the compelling comparison with Luke 16:9, with its "mammon of

35. The word translated both "how small" and "how great" (ἡλίκος) denotes size and contrast. It can mean either "how large" or "how tiny," because its root refers merely to the extremity of some measurement.

36. Leonard E. Elliott-Binns, "The Meaning of ὕλη in James 3:5," *NTS* 2 [1955]: 48 – 50) argues that brushwood and undergrowth, not tall trees, are in view, but this scarcely changes the meaning of the illustration.

37. Moo (*The Letter of James*, 156) points out that here James has abandoned his similes in favor of "straightforward metaphor."

38. Martin (*James*, 113) gives a list of texts from Jewish literature that compared the tongue to fire, including Pss 10:7; 39:1 – 3; 120:2 – 4; Pr 16:27; 26:21; Isa 30:27; Sir 28:13 – 26. Davids (*The Epistle of James*, 141) notes that fire is often used as a metaphor for passions that are out of control, but agrees with Martin that this is more apparent in other texts.

39. Martin, *James*, 114 – 15; Cf. Burchard, *Der Jakobusbrief*, 144: "the world of unrighteousness" is in apposition to "fire."

40. See Moo, *The Letter of James*, 158. "The unrighteous world" is thus also emphatic, due to its unusually early position in the sentence. For "makes itself" or "is made" (καθίσταται) with a loosely attached predicate nominative, see several of the examples in BDAG, 492, s.v. "καθίστημι/καθιστάνω," sec. 3.

41. This reading is supported by the Latin Vulgate; cf. the NAB: "It exists among our members as a whole universe of malice."

42. Moo, *The Letter of James*, 157.

unrighteousness" (μαμωνᾶ τῆς ἀδικίας), where the genitive has replaced an adjective.[43] The NET phrases it nicely: "The tongue represents the world of wrongdoing among the parts of our bodies."

The next question is whether the verb in this sentence (καθίσταται) is a true middle (i.e., the tongue "appoints itself") or a passive (it "is appointed"). If one takes it as middle, then we have to accept some degree of volition on the part of the tongue itself, which makes it that much more unruly. If one accepts a passive form, then we need to ask who sets the tongue in our members. Does one blame God for this evil in our midst, or is there someone else to account for this unruly member? Baker suggests understanding καθίσταται as passive, so that James here is merely saying that we are the way God has made us.[44] But God did not create us to be sinful, so the middle voice makes more sense.[45] The tongue, as the embodiment of our sinful nature, appoints itself in this evil role. Lastly on this particular clause, do we interpret "members" (μέλεσιν) corporately or individually? If corporately, then this clause uses "tongue" to refer to the speech of an entire congregation, perhaps focusing specifically on the leader.[46] If individually, then "tongue" denotes the speech of an individual and the role it plays within that person's life. The latter appears clearer.

James continues his denunciation with three adjectival participial phrases that further unpack the dangers of ill-conceived speech. The present tenses suggest a continual aspect to the problems that the tongue can cause. It continually corrupts or defiles the person who speaks wrongly, it increasingly damages others just as a fire burns out of control, and it is repeatedly kindled by hell itself.[47] Again, "body" (σῶμα) can be taken corporately or individually, referring either to the church as the body of Christ (in a Pauline sense), or to the individual person that the tongue so taints. It seems best to continue to understand this term in a more individual manner, so that James is talking about forces internal to each person.[48]

The expression "the course of existence" (τὸν τροχὸν τῆς γενέσεως) is difficult to translate, and some have taken it to reflect a philosophical background in Orphic lore. There the wheel that the goddess Fortune controlled depicted cycles of life, death, and reincarnation, and the rises and falls of circumstances within each life.[49] However, it seems better to understand this term more informally, in terms of the whole course of our existence (cf. the famous "circle of life" in the movie *The Lion King* or the NAB: "Its flames encircle our course from birth"), rather than reading in this technical background. The expression seems already to have been popularized and decontextualized (if it ever had any technical meaning) by James's day. The tongue, in its destructive path, wreaks havoc and corrupts one's entire life.

The term "Gehenna" (γεέννα) literally refers to the valley of *Gehinnom* (in Aramaic), outside of Jerusalem, stigmatized because of child sacrifices to Molech previously practiced there (cf. 2Ki 23:10; 2Ch 28:3; 33:6; Jer 7:31 – 32; 19:5 – 6; 32:35).

43. Davids, *The Epistle of James*, 142.

44. Baker, "James," 76.

45. Dibelius, *James*, 194.

46. Martin, *James*, 115.

47. Stulac (*James*, 126) perceives a deteriorating progression in the four clauses/phrases predicated about the tongue — from a multitude of evils in speech to corruption of the whole person to destruction of the person's life to the damnation of hell. This neatly parallels the progression seen in 1:13 – 15.

48. Baker ("James," 76) comments that "the imagery compares to a person drinking a red dye that quickly spreads to discolor every molecule of his body. The spiritual message is that the evil of the tongue contaminates our whole lives, and there is nothing we can do about it. It is a permanent stain."

49. See further Dibelius, *James*, 196 – 98; Adamson, *The Epistle of James*, 160 – 64.

50. Moo (*The Letter of James*, 160) sees in γεέννα another

Figuratively, it means "hell."[50] While it does not necessarily connote the demonic realm, James will shortly label false wisdom as diabolical (3:15), so it is understandable why many have viewed James as linking Gehenna with the abode of Satan, who tempts humans to speak wickedly and believe that which is false.[51] Richard Bauckham, however, thinks James's point is about the *punishment* for wicked speech (unrepentant offenders winding up in hell), not about the *origin* of such speech, and this interpretation may be preferable. It follows the principle of the crime fitting the punishment (the tongue that starts a "fire" ends up being punished by "fire") and finds a close parallel in *Psalms of Solomon* 12:1–4.[52]

James 3:7 For every kind of animal and bird, reptile and sea creature is tamed and has been tamed by humankind (πᾶσα γὰρ φύσις θηρίων τε καὶ πετεινῶν, ἑρπετῶν τε καὶ ἐναλίων δαμάζεται καὶ δεδάμασται τῇ φύσει τῇ ἀνθρωπίνῃ). James moves to a different analogy from the realm of wild animals to depict the out-of-control nature of the tongue. While "kind" (φύσις) can refer to "nature," as in the character of something, here it refers to every "type" or "species" (cf. NRSV) of animal within the particular categories. The list of creatures employs partitive genitives, implying "every kind of animal out of the following groups." The division of the animals into these four categories originates in Gen 1:26 and 9:2. James's allusion to creation recalls the divine mandate to the first humans to "subdue" the world. While the animal world remains under humanity's control, thus preserving the creation order, the tongue does not.

The first verb, "is tamed" (δαμάζεται), represents a gnomic present, affirming merely the possibility that these animals can be tamed.[53] The second verb, "has been tamed" (δεδάμασται), may function as a hyperbole. James is not trying to argue that humanity has tamed every single animal at some point or other, but, more than even in his day, humanity *has* domesticated the natural world through its construction of cities, roads, farms, and the like.[54] Moreover, already in the first century people had tamed a large number of the animals for their own purposes. Psalm 8:6–8 further shows the idea of subduing animals not only for agriculture, but also as hunters sought prey in the wild.[55] Just as the first use of "kind" (φύσις) in this verse meant "a species of" animal, the second use likewise refers to "humankind" (the species of humanity), not to "the nature of humans." Baker suggests that, by the repeated use of φύσις, both for the animals and for people, James is using irony to

---

connection to Jesus' teaching, because "only in the teaching of Jesus do we find this word elsewhere in the NT (11 times)," and Jesus "used the word to refer to the place of ultimate condemnation." Given Jesus' conception of Gehenna as a place of unquenchable fire, James's use of the term for the ignition of the fiery tongue follows naturally.

51. Baker ("James," 77) views γεέννα here as "a euphemism for Satan," such that "the human tongue is Satan's garrison for dispatching his harmful designs on the individual and on society." Davids (*The Epistle of James*, 143) argues for interpreting James as perhaps the first person to identify Satan as resident in hell. Moreover, "the evil in a person, already spoken of as the world or evil impulse, is now traced for the first time to its ultimate source in Satan."

52. Richard Bauckham, "The Tongue Set on Fire by Hell (James 3:6)," in *The Fate of the Dead: Studies in the Jewish and Christian Apocalypses* (Leiden: Brill, 1998), 119–31.

53. Porter (*Verbal Aspect in the Greek of the New Testament*, 224) refers to Jas 3:3–12 as "perhaps the largest section of omnitemporal [his term for gnomic] Present usage in the NT." In a sense, every verse in this section contains at least one verb that reflects a proverbial kind of action that remains consistently true at all times.

54. The combination of the present and perfect tenses of "tame" stresses all the more "the control human beings have exercised on the animal world from the very beginning" (Hartin, *James*, 179).

55. Hiebert (*The Epistle of James*, 220) and Townsend (*The Epistle of James*, 62, following the REB) both prefer "subdue" to "tame," because the focus is on humanity's dominance over creation.

depict humanity as just one more creation of God, potentially no better than the animals.[56]

James 3:8 But no one of humans is able to tame the tongue; it is an uncontrollable evil, full of deadly poison (τὴν δὲ γλῶσσαν οὐδεὶς δαμάσαι δύναται ἀνθρώπων, ἀκατάστατον κακόν, μεστὴ ἰοῦ θανατηφόρου). While humans have been able to subjugate all sorts of wild animals, no one has ever mastered the tongue. In the first clause of this verse, the main ambiguity involves "humans" (ἀνθρώπων), possibly a possessive genitive modifying "tongue" (γλῶσσαν), but more likely a partitive genitive modifying the nearer word for "no one" (οὐδεὶς). The genitive noun has been moved to the end of the statement, however, to emphasize an implied contrast. This implies that we need to look outside humanity for help in taming the tongue. While no one *of humans* can subdue our speech, God can control it for us.[57]

James continues his description of the tongue by likening it to a fatal attraction.[58] We first saw the term "uncontrollable" (ἀκατάστατον) in 1:8, where it was used of the restlessness of waves. Here it has an even worse connotation. To communicate this out-of-control aspect, a stronger translation than "restless" should be used. In addition to "uncontrollable," it can mean "unstable." Thus the imagery can convey the idea of something that may at any point lash out, a disorderly and unpredictable organism. The image of death-bearing poison is dramatic, especially considering that tongues normally are used to taste life-giving food and drink! The metaphor suggests the image of a serpent, poised to strike, much like the destructive, deceptive words of the snake to Eve in the garden of Eden, which poisoned paradise. Psalm 140:3 further declares that violent evildoers "make their tongues as sharp as a serpent's; the poison of vipers is on their lips."

James 3:9 By it we bless the Lord and Father and by it we curse humans made in the image of God (ἐν αὐτῇ εὐλογοῦμεν τὸν κύριον καὶ πατέρα καὶ ἐν αὐτῇ καταρώμεθα τοὺς ἀνθρώπους τοὺς καθ' ὁμοίωσιν θεοῦ γεγονότας). James finally portrays the major problem that makes the tongue so evil — its duplicity. Blessing the Lord and cursing people reflect the best and worst of human speech. While it is tempting to read "the Lord" (κύριον)[59] as a reference to Jesus, the shared article τόν referring to both "Lord" and "Father" (πατέρα)

56. Baker and Ellsworth, *Preaching James*, 87 – 88.

57. Townsend (*The Epistle of James*, 63) alleges that this contrast, which goes back at least as far as Augustine, while true, "is almost certainly not in James's mind," but he gives no reasons for this conviction. Moo (*The Letter of James: An Introduction and Commentary*, 127) quotes Augustine's view (from *On the Creation* 8) as if it were worth some credence, but fifteen years later (Moo, *The Letter of James*, 161) doubts this. Contra Moo's later position, affirming that God can help us control what we cannot manage in our own strength hardly commits us to believing in perfectionism in this life. Cf. esp. J. L. P. Wolmarans, "The Tongue Guiding the Body: The Anthropological Presuppositions of James 3:1 – 12," *Neot* 26 (1992): 526.

58. Here is a textual variant, rated a {B} by the UBS. The term "uncontrollable" or "unstable" (ἀκατάστατον) has the textual support of ℵ, A, B, K, and P, among others. Meanwhile, the other option (ἀκατάσχετον), which has only the stronger connotation of "uncontrollable," appears in C, Ψ, [*Byz*], and a number of minuscules and Fathers. The latter reading supports the argument that James was dealing with the negative connotation of an uncontrollable nature, even if he originally wrote the term with a broader range of meaning (ἀκατάστατον). A scribe would more likely have changed this to the stronger and more unambiguously negative term (ἀκατάσχετον) than changing the clear word to the more ambiguous one.

59. This is the third textual decision the UBS presents in this passage; this time rated an {A}. Here the contrast is between "Lord" (κύριον), which nearly all of the oldest manuscript support, and "God" (θεόν), which is best supported by *Byz*, along with a number of minuscules. The latter reading most likely was introduced intentionally to smooth out any confusion. Once again, the scribes would more likely have changed the ambiguous word (κύριον) to the unambiguous one (θεόν) rather than the reverse.

makes this unlikely; since Jesus is never referred to in Scripture as "Father."[60] This blessing is most likely a liturgical acclamation of God in worship, especially given James's formal language within the quote.[61]

The term for "we curse" (καταρώμεθα) does not necessarily include the idea of an official, public curse placed on those who have rejected the church, as synagogues later intoned on members who had become followers of Jesus. More likely, the NT prohibitions against cursing simply were "aimed at those who struck out in anger (see Mt 5:21 – 26) against other Christians."[62] James's disgust here is founded on the self-defeating idea of cursing someone made in the "image of God." This implies, derivatively, that human beings, despite the fall, retain vestiges of God's image, and so to curse a fellow human, whether or not Christian, is to curse the reflection of the divine. But James's main concern involves how the double-mindedness that his entire epistle combats "transposes itself into double-tonguedness."[63]

James 3:10 From the same mouth come blessing and cursing. My brothers and sisters, these things ought not to be so! (ἐκ τοῦ αὐτοῦ στόματος ἐξέρχεται εὐλογία καὶ κατάρα. οὐ χρή, ἀδελφοί μου, ταῦτα οὕτως γίνεσθαι). James summarizes this contradictory state of affairs and then denounces it. The denunciation declares that the same person should not be capable of both blessing and cursing.[64] James's language strongly rebukes those who speak in this duplicitous manner, urgently insisting that this behavior has no place among Christians.[65] People turn deceitful when they speak with forked tongues. Like Jesus, James insists that what comes from people's mouths illustrates their hearts, so that this kind of double-speak reveals the vacillating allegiance condemned in 1:5 – 8.

James 3:11 Does a spring from the same opening pour forth both sweet and bitter [water]? (μήτι ἡ πηγὴ ἐκ τῆς αὐτῆς ὀπῆς βρύει τὸ γλυκὺ καὶ τὸ πικρόν;). To illustrate the abnormality of duplicitous speech, James again turns to illustrations from nature. The initial, untranslated μήτι introduces a question that expects a negative answer. Here our mouths are compared to springs of water, but springs provide either salt water or sweet water; they cannot produce both. To mix in even a little salt makes all the water salty. In the natural world, springs cannot quickly switch from gushing forth (βρύει; cf. NAB) contaminated water to producing clean water. So, too, if our words stem from our heart, they should be entirely pure, not mixed with evil. Such mixing befouls every part of us.

60. Granville-Sharp's rule asserts that when there is a single article with a pair of nonproper, singular, personal nouns joined by a conjunction, then the nouns always refer to the same person/thing. If "Lord" and "Father" *are* taken as proper nouns here, then the rule does not as strictly apply, but the two descriptors are still closely related and probably refer to the same entity, God.

61. Cf. Hiebert, *The Epistle of James*, 222.

62. Martin, *James*, 119. More broadly, Keener (*The IVP Bible Background Commentary*, 697) envisions James censuring "incendiary rhetoric or a battle cry, cursing mortal enemies," even though these forms of speech had become deeply embedded in the Jewish tradition of patriotism from the times of the Maccabees onward.

63. Tidball, *Wisdom from Heaven*, 106. If the denunciations of other people proved sufficiently extreme, they "may have taken to themselves the eschatological prerogatives of Christ in sentencing the damned" (Scaer, *James*, 101).

64. In vv. 9 – 10 there is a clear echo of Jesus' teaching in Mt 12:33 – 37, concerning how someone with an evil heart cannot speak good and how one's words come from one's heart. One's speech consistently reflects the state of one's heart, hence the concern with such duplicitous speech. James's teaching also echoes Mt 15:18 on how speech from an impure heart defiles.

65. On the strength of James's denunciation, see Adamson, *The Epistle of James*, 146 – 47.

James 3:12 Is it possible, my brothers and sisters, for the fig tree to produce olives or the grapevine figs? Neither does a salty [spring] make sweet water (μὴ δύναται, ἀδελφοί μου, συκῆ ἐλαίας ποιῆσαι ἢ ἄμπελος σῦκα; οὔτε ἁλυκὸν γλυκὺ ποιῆσαι ὕδωρ). James concludes his string of analogies to the ridiculous nature of the tongue with three further examples of how the world of nature must remain true to itself.[66] James's point is that no plant can produce the fruit that belongs to a different plant,[67] just as one kind of water cannot transform itself into another kind.[68] In the same way, our tongues, which have been natural conduits of evil ever since the fall, cannot produce good on their own.

The last clause in this verse contains two nominative adjectives, so that either could be the grammatical subject. It seems better to understand James's illustration in terms of the near impossibility of making saltwater into sweet, since it is easy enough to make sweet water salty.[69] But there is also the contrast that comes from Jesus' teaching, that those who are "good" internally will produce good speech, while those who are unredeemed in their hearts will remain poisonous in their speech. James is looking for consistency of behavior, not perfection (see 3:2). Just as one can depend on a fig tree to grow figs and on a fresh-water spring to pour forth fresh water, the maturing believer should increasingly converse constructively rather than destructively.

> Thus the implication of the metaphors [in vv. 9 – 12] shifts from the initial claim that one person cannot utter both good and bad statements (blessing God and cursing people) to the claim that a person of one kind cannot utter statements of another kind and finally to the claim that a bad person cannot utter good statements. This is an intelligible and logical progression of thought.[70]

Theology in Application

The Problem of Too Many Teachers (3:1 – 2a)

In beginning this passage by warning that fewer in his churches should become teachers, James may be reflecting on Jesus' words later recorded in Mt 23:2 – 7. There Christ laments that various Jewish teachers do not practice what they preach as they make life difficult for those under them (vv. 2 – 4), and that they overly value the status and respect that come with their position (vv. 5 – 7). The rest of the NT contains numerous examples of good and bad teachers. Teaching can be a spiritual gift exercised for the edification of the church (Ro 12:7; 1Co 12:28; Eph 4:12) or a

66. Here the textual variants probably stem from the highly elliptical nature of the most probably original form of the concluding statement, "neither salty sweet to make water" (οὔτε ἁλυκὸν γλυκὺ ποιῆσαι ὕδωρ), rated a {B} in the UBS. The variants reflect attempts to fill in the ellipses and explain James's meaning more clearly.

67. Figs, olive oil, and wine were the three chief products from Israel's horticulture (cf. Hiebert, *The Epistle of James*, 225).

68. Martin (*James*, 121) suggests a background in Jesus' use of nature (Mt 7:16 – 20; 12:33 – 35; Lk 6:43 – 45) for James's illustrations here.

69. Davids (*The Epistle of James*, 148) argues that "ἁλυκὸν must stand for a brackish *spring* and the ποιῆσαι, at best unusual for what a spring does, must have been chosen to make the parallel with v 12a explicit." The somewhat unusual word order (for Hellenistic Greek) again places emphasis on the unusually early word, "salty," in the final clause.

70. Bauckham, *James*, 90.

self-appointed role for which one is unqualified — doctrinally and/or behaviorally (see esp. the false teachers opposed in Jude, 2 Peter, and 1 – 3 John).

On the greater responsibility and accountability that teachers have, by virtue of the dominant role that speech plays in their vocation, James may have remembered teachings like those enshrined in Lk 12:48b and Mk 12:36 – 40. Of course, teachers in the ancient Mediterranean world were far more than transmitters of tradition; they were models to be imitated in every walk of life, as Paul repeatedly exemplifies by calling people to imitate his own ministry of service (e.g. 1Co 4:16; 1Th 1:6), even to the degree that he can soberly affirm he is imitating Christ (1Co 11:1).[71]

Today's teachers frequently need to recover this holistic form of ministry. Too many are so cloistered from the crowds they instruct that few people ever know what they are really like behind the scenes. The inflated "hero-worship" that excellent, well-known teachers receive can easily create an overexalted sense of one's worth and inerrancy! Soon the teacher becomes autocratic, accepting no one else's opinion on really important issues and accusing those who disagree of being less spiritual or insubordinate.[72] James's letter should instill in us the exactly opposite traits: greater humility of demeanor and opinion. Our lives should be an open book, worthy enough for others to examine and replicate. Of course we will sin, but part of discipleship is learning from a good model of repentance, too.

The seminary where both of us have taught has in its mission statement the three key tasks of equipping leaders to "think biblically, live faithfully, and lead wisely for a lifetime."[73] Robert Wall correctly detects all three of these in James, but he also recognizes the priority of living faithfully: "James seems more interested in personal character than in professional competency." What ultimately decides the value of a teacher's faith is whether he or she "is 'wise and understanding' rather than merely orthodox."[74] More simply put, these three objectives remain: content, competence, and character.[75] But the greatest of these is character!

The Positive Potential of Speech (3:2b – 5a)

Before James scares *everyone* away from teaching or even from speaking at all,[76]

71. Cf. further David S. Dockery, "True Piety in James: Ethical Admonitions and Theological Implications," *CTR* 1 (1986): 151 – 70.

72. Hughes, *James*, 127 – 28. Cf. Evans, "James," 778: "Never being able to admit to a mistake or willing to lose an argument is by no means a sign of strength, and the threatening, do-not-dare-to-contradict-me approach is not a sign of wisdom. Destroying other people by aggressive and wounding words or using prayer as a means of trying to blackmail God into acceding to selfish demands is spiritual adultery, a betrayal of all that life in Christ implies."

73. The exact wording is most indebted to the 2001 formulations of Craig R. Williford, then president of Denver Seminary.

74. Wall, *Community of the Wise*, 162.

75. The alliterative terms were chosen by the late president of Denver Seminary, Clyde B. McDowell, to summarize its mission statement when he was still a local pastor and adjunct professor at the school in 1992.

76. Gench (*Hebrews and James*, 112) reminds us that v. 2 teaches us to "bridle," not "zipper," the tongue!

he reminds us of the extraordinary amount of good that skilled instruction and sensitive speaking can accomplish. Tiny bits and rudders enable equestrians and ships' captains to guide much larger, unruly modes of transportation exactly where they want them to go a substantial majority of the time (vv. 3 – 4). Whether the informal teaching of a parent to a child or the formal instruction of a professor in the classroom, the opportunity to mold the lives of others for kingdom values is an enormous privilege and as rewarding a vocation as any on earth. One good student who moves into an influential position in the world can multiply her or his teacher's ministry in almost unlimited fashion in good and godly ways.[77]

The book of Proverbs recognizes the positive power of speech as well as its potential destructiveness. Chapters 1 – 9 stress the need to learn from parental instruction. The rest of the book contains a raft of individual gems of wisdom:

- The mouth of the righteous is a fountain of life (10:11a).
- A gentle answer turns away wrath (15:1a).
- Plans fail for lack of counsel, but with many advisers they succeed (15:22).
- Whoever heeds life-giving correction will be at home among the wise (15:31).
- Gracious words are a honeycomb, sweet to the soul and healing to the bones (16:24).

These are but a small sample of similar teachings in Pr 10 – 31. Applications abound. Every successful interpersonal relationship reflects healthy communication skills. The key to growing intimacy in a marriage is identical to that which creates a harmonious, productive workplace: loving, transparent, positive, trusting, empathetic speech that keeps short accounts, deals with problems as they arise, and then forgets them and moves ahead.[78] The tongue is so powerful that it indeed shapes one's entire personality (cf. also v. 6).[79]

The Negative Potential of Speech (3:5b – 8)

For this very reason, speech can prove highly destructive as well. A long list of biblical and apocryphal proverbs could be enlisted for proof here, too.

- A harsh word stirs up anger (Pr 15:1b).
- The mouth of the fool gushes folly (15:2b).
- A perverse tongue crushes the spirit (15:4b).

77. For a striking example, see R. Wayne Stacy, "The Power to Bless: James 3:1 – 12 (A Sermon)," *RevExp* 97 (2000): 233 – 34.

78. For excellent advice along these lines, see William E. Hulme, "Mind Your Tongue: Reflections on Christian Conversation," *WW* 6 (1986): 249 – 55.

79. Hubbard, *The Book of James*, 75.

The list is almost endless. Particularly apposite to Jas 3:5 – 6 is Pr 16:27: "Scoundrels plot evil, and on their lips it is like a scorching fire" (TNIV). Compare also 18:21 (which recalls Jas 3:7 – 8): "The tongue has the power of life and death." In Sirach, one can contrast Sir 5:13 – 6:1 with 14:1 or 19:15 with 22:27. Particularly passionate in its warnings against the "whisperer," "double-tongued," and "backbiter" is 28:13 – 26.[80]

The rotten fruit of an untamed tongue include "gossiping, belittling, cursing, bragging, manipulating, false teaching, exaggerating, complaining, flattering and lying."[81] Stulac astutely observes:

> Spread gossip, and people will not trust you. Speak with sarcasm and insults, and people will not follow you. Yet what is especially on James's mind is not the reaction of others to your speech but the spreading of sin from your speech to the rest of your life. Be hateful with your tongue, and you will be hateful with other aspects of your behavior. If you do not discipline and purify your speech, you will not discipline or purify the rest of your life.[82]

In America, we cherish freedom of speech. But with freedom comes responsibility. Responsible citizens in a democracy, and Christians in any form of society, must learn what is helpful and even necessary to say, even when unpleasant — such as in challenging injustice against others — and what remains only destructive.[83] Evangelical Christians have at times had a poor track record of speaking the truth *in love* in situations such as these, even as more liberal Christians have often failed to speak *the truth* in love. And almost all people suffer from the tendency to pass on interesting rumors to others without scrupulously checking their accuracy, especially in the Internet age, which produces a torrent of misinformation, half truths, and personal opinions all subtly mixed together with genuine facts for just about any Google search that one executes![84]

The Possibility of Inconsistency (3:9 – 12)

That all humanity, even in its unredeemed state, still reflects the image of God (v. 9), however imperfectly, challenges the stereotypical agendas of both the political and religious "right" and "left." Abortion and euthanasia offend God deeply because

80. See further Barclay, *The Letters of James and Peter,* 82 – 83.

81. Barton, Veerman and Wilson, *James,* 77.

82. Stulac, *James,* 125.

83. Cf. Perkins, *First and Second Peter, James and Jude,* 115: "we have come to wonder whether all forms of speech should be permitted in public, on rap records, in the media, and the like. Speech that expresses hatred toward or demeans others because of their racial origins, sexual preference, gender, or religion is being restricted." Unfortunately, sometimes these restrictions are inconsistently implemented, so that Christians seem to remain the one group against which anything slanderous may be spoken with impunity.

84. Deiros (*Santiago y Judas,* 177 – 78) highlights how governments throughout the world deliberately spread lies and half truths to generate support among their people for controversial programs and policies.

they take lives made in his image. But abuse or neglect of the poor and outcast (including the homosexual) proves equally offensive because such treatments likewise demean individuals God made to reflect himself. A theology of just war inevitably sentences countless lost souls who die in battle to hell on the spot, while full-fledged pacifism permits tyrants to pronounce the same sentences by means of unchecked terrorism of many kinds.

James's exhortation here, however, applies the doctrine of the *imago Dei* to our speech. We need to recover the abhorrence of believers praising God while cursing people that James displayed in v. 10a.[85] Duplicity of speech is condemned in Ps 62:4 and in intertestamental texts like Sir 5:13 and the Dead Sea Scrolls' *Rule of the Community* (1QS 10.21 – 24). V. 10b, however, reminds us that our behavior does not have to remain this bad.

The imagery of vv. 11 – 12 calls us "to restore integrity and discipline to Christian speech. Change is possible ... or else so much energy would not have been expended on this topic of disciplined speech."[86] The imagery of these verses further reminds us of Jesus' teaching in Mt 7:16 – 20: we will be known by our fruit. A truly good tree cannot bear bad fruit. From a bird's-eye view, what will ultimately characterize the overall life of a redeemed person is constructive speech.

85. Cf. Stulac, *James*, 128 – 29: "Consider the habitual verbal abuse that occurs in our churches — how commonplace it is for us to speak of others with ridicule or with cutting remarks, how quickly we accuse others of evil motives when they do things we don't like and how easily we can have angry fights in our churches. Where is our biblical sense of shock at all of this?" Prayer requests can lightly mask gossip, passing on information others would not want spread. The movie *Saved* offers some bitter, though humorous, parodies of this behavior.

86. Gench, *Hebrews and James*, 111.

CHAPTER 7

James 3:13 – 18

Literary Context

James 3:13 – 18 continues to unpack the second major theme of the letter — wisdom and speech. Those who see the warnings of 3:1 – 12 primarily or exclusively addressing teachers find no difficulty in extending this focus to include the rest of the chapter. Teachers certainly need to acquire and model "the wisdom from above" rather than engaging in rivalry, boasting, falsehood, disorder, and the like — sins readily committed by the tongue.

At the same time, no category of Christian should be excluded from James's purview here. Dissension in Christian contexts often stems from people who have no regular teaching role. Indeed, it seems that often those who divide congregations are not those who teach and appreciate the difficulty of the task but those considerably less involved in leadership or ministry with the time on their hands to carp too critically about those they ought to be supporting and encouraging! So we do best to see James addressing all Christians in this paragraph, even if his words have special bearing on teachers.[1]

The theme of wisdom, of course, first appeared in 1:5 – 8 and then again in 1:19 – 26. The humility enjoined in 3:13 echoes the language of 1:21. Now, however, believers are performing the good works that flow from salvation (recall 2:14 – 26) with humility, not just receiving the word implanted in them. The bitter spirit that 3:14 warns against builds on the imagery of the "bitter" water of v. 11. So, too, the prohibition against boasting reemploys the terminology of triumph from 2:13, but in a fully negative sense here. Such false wisdom cannot come down from above (3:15) because heaven sends only good gifts (1:13 – 18). The rebellion or disorder of 3:16 (ἀκαταστασία) comes from the same root as the "unstable" (ἀκατάστατος) person of 1:8 and the "uncontrollable" (ἀκατάστατον) tongue of 3:8. Heavenly wisdom's mercy (3:17) harks back to the mercy that triumphs over judgment in 2:13, while "not discriminating" (v. 17) counters the sins of doubting in 1:6 and of showing prejudice in 2:4.

1. Cf. Townsend, *The Epistle of James*, 68.

Similarly, 3:13 – 18 prepares the way for James's rebukes in 4:1 – 12 that find too many in his congregations acting like "friends of the world" (see esp. 4:4; cf. "earthly" in 3:15) rather than friends of God. The fights, quarrels, and jealousies of 4:1 – 2 are most likely verbal (see below, p. 187), reflecting the bitter jealousy and party strife of 3:14. The need for humility in 3:13 anticipates the same virtue in 4:6, which God will graciously reward. The diabolical wisdom of 3:15 can be resisted (4:7), just as an evil heart (3:14) can be transformed for the better (4:8). Not speaking against one another (4:11 – 12) plays a crucial role in this transformation. Avoiding improper judgments against others does likewise (3:17).

Links between 3:13 – 18 and later material in the epistle appear less frequently but include the recurrence of the warning against boasting (3:14; cf. 4:13 – 17, esp. v. 16, this time in the context of one's future plans). Peacefulness and gentleness (3:17 – 18) eschews the violence often relied on to retaliate against injustice and perseveres in longsuffering patience instead (5:7 – 11). In the process, one's heart is strengthened (5:8) rather than embittered (3:14).

Main Idea

By their good conduct, Christians should demonstrate heavenly rather than worldly wisdom. Specifically, they will exhibit purity and peacefulness rather than jealousy and strife.

Translation

(See next page.)

James 3:13-18

13a	Rhetorical Q.	**Who is wise and understanding among you?**
b	Exhortation	**They must show ... their works**
c	means	by good conduct
d	manner	in the humility of wisdom.
14a	Condition (of 14c)	But if you have bitter jealousy and selfish ambition
b	place	in your heart,
c	exhortation	**do not boast and lie**
d	disadvantage	against the truth.
15a	Assertion	**This is not the wisdom**
b	source	coming down from above, but
c	contrast	earthly,
d	series	natural,
		demonic.
16a	Place (of 16b)	For wherever there are jealousy and selfish ambition,
b	basis (of 15)	**there are disorder and every base deed**.
17a	Contrast (w 15)	But **the wisdom from above is first pure**, then peaceful,
b	series	gentle,
		willing to submit,
		full of mercy and good fruits,
		impartial,
		genuine.
18a	Result	And **a harvest of righteousness is sown**
b	manner	in peace
c	sphere (advantage + agency)	among those making peace.

Structure

This paragraph subdivides into an ABA structure, with James's discussion of true, godly wisdom sandwiching his warnings against ungodly, false wisdom. V. 13 forms the thesis sentence for the paragraph. The rhetorical question and command create the equivalent of a conditional sentence: "If people want to be wise, they must demonstrate it by humble, beneficial conduct." The opposite alternative (vv. 14 – 16) is introduced as part of a sentence that *is* explicitly conditional (v. 14). This declaration also provides the rationale for the definition of true wisdom: jealousy and rivalry work against the truth, so the wise person will defer to and co-operate with others.

Above all, those with God's understanding will not boast about the evil things they do (and even the wisest still sin more often than they would like to, or would like to admit that they do). Those who do boast about evil do not reflect heaven-sent wisdom (v. 15a) but that which at best is merely of human manufacture and at worst diabolical (v. 15b). While many behavioral outworkings of this wisdom from below may manifest themselves, the self-centeredness that spurs on jealousy and rivalry remains at the heart of the problem. When these two traits are allowed free rein, every other sort of wicked deed may follow (v. 16).

The antidote, fleshing out the opening call to good conduct with a humble demeanor, begins with purity (v. 17a). Almost by definition, pure, unmixed goodness and devotion to God must take precedence over any other trait, for if people are easy to get along with and full of good behavior but uncertain about their fundamental spiritual allegiance, they never do anything of distinctively *kingdom* value. Peacefulness seems to sum up the next three traits, followed by the references to good works. Then come two characteristics that show one's genuineness, so that we are back to the theme of purity again (v. 17b). The benefits of peacemaking round out the paragraph. What may have once been a stand-alone proverb epitomizes the results of "wisdom from above" here (v. 18).

Exegetical Outline

- IV. Restatement of the Three Themes (2:1 – 5:18)
  - B. Wisdom and Speech (3:1 – 4:12)
    - 1. The Power of the Tongue (3:1 – 12)
    - ➡ **2. Wisdom from Above and Wisdom from Below (3:13 – 18)**
      - a. Wise persons demonstrate their wisdom through good conduct (v. 13).
      - b. Christians should avoid worldly wisdom (vv. 14 – 16).
        - i. They ought not to boast or lie about bitter, jealous attitudes among believers (v. 14).
        - ii. The source of this so-called "wisdom" is the world, the flesh, and the devil (v. 15).
        - iii. Such attitudes typify a much larger morass of rebellion and evil (v. 16).
      - c. Christians should embrace heavenly wisdom (vv. 17 – 18).
        - i. True wisdom must above all reflect moral purity (v. 17a).
        - ii. This wisdom also includes many good works reflective of an even-tempered, well-balanced personality (v. 17b).
        - iii. True wisdom places a special priority on peacemaking (v. 18).

Explanation of Text

James 3:13 Who is wise and understanding among you? They must show by good conduct their works in the humility of wisdom (τίς σοφὸς καὶ ἐπιστήμων ἐν ὑμῖν; δειξάτω ἐκ τῆς καλῆς ἀναστροφῆς τὰ ἔργα αὐτοῦ ἐν πραΰτητι σοφίας). In this verse, James changes tactics, and seemingly topics as well. However, if one remembers that control of the tongue is a popular theme in *wisdom* literature, then the transition is actually smooth. James asks rhetorically who qualifies as a sage.

The two terms "wise" (σοφός) and "understanding" (ἐπιστήμων) seem interchangeable, so that it could appear that James is both redundant and over-intellectualizing the faith. But "wise" (σοφός) has its background in the Hebrew word *ḥokmâ*, in which theory and practice intersect. In the OT, "wisdom" leads to the fear of God (and vice-versa; see above, p. 61), not merely cognitive knowledge. The second term, "understanding" (ἐπιστήμων), is a NT *hapax*, but seems to have an even more practical bent, pertaining to "being knowledgeable in a way that makes one effectual in the exercise of such knowledge, *expert, learned, understanding*."[2] Kistemaker argues that "understanding" (ἐπιστήμων) qualifies "wise" (σοφός) to mean a "wise person [who] also has experience, knowledge and ability."[3]

These two words appear together in the LXX three times (Dt 1:13, 15; 4:6). While the first two passages refer to the qualities a leader ought to possess, the third expands the application to the people in general. James likely uses these terms similarly to refer both to the leaders of the church and to the entire congregation. Not only the leaders of a church, but every Christian ought to seek both knowledge about God as well as "practical moral and spiritual insight."[4] James is asking his congregations to evaluate themselves and discern who the truly wise ones among them are, who both know what is right and practice it.[5]

James then answers his rhetorical question by stressing the results ("good conduct") and demeanor ("humility") of godly wisdom. This section begins with the third-person aorist imperative "must show" (δειξάτω). While this form is often translated with the permissive "let," it is better in this context to understand it as "must." Echoing the faith and works discussion of 2:14–26, James insists that people's "good conduct" is the inevitable outgrowth of true wisdom.

The "humility of wisdom" (πραΰτητι σοφίας) would have been an odd expression in the first-century Hellenistic world. Meekness was not a well-respected trait in much Greek thought. The NT writers, however, followed Jesus' teaching and understood meekness or humility to involve "a healthy understanding of our own unworthiness before God and a corresponding humility and lack of pride in our dealings with our fellow-men."[6] Stulac calls it a "yielding of oneself in ready teachability and responsiveness to God's word."[7] "Of wisdom" (σοφίας) probably represents a genitive of source or origin (cf. NET: "the gentleness that wisdom brings"), since the entire paragraph contrasts the two opposing ways of being and their origins.[8]

2. BDAG, 381. Cf. REB: "Who is wise or learned...? Let him give practical proof of it."

3. Kistemaker, *James and the Epistles of John*, 117.

4. Hiebert, *The Epistle of James*, 227.

5. Cf. Andria, "James," 1513: "Wisdom is not a philosophical theory but something that has to be demonstrated in daily life. And it, too, follows from applying the truth of the word."

6. Moo, *The Letter of James: An Introduction and Commentary*, 132.

7. Stulac, *James*, 134.

8. Burchard, *Der Jakobusbrief*, 125. Popkes (*Der Brief des

Johnson points to two previous passages in this letter for background to the expression — the prayer for wisdom in 1:5 and "the exhortation to 'receive with meekness' the implanted word in 1:21." Thus the humility in question is that which grows out of divine wisdom. "The term *praus* is not accidental: the entire passage takes up the contrast between the qualities of mildness associated with God's wisdom and the harshness of a worldly wisdom based on envy."[9] According to James, for people to be truly wise, they must exhibit humility.

James 3:14 But if you have bitter jealousy and selfish ambition in your heart, do not boast and lie against the truth (εἰ δὲ ζῆλον πικρὸν ἔχετε καὶ ἐριθείαν ἐν τῇ καρδίᾳ ὑμῶν, μὴ κατακαυχᾶσθε καὶ ψεύδεσθε κατὰ τῆς ἀληθείας). James then launches a warning against the traits opposite to those that characterize wisdom, all of which recur in v. 16. The first-class condition suggests that James's congregations may actually be harboring these attitudes, though the clause could simply assume the truth of the protasis for the sake of argument. The quarrels discussed in the next section (4:1–10) make it virtually certain that some in James's churches are struggling with these very issues.[10]

The term "zeal" (ζῆλος) ranges in meaning from the positive concepts of "enthusiasm" and "ardent concern" to the negative ones of "jealousy" and "envy." Given that here the zeal is "bitter" (πικρὸν) and paired with "selfish ambition" (ἐριθείαν), the term is clearly negative in this context, hence, "jealousy." This kind of envy seeks the best for oneself, regardless of what might be good for another person, always wishing for others to have less than oneself, whether with possessions or with opportunities. In a group setting, "bitter jealousy" may manifest "a fierce desire to promote one's own opinion to the exclusion of those of others."[11]

Combined with "selfish ambition" (ἐριθείαν), a word commonly used in settings of sectarian rivalry or partisan politics,[12] the image appears of people in angry competition, undermining one another and each fighting for their own rights, a far cry from "the humility of wisdom." These problems originate "in your heart" (ἐν τῇ καρδίᾳ ὑμῶν), with the singular "heart" modified by the plural "your." Most likely James implies that the problem involves a rotten core of key individuals within the church. At the very least, each entire congregation is, for the most part, being viewed collectively as reflecting wrong attitudes. Because the images of bitter jealousy and selfish ambition are often linked to competition among various leaders, and because this entire chapter began with James's challenges to teachers, he may well be pointing his finger at a widespread problem stemming from those who would instruct and guide the church for the wrong reasons.

The second half of this verse issues a rebuke to those who are feeling secure in their positions of competing against others. While "not" (μή) with a present imperative does not *necessarily* mean "to stop" a current action, in this situation it seems probable that these failings do already exist and that James wants to steer his churches in a different direction. Hiebert insists that James's "singular negative (*mē*) must be taken with both verbs; the negative with the present imperative verbs

Jakobus, 246) supports the other main alternative, a descriptive genitive (yielding the translation "wise humility").

9. Johnson, *The Letter of James*, 270. Cf. idem, "James 3:13–4:10 and the *Topos* Περὶ Φθόνου," *NovT* 25 (1982): 336, quoting Socrates: "Envy (or jealousy) is an ulcer of the soul."

10. R. Alan Culpepper, "The Power of Words: The Tests of Two Wisdoms," *RevExp* 83 (1986): 415.

11. Ropes, *A Critical and Exegetical Commentary on the Epistle of St. James*, 245.

12. Townsend, *The Epistle of James*, 69–70.

demands that these actions, expressive of their attitude, must cease."[13]

The main question here is whether both the verbs "boast" (κατακαυχᾶσθε) and "lie" (ψεύδεσθε) or just "lie" goes with "against the truth" (κατὰ τῆς ἀληθείας).[14] While some support the idea that the prepositional phrase modifies both verbs, they do not account for the redundancy of the two "against" (κατά-) expressions.[15] Others see the boasting as referring back to "wisdom" (σοφία), with the resulting translation "don't sin against the truth by boasting of your wisdom."[16] While Burdick goes so far as to suggest that the people were boasting *of* their "bitter envy and selfish ambition,"[17] it seems more natural, given all of James's teaching to this point, to see the boasting as people pridefully claiming wisdom not really theirs (cf. NJB: "do not be boastful or hide the truth with lies"; HCSB: "don't brag and lie in defiance of the truth").[18]

James 3:15 This is not the wisdom coming down from above, but earthly, natural, demonic (οὐκ ἔστιν αὕτη ἡ σοφία ἄνωθεν κατερχομένη ἀλλὰ ἐπίγειος, ψυχική, δαιμονιώδης). James continues for a moment in this negative vein. Referring back to the envy and boasting, he identifies the true source of this behavior. The term "from above" (ἄνωθεν) points the audience back to 1:17 – 18, where God was seen as the One who pours out good gifts from above. This link encourages the interpretation of wisdom as the preeminent gift from above. It also clearly indicates a divine origin for wisdom. Likewise, the participle "coming down" (κατερχομένη) echoes the "coming down" (καταβαῖνον) of 1:17, underlining again the heavenly source.

The participle here can be taken periphrastically, that is, as the predicate use of the adjectival participle ("this wisdom *is not coming down* from above") or adverbially ("this wisdom is not from above, *coming down*"). While the latter is grammatically possible, even replicating the Greek word order, it leaves "coming down" without much meaningful connection to the rest of the sentence. The former makes good sense, but the syntax causes problems for it.[19] The adjectives in the second part of the verse suggest a still better option — the attributive use of the adjectival participle ("this is not wisdom *which comes down* from above").[20]

The key to understanding the "unholy triad" of descriptors of the source of the false wisdom is that it does *not* originate with God. "Earthly" (ἐπίγειος) in the NT consistently refers to that which is inferior.[21] Wisdom that is "earthly" shuts out God and limits its scope to things on this earth. According to James, "a wisdom that excludes consideration

13. Hiebert, *The Epistle of James*, 230.

14. The NIV takes each separately, saying "do not boast *about it* and deny the truth," while the NASB understands "and lie" (καὶ ψεύδεσθε) consecutively (denoting a result) as "do not be arrogant *and so* lie against the truth."

15. See Dibelius, *James*, 210; Wall, *Community of the Wise*, 184.

16. Martin, *James*, 131. Cf. Moo, *The Letter of James: An Introduction and Commentary*, 133; Nystrom, *James*, 207.

17. Donald W. Burdick, "James," in *The Expositor's Bible Commentary*, ed. Frank E. Gaebelein, vol. 12 (Grand Rapids: Zondervan, 1981), 190.

18. Cf. Plato, *Philebus* 49A, in which Socrates asks rhetorically, "And of all the virtues, is not wisdom the one to which people in general lay claim, thereby filling themselves with strife and false conceit of wisdom?"

19. Porter (*Verbal Aspect in the Greek of the New Testament*, 457) observes that "the intervening subject [between 'is' (ἔστιν) and "coming down" (κατερχομένη)] makes periphrasis highly unlikely."

20. Maier, *Der Brief des Jakobus*, 167. The problem here is that one would expect an articular noun to be modified by an articular participle if the participle were functioning attributively in this position. But the article with σοφία is needed to indicate the predicate function of the demonstrative ("wisdom from above is *this*") more so than to make the wisdom definite, so this principle may prove less applicable here.

21. Davids, *The Epistle of James*, 152.

of God is, in fact, not simply 'earthly' in a neutral sense, but represents a kind of closure." It is "earthbound" or restricted to this world.[22]

The middle term, "natural" (ψυχική), is often contrasted with "spiritual" (πνευματική) in Scripture, so that the significance of "natural wisdom" is that it lacks the life of the Spirit.[23] While "sensual" (HCSB) may work as a translation, it must be understood that "the term does not refer to the gross lusts of the flesh, but rather denotes that which is essentially human as contrasted to the spiritual in life here on earth apart from God."[24] In order to avoid this misunderstanding, we have chosen the term "natural" (NASB) to contrast with the "supernatural" implications of "spiritual" (πνευματική). "Natural" refers to those who are merely human; "supernatural," to those who also have the Spirit living in them.

The last term, "demonic" (δαιμονιώδης), suggests that this wisdom is demon-inspired.[25] This term recalls the diagnosis in 3:6 of the tongue being "set on fire by hell" and anticipates the warning in 4:7 to "resist the devil." In his proscription of "lying against the truth," James has "cited already another characteristic of demons" — their actions betray the origin of their "wisdom."[26] James exposes his congregation's faulty worldview as the complete antithesis of anything godly: it is earthbound, spiritually dead, and demon-instigated. These three adjectives form the biblical source of the well-known English triad of "the world, the flesh, and the devil."

James 3:16 For wherever there are jealousy and selfish ambition there are disorder and every base deed (ὅπου γὰρ ζῆλος καὶ ἐριθεία, ἐκεῖ ἀκαταστασία καὶ πᾶν φαῦλον πρᾶγμα). Concluding his discussion of false "wisdom,"[27] James declares that envy opens the door to all manner of wickedness. He leaves no room for people who seek their own glory within the church. He links jealousy and selfish ambition to the demonically inspired false "wisdom," while drawing out the implications of our selfish actions. Often, when Christians strive for a higher position in church, they do not imagine that their actions will actually create more problems. We may well think that we are the solution and that if we get our way, we will help the church improve. Instead, James declares that self-seeking will invariably produce chaos and lead people to baser actions rather than to nobler ones.

This is James's third use of the root of "disorder" (ἀκαταστασία) — recall 1:8, "unstable" (ἀκατάστατος), and 3:8, "uncontrollable" (ἀκατάστατον). This root ranges in meaning from the comparatively mild sense of "turbulent" to a violent form of "seditious."[28] Ropes describes the noun here as connoting "something of the bad associations of our word 'anarchy,'"[29] and Martin depicts it as the "breakdown of order bordering on unruliness."[30] Whereas it has absorbed the idea of instability from its related adjective, the noun focuses more on the results of restlessness. This chaos ruins both the credibility of the church in the eyes of the world and the ability of the church

22. Johnson, *The Letter of James*, 272.

23. Townsend, *The Epistle of James*, 70.

24. Hiebert, *The Epistle of James*, 232.

25. See Martin, *James*, 132. It can also be argued that the -ωδες ending suggests demon-like rather than demon-inspired.

26. Davids, *The Epistle of James*, 152.

27. It is interesting to note that James never uses the noun σοφία to refer to the false "wisdom"; rather, it is only implied within the text. Cf. Church, "James," 375. Hartin (*A Spirituality of Perfection*, 73), following Cargal (*Restoring the Diaspora*, 153), labels this "anti-wisdom."

28. William D. Mounce, ed., *Mounce's Complete Expository Dictionary of Old and New Testament Words* (Grand Rapids: Zondervan, 2006), 1075.

29. Ropes, *A Critical and Exegetical Commentary on the Epistle of St. James*, 248.

30. Martin, *James*, 126.

to minister effectively to its own congregation. When we fight for power in Christian circles, evil establishes a foothold. When we operate with worldly values, seeking our own honor and status, we even offer Satan an entrance into the house of God! Our actions no longer demonstrate our faith (as throughout ch. 2), but rather show our commitment to the world and its standards of behavior (setting up ch. 4).

"Base" (φαῦλος) means "evil, wrong, bad, vile."[31] The word for "deed" (πρᾶγμα) can sometimes refer to a lawsuit (recall the κριτήρια of 2:6), suggesting that "the malicious speech of an insider has the same deleterious effect upon the community's life as that provoked by the rich outsider who hauls the poor believer before the law-court in order to shame those who follow Christ."[32] Leaders and all Christians alike can scarcely take this warning too seriously!

James 3:17 But the wisdom from above is first pure, then peaceful, gentle, willing to submit, full of mercy and good fruits, impartial, genuine (ἡ δὲ ἄνωθεν σοφία πρῶτον μὲν ἁγνή ἐστιν, ἔπειτα εἰρηνική, ἐπιεικής, εὐπειθής, μεστὴ ἐλέους καὶ καρπῶν ἀγαθῶν, ἀδιάκριτος, ἀνυπόκριτος). Finally, James returns to unpack the topic of true wisdom. He begins by emphasizing the origin of this wisdom, placing "from above" (ἄνωθεν) first and reversing his previously used word order (see v. 15). In contrast to the wisdom that originates within the bounds of this world or even in the minds of demons, the wisdom worth seeking comes from heaven. Gifts from God come "from above" (1:17).

There is some debate over the significance of the order of the subsequent adjectives, especially concerning the placement of "pure" (ἁγνή), but most believe that wisdom's attributes all follow from and are subsequent to that initial term of purity. The root of this word (ἁγνός) denotes ethical blamelessness, and "wisdom which is free from any stain or blemish would be incapable of producing anything evil."[33] Purity means both that one is "free of the moral and spiritual defects that are the marks of the double-minded,"[34] and that one is "unstained from the world" (cf. 1:27).[35] If "nothing which shows itself as half-good, half-bad, can be accounted wisdom,"[36] then wisdom must show itself as pure, unmixed with anything worldly or demonic. It remains singularly focused on God, without any tugs of loyalty elsewhere. One may be peaceful, gentle, full of mercy, and the like, but unless these character traits come from genuine Christian faith, they prove meaningless from the eternal perspective of God's kingdom.

The remaining characteristics of heavenly wisdom proceed from the principle of purity. These traits emerge as "moral purity ... expanded by means of a list of adjectives arranged to take advantage of assonance."[37] Assonance, the repetition of identical or similar vowel sounds in close proximity to one another, especially at the beginnings of words, seems to be the primary organizing principle for this list. A sequence of this sort would create a useful mnemonic tool, helping people remember all the various elements of wisdom.[38] Yet while James does arrange his attributes for

31. Barclay M. Newman Jr., ed., *A Concise Greek-English Dictionary of the New Testament* (New York: United Bible Societies, 1971), 192.

32. Wall, *Community of the Wise*, 187.

33. Moo, *The Letter of James: An Introduction and Commentary*, 135.

34. Martin, *James*, 133. Cf. Keenan, *Wisdom of James*, 118: pure "first from wavering discrimination and double-mindedness, and thus from instability."

35. Wall, *Community of the Wise*, 188.

36. Ropes, *A Critical and Exegetical Commentary on the Epistle of St. James*, 249.

37. Davids, *The Epistle of James*, 154.

38. Wall (*Community of the Wise*, 189) thus argues that the "function of this catalogue is primarily rhetorical and impressional."

aesthetic and rhetorical purposes, their theological significance is in no way diminished. A person who lived out this list "would indeed be inspired by God and be a binding force in the Christian community."[39] This true, heavenly wisdom is everything that the earthly "wisdom" was not, the complete antithesis of the self-seeking, self-serving attitudes of vv. 14 – 16. With purity as the prerequisite for the rest of the virtues, God's holiness is demonstrated as "heavenly wisdom [that] enters this sinful world but is not affected by it."[40]

The various adjectives do give James's audience a clear picture of the characteristics of wisdom. Besides being pure, wisdom ought to be "peaceful" (εἰρηνική), the opposite of the combative, false "wisdom," which is full of strife. True wisdom is also "gentle" (ἐπιεικής) — "considerate" (REB) or "lenient" (NAB). This quality "describes the kind of person who though wronged and possessing the 'right' not to bend nevertheless forgoes his right."[41] It is willing to submit (εὐπειθής), in contrast to the selfish ambition of wisdom from below. This term also conveys a person "open to reason" (ESV), "compliant" (HCSB), and "accommodating" (NET).[42] Like false wisdom, true wisdom is revealed by its results. But, instead of producing strife and evil actions, true wisdom proves full of mercy and good fruits.

Switching from words dominated by long e-sounds to those characterized by the a-sound. James also notes that true wisdom is "impartial" (ἀδιάκριτος), as in 2:4. He may also have the sense of "nonjudgmental" in mind, given his teaching in 4:11 – 12, still to come.[43] Finally, true wisdom utterly lacks any hypocrisy or double-mindedness but is rather entirely what it purports to be: "genuine" (ἀνυπόκριτος).[44] Motyer translates these concluding characteristics as "without uncertainty" and "without insincerity," noting that "the former word demands a firm commitment of mind and heart; the latter, an equally firm commitment to a matching life."[45] A believer consistently characterized by these virtues would truly impact the world for God's kingdom. On the parallels between these traits and Paul's fruit of the Spirit and their implications, see below, pp. 178 – 79.

James 3:18 And a harvest of righteousness is sown in peace among those making peace (καρπὸς δὲ δικαιοσύνης ἐν εἰρήνῃ σπείρεται τοῖς ποιοῦσιν εἰρήνην). The final verse of this passage sounds proverbial, thus leading some to question its connection with the preceding material. The initial conjunction (δέ), while possibly adversative ("but"), is more likely continuative ("and"), so that this proverb functions as the logical conclusion to the discussion of wisdom. Johnson argues that δέ suggests a slight contrast in that James "returns to the necessity of *acting* on the positive qualities associated with the wisdom from above," so that this verse does not add a further description of true wisdom, but adds the thought of its results to complete the picture.[46] Just as James provided a description of false wisdom (v. 14) and consid-

39. Davids, *The Epistle of James*, 155.

40. Kistemaker, *James and the Epistles of John*, 122.

41. Hughes, *James*, 158.

42. Culpepper ("The Power of Words," 415) contrasts "gentle" and "compliant," by observing that the former applies to "a position of strength" in which "the wise person is considerate of those who might otherwise be dominated or manipulated," while the latter applies to "a position of weakness" in which "the wise one is not stubborn but reasonable, yielding and obedient."

43. Baker and Ellsworth (*Preaching James*, 101) likewise see both senses: "'without a trace of partiality' is the antonym of... 'made distinctions' in 2:4. It means to not be judgmental or divisive.... It calls for actions that embrace other people without cultural, economic, or social prejudice."

44. Moffatt's *A New Translation of the Bible* renders these last two adjectives as "unambiguous" and "straightforward."

45. Motyer, *The Message of James*, 136.

46. Johnson, *The Letter of James*, 275.

ered its consequences (v. 16), so too here: first he portrays the traits of true wisdom (v. 17) and then depicts its results (v. 18).

Grammatically, the final dative expression (τοῖς ποιοῦσιν) is ambiguous, representing either a dative of agency ("by those making peace") or a dative of advantage ("for those making peace"). While some argue that a dative of advantage is more natural or that the dative of agency is redundant,[47] others defend the repetition as "emphatic tautology ... used for rhetorical effect."[48] These different nuances are difficult to bring out in translation, and, as Hiebert argues, "perhaps James deliberately left the construction unlimited by a preposition in order to leave room for both meanings. The fruit of righteousness is not only sown by the peacemakers, but they also enjoy the results of their work."[49] Thus, peacemakers "produce, in the atmosphere of peace they create, *the harvest* (fruit) *of righteousness*."[50] Especially when one thinks of "fruit" (καρπός) as the crop that is harvested, the expression "of righteousness" (δικαιοσύνης) more likely reflects an appositional genitive than one of source. The harvest *is* the righteous behavior that peacemakers facilitate.[51]

The centrality of peace in this verse creates another difficulty, however. The main subject seems to change from "wisdom" to "peace." It is true that the simple catchword link with "peaceful" (εἰρηνική) in v. 17 helps to explain the transition but, beyond that, "since the whole chapter has concerned those fighting, arguing, and disturbing the peace and unity of the community, this saying is hardly simply suggested by the catchword εἰρήνη-εἰρηνική, but rather forms a suitable conclusion underlining the main point."[52]

The farming image contrasts strongly with the earlier images of fire, instability, and chaos. "Peace is the idea that gathers together a number of disparate ideas that are at work in this passage, as the wisdom of God leads to the peace and wholeness God desires of and for us."[53] Throughout all of Scripture, the idea of peace centers on the idea of "wholeness," an idea that is "thoroughly Hebraic, meaning much more than a mere absence of disquiet. The prime notion is positive, embracing prosperity, contentment as well as security."[54] This concept of peace goes far beyond a shallow avoidance of problems and uncomfortable issues. Neither will wisdom "pursue peace at the expense of purity. It will not compromise with sin to maintain peace. But even when fighting against sin, it hungers for peace, yearning to heal all divisions by its wise counsel."[55] In essence, peace is the ultimate goal of wisdom, and wisdom only reaches its fullest potential in the midst of peace.

47. Cf. Laws, *The Epistle of James*, 165; Martin, *James*, 135.

48. Davids, *The Epistle of James*, 155. Cf. Moo, *The Letter of James: An Introduction and Commentary*, 137.

49. Hiebert, *The Epistle of James*, 237. Cf. Maier, *Der Brief des Jakobus*, 172. The NET may have both datives in mind with its rendering, "among those who make peace." A dative of sphere allows for both agency and advantage.

50. Moo, *The Letter of James: An Introduction and Commentary*, 137.

51. Cf. Hartin, *James*, 195.

52. Davids, *The Epistle of James*, 155.

53. Nystrom, *James*, 210.

54. Adamson, *The Epistle of James*, 157.

55. Hiebert, *The Epistle of James*, 234–35.

In Depth: Does Wisdom Equal the Spirit in James?

Readers familiar with Gal 5:22 – 23 can scarcely avoid thinking of Paul's "fruit of the Spirit" as they read James's description of wisdom from above. Paul lists "love, joy, peace, patience, kindness, goodness, faithfulness, gentleness and self-control." Only two of the actual Greek roots reappear in Jas 3:13 – 18—"peace" and "gentleness" (or "humility"), but the concepts closely overlap with the virtues James commends. What is more, James refers to the "fruit" (καρπός) of righteousness (v. 18), using the identical term that Paul does for the Spirit's fruit, and James contrasts his collection of positive character traits with their diametric opposites (the earthly, natural, and demonic wisdom), just as Paul juxtaposes his list of fruit with an equally detailed catalogue of the "acts of the sinful nature" (Gal 5:19 – 21).

Curiously, there is no unambiguous reference to the Holy Spirit anywhere in James. The two uses of "spirit" (πνεῦμα) in this letter come in 2:26, a clear reference to the human spirit giving life to the body, and in 4:5, where we will argue the human spirit is likewise in view (see below, pp. 190 – 92). Given that James's "wisdom from above" obviously comes from God in heaven, who regularly throughout Scripture mediates his gifts to humans by means of his Spirit, one can understand why commentators have wondered whether Wisdom personified might be James's equivalent to the divine Spirit.[56]

Old Testament and intertestamental wisdom literature developed in their understanding of the Holy Spirit, such that ancient views of God's *rûaḥ*, not always clearly personal, became more and more personified, then hypostatized (taking on a somewhat independent life as an entity distinct from God), and then increasingly linked with Wisdom, which underwent a similar development. In Pr 8 – 9, for example, based on the feminine gender of the Hebrew word (*ḥokmâ*), Wisdom appears metaphorically as a woman calling out to the townspeople in Israel to come and learn from her, while avoiding "Dame Folly," particularly with her attempts to seduce young men into houses of prostitution.

In the intertestamental literature, especially in Wisdom of Solomon and Sirach, Wisdom speaks more and more like a divine being herself, in language sometimes strikingly similar to that of Jesus two centuries later (most notably, cf. Sir 51:23 – 27 and Mt 11:27 – 30). In Lk 11:13, Jesus promises the Holy Spirit to those who ask the Father for him, a promise which Mt 7:11 generalizes to include all "good gifts." When Jas 1:5 commands believers to ask God for wis-

56. In the last half-century, this perspective is particularly associated with J. Andrew Kirk, "The Meaning of Wisdom in James: Examination of a Hypothesis," *NTS* 16 (1969 – 70): 24 – 38. Cf. esp. Davids, *The Epistle of James*, 55 – 56, 71 – 72, 152.

dom, and we hear an echo of the Jesus' tradition in the promise that it will be given to those people, the parallels between Wisdom and the Spirit become remarkably close.[57]

Still, no other passage in the NT ever suggests that Jesus' followers after Pentecost (Ac 2, when they received the permanent indwelling of the Spirit) ever had to or were even able to ask for the Spirit to come again. They might need to be repeatedly *filled* with, or fully empowered by, the Spirit (Eph 5:18; cf. Ac 2:4; 4:8, 31; 9:17; 13:9), but the Spirit always resided within them. James, however, does envision situations in which a believer might "lack" wisdom and thus need to ask for it from the "giving God" (1:5). If James does not fully equate Wisdom with the Spirit, he nevertheless appears to understand them in similar ways and probably would have agreed that the Spirit is the preeminent (and perhaps exclusive) dispenser of the Father's wisdom for Christian living.

All the more reason not to follow the pursuits of earthly or even demonic "wisdom"; one cannot simultaneously be a friend of God and of the world (4:4). If one ought not join the "members of Christ" (a believer's body parts) with a literal prostitute (1Co 6:15), one ought not prostitute (or adulterate) oneself metaphorically by coveting other sinful or wasteful pleasures (again, cf. Jas 4:4). If one does, he or she is linking the Spirit (as the source of heavenly wisdom) with "the world, the flesh, and the devil" in a similarly outrageous "mixed marriage"!

Theology in Application

All of the background to "wisdom" presented earlier (see pp. 61 – 63) informs 3:13 – 18 as well. Particularly significant is Job 28:28, which combines the classic refrain, "The fear of the Lord — that is wisdom" with "to shun evil is understanding" (cf. also Pr 1:7). Proverbs 15:33, like Sir 1:27 and 3:17, also contains combinations of concepts like wisdom and meekness or works and humility.[58] Of the teachings of Jesus, one thinks especially of Mt 11:29, which includes his affirmation that he is "gentle and humble in heart." Jealousy proved the undoing of certain Jewish leaders in Ac 5:17 and 13:45. The warning against arrogant boasting meshes with Jeremiah's call to boast only in the Lord (Jer 9:24).

By contrast, "wisdom from above" is described in language reminiscent of numerous passages in intertestamental wisdom literature (e.g., Wis 7:25; 9:4, 8; Sir 1:1; 24:3). Sowing a harvest of righteousness mirrors Jesus' seed parables — the sower, the seed growing secretly, the mustard seed, and the wheat and weeds — which,

57. See Kamell, "Wisdom in James," esp. 123 – 53.

58. Bauckham, *James*, 84.

along with their interpretations, dominate Mt 13 and Mk 4. The emphasis on peacemaking harks back to the beatitude that blesses the peacemakers (Mt 5:9). Even more closely parallel is Isa 32:17 — "The fruit of that righteousness will be peace; its effect will be quietness and confidence forever" (TNIV). Interestingly, both of the pictures we have of James's leadership in Acts show him striving to make peace between warring factions in the church — specifically, Paul and his supporters and the conservative Jewish Christians of Jerusalem (Ac 15:13 – 21; 21:18 – 25).[59]

Ironically, as access to information and knowledge continues to explode, most notably through the Internet, the prevalence of true wisdom seems to wane.[60] When writers had to pass the strict criteria of reputable publishers in order to see their works make it into print, the reading public could assume a measure of truth in much of what appeared. Now, when anyone can create a website and promulgate any fantasy as sober truth, it becomes increasingly hard to know whom and what to believe. Countless people around the world gullibly accept the fiction of *The Da Vinci Code* (or comparable works) about Christian origins without any research of their own, while rejecting (or remaining blithely unaware of) the painstaking demonstrations by historians and archaeologists of the accuracy of countless texts of Scripture![61]

Even scarcer are those who demonstrate true wisdom and understanding in a spirit of humility. Centuries ago, the Venerable Bede opined, "Someone who lives in a humble and wise way will give more evidence of his standing before God than any number of words could ever do."[62] Sadly, far more common are teachers (and other speakers) in Christian circles who are clearly full of themselves, above the critiques of others, and confident that they are always right, even with issues on which godly, Bible-believing Christians have never agreed. Such behavior fits James's description of the "wisdom" that is earthbound and demonic, not that which is heaven-sent.[63] Gerhard Maier summarizes well when he describes the "surprise" this passage contains: "One recognizes Christian wisdom from a person's mode of life. This means likewise *not* from his or her intelligence, rhetoric or relevance!"[64] Many congregations need to apply this when they choose their leaders, preferring at times the humble shepherd to the more charismatic orator.

The jealousy and selfish ambition of this "wisdom" from below suggests that it is characterized by "extreme and destructive individualism" that "always makes a pri-

59. Motyer, *The Message of James*, 135.

60. Tidball, *Wisdom from Heaven*, 54.

61. For the meticulous confirmation of huge numbers of details in the historical narratives of Scripture, see esp. Kenneth A. Kitchen, *On the Reliability of the Old Testament* (Grand Rapids: Eerdmans, 2003); *Gospel Perspectives*, 6 vols., ed. R. T. France, David Wenham, and Craig Blomberg (Eugene, OR: Wipf & Stock, repr. 2003 – 4); and Colin J. Hemer, *The Book of Acts in the Setting of Hellenistic History*, ed. Conrad Gempf (Tübingen: Mohr, 1989). For semipopular level summaries, cf. Walter C. Kaiser Jr., *The Old Testament Documents: Are They Reliable and Relevant?* (Downers Grove, IL: IVP, 2001); and Craig L. Blomberg, *The Historical Reliability of the Gospels* (Downers Grove, IL: IVP, rev. 2007).

62. Cited in Bray, *James, 1 – 2 Peter, 1 – 3 John, Jude*, 42.

63. Hubbard, *The Book of James*, 80.

64. Maier, *Der Brief des Jakobus*, 165 (translation ours; italics his).

ority of Number One and looks out for its own interests."[65] Four manifestations of this destructiveness particularly beset the teacher or scholar: arrogance, bitterness, fanaticism, and self-centered rivalry.[66] More generally, "there is a kind of person who is undoubtedly clever, with acute brain and skilful tongue; but his effect, nevertheless, in any committee, in any church, in any group, is to cause trouble and to disturb personal relationships. It is a sobering thing to remember that the wisdom he possesses is devilish rather than divine."[67] Until God's people recognize that Jesus' model for church discipline (Mt 18:15 – 18) applies to such individuals (Tit 3:10 – 11), effective ministry will be thwarted, good people will be needlessly hurt, and Satan and his minions will laugh and mock us from their spiritual strongholds.

The right approach focuses on purity and peace, in that order. Without the purity of God's people, peace proves relatively meaningless. In today's era of pluralism and relativism, we need to remember that we do "what is wise *first of all* because it is right."[68] But, as in Eph 4:15, we must speak and do what is true *in love*. One can carry out even the most unpleasant processes of church discipline in a calm, compassionate and rational spirit, whether or not the offending party behaves in kind.[69] And if "gentle" also means "lenient," then the wisdom from above applies God's laws by moderating "rigorous justice by sympathetic understanding or excusing of mitigating circumstances."[70] This idea possibly parallels the odd twist of 2:13 (after 2:1 – 4) — commanding impartiality and yet promising that mercy will triumph over justice.

Nystrom provides excellent examples of what peace does not look like in church life — when "tough love" is avoided[71] — while Glen Stassen's "Just Peacemaking" movement has demonstrated how proactive measures for establishing peace and reconciliation can accomplish much good in even some of the most intractable social and political settings.[72] On the smaller scale of intrachurch conflict, see especially Ken Sande's *The Peacemaker*, along with his Christian organization for mediating and arbitrating in such disputes.[73] Harold Songer aptly stresses that the righteous do not merely "keep the peace," which sometimes means failing to confront problems that should be addressed. Rather, they "make peace," which may mean temporarily disrupting a community in order to deal with root problems, so that genuine peace may ensue.[74]

65. Tidball, *Wisdom from Heaven*, 45.

66. Barclay, *The Letters of James and Peter*, 91 – 92.

67. Ibid., 94.

68. Stulac, *James*, 137.

69. Cf. Lea, *Hebrews and James*, 306.

70. Kugelman, *James and Jude*, 43.

71. Nystrom, *James*, 210 – 20.

72. Glen H. Stassen, *Just Peacemaking: Transforming Initiatives for Justice and Peace* (Louisville: WJKP, 1992); idem, *Just Peacemaking: Ten Practices for Abolishing War* (Cleveland: Pilgrim, 1998).

73. Subtitled *A Biblical Guide to Resolving Personal Conflict* (Grand Rapids: Baker, rev. 1997).

74. Harold S. Songer, "James," in *The Broadman Bible Commentary*, ed. Clifton J. Allen, vol. 12 (Nashville: Broadman, 1972), 126. This argument has been applied to the occasional need for just wars by entire nations also.

CHAPTER 8

James 4:1 – 12

Literary Context

These twelve verses further unfold the second main section of the letter body, which elucidates the theme of wisdom and speech. James 4:1 – 10 flows so naturally from 3:13 – 18 that some commentators keep the two subsections together as a single passage.[1] Having just warned against the evils that result from jealousy and rivalry (3:14, 16), James now points out what some in his churches have seemingly allowed those motives to produce — coveting and quarreling — which resemble devotion to this fallen world rather than to God (4:1 – 6). Vv. 7 – 10 offer the antidote: resist the devil (recall the link between the world and the devil in 3:15) and submit to God (as with those who exhibit wisdom from above, cf. 3:13, 17 – 18). Vv. 11 – 12 remind the reader that James has not lost sight of the key illustration of the kind of wisdom one manifests, namely, one's speech. Speaking against one another is a primary example of how people act on their selfish ambition. But just as it impugns those created in God's image and thus implicitly attacks God himself (3:9), it also opposes God's law that prohibits slander and false judgment, again critiquing the God who gave the law.[2]

Connections with still earlier material in James likewise appear. The "lusts" of 4:1 – 3 recall the evil desires of 1:14 – 15. The "warring" in one's "members" in 4:1 utilizes the identical term as in 3:5 – 6, in which the tongue proved so dangerous among the various parts of the body. The combination of murder and adultery in 4:2 and 4 echoes the pairing in 2:11 of the two commandments in the Decalogue that prohibit those actions. Becoming God's friend (4:4) reminds us of Abraham's

1. E.g., Johnson, *The Letter of James*, 267 – 90.

2. Where vv. 11 – 12 belong is perhaps the most difficult question involving the outlining of individual pericopes in the entire letter. Edgar (*Has God Not Chosen the Poor*? 197 – 209) makes 4:11 – 5:11 a major subsection, perceiving three eschatologically grounded warnings and related exhortations rising in intensity. Baker and Ellsworth (*Preaching James*, 118 – 36) link 4:11 – 5:6 together as three ways to snub God's sovereignty. Nystrom (*James*, 248 – 66) combines 4:11 – 12 with 13 – 17 as a subunit, addressing "two problems in the community." Brosend (*James and Jude*, 416 – 22) takes vv. 11 – 12 as an independent segment with connections forward and backward, while Townsend (*The Epistle of James*, 84) detects no connections with the immediate context of these two verses! But a majority of commentators assert that vv. 11 – 12 round out the discussion of speech before James moves on to two passages closely linked by the misuse of wealth (4:13 – 17 and 5:1 – 6).

similar commendation (2:23). The humble person who receives God's grace (4:6) parallels the "humiliated" of 1:10 who will be exalted, a thought repeated in even more parallel language in 4:10. Cleansing hands and hearts (4:8) applies the language of ritual purity to moral issues, just as 1:27 did when it enjoined keeping oneself unstained by the world. The command for the wicked to humble or humiliate themselves in repentance (4:9) employs the same concept (and a partially synonymous verb) as 1:10 when it predicts the eschatological humiliation of the unrepentant wicked.

The rebuke concerning improper judgment (4:11 – 12) employs the same κριν-word group as the censures against vacillation in 1:6 and discrimination in 2:4, like the virtue commended in 3:17 of being impartial and nonjudgmental. The declaration that there is only one lawgiver and judge (4:12a) applies the confession of monotheism, spelled out even more explicitly in 2:19, while the rhetorical question condemning judgmentalism (4:12b) applies the Levitical command to love one's "neighbor" (2:8).

Fewer parallels link this passage with what comes next; many thus see James as turning to a new topic in 4:13 – 17. But these verses clearly continue the theme of proper and improper speech by stressing what those planning for the future should and should not *say* (see vv. 13 and 15). The need to qualify one's prayers with the right attitude or motives (4:3) can be generalized to include leaving room for God's will to override ours for any reason (4:15). The arrogant boasting of 4:16 flows naturally from the improper motives of praying for possessions for merely selfish indulgence (4:3). Indeed, the rich oppressors of 5:1 – 6 demonstrate the extremes to which one can carry spending money just on oneself. James 5:6 further illustrates the likelihood of the murder in 4:2 being metaphorical. The patience James commands oppressed believers to exemplify in 5:7 – 11 roughly parallels the submission needed in 4:7 – 10. One more improper form of speech, finally, will be prohibited in 5:12 — the taking of oaths one is likely to break.

IV. The Three Themes Expanded (2:1 – 5:18)
- B. Wisdom and Speech (3:1 – 4:12)
  1. The Power of the Tongue (3:1 – 12)
  2. Wisdom from Above and Wisdom from Below (3:13 – 18)
  3. **The Misuse of Speech in Quarrels and Slander (4:1 – 12)**
     - **a. Friendship with the World (4:1 – 6)**
     - **b. Submission to God (4:7 – 10)**
     - **c. Speaking against Others (4:11 – 12)**
- C. Trials and Temptations (4:13 – 5:18)

Main Idea

Christians should reject strife and humbly submit to God in order to be his rather than the world's friends. A key test case for demonstrating this transformation involves how one speaks to and about other people.

Translation

James 4:1-12

1a	Question	**From where come the wars and from where come the fightings among you?**
b	Answer	**Is it not from this—from your passions** warring in your members?
2a	Assertion	**You desire** and **you do not have,**
b	Result (of 2a)	**[so] you murder**;
c	Restmnt. (of 2a)	and **you envy and are not able to obtain,**
d	Result (of 2c)	**[so] you fight and war.**
e	Restmnt. (of 2a)	**You do not have**
f	cause (of 2e)	because you do not ask.
3a	Expansion (of 2f)	**You ask and do not receive**
b	cause	because you ask wrongly,
c	purpose	so that you may spend on your pleasures.
4a	Rhetorical Q.	You adulterous people, **do you not know that**
	contrast	**friendship with the world is enmity with God?**
b	Condition (of 4c)	If someone therefore wishes to be a friend with the world,
c	resatement (of 4a)	**they establish themselves as an enemy of God.**
5a	Expansion (of 4a)	Or **do you think the Scripture says in vain that**
b	content	God jealously longs for the spirit
c	identification	that he made to live in us,
6a	contrast	but he gives a greater grace?
b	Restatement (of 5a)	Therefore **it says:**
c	restatement (of 5bc)	"God opposes the proud,
d	restatement (of 6a)	but he gives grace to the humble." (Pr 3:34)
7a	Inference	(1) **Submit (yourselves)** therefore **to God**;
b	contrast	(2) **resist the devil,**
c	result	and **he will flee from you.**
8a	Parallel (to 7a)	(3) **Draw near to God**
b	result	and **he will draw near to you.**
c	Grounds (of 7a,8a)	(4) **Cleanse your hands**, sinners,
d	parallel	and (5) **purify your hearts**, double-minded ones.

9a	Expansion (of 8cd)	(6) **Be miserable and** **mourn and** **weep.**
b	Restatement	(7) **Let your laughter be turned to sadness and** **your cheer into gloominess.**
10a	Restmnt. (of 7a)	(8) **Humble yourselves before the Lord**
b	result	**and he will lift you up.**
11a	Exhortation	**Do not speak against one another**, brothers and sisters.
b	Basis	**The one who speaks against a brother or sister or** **judges his/her brother or sister,** **speaks against the law and** **judges the law;**
c	condition (of 11d)	but if you judge the law,
d	result	**you are not a doer of the law** but a judge.
12a	Assertion	**There is one lawgiver and judge**
b	description	who is able to save and to destroy;
c	rhetorical Q.	but **who are you,**
d	description	who are judging your neighbor?

Structure

James 4:1 – 6 presents a key problem for those who would exhibit wisdom from above. They still fight with fellow Christians. How can this be? James raises and answers his own question — from the lustful desires that remain part of humanity's fallen nature, even after redemption (v. 1). These desires regularly attach themselves to what people do not already possess, leading to all kinds of quarrels — from verbal assaults to literal warfare (v. 2a-b). One reason many lack what they want is that they have not asked God in prayer (v. 2c). Alternately, they have asked him but with self-centered motives (v. 3). Such behavior resembles the characteristic behavior of the unredeemed, not the regenerate (v. 4)! If this sounds too harsh, James backs up his claim by paraphrasing (vv. 5 – 6a) and then quoting (vv. 6b-c) Scripture that supports him (Pr 3:34 LXX).

James then unleashes a staccato barrage of short commands, identifying the solution to these sinners' plight (vv. 7 – 10). Vv. 7a and 10a create an inclusio around this paragraph with his call that they submit and humble themselves before the Lord. With the first call, he promises that resistance to the devil will ensure his flight (v. 7b); with the final one, that God will exalt such an individual (v. 10b). In between, he unfolds what is involved in the submission and resistance of v. 7: drawing near to God with cleansed hands and hearts (changed actions and attitudes — v. 8). Then he anticipates his final command by explaining what the humbling oneself of v. 10 means: appropriate mourning for past sins (v. 9).

Vv. 11 – 12 conclude this passage. As in 3:1 – 12, James returns to specific sins of the tongue (vv. 11 – 12), as he forbids false or overly judgmental speech against others (v.11), which is another product of "wisdom" from below (3:14 – 16). For God alone is judge, and only he knows how to judge a person with complete truth (v. 12). Submitting to him in this role shows true wisdom from above.[3]

Exegetical Outline

IV. The Three Themes Expanded (2:1 – 5:18)

B. Wisdom and Speech (3:1 – 4:12)

➦ **3. The Misuse of Speech in Quarrels and Slander (4:1 – 12)**

a. Christians should reject strife as stemming from friendship with the world (vv. 1 – 6).
   i. The question raised and answered: Where does strife come from? From our evil natures (v. 1).
   ii. The behavior observed: Strife among Christians does not satisfy their desires (vv. 2 – 3).
   iii. The question and answer rephrased: Where does all this selfishness come from? From friendship with the world, which is incompatible with friendship with God (v. 4).
   iv. The appeal to Scripture: God does not want us to act this way and makes it possible for us not to act this way (vv. 5 – 6).

b. Christians should humbly submit to God in response to his friendship (vv. 7 – 10).
   i. The main point stated: Submit to God (v. 7a).
   ii. Three commands on how to do this (vv. 7b – 9).
   iii. The main point restated: Humble yourselves before God (v. 10).

c. Christians should reject slander as one particularly insidious manifestation of strife (vv. 11 – 12).
   i. Slandering fellow believers slanders God's law, which prohibits such action (v. 11a).
   ii. This usurps God's role as sole judge by placing believers in a position of judging God's law instead of obeying it (vv. 11b – 12).

3. At the same time, the "warnings in vv. 11 – 12 grow out of the rebuke of pride and the call for humility in vv. 7 – 10" (Lea, *Hebrews and James*, 322).

Explanation of Text

James 4:1 From where come the wars and from where come the fightings among you? Is it not from this — from your passions warring in your members? (Πόθεν πόλεμοι καὶ πόθεν μάχαι ἐν ὑμῖν; οὐκ ἐντεῦθεν, ἐκ τῶν ἡδονῶν ὑμῶν τῶν στρατευομένων ἐν τοῖς μέλεσιν ὑμῶν;). James begins this next section with another rhetorical question for his audience. In direct contrast to the previous discussion of peace in 3:18, he here addresses the infighting in his audience. Johnson sees this as the continuation of the preceding contrast between quarreling and peacemaking, following a Hellenistic *topos* or set-piece discussion of envy. As such, the question regarding wars and fightings "should be seen as one of the standard features of that *topos*, based less on the supposed activities of his readers than the logic of the argument."[4]

It seems odd, however, that James would expand a *topos* of this kind with no immediate relevance to his audience, and it is better to assume there were at least some arguments occurring in his congregations. Some commentators imagine literal violence, especially if James were writing in the early 60s as the Zealot movement was getting more organized.[5] But as in English, the Greek words for wars and fightings can be metaphorical as well. If this letter was written from the 40s, these terms almost certainly must be referring to quarrelling in the sense of verbal sparring and criticism. In this case, the theme of right and wrong speech continues to punctuate 3:1 – 4:12.

Continuing his monologue, James answers his own question with another one. The word for "not" (οὐκ) implies that he expects a positive answer: the quarrels *do* come from our passions. The combination of "from where?" and "from this" (πόθεν; ἐντεῦθεν) can more easily be translated with the older English terms "whence" and "hence" (KJV), for which we have no simple equivalents today. The word for "passion" (ἡδονή) is the source of the English word "hedonism," but in James's day it simply implied an intense pleasure or enjoyment (cf. REB "appetites"), though more and more it was coming to have connotations of lusts, especially involving improper sexual desires. The expression "warring in your members" could refer to internal strife within a person, external conflict between fellow Christians, or both.[6]

James 4:2 You desire and you do not have, [so] you murder; and you envy and are not able to obtain, [so] you fight and war. You do not have because you do not ask (ἐπιθυμεῖτε καὶ οὐκ ἔχετε, φονεύετε καὶ ζηλοῦτε καὶ οὐ δύνασθε ἐπιτυχεῖν, μάχεσθε καὶ πολεμεῖτε, οὐκ ἔχετε διὰ τὸ μὴ αἰτεῖσθαι ὑμᾶς). If James has not turned from treating internal tensions to external ones already in v. 1, he clearly does so now.[7] V. 2 begins to diagnose the squabblers' problems. The punctuation of this verse may be the most difficult exegetical problem. The NIV follows the UBS's punctuation most closely, translating, "You want something

4. Johnson, *The Letter of James*, 275 – 76.

5. See esp. Martin, *James*, 144. Cf. Michael J. Townsend, "James 4:1 – 4: A Warning against Zealotry?" *ExpTim* 87 (1975 – 76): 211 – 13.

6. The former is the usual interpretation, but, in support of the latter, see, e.g., Wall, *Community of the Wise*, 195. Barclay (*The Letters of James and Peter*, 98) explains how both could easily have come into play: "the feverish search for pleasure issues in long-drawn-out resentments which are like wars, and sudden explosions of enmity which are like battles." Similarly, Cargal, *Restoring the Diaspora*, 155. *Apoc. Elijah* 1:16 provides a particularly close parallel in the context of explaining the purpose of fasting: "Remember that from the time when he created the heavens, the Lord created the fast for a benefit to men on account of the passions and desires which fight against you so that the evil will not inflame you."

7. Perkins, *First and Second Peter, James, and Jude*, 123.

but don't get it. You kill and covet, but you cannot have what you want. You quarrel and fight." Meanwhile the NASB tries to smooth out a little of the text's abruptness in an understandable way: "You lust and do not have; so you commit murder. And you are envious and cannot obtain; so you fight and quarrel" (cf. also NRSV, TNIV).

Davids argues for the former translation because he perceives a chiastic structure when v. 3 is combined with this punctuation of v. 2: "you desire and you do not have" (v. 2a) matches "you ask and do not receive ..." (v. 3), while "you murder and envy and cannot obtain" (v. 2b) parallels "you fight and quarrel [and] do not have because you do not ask" (v. 2c).[8] But the conceptual break in vv. 2 – 3 comes between the statement of the problem and the reason for the problem, which splits Davids' third segment (v. 2c) right down the middle. Plus, for his understanding to flow smoothly, one must insert an "and" at this very seam, which in fact the text does not contain. The latter translation, therefore, is preferable. It meshes neatly with the flow of James's thought, especially in highlighting the consequences of our actions and desires. As Moo points out, a pattern that understands "the struggles that are wracking the community ... [as] the product of their envious desire to get what they don't have" fits better with James's overall teaching (cf. 3:14 – 16), as well as avoiding the problem of having "murder" appear in an anticlimactic position (before "envy," as in the NIV ["covet"]).[9] Laws argues that this verse instead points out the "serious and inevitable consequences" of envy.[10]

The term "desire" (ἐπιθυμέω) does not have to be negative, but, as with "passions" in v. 1, seems here to imply a strong and unhealthy craving to secure something not currently one's own. The term "murder" (φονεύω) proves more difficult, because there is not much evidence of a figurative meaning for this word. Yet James may use this harsh language to shock his audience, but at the same time echo Jesus' teaching in Mt 5:21 – 22 that to hate another person is to commit murder in one's heart (cf. also the vivid metaphorical language of Ps 59:6).[11]

James's first subsection in these verses may end after πολεμεῖτε, two-thirds of the way into v. 2, given the inclusio formed by and the chiasm contained in the repeated words "wars ... fightings ... fight ... war" (πόλεμοι ... μάχαι ... μάχεσθε ... πολεμεῖτε). Throughout these verses, the common theme is selfish desire and envy. In this way, James's thoughts hark back to 3:14 – 16 and the evil effects of a selfish focus. It is interesting that James uses the middle form of αἰτέω, which could well be intensive, in order to express the idea that "you don't have because you yourselves don't *really* ask."[12] It is possible again that James is echoing his brother's teaching in Mt 7:7 – 8 and expanding on the theme of asking. Jesus taught his followers

8. Davids, *The Epistle of James*, 157 – 58.

9. Moo, *The Letter of James*, 182; contra Martin (*James*, 146), who understands James as trying to counter a pattern of physical violence within the community.

10. Laws, *The Epistle of James*, 172.

11. The "wars" (πόλεμοι) of v. 1 are probably metaphorical, the "fightings" (στρατευομένων) certainly are, and in v. 4, "adulteresses" (μοιχαλίδες) are also metaphorical. Thus it seems reasonable to see James's language here as that of strong metaphor to make a point. Andria ("James," 1514) sees James as "exaggerating" to stress "the gravity of the situation." Johnson (*The Letter of James*, 277) points to the Hellenistic *topos* of envy where murder is the logical conclusion of envy (see also his article, "James 3:13 – 4:10 and the *Topos* Περὶ Φθόνου"). On the other hand, *1 Clement* 4:7 gives a clear example wherein "jealousy and envy" (ζῆλος καὶ φθόνος) did lead to fratricide (ἀδελφοκτονίαν) in the case of Cain and Abel, hence this language does not necessarily have to be figurative or exaggerated. The precedent for this sort of behavior was set from the beginning of the Hebrew Bible.

12. Cf. Hiebert, *James*, 248, n. 28. Most commentators, however, see the alternation from middle to active to middle forms of this verb in vv. 2 – 3 as merely stylistic.

that those who asked from God would receive, and it seems reasonable to envision that twenty years later some are upset because they are not obtaining what they want. First, James reminds them, they need to *ask* in order to receive![13] Moreover, the present tense of the verb may suggest that at times they must ask continuously or persistently. We may often need to persevere in our prayer in order to receive (cf. Lk. 18:1 – 8).

James 4:3 You ask and do not receive because you ask wrongly, so that you may spend on your pleasures (αἰτεῖτε καὶ οὐ λαμβάνετε διότι κακῶς αἰτεῖσθε, ἵνα ἐν ταῖς ἡδοναῖς ὑμῶν δαπανήσητε). Some in James's audience, however, might argue in reply that they *have* been praying and asking and they still have not received what they asked for. Thus James continues to expand on this theme. In this verse he gives another reason for unanswered prayer. Here the issue involves evil motives — asking "wrongly" (κακῶς). James makes another interesting switch in voice from active (αἰτεῖτε) to middle (αἰτεῖσθε), possibly in order to draw out the selfishness involved in their requests. They do not pray altruistically, but rather pray emphatically (intensively) but wrongly for their own wants and desires.[14]

James's explanatory purpose clause makes this tension explicit. They are apparently asking for material "things" so that they can spend their money and flaunt their possessions. James makes it clear that believers ought *not* to be asking for selfish gain and that God does not honor those requests. How dramatically this verse contrasts with the so-called "health and wealth" gospel! The evil in James's audience's asking is evident, because "the gift-giving God is here manipulated as a kind of vending machine precisely for the purpose of self-gratification."[15]

James 4:4 You adulterous people, do you not know that friendship with the world is enmity with God? If someone therefore wishes to be a friend of the world, they establish themselves as an enemy of God (μοιχαλίδες, οὐκ οἴδατε ὅτι ἡ φιλία τοῦ κόσμου ἔχθρα τοῦ θεοῦ ἐστιν; ὃς ἐὰν οὖν βουληθῇ φίλος εἶναι τοῦ κόσμου, ἐχθρὸς τοῦ θεοῦ καθίσταται). At this point the issue comes to a head. James brands those in his churches who are behaving so selfishly with the intentionally insulting term "adulteresses," invoking language from OT prophetic literature in which Israel and Judah were likened to adulteresses flaunting themselves in relationships with idols while claiming to worship God.[16] While the feminine term sounds odd when referring to men and women together in a group,[17] in keeping with biblical tradition James personifies the entire church as the "bride" of Yahweh or Christ. At best she has become distracted from and at worst unfaithful to her groom.

13. This failure to ask the correct source of gifts could indicate a faulty theology of God, one that James has already addressed in 1:5 – 7, 16 – 17. Moo's hypothesis (*The Letter of James*, 184), suggesting that what they desire and do not have is the "kind of wisdom that will enable them to gain recognition as leaders in the community," proves interesting, but it is not the most straightforward reading of the text (esp. given v. 3).

14. Hiebert, *The Epistle of James*, 248. Cf. also Robertson (*Grammar of the Greek New Testament*, 805). But, as noted above, most commentators see only stylistic variation.

15. Johnson, *The Letter of James*, 278.

16. See Moo (*The Letter of James*, 187) for a lengthy list of examples and texts from the OT.

17. Here the textual variant is clearly an attempt to deal with the feminine "adulteresses" (μοιχαλίδες), by substituting the combination of masculine and feminine terms. While there is precedent for James using both a masculine and feminine term when addressing his audience (recall 2:15), here the pairing clearly forms the easier reading evidently inserted to clarify a feminine plural term being used to address a mixed audience of both men and women. The feminine plural vocative μοιχαλίδες is a common Septuagintalism. The external evidence likewise supports the {A} rating, because ℵ*, A, and B all agree on this reading.

"The world" (τοῦ κόσμου) and "God" (τοῦ θεοῦ) are objective genitives, following the active nouns "friendship" (φιλία) and "enmity" (ἔχθρα). Friendship in antiquity was usually taken far more seriously than in today's Western world, as a lifelong pact between people with shared values and loyalties.[18] The expression "friend ... of the world" (φίλος ... τοῦ κόσμου) explains the metaphorical adultery. The audience has the wrong object for a lover — the fallen world system and values of the unregenerate.[19] Perhaps the closest parallel to this image appears in 1Jn 2:15, which forbids us to love the world. Friendship in James's day indicated identification to and relationship with something or someone, so to be friends with the world means to identify with its standards and priorities.[20] Motyer warns that we must not think "we can live in intimate fellowship with [God] when the set of our hearts (*whoever wishes*) is towards *the world*."[21] Rather, such people "establish themselves" (καθίσταται — as in 3:6) as God's enemies.[22] This contrast between friendship with the world and with God arguably is the theme of the entire letter; Johnson has shown how every other major topic can be subsumed under it.[23]

James 4:5 – 6a Or do you think the Scripture says in vain that God jealously longs for the spirit that he made to live in us, but he gives a greater grace? (ἢ δοκεῖτε ὅτι κενῶς ἡ γραφὴ λέγει, Πρὸς φθόνον ἐπιποθεῖ τὸ πνεῦμα ὃ κατῴκισεν ἐν ἡμῖν, μείζονα δὲ δίδωσιν χάριν;). In order to support his invective in vv. 1 – 4, James turns to Scripture. Most assume that the "quotation" extends only to the end of v. 5. But there is no OT passage that closely parallels v. 5b. A minority of commentators, therefore, have translated "Scripture" (γραφή) as merely "writing";[24] but with the overwhelming frequency of the term in the NT meaning what we call the OT and with the verb "says" repeated in the middle of v. 6 in a similar formula introducing what is unequivocally Scripture, this solution seems much less likely. The UBS cites Ex 20:5 as a possible parallel, which states that God is "a jealous God" (cf. also Ex 34:14; Zec 8:2), so Jas 4:5 could reflect an expanded paraphrase of sorts.

A few scholars have detached v. 5a from 5b, creating two separate sentences: "Or do you think the Scripture speaks in vain [referring back to the teaching of v. 4]? The Spirit tends toward envy ... [or however this clause is rendered]."[25] Yet after "the Scripture says," we expect to discover the contents of that reference. And without this, v. 5b follows on from v. 5a with no obvious logical connection. Laws thus suggests that v. 5b forms a parallel question, also requiring a negative answer:

18. See esp. John T. Fitzgerald, ed., *Friendship, Flattery, and Frankness of Speech: Studies on Friendship in the New Testament World* (Leiden: Brill, 1996). On the importance of harmony among friends, especially in group settings, see Donald J. Verseput, "Plutarch of Chaeronea and the Epistle of James on Communal Behaviour," 502 – 18.

19. Cf. Luke T. Johnson, "Friendship with the World/Friendship with God: A Study of Discipleship in James," in *Discipleship in the New Testament*, ed. Fernando F. Segovia (Philadelphia: Fortress, 1985), 173.

20. Cf. Church, "James," 386.

21. Motyer, *The Message of James*, 147.

22. Cf. REB "makes himself." But the word's root carries the stronger sense of the NJB's "constituted." Johnson ("Friendship with the World/Friendship with God," 171) suggests "establish."

23. Ibid., 176 – 83.

24. Some (e.g., Kugelman, *James and Jude*, 49; Tsuji, *Glaube zwischen Vollkommenheit und Verweltlichung*, 84 – 85) take γραφή as extrabiblical "writing," recalling how Jude quotes or alludes to pseudepigraphal texts, but no text noticeably close to this one has ever been discovered. Also, just as Jn 7:38 refers to a cluster of OT themes with possible snippets of various texts under the rubric of γραφή, it is possible that James is alluding to a recurring scriptural theme without having any one specific text in mind. Cf. also 1Co 2:9 and Eph 5:14 (Barton, Veerman, and Wilson, *James*, 97).

25. E.g., Hiebert, *The Epistle of James*, 253 – 56.

"Is the human spirit's longing directed by envy?"[26] But this approach has the added weaknesses that (1) nothing in the grammar of v. 5b suggests it should be punctuated as a question, and (2) the more obvious answer to this question would be "yes," not "no"!

Perhaps, then, we should take "spirit" (πνεῦμα) as God's Spirit and translate 5b as "does the Spirit which he caused to live in us long enviously?" with the implied answer negative.[27] Johnson resolves the problem with taking v. 5a as a question by viewing it as a statement introducing v. 6b, with vv. 5b – 6a as an intervening parenthesis with question and statement.[28] But the other problems with Laws' approach bedevil Johnson's interpretation, too, and no references to "Scripture says" elsewhere in the NT are this far separated from the passages they introduce.

The majority of commentators, therefore, understand v. 5b to reflect the quotation of "Scripture," however allusive (and elusive)! There are then three main translations suggested: (1) "the spirit he caused to live in us envies intensely"; (2) "the Spirit he caused to live in us longs jealously"; and (3) "God jealously longs for the spirit he made to live in us."[29] While (1) fits with the jealousy discussed in vv. 1 – 2, given that the immediate context is the hostility between God and the world, the latter two options seem stronger. Besides, even if some writing could be found that taught (1),[30] how might someone imagine this "writing" (or Scripture) to speak in vain?

While some reject an interpretation that has either God or the Holy Spirit described as "jealous," the background of God's jealousy in Ex 20:5 makes it possible here to apply a normally negative term ("envy" — φθόνος) to a holy God. "Longs" (ἐπιποθεῖ), after all, often refers to a strong desire that is not necessarily evil. A God who is jealous in such a way as to consume his people with fire, burning in anger against them and bringing disaster on them when they rebel against him (cf. Dt 4:24; Jos 24:19; Isa 26:11; Ez 16:42), can surely be said to long enviously for their spirits to return to him.[31]

While the choice of either (2) or (3) preserves the larger narrative flow of the passage, it seems more within James's style that God would be the subject of the sentence. James has not directly alluded to the Holy Spirit yet in his epistle, so his

26. Laws, *The Epistle of James*, 178 – 79; for more detail, see her earlier, "Does the Scripture Speak in Vain? A Reconsideration of James iv.5," *NTS* 20 (1973): 210 – 15. More recently, cf. Isaacs, *Hebrews and James*, 227.

27. P. Thomson, "James iv. 5," *ExpTim* 29 (1917 – 18): 240. Cf. the 1881 edition of the RV. Thomson was simplifying a suggestion of A. Haire Forster ("James iv. 5, 6," *ExpTim* 29 [1917 – 18]: 139) that required the addition of an "or" into the text.

28. Johnson, *The Letter of James*, 280 – 82; Sleeper, *James*, 109.

29. See Moo (*The Letter of James*, 188 – 90) for an extensive discussion of the exegetical issues and options surrounding this half-verse, with evidence supporting the claims we make here. He ultimately defends the same approach as we do (but not with respect to where the quotation ends).

30. See esp. the argument in Richard Bauckham, "The Spirit of God in Us Loathes Envy: James 4:5," in *The Holy Spirit and Christian Origins*, ed. Graham N. Stanton, Bruce W. Longenecker, and Stephen C. Barton (Grand Rapids: Eerdmans, 2004), 270 – 81. Bauckham composes a possible underlying Hebrew source for the quotation with a verb that could mean "abhor" as well as "long for," notes numerous parallels between James and what we know from quotations in other ancient literature of the contents of the lost book of Eldad and Medad (cf. Nu 11:25 – 30), and imagines a possible reference gleaned from this "writing" (γραφή) (as *1 Clement* also calls it), which would speak of the Holy Spirit abhorring the kind of envy illustrated in the Numbers passage and presumably elaborated in the lost book. But one cannot easily come to this conclusion via the *Greek* text of James, nor does Bauckham respond to the strongest arguments in favor of the consensus view or interact with Carpenter (see below, 192) at all.

31. Burchard, *Der Jakobusbrief*, 173. Robertson (*Greek Grammar of the New Testament*, 626) translates this controversial expression (πρὸς φθόνον) as "jealously."

sudden appearance might be questioned, while God must be the subject of "caused to live,"[32] so it is most natural if he remains the subject throughout the half-verse. This understanding also fits with the beginning of v. 6, where God is again the implied subject. In this event, it seems better to understand "spirit" (πνεῦμα) as the human spirit, for James just finished calling his audience "adulteresses" in their relationship with God and is not likely to be thinking of the Holy Spirit living in them at this point. Option (3) thus remains best, and Spicq consequently translates these three words (πρὸς φθόνον ἐπιποθεῖ) as "loves intensely and exclusively."[33]

But we are still left with the odd "quotation." Granted that numerous OT texts call God jealous, is there any way to account for the specific reference to the spirit he caused to live within us?[34] Craig Carpenter has suggested an intriguing approach that we believe merits further consideration. What if the quotation beginning in v. 5b extends all the way through v. 6a (cf. the UBS placement of the question mark only after "but he gives greater grace")? Clearly v. 6a sounds like Scripture; it closely mirrors the second line of the text of Pr 3:34 quoted in the second half of this same verse. Three of the four Greek words are identical to the LXX — "but he gives grace" (δὲ δίδωσιν χάριν). The first line of the proverb in v. 6b in fact conceptually resembles v. 5b. "God opposes the proud," precisely because he jealously longs for our human spirits to turn to him. Perhaps vv. 5b – 6a *together* represent the Scripture that does not speak in vain, because they paraphrase the very passage from Proverbs that James then cites explicitly in v. 6b.[35] And those who have thought that this Scripture spoke in vain — to no effect — will discover one day that God's resistance to them has proved unthwartable. But no interpretation is free from problems, so preachers and teachers should beware of making any major point in a message dependent on the unique form of any one of the approaches to vv. 5b – 6a presented here.

James 4:6b-d Therefore it says: "God opposes the proud, but gives grace to the humble" (διὸ λέγει, Ὁ θεὸς ὑπερηφάνοις ἀντιτάσσεται, ταπεινοῖς δὲ δίδωσιν χάριν). On any interpretation of the previous verse and a half, James now moves to cite an unambiguous text of Scripture, Pr 3:34, in the form found in the LXX. Here he clarifies who receives God's grace — the humble, those who remain faithful in their dependence on him rather than on self or any other false gods. Here again we see the image of God as the good giver, which James has consistently brought before his audience. Instead of wanting the things of the world, we should remember, even while living in this world, that God gives the gifts that are truly worth having.

The first dative substantive, "proud" (ὑπερηφάνοις), functions as the direct object of "opposes" (ἀντιτάσσεται). The second one, "humble" (ταπεινοῖς), represents the more common dative of indirect object (or one of its subcategories, a dative of advantage). As earlier in 1:9, ταπεινοῖς suggests a social as well as spiritual condition, not just "humble" but "humiliated" — by poverty, oppression, and the like. God gives his gifts only to

32. The textual issue here primarily surrounds two verbs that would have sounded almost alike. The UBS choice, "made to live" (κατῴκισεν), is a causative and has the support of 𝔓[74], ℵ, B, and Ψ; while the second option, "lived" (κατῴκησεν), is intransitive and has little early manuscript support. The third option is just a spelling variant of the second.

33. C. Spicq, "Ἐπιποθεῖν, desirer ou chérir?" *RB* 64 (1957): 184 – 95.

34. Some commentators simply give up and assume that James has garbled his source material at this point. So, e.g., Wiard Popkes, "The Composition of James and Intertextuality: An Exercise in Methodology," *ST* 51 (1997): 99 – 103.

35. See Craig B. Carpenter, "James 4.5 Reconsidered," *NTS* 47 (2001): 189 – 205, esp. 199 – 203.

those who are humble, or humbled, enough both to ask for and to receive them. But, James states, his grace is "greater" (v. 6a). Because it is not clear what kind of comparison is in view, this may be a case of the comparative form used for the positive ("great"). As Guthrie suggests, "the grace God gives is ... 'extraordinary.'"[36]

James 4:7 Submit (yourselves) therefore to God; resist the devil, and he will flee from you (ὑποτάγητε οὖν τῷ θεῷ, ἀντίστητε δὲ τῷ διαβόλῳ καὶ φεύξεται ἀφ' ὑμῶν). James now turns explicitly to the remedy for friendship with the world. The initial command to submit follows closely on the idea of God supporting the humble, as the "therefore" (οὖν) indicates.[37] A willingness to submit to authority shows one's humility as genuine. Here the verb ὑποτάγητε, though passive in form, most likely means to allow oneself voluntarily to become subject (i.e., to "be subjected" by God), thus virtually equivalent to a reflexive middle.[38] While "submit" is a loaded term in our culture, here perhaps the best understanding would be the image of ordering our lives under God's authority and will.[39] The commands he has promulgated we must obey.

Conversely, James orders his followers to "resist the devil," an interesting command in light of his other injunctions on *fleeing* temptations.[40] One must note the contrast, however, in that while we are commanded to resist the devil, we are not told to remain in the place where his temptations prove strongest in order to fight them (though, as with Jesus himself in the wilderness and in Gethsemane, at times there may be no God-pleasing alternative). Often we must run away, either literally or metaphorically. In other situations, we must simply live morally in the midst of immorality.[41] Together, the two halves of v. 7 provide the two complementary means of resisting the devil, because submission to God is itself an act of resistance to the devil. As James already spelled out in v. 4 by calling his audience "adulteresses," submission to God and allegiance to the devil are mutually exclusive. Moreover, as people align their lives with God, the result becomes a growing resistance to the temptations of the devil and he loses any foothold and must flee.[42]

There are two principles, however, that this verse does not imply. First, it does not indicate that if we resist the devil by pure thoughts and actions our lives will then be smooth, because the devil will leave us entirely alone after he has fled from us. It does promise, however, that if we resist him, he will have no true power over us, that is, over our

36. Guthrie, "James," 255.

37. Davids (*The Epistle of James*, 165) argues that "the οὖν clearly shows that these imperatives (10 in all in 4:7 – 10) are an expansion of the Pr. 3:34 quotation and the previous parenesis." Laws (*The Epistle of James*, 180 – 81) disagrees and finds a merely tangential relationship between the two sections but, both conceptually and grammatically, Davids' position proves the stronger. Moo (*The Letter of James*, 192) concurs, arguing from the verbal links of the root *tapein-* which "effectively ties the series of commands to the promise of grace in the quotation of v. 6."

38. Cf. Hiebert, *The Epistle of James*, 261, 265.

39. Cf. Moo, *The Letter of James*, 192: "to *submit* to God means to place ourselves under his lordship, and therefore to commit ourselves to obey him in all things."

40. While the verbs are different, Martin (*James*, 152) points out the conceptual parallel between God's attitude toward the proud in v. 6a and our attitude towards Satan. Baker ("James," 91) argues that "the second command, 'Resist the devil,' is the necessary complement to the idea of submitting to God. Just as friendship with God and the world are mutually exclusive, so withstanding the onslaughts of Satan is the flipside to pledging loyalty to God."

41. Keener (*The IVP Bible Background Commentary*, 699) notes that "ancient magical texts spoke of demons' fleeing before incantations, but the idea here is moral, not magical." One recalls similar concepts in Eph 6:10 – 20.

42. The second half of v. 7 also provides a good example of the conditional use of the imperative. "Resist the devil and he will flee from you" is semantically equivalent to "If you resist the devil — and you should — then he will flee from you" (Wallace, *Greek Grammar beyond the Basics*, 491).

souls (cf. 1 Jn 4:4). Second, James is not issuing a rallying cry for believers to be engaged in dramatic spiritual warfare on every front. While there are definitely times and places for intense, concerted prayer against the enemy and even for casting out demons, some people take this verse to imply that they ought to fight Satan's dominion in their lives over the slightest headache. If we truly submit to God, he will make clear when we need to use direct rebukes or exorcistic activity against the powers of darkness. More often than not, we should "merely" flee or leave a temptation-producing situation. In either event, God promises us the ability to bear up under the devil's wiles without yielding to them (1Co 10:13).

James 4:8 Draw near to God and he will draw near to you. Cleanse your hands, sinners, and purify your hearts, double-minded ones (ἐγγίσατε τῷ θεῷ καὶ ἐγγιεῖ ὑμῖν. καθαρίσατε χεῖρας, ἁμαρτωλοί, καὶ ἁγνίσατε καρδίας, δίψυχοι). James continues unleashing his barrage of commands. The first half of v. 8 mirrors v. 7b in form, but communicates the obverse of its contents. Instead of commanding resistance to the devil and guaranteeing his flight, James calls for movement toward God and promises that God will reciprocate. He uses the same verb, "draw near" (ἐγγίζω), to indicate both our actions and God's response. But "drawing near" to God is not just a mental or emotional activity for James. Instead, it is a practical response to God: controlling one's tongue (1:19, 26; 3:2), caring for the poor (1:27; 2:16 – 17), growing in wisdom and peace (1:5; 3:16 – 18), and communing with him in prayer (4:2 – 3, 15; 5:13 – 18).[43] The more we seek to live according to God's wisdom, the closer we will grow to his purity and holiness.[44] As we cultivate his heart in ourselves, we will automatically begin to see the world through God's eyes and be humble. As James has already shown, God gives grace to the humble; therefore, he will give strength and "be near" to those who live thus.[45]

To reinforce the practical nature of "drawing near to God," James adds a call based in OT imagery of cleansing and purifying, originally from Israelite cultic practice. But James takes these terms of ritual purity and transposes them into a moral context. Baker points out that these two commands indicate both the "external changes" and the "internal cleanup that is required" in a repentant sinner.[46] James no longer calls his audience by the usual endearing "brothers and sisters" (ἀδελφοί); instead, he calls them "sinners" and "double-minded." We first saw the latter term (δίψυχοι), a word perhaps of James's creation, in 1:8. Here its meaning is broadened to refer to the two-natured person of 4:4.[47]

It is interesting to note that James now uses it in conjunction with the idea of purifying one's heart. Purity applies to that which is unmixed, untainted, and single in its devotion and actions (cf. 3:17). In calling people to purify their hearts, James calls them to remove everything from their thoughts

43. Hughes, *James*, 187.

44. Indeed, living in God's presence is our first act of obeying the call to submission in v. 7 (Motyer, *The Message of James*, 152).

45. Martin (*James*, 153) suggests that "though ἐγγίσατε is a command it may well be that James assumes that if one resists the devil then *eo ipso* [i.e., inevitably] one comes near to God. Such thinking is consistent with his 'either/or' disjunction in vv 4 – 6."

46. Baker, "James," 91.

47. Porter ("Is *Dipsuchos* [James 1,8; 4,8] a 'Christian' Word?" 474) argues that the two uses in 1:8 and 4:8 are the original uses of this term, seeing the "author of the book of James as a creative user of the Greek language, probably himself inventing a lexical item to express a concept he wished to grammaticalize in a single lexical form, which had subsequent widespread though exclusive use within a Christian linguistic environment," thus creating a specifically "Christian" term.

and actions that show them not single-mindedly pursuing God and his will in the world. The REB appropriately translates "double-minded" (δίψυχοι) as "you whose motives are mixed," while Hughes observes that the antidote introduced here for such dual allegiance is repentance.[48]

James 4:9 Be miserable and mourn and weep. Let your laughter be turned to sadness and your cheer into gloominess (ταλαιπωρήσατε καὶ πενθήσατε καὶ κλαύσατε. ὁ γέλως ὑμῶν εἰς πένθος μετατραπήτω καὶ ἡ χαρὰ εἰς κατήφειαν). James next calls his listeners to make a public display of this repentance from their double-mindedness. Instead of taking pride in themselves, which led to fighting and competition for leadership, they should mourn that their arrogance has led to such debasement.[49] James speaks with a prophetic voice, ordering them to move beyond merely correct outward actions to appropriate heart attitudes of sorrow for their willful, wicked behavior.[50] He instructs them to cease their laughter and joy; this must become a time of remorse and regret over sin.[51] The NJB nicely captures the sense: "Appreciate your wretchedness and weep for it in misery."

James does not claim that there are never times for joy, but he maintains that *this* is the time for repentance, a "reaction ... for purposes of restoration. Those who follow such a path will be qualified to laugh and rejoice" at the time of the eschatological reversals.[52] Once we realize the grievous nature of our sins, we ought to "be upset and show it when we realize just how far away we let ourselves get from God," crying "at the horror of" our sins.[53]

James 4:10 Humble yourselves before the Lord and he will lift you up (ταπεινώθητε ἐνώπιον κυρίου καὶ ὑψώσει ὑμᾶς). Finally, we reach the conclusion of the discussion of humility versus pride, started back in 3:14, as James rephrases his call for submission and God's promise of exaltation. It is not for us to compete for position for the sake of our own selfish ambition; instead, it is for God to exalt as he wills. The theme of humility here proves essential to James's thought: God gives grace to us when we are humiliated and exalts us, but we in turn are asked to humble ourselves. Having introduced this theme due to the arguments and rivalry occurring in his churches (recall 3:14 and 4:1 – 2), James concludes it with humility as his answer to these problems. People who are humble do not seek their own "rights" to positions of leadership, but allow God to encourage and lift them up as he sees fit. Thus, humility comprises an essential attribute for community.

In contrast with pride and selfish ambition in the church, "only self-abasement and repentance is needed to gain the true exaltation which comes not from the world, but from God (cf. 1:9 – 11)."[54]

48. Hughes, *James*, 188.

49. Moo (*The Letter of James*, 195) explains: "A carefree, 'devil-may-care' attitude is typical of those who are 'friends with the world.' They live a hedonistic philosophy ... but even the committed Christian can slip into a casual attitude toward sin, perhaps presuming too much on God's forgiving and merciful nature. James's words in this passage directly counter any such attitude. He wants us to see sin for what it is." Sir 34:31 provides an apt warning: "If one fasts for his or her sins and goes and does the same things, who will listen to their prayer? And what has that one gained by humbling himself?" Just as James urges, repentance without changed behavior does not bring one closer to God; true repentance is revealed by one's works.

50. See Martin (*James*, 154) for comparisons with other prophetic texts.

51. "Laughter seems to describe the loud gaiety of worldly people. Their frivolity will become gloomy when they recognize their foolish choices. Laughter and joy are not evil. However, the particular moments when we meet God as sinners demand a serious repentance rather than hilarious celebration" (Lea, *Hebrews and James*, 322).

52. Martin, *James*, 155.

53. Baker, "James," 92.

54. Davids, *The Epistle of James*, 168. Cf. esp. Lk 18:9 – 14.

"Humility is not passivity, but receptivity. It is certainly not groveling before God or others; it is simply accepting truth, learning from every situation, growing in simplicity and in wisdom."[55] As throughout the Bible, God's people must work hard to please him, but by his great grace (recall v. 6) that work accomplishes something of eternal value.[56] James has now completed his inclusio, begun in v. 7 (see above, pp. 184–85).[57]

James 4:11 Do not speak against one another, brothers and sisters. The one who speaks against a brother or sister or judges his/her brother or sister, speaks against the law and judges the law; but if you judge the law, you are not a doer of the law but a judge (μὴ καταλαλεῖτε ἀλλήλων, ἀδελφοί. ὁ καταλαλῶν ἀδελφοῦ ἢ κρίνων τὸν ἀδελφὸν αὐτοῦ καταλαλεῖ νόμου καὶ κρίνει νόμον· εἰ δὲ νόμον κρίνεις, οὐκ εἶ ποιητὴς νόμου ἀλλὰ κριτής).[58] Here a slight jump in thought occurs, in some ways paralleling the partiality discussion in 2:1 – 13. James returns to specific sins of speech, suggesting that he is still following the train of thought he began in 3:1 rather than a more general discussion of law-keeping. The verb "speak against" (καταλαλέω) can sound overtones of unjustified speech against someone (hence NIV "slander"), and it can parallel the more negative meanings of "judge" (κρίνω — such as "condemn;" cf. NJB). But it may also refer to broader oral mistreatment, including "destructive verbal attacks, gossip behind another person's back and false accusations."[59] Thus various other translations include "criticize" (NLT), "speak evil against" (NRSV, ESV), "malign" (Berkeley), "disparage" (TCNT), and "backbite" (Tyndale).[60] This command against speaking evil of another has ample precedent in earlier Jewish texts.[61] Leviticus 19:16 explicitly prohibits slander, while v. 18 on neighbor-love (see Mt 19:19) may well be the most central law that is broken when we judge one another.[62]

Conceptually, how does slandering or condemning others show that we judge the law? Most likely the implication is that by choosing to ignore various commands in the law, especially the law of neighbor love for which James has a deep concern, we put ourselves into the position of deciding which of them we really think ought to be obeyed, rather than allowing the law to shape our lives. "Such a person ... sets himself 'outside' and 'above' the law."[63] This verse also indicates a deeper problem in that "the one who judges another member of the community can hardly be said to have humbled him- or herself or to have drawn near to God, the 'one' who is able to save."[64] The fact that

55. McDonnell, *Catholic Epistles and Hebrews*, 30 – 31.

56. Cf. Evans, "James," 778: "Because God 'gives all the more grace,' the devil can be defeated. Will power is involved, the believer must actively resist, but God's grace makes successful resistance possible."

57. See Davids, *The Epistle of James*, 165; Martin, *James*, 152.

58. Baker ("James," 93) gives a lengthy list of texts that forbid Christian judging. He also makes the important distinction between critiques done out of love to help us grow and the criticism "done out of spite, anger, arrogance, and disdain. The intent is to hurt someone, with words substituting for an actual weapon" (94). The former is done from godly concern, the latter from sinful pride.

59. Stulac, *James*, 152.

60. "Face-to-face rebuke was necessary at times. Christians do make mistakes. James himself had spent several chapters pointing out the mistakes of his friends. But he did it to their faces, and he did it for their good. Backbiting fails at both these points and its results are always damaging" (Hubbard, *The Book of James*, 99 – 100).

61. See Martin (*James*, 163) for an excellent list.

62. On slander, see further Ps 15:3 and Pr 10:18; for intertestamental background, cf. esp. Wis 1:11: "Beware then of useless murmuring, and keep your tongue from slander; because no secret word is without result, and a lying mouth destroys the soul."

63. Ibid., 164. The present tenses in this clause are again gnomic or, more precisely, timeless (Porter, *Verbal Aspect in the Greek of the New Testament*, 238).

64. Brosend, *James and Jude*, 117.

"law" (νόμος) remains anarthrous throughout this section suggests that perhaps James speaks qualitatively here, seeing God's will *as* law.[65] Indeed, instead of thinking of Torah by itself, he may be harking back to Torah as fulfilled in Christ, the gospel message, and the new covenant as the (qualitatively) royal law, as in 2:8 – 13.[66]

James 4:12 There is one lawgiver and judge who is able to save and to destroy; but who are you, who are judging your neighbor? (εἷς ἐστιν [ὁ] νομοθέτης καὶ κριτὴς ὁ δυνάμενος σῶσαι καὶ ἀπολέσαι· σὺ δὲ τίς εἶ ὁ κρίνων τὸν πλησίον;). James's rationale for not judging stems from the character of God: by setting oneself up as having the right to decide which laws ought and ought not be obeyed, one's sins of speech disclose an even greater problem, that is, usurping God's role (in direct opposition to the first commandment and in parallel with the original fall).[67] God is the one who establishes what is right (as lawgiver) and also the one who punishes the wrongdoer (as judge). "Usurping his judging authority by judging a person is really a blaspheming of God."[68] However,

> James is not prohibiting the proper, and necessary, discrimination that every Christian should exercise. Nor is he forbidding the right of the community to exclude from its fellowship those it deems to be in flagrant disobedience to the standards of the faith.... James [here] rebukes jealous, censorious speech by which we condemn others as being wrong in the sight of God [an assessment that only God can make].[69]

Again, we have a mini-inclusio, with "neighbor" (πλησίον) at the end of v. 12 harking back to the "one another" (ἀλλήλων) at the beginning of v. 11. James's closing question appears to be sarcastic and rhetorical, addressing the one who dares to speak against another: "To do so is to set oneself as superior to the one spoken against, is to deny the claim of the law to love the neighbor, and is to presume a role that can be held only by God."[70] If James did include the article with "lawgiver,"[71] we have another probable allusion to the Shema, with the possible translation "the lawgiver and judge is one," that is, unwavering in focus (recall 2:19 and the discussion of the grammar there).[72] We should be growing in similar single-mindedness.

65. Hiebert, *The Epistle of James*, 268.

66. Cf. Tidball, *Wisdom from Heaven*, 111.

67. Commands against slander appear in countless religions and philosophies. James's distinctive lies in his grounding his prohibition in the nature of God rather than in the character of interpersonal relationships among humans. See Giovanni C. Bottini, "Uno solo e' il legislatore e giudice (*Gc* 4, 11 – 12)," *SBFLA* 37 (1987): 99 – 112.

68. Davids, *The Epistle of James*, 170.

69. Moo, *The Letter of James*, 199.

70. Brosend, *James and Jude*, 119. Williams' NT reads, "You are not a practicer but a critic of the law," while Knox's yields, "Thou art setting thyself up to be its censor, instead of obeying it." Hughes (*James*, 198) calls this one of the worst sins, because it exalts oneself above the law and thus above God, the author of the law.

71. The textual debate here involves the inclusion or omission of the article before "lawgiver." Metzger (*Textual Commentary on the Greek New Testament*, 613) analyzes the situation thus: "Because manuscript evidence for and against the inclusion of ὁ before νομοθέτης is rather evenly balanced, with no compelling considerations arising from either palaeography or syntax, the Committee retained the article but enclosed it within square brackets."

72. Cf. Martin, *James*, 164, though this interpretation does not require us to follow him in seeing James here as opposing the "pseudo-Paulinist Christians" who claim an antinomian position. One might be tempted to think that James meant that the lawgiver was one and the same as the judge, but this would have required the third-person plural verb: "the lawgiver and judge *are* one."

Theology in Application

Friendship with the World (4:1 – 6)

The biblical foundation for vv. 1 – 3 is the tenth commandment, which forbids covetousness (Ex 20:17).[73] Jesus himself develops a metaphorical definition of murder as including hateful speech in Mt 5:21 – 22. An even closer parallel appears in Sir 28:17 – 18: "The blow of a whip raises a welt, but a blow of the tongue crushes the bones. Many have fallen by the edge of the sword, but not so many as have fallen because of the tongue."[74] Christ's promises that those who ask of God will receive (Mt 7:7 – 11, Lk 11:9 – 13) may well be in view behind Jas 4:3. The image of God's faithless people as an adulterous wife punctuates the prophets, most notably in Hosea (see esp. Hos 1 – 3), in which the prophet's prostitute-wife directly symbolizes Israel. Ezekiel 23 offers another particularly vivid chapter that develops this image.[75]

John Schmitt prefers Pr 30:20 as the most relevant underlying Scripture, because there the adulteress "eats and wipes her mouth" (euphemisms for her genitals?) and claims to have done nothing wrong, the very attitude of remorselessness that James presumably seeks to combat.[76] Jesus likewise refers to his contemporaries as an adulterous generation (see esp. Mt 16:4; cf. 12:39; Mk 8:38). The contrast between friendship with the world and with God resembles the calls to choose Lady Wisdom over Dame Folly in Pr 8 – 9 and to worship God rather than mammon during Jesus' ministry (Mt 6:24; Lk 16:13).[77] The possible Scriptures behind Jas 4:5 have already been presented, and we have opted for seeing this as a paraphrase or commentary on Pr 3:34, subsequently quoted in v. 6.[78]

James's rebuke of quarrelling Christians does not mean believers cannot have healthy disagreements among themselves. Doctrinal controversies, church policies and strategies, worship preferences, and countless other topics can hardly avoid debate when Christians share their honest opinions with one another. Unity scarcely

73. Cf. Sleeper, *James*, 105 – 6.

74. Quoted and seen as the key background text by Kugelman, *James and Jude*, 46 – 47.

75. For a full treatment of this theme throughout Scripture, see Raymond Ortlund Jr., *Whoredom: God's Unfaithful Wife in Biblical Theology* (Leicester: IVP; Grand Rapids: Eerdmans, 1996). In this original edition, Ortlund begins his introduction by confessing, "The title of this book offends its author" (p. 8). But he goes on to explain its appropriateness, in light of the offensiveness of the faithlessness to which it refers. Ironically, someone was not convinced, and perhaps they were even offended, because the reprint edition (Downers Grove, IL: IVP, 2003) changed the book's title to *God's Unfaithful Wife: A Biblical Theology of Spiritual Adultery* and altered the introduction so that no indication of its original title remains!

76. John J. Schmitt, "You Adulteresses! The Image in James 4:4," *NovT* 28 (1986): 327 – 37.

77. See, respectively, Timothy B. Cargal, "When Is a Prostitute Not an Adulteress? The Language of Sexual Infidelity in the Rhetoric of the Letter of James," in *A Feminist Companion to the Catholic Epistles and Hebrews*, ed. Amy-Jill Levine (Cleveland: Pilgrim, 2004), 114 – 26; Tamez, *The Scandalous Message of James*, 49.

78. One other possibility for v. 5b, taken by itself, is Ge 6:5, in which the Lord sees how wicked human spirits have become. See Lewis J. Prockter, "James 4.4 – 6: Midrash on Noah," *NTS* 35 (1989): 625 – 27. But in Genesis judgment ensues, rather than a jealous longing by which God tries to woo people back to himself.

requires unanimity on all topics, merely the agreement not to let disagreements destroy deeper bonds.[79] But the bigger problem, sadly, in many Christian contexts is the lack of sufficient unity and commitment to one another in the first place. The questions Luke Johnson poses to Christian scholars apply equally clearly to all who expound Scripture: "To what extent does [teaching] operate on the basis of envy and arrogance ... shaped by competition rather than collaboration...? And how do our own aspirations, professions, and practices, [*sic*] contribute to the shaping" of both the academy and the church?[80] While commentators disagree as to how literal the fights and wars in vv. 1 – 2 should be understood, all acknowledge that in extreme cases professing believers have tried to settle their disputes with inappropriate force, whether personal or institutionalized.[81]

Vv. 2 – 3 introduce two key principles concerning prayer, which will need to be supplemented after we consider vv. 13 – 17. On the one hand, God's people miss out on many blessings for themselves and others by not praying as often or as persistently as they should.[82] Or they *do* pray with sufficient frequency or fervency but out of self-centered motives and thus still do not receive. Clear instances are easy to discern, at least in others — for example, the desires for too luxurious a standard of living, for promotion or status, for reward or recognition, or for freedom from even the slightest trace of suffering. It is much harder to admit that our own seemingly more noble requests for good health (so we can serve Christ better), good finances (so we can care for our families properly or give more away), or a good job (so we can exercise our spiritual gifts best there) can easily wind up being motivated by the even more fundamental yet ultimately selfish desires to feel good, to be able to buy whatever we want, or to gain a good reputation with others.[83] On the other hand, as we will see toward the end of ch. 4, sometimes perfectly appropriate requests simply do not form part of God's will because of his more overarching designs.

79. Cf. Stulac, *James*, 139.

80. Luke T. Johnson, "Reading Wisdom Wisely," *LS* 28 (2003): 111.

81. See esp. Richardson's thoughtful applications (*James*, 175 – 76) to the social as well as the personal realm.

82. Guthrie's comments about the "general prayerlessness" of James's congregations ("James," 253) often apply to ours as well: "They have intense desires that are promoting relational havoc in the church, and yet the desires find no answer because they have ceased to go to the source of real fulfillment — God himself."

83. Blaise Pascal shows an example of correct prayer according to the will of God while humbly confessing the things he had sought for selfish reasons: "Yea, Lord, I confess that I esteemed health as a good, not because it is a means of serving you, but because with it I could exercise less restraints and self-discipline to enjoy the things of this life and to better relish its fatal pleasures. Grant me the grace to rectify my reason and conform my feelings to your ways. So may I account myself happy in affliction, so that while I am incapable of external actions, you may so purify my thoughts that they may no longer contradict your own. Thus may I find you within myself, while my bodily weakness incapacitates me from seeking you without.... I pray neither for health nor sickness, life nor death. Rather I pray that you will dispose of my health, my sickness, my life, and my death, as for your glory, for my salvation, for the usefulness to your church and your saints, among whom I hope to be numbered. You alone know what is expedient for me. You are the Sovereign Master. Do whatever pleases you. Give me or take away from me. Conform my will to yours, and grant that with a humble and perfect submission, and in holy confidence, I may dispose myself utterly to you. May I receive the orders of your everlasting, provident care. May I equally adore whatever proceeds from you" (taken from Blaise Pascal, *The Mind on Fire*, ed. James M. Houston (Minneapolis: Bethany, 1997), 185 – 86.

Friendship with God rather than the world does not mean separation from the world, because Jesus commanded his disciples to be its salt and light (Mt 5:13 – 16). But it does require separation from the sinful practices of the world. The most difficult application question arising from vv. 4 – 6 is whether a "friend of the world" can ever be a *true* Christian. Much, of course, will depend on one's larger convictions on the historic debates between Arminianism and Calvinism. In the former camp, Tidball has no difficulty affirming that "friendship with the world leads to unbelief and apostasy and puts one on the wrong side of God."[84] In other words, Christians can choose to renounce their faith altogether. On the latter side, Motyer equally straightforwardly declares that "we who are AD children can live BC lives."[85] In other words, we may be saved but still often not live like it.

But even the Calvinist typically concurs that a time comes when professed Christians so consistently and characteristically live in such non-Christian ways, without any remorse, that one has to question whether any true conversion ever occurred at all.[86] Pride rather than humility may form one telltale sign (v. 6), a pride that implies a "vast contempt for all" of one's fellow humans and that "shuts itself off from God for three reasons": "it does not know its own need," "it cherishes its own independence," and "it does not recognize its own sin."[87] At the same time, the grace of Christ remains greater than every human weakness, ready at the slightest sign of repentance to intervene and transform sinners, reconciling them to God, however rebellious their pasts have been.[88]

Submission to God (4:7 – 10)

Earlier James placed the blame for succumbing to temptation squarely on the shoulders of the sinning individual (1:13 – 15). Nevertheless, he knows Satan's role full well, as v. 7 discloses. Interest in this arch-adversary and accuser increased notably in intertestamental times. Known best from Job in the OT literature, the devil emerges in Second Temple Judaism as a key opponent of human well-being. Still, he can (and must) be resisted, and he will flee (see esp. the *Testament of the Twelve Patriarchs*, e.g., *T. Dan* 5:1, *T. Naph.* 8:4).[89]

That this proclamation follows after the assurance of God's grace reminds us that we do not resist the devil nor does he flee from us by our own strength but only through the Lord. Submitting to God proves diametrically opposite to the world's call to self-assertion, autonomy, and power. Even Christians crusading for a good cause or zealous in their altruism can become so fanatic in promoting their

84. Tidball, *Wisdom from Heaven*, 157.

85. Motyer, *The Message of James*, 147 (by which he is *not* introducing a dispensationalist perspective to periods of history).

86. Cf. Hughes, *James*, 176.

87. Barclay, *The Letters of James and Peter*, 105.

88. Cf. Hughes, *James*, 179 – 80.

89. Sleeper, *James*, 111; Perkins, *First and Second Peter, James, and Jude*, 125.

own personal agendas that they unwittingly wind up resisting God rather than the devil.[90] Believers must always be ready to set aside their own crusades in submission to God, not elevating their surety of what God wants so high that they cannot be corrected.

The calls to draw near to God, to cleanse one's hands, and to purify one's hearts all draw on the ritual language of the temple cult (see esp. Isa 1:11 – 17; cf. also Ex 30:19 – 21; Lev 16:4).[91] Expressions for ritual purification were used metaphorically to refer to moral holiness already in the OT (e.g., Ps 26:6; Isa 1:16). But this is not separation from sinners, only from sin.[92] Jesus would likewise bless "the pure in heart" (Mt 5:8), while calling his followers to remain the "salt of the earth" and "the light of the world" (vv. 13 – 16).[93] James 4:9 may draw on the beatitudes as well, with its blessing for mourners (Mt 5:4; cf. already Job 5:11), and/or Jesus' corresponding woe to those who laugh (Lk 6:25).

The benefits of humility, unpopular though this quality was in Greco-Roman circles, were well sketched out in the Jewish Scriptures (cf. Job 22:29; Pr 29:23; Isa 57:15) and beyond (Sir 2:17, 3:17).[94] Jesus, of course, promised the exaltation of the humble in several respects (see esp. Mt 23:12; Lk 14:11; 18:14). Paradoxically, however, one cannot be motivated by the desire for reward and still remain genuinely humble. One must treat others as better than oneself (cf. Php 2:4; Jas 2:8) because one truly recognizes that everything one is and has stems from God's lavish grace. Gratitude engenders selfless service far better than does any hope for recompense.

Speaking against Others (4:11 – 12)

James's warnings against destructive speech owe their origins to the commandment in the Decalogue against bearing false witness (Ex 20:16). If one is to love one's neighbors (Lev 19:18), then one cannot simultaneously slander them (19:16). Yet Leviticus also reminds us between these two verses that there are times for the frank rebuke of a truly erring sinner (19:17). Even then it should be done with enough love that we could imagine ourselves accepting similar treatment if we were in the wrong (Gal 6:1; Mt 7:12).[95] Thus James is not calling believers never to judge, in the sense of not analyzing others' behavior and beliefs, nor even in the sense of refusing to take corrective action, but rather not to be characterized by a judgmental or censorious spirit.

The same point emerges from Mt 7:1 – 6 and 1Co 5:1 – 5. The fullest explanation

90. Cf. Townsend, *The Epistle of James*, 75.

91. Darian Lockett, "'Unstained by the World': Purity and Pollution as an Indicator of Cultural Interaction in the Letter of James," in *Reading James with New Eyes*, ed. Kloppenborg and Webb, 49 – 74.

92. Darian Lockett, *Purity and Worldview in the Epistle of James* (London: T&T Clark, 2008).

93. For extensive application of this theme, see Nystrom, *James*, 231 – 35.

94. Barclay, *The Letters of James and Peter*, 109 – 10.

95. Cf. Brosend, *James and Jude*, 121.

of the correct balance comes in Mt 18:15 – 35. Unrepentant believers may need church discipline, in extreme situations even excommunication (vv.15 – 18), but fellow Christians hurt by those individuals must forgive "seventy-seven times" (vv. 21 – 22), lest in turn God will not forgive their own sins (vv. 23 – 35).[96] The problem in most Christian contexts, however, is not in dealing with the extreme, clear-cut cases, but in finding fault with fellow believers in the grayer areas. Stulac suggests three ways in which Christians are often too quick to criticize: "judging the motives behind others' words or actions in church business, judging how others spend money and judging how others are rearing their children."[97]

Behind v. 12 lies again the Shema of Dt 6:4, with its declaration of monotheism and the single-mindedness of God (cf. also Mt 10:28; Lk 12:4).[98] On God as the One who alone saves or destroys life, see Dt 32:39; 1Sa 2:6; 2Ki 5:7; Ps 68:20.[99] As with not judging other people, not judging the law does not absolve us from our responsibility to analyze, interpret, or assess its meaning and significance. It *does* mean, however, that we do not set ourselves up as an authority over God's Word such that we can reject its claim on our lives after we have determined what its contemporary application implies for us at any point.

96. See further Blomberg, "On Building and Breaking Barriers."

97. Stulac, *James*, 155.

98. Edgar, *Has God Not Chosen the Poor?* 198.

99. Hartin, *James*, 218.

CHAPTER 9

James 4:13 – 17

Literary Context

At last James is ready to unpack his third main theme, that of trials and temptations (4:13 – 5:18). This closing section of the letter's body also returns to problems caused by the pursuit of wealth, at least in 4:13 – 5:6. But whereas the main lesson for believers to learn in 2:1 – 26, when James formally expanded on riches and poverty, was that they ought not discriminate in favor of the rich and neglect the poor whom they could help, here the main focus is on how James's audience should respond when *they* are on the receiving end of exploitation and oppression.

Despite formal parallels with 5:1 – 6, the present section really is not about wealth or poverty but about the temptations of autonomous planning more generally and thus a failure to take God's will into account.[1] In 5:1 – 6, rich *unbelievers* are causing their trials and the believers must resist the temptation to fight back or make unrealistic promises but instead to trust in Christ's return and the judgment day to right their wrongs (vv. 7 – 12). If their trials result from physical sickness rather than oppression, they must pray to God for healing and forgiveness if that is necessary (5:13 – 18).

As with all the other main subsections of this letter, however, James intertwines sufficient parallels in themes and wording that we can perceive connections between what comes before and after any given passage. The transience of the merchants (4:13 – 14) recalls how the rich person might well pass away right in the midst of the (financial?) activities of life (1:10 – 11). The arrogant boasting of 4:16 represents a central aspect of the earthly wisdom of 3:14 – 16. The conclusion of a short paragraph with a proverbial statement not tightly integrated with the preceding material (4:17) matches what we saw with 3:18. And it is possible to see all of ch. 4 linked together loosely via the theme of submission to God,[2] or to view 4:13 – 17 as

1. Wealth can clearly exacerbate this temptation, however. Thus Davids (*The Epistle of James*, 171) labels 4:13 – 5:6 "testing through wealth," with "the test of wealth" and "the test by the wealthy" (174) as his subheadings for 4:13 – 17 and 5:1 – 6, respectively.

2. William L. Blevins, "A Call to Repent, Love Others and Remember God: James 4," *RevExp* 83 (1986): 419 – 26.

the last subsection on proper speech (don't boast in what you *say* but *declare*, "If it is the Lord's will"), concluding the material begun in 3:1.[3]

The closest formal link between 4:13 – 17 and ch. 5 comes with the identical introductory call, "Come now," linking 4:13 and 5:1. More generally, we can view a development of thought from 4:1 – 5:6 with God's giving grace to the humble (4:6) leading to our need to humble ourselves (4:10), and God's resistance of the proud (4:6) leading to his mild rebuke of the merchants in 4:13 – 17 and his severe condemnation of the rich exploiters in 5:1 – 6.[4]

IV. The Three Themes Expanded (2:1 – 5:18)
- C. Trials and Temptations (4:13 – 5:18)
  - ➦ **1. Planning apart from God's Will (4:13 – 17)**
  - 2. Responding to Oppression (5:1 – 12)
  - 3. Anointing Prayer for Serious Illness (5:13 – 18)

Main Idea

Christians should not plan for the future as if they are in complete control of their own lives but should consistently make a healthy allowance for God's sovereignty. Awareness of this principle makes failure to implement it all the more culpable.

Translation

(See next page.)

Structure

More so than with any other section of James that is this large, the grammar and the semantic function of each portion of this paragraph stand in some tension with each other. Strictly speaking, the main verb of the whole paragraph is "Come," but "Come now" merely functions as a call to pay close attention to what appears next. It is possible, though incredibly unwieldy, to punctuate all of vv. 13 – 15 as an

3. E.g., Felder, "James," 1799.

4. Luís Alonso Schökel, "James 5,2 [*sic*] and 4,6," *Bib* 54 (1973): 73 – 76.

James 4:13-17

13a	Exclamation	**Come** now, **you who say**	"**today** or
b	series		**tomorrow**
			we will go to such and such a city and
			we will spend a year there and
			we will do business and
			we will make a profit."
14a	Problem	**You do not know**	**about tomorrow**,
b	apposition		what your life will be.
c	illustration	For **you are a mist** which	appears for a little while, and then
d	contrast		disappears.
15	Resolution	Rather **you should say, "If the Lord wills, then we will**	**both live**
			and do this or that."
16a	Action	But now **you boast in your arrogance**;	
b	assertion	**all such boasting is evil**.	
17a	Inference	Therefore **it is sin** for anyone who	knows a good thing to do and
b	contrast		does not do it.

exclamation, "Come now, you who say [x] instead of saying [y]."[5] But virtually all translators render the infinitive of v. 15 as independent and thus imperatival.

Vv. 14a and b can be divided into a saying and a question ("You don't know.... What is your life?"), but we have taken the second part as appositional to the first: the thing we don't know about tomorrow is what our life will contain or be like. This leaves v. 13 as an exclamation of dismay concerning those who four times insist that "we will" do something, even for up to a year, when the future remains so uncertain. The problem this poses is resolved by leaving room for God's will to overturn ours (v. 15) rather than by never making plans. Some within James's congregations, however, are currently behaving with arrogance toward God in their lifestyle (v. 16a). Worse still, they not only leave God out of their planning, they actually boast about their autonomy (v. 16b). Lest there be any doubt of the evil of this approach, James's closing rebuke removes all possibility that they can plead ignorance of the right process. The inference that necessarily follows is that they are sinning if they fail to include God in their planning (v. 17).[6]

5. Cf. Hiebert, *The Epistle of James*, 277.

6. Isaacs, *Hebrews and James*, 235.

Exegetical Outline

IV. The Three Themes Expanded (2:1 – 5:18)

C. Trials and Temptations (4:13 – 5:18)

➡ **1. Planning apart from God's Will (4:13 – 17)**

a. Christians should not presume to know the future but should always leave room for God's will to overrule theirs (vv. 13 – 15).

i. The wrong attitude is to pronounce confidently on all coming events (vv. 13 – 14).

ii. The right attitude is to plan but to make allowance for God's will to change those plans (v. 15).

b. Such presumption about the future is in fact boasting in one's own arrogance (vv. 16 – 17).

i. For Christians, all such boasting is particularly evil (v. 16).

ii. This is because Christians know better (v. 17).

Explanation of Text

James 4:13 Come now, you who say "today or tomorrow we will go to such and such a city and we will spend a year there and we will do business and we will make a profit" (Ἄγε νῦν οἱ λέγοντες, Σήμερον ἢ αὔριον πορευσόμεθα εἰς τήνδε τὴν πόλιν καὶ ποιήσομεν ἐκεῖ ἐνιαυτὸν καὶ ἐμπορευσόμεθα καὶ κερδήσομεν). James begins this section by calling his audience to pay particular attention to his next injunctions. "Come now" (ἄγε νῦν) commonly introduced arguments addressing imaginary opponents or "prefacing harsh words in satire."[7] One of the primary questions of this section (4:13 – 17) concerns whether or not the people addressed should be regarded as Christians. Those who argue that being wealthy and being a Christian are mutually exclusive would say, "No, these addressees cannot be believers."[8] Others argue that it makes no sense for James to be correcting those outside of his congregations, as they would have no reason to care or listen.[9] As this passage continues, we will examine the various pieces of evidence for each side.

This verse does introduce, however, the concept that wealth allows people an independence from

7. Keener, *The IVP Bible Background Commentary*, 700.

8. E.g., Maynard-Reid (*Poverty and Wealth in James*, 69) argues that while there are three groups of "rich" described in James (chs. 2, 4, and 5), these are not distinct classes but rather different functions of the same individuals. His arguments for this group not being Christian are simplified as follows (pp. 70 – 75): (1) "Come now" (ἄγε νῦν) is definitely brusque and not a friendly greeting; (2) "we will do business" (ἐμπορευσόμεθα) elsewhere in the NT appears only in 2 Pe 2:3, where it means to cheat or deceive; and (3) the bulk of trading and commercial activities was limited to the native aristocracy of large landowners (thus linking this group in 4:13 – 17 to the group in 5:1 – 6). Edgar (*Has God Not Chosen the Poor?* 198 – 99) adds (4) the repetition of "Come now" in 5:1, more clearly addressed to absent unbelievers (by the literary device of apostrophe); (5) the lack of any reference to "brothers" or "sisters" (fellow Christians); and (6) the profit motive of the ungodly plans.

9. Moo (*The Letter of James*, 201) agrees: "James chastises these merchants for failing to look at life from a Christian perspective (v. 14), urges them to acknowledge the Lord's sovereignty and providence as they make their plans (v. 15), and suggests that they know what they ought to do in this matter (v. 17). James would hardly address non-Christians in this way." It is better, therefore, with Adamson (*The Epistle of James*, 180) to see these people as believers who are temporarily, if unwittingly, adopting a "practical atheism" by leaving God out of their planning while knowing better.

God that can be dangerous for their spiritual state, and James wishes to convict people about this arrogant autonomy. Using the vocative substantival participle, "you who say" (οἱ λέγοντες), to address his audience, James is then able to give a fuller picture of the group he wishes to chasten. "As so often in James, it is speech as revealing the orientation of the heart that is the special target."[10] And who is this group? They are the people who plan their lives, their futures, without thought of God and his plans or sovereignty.

The general statements of "today or tomorrow" and "such and such" reveal that James writes this about anyone who makes any plans separate from God. The consistent use of the future tense indicative verbs — "we will go" (πορευσόμεθα), "we will spend" (ποιήσομεν), "we will do business" (ἐμπορευσόμεθα), and "we will profit" (κερδήσομεν) — shows a confidence that these plans *will* be carried out. There is no conditional clause to mitigate the certainty these planners exhibit. They intend to travel and stay in a foreign city in a time when travel was not always safe, and they then expect to do profitable business there.[11] They have the time and the places all set, everything is secure, and they do not think at all of how God might regard their plans. Their boasts reveal their arrogant attitude toward God and the truth of his sovereignty over their lives.[12] "The problem James has with such an attitude does not stem from the fact that these business people are following a 'secular' vocation.... What galls our author is that such an attitude reflects a proud complacency that suggests a 'this-worldly planning' and a blatant desire to become rich."[13] It is not their occupation, but their attitude, that has become secular.

James 4:14 You do not know about tomorrow, what your life will be. For you are a mist which appears for a little while, and then disappears (οἵτινες οὐκ ἐπίστασθε τὸ τῆς αὔριον ποία ἡ ζωὴ ὑμῶν· ἀτμὶς γάρ ἐστε ἡ πρὸς ὀλίγον φαινομένη, ἔπειτα καὶ ἀφανιζομένη). James points out the folly of succumbing to the temptation to make plans without God. His indictment begins with the indefinite relative pronoun (οἵτινες), which gives the qualitative sense of "people such as you." He then uses the least common of the three main NT verbs for "knowing" (ἐπίσταμαι), with the basic meaning of "understand," but which does not necessarily indicate the intellectual or content-based knowledge that can attach to "know [that]" (οἶδα) or the personal and often practical knowledge of "know [someone]/know how" (γινώσκω). The verb James chooses is simpler in its range of meanings than the other two (just like its cognate "understanding" [ἐπιστήμων] in comparison to "wise" [σοφός] [see above, p. 171]).

There are two primary translations for the first half of the verse: "You do not even know what tomorrow will bring. What is your life?" (cf. NRSV, ESV), or the one offered above (cf. HCSB: "You don't even know what tomorrow will bring — what your life will be!"). The one we have chosen follows the UBS committee's decision on the various textual

10. Johnson, *The Letter of James*, 295.

11. Moo (*Letter of James*, 202) has a helpful warning: "It would be terribly tempting ... to find here a rebuke of those who are out to make a profit at all.... Whatever we might think about the compatibility of Christianity and the profit motive of capitalism, it would be wrong to find any critique here.... James is not rebuking these merchants for their plans or even their desire to make a profit. He rebukes them rather for the this-worldly self-confidence that they exhibit in pursuing these goals — a danger, it must be said, to which businesspeople are particularly susceptible."

12. Cf. Raymond A. Martin, "James," in Raymond A. Martin and John H. Elliott, *James, I-II Peter, Jude* (Minneapolis: Augsburg, 1982), 43: "another evidence of arrogance — the feeling that we control our own destiny; the inability or unwillingness to admit our dependence on God every day of our lives."

13. Martin, *James*, 165.

and punctuation variants.[14] The debates, however, are finely balanced.[15] Fortunately, the main point of the verse is clear on any of the main readings.

Mist or "vapor" (ἀτμίς) formed a natural analogy for the ephemeral in the dry Palestinian climate, in which water droplets in the air formed from condensation near the sea but then quickly disappeared. Mist was a prevalent OT metaphor for the transitory, drawn from the world of nature (along with others like grass, shadow, cloud, and smoke).[16] Augustine elaborates: "Restoring health for a time to a man's body amounts to no more than extending his breath for a little while longer. Therefore it should not be considered of great importance, because it is temporal, not eternal."[17] James here employs another play on words, using the same root word in Greek for both the positive appearing (φαινομένη) and the negative disappearing (ἀφανιζομένη). Since we have these similarly parallel terms in English, it is worth preserving the wordplay in translation.[18]

James 4:15 Rather you should say, "If the Lord wills, then we will both live and do this or that" (ἀντὶ τοῦ λέγειν ὑμᾶς, Ἐὰν ὁ κύριος θελήσῃ καὶ ζήσομεν καὶ ποιήσομεν τοῦτο ἢ ἐκεῖνο). James now enunciates the positive action that these merchants ought to take. This is the verse that makes it most readily apparent that these addressees are probably Christians. On the one hand, it is just possible to understand this verse as a charge to the poor Christians within James's congregations concerning how *they* should act when they plan for the future, in contrast to the rich non-Christians whom James condemns in vv. 13–14. On the other hand, there is no clear shift in the addressees, and it seems more logical to understand the "you" (ὑμᾶς) as referring to the same group already directly addressed in v. 13 and referred to with the second person plural verb in v. 14. If James commands this group of businesspeople to consult God's will during their work, it only makes sense for them to be believers for two reasons. First, nonbelievers

14. There are three different textual variants in this verse. The first regards the inclusion of the article "the [thing]" (τό) before "of the morrow" (τῆς αὔριον) and secondarily the form of the article. The first alternative here ("the things" [τά] instead of "the thing" [τό]) appears to reflect assimilation with Pr 27:1, and the lack of an article altogether seems to be a tendency of B. Thus the accepted variant, with the singular article that is reasonably well attested, is most likely the original reading. The second variant, involving the inclusion of "for" (γάρ) or "but" (δέ) after "what kind" (ποία), seems to be an attempt to clarify the ambiguity of whether ποία introduces an independent question or is dependent on "you know" (ἐπίστασθε). With the connective, the previous clause cannot easily form a question. The third variant concerns the itacism of "it will be" (ἔσται) and "you are" (ἐστε). The third person singular future was more likely to be introduced by a copyist after interpreting the previous clause as a question. The omission in א is most likely an oversight, while the presence or lack of the article does not change the meaning (and B, as just noted, has a tendency to drop the article).

15. Moo (*The Letter of James*, 203) argues that "what sort" (ποῖος) more naturally leads to a separate question, as in the RSV and *contra* the NASB. Johnson (*The Letter of James*, 296), however, after examining the variants and translation options, argues that "on the whole ... it seems better to follow the text and punctuation of the 26th edition of Nestle-Aland [identical to the UBS 3rd ed.], as in the translation given here, despite its awkwardness."

16. Indeed, "mist" (ἀτμίς) can even be translated as "smoke" (cf. NET, HCSB). But for seafaring merchants, "mist" is the more natural meaning (Townsend, *The Epistle of James*, 87). The philosopher Jean-Luc Marion (*God Without Being*, trans. Tomas A. Carlson [Chicago: Univ. of Chicago Press, 1991], 222, n. 20) sees Ecclesiastes in the background here with its declaration of "meaningless." He observes that "*atmis* usually translates *hebhel*, only the LXX makes the exception in preferring *mataiotēs*—the point in common of translations consists in indicating that the thing does not hold.... James 4:14 therefore is closest to the Qoheleth in saying: *atmis ... pros oligon phainomenē epeita kai aphanizomenē*; which the Vulgate re-transcribes—Jerome very logically using the same Latin term to render *atmis* and to render *hebhel*—as *vapor... ad modicum parens et deinceps exterminabitur.*"

17. Quoted in Bray, *James, 1–2 Peter, 1–3 John, Jude*, 52.

18. Martin (*James*, 166), who also gives an excellent list of parallels in both Judeo-Christian and Greco-Roman literature to the concept that life is short and we do not control tomorrow.

would have no reason to care about God's will for their lives, and second, nonbelievers would have even less reason to listen to James's commands.[19]

"Should say" (λέγειν) renders the infinitive as imperatival, which requires it to be independent from any other finite verb nearby. This verse again reveals James's position that our speech discloses the attitudes of our hearts. More important than the mere verbalization of these words is an attitude of humility before God that becomes the fixed position of our hearts in all of our planning. The expression "if the Lord wills" (ἐὰν ὁ κύριος θελήσῃ), while common enough in ancient Mediterranean culture to have come from many possible sources, is an OT idea, and the concept appears frequently in the NT (e.g., Mt 7:21; 26:42; Jn 4:34; Ac 18:21; 1Co 1:1).[20]

This expression should be interpreted neither as a pious addendum to be repeated mindlessly nor as an expression of fatalism that excuses us from taking responsibility for our actions. Rather, it ought to convict our hearts of God's sovereignty in every area of our lives even as we seek to please him by following his will as best as we can discern it.[21] The third-class condition introduced by "if" (ἐάν) here is significant in that this phraseology is clearly not presuming on God's grace — one's own plans may or may not reflect the Lord's purposes. The verb "we will live" (ζήσομεν) shows that we should not take even living for granted, because our very lives depend on God's grace for their continuance. Motyer argues that the verbs in this verse point to our own ignorance, frailty, and dependence on God, essential attitudes for all believers.[22]

James continues with the generic "this or that" (τοῦτο ἢ ἐκεῖνο), akin to the generalized "such-and-such" in v. 13, which shows that this "exhortation applies to every circumstance."[23] It is important to stress that the proper attitude James enjoins does not exclude planning; instead it demands that one submit to God's will during and after one's planning, "recognizing both human finiteness and divine sovereignty."[24]

James 4:16 But now you boast in your arrogance; all such boasting is evil (νῦν δὲ καυχᾶσθε ἐν ταῖς ἀλαζονείαις ὑμῶν· πᾶσα καύχησις τοιαύτη πονηρά ἐστιν). In contrast with the proper course of action, James shows these traveling merchants the implications of their present behavior. Again, he returns to convicting his hearers, which also leads to the conclusion that his listeners here are (at least primarily) Christians. These believers, however, are not operating their lives and businesses as James thinks they should. The verb for boasting (καυχάομαι), which occurred in compound form in 3:14, is generally a negative term for presumptuous bragging.

19. Points regularly made by a majority of commentators. The former could be offset if the "unbelievers" were Jewish rather than pagan, but the latter would still stand. Some Greco-Romans would have spoken about God's will, but most would have thought of gods or goddesses in the plural.

20. Moo (*The Letter of James*, 205) argues that James's use of "Lord" (κύριος), rather than the more general "G/god" (θεός), places this expression within the Judeo-Christian tradition. Knut Backhaus ("Condicio Jacobaea: Jüdische Weisheitstradition und christliche Alltagsethik nach Jak 4, 13–17," in *Schrift und Tradition*, ed. Knut Backhaus and Franz G. Untergassmair [Paderborn: Schöningh, 1996], 135–58) observes that a key Christian distinctive can be summed up as a theocentric perspective that puts God's will at the very heart of life while at the same time recognizing wisdom and guidance for daily living as potentially coming from any surrounding circumstance or way of thinking.

21. Martin (*James*, 167) explains, "Just as with any Christian teaching, this phrase can become no more than a vain, thoughtless repetition, a kind of fetish. What James is urging here is a conviction (worked out in a congruent lifestyle) that leads one to acknowledge that indeed God is in control of life's decisions."

22. Motyer, *The Message of James*, 161.

23. Johnson, *The Letter of James*, 297.

24. Davids, *The Epistle of James*, 173.

The ambiguity in the first half of this verse surrounds "in your arrogance" (ἐν ταῖς ἀλαζονείαις). One option is to understand James as saying that these people boast *concerning* or *about* their arrogance, as though their independence or self-determination is itself a matter of pride.[25] The second option is to understand the prepositional phrase as adverbial, describing the manner in which they are boasting — *in a state* of arrogance.[26] While the latter option probably does indicate the condition of their hearts, the flow of the passage (that we are dependent on God for all his graces) urges the former understanding, namely, that these business people are bragging about their ability to plan their own lives independently of any divine guidance. Moo, moreover, convincingly argues that "boast in" (καυχάομαι + ἐν) in the NT is always followed by the object in which one boasts and that the plural (lit., "arrogances" [ἀλαζονείαις]) supports this understanding — that is, they boast in their repeated acts of arrogance.[27]

James roundly condemns this attitude, arguing that when people boast about their own autonomy, they sin. We should note that he does not say that *all* boasting is sin, but rather that *this specific type* of boasting in one's independence is sin. The NT teaches us in numerous places the things about which we *can* boast: Christ's death, our own weakness, God's strength, and the like. The boastful attitudes of these businesspeople, by contrast, illustrate the ideas of 4:4 and what it means to be a friend of the world.[28] These traders are more concerned with physical wealth and their own plans than with humility before God.

James 4:17 Therefore it is sin for anyone who knows a good thing to do and does not do it (εἰδότι οὖν καλὸν ποιεῖν καὶ μὴ ποιοῦντι, ἁμαρτία αὐτῷ ἐστιν). V. 17 stands as a seemingly strange conclusion to this passage. The "therefore" (οὖν) links this verse with what precedes it, but it also reads like an individual maxim that could fit in many different contexts. This verse refers most specifically to actions or, rather, to a failure to act in ways that people know they ought. In this context, James has urged his audience to take God's will into account in all of their planning for life, so that to fail to stand in humility before God's sovereign will at all times is to fail to do a "good" thing that they now understand.[29]

The concept of "doing the good" was a familiar OT concept of practicing the law (the "good") and fits well with a Jewish-Christian audience. The "good" (καλὸν), while definitely embracing the thought of leaving room for the Lord's will at all times, in James's thought most likely includes other actions of good as well, most notably deeds of charity and caring for the poor.[30] The merchants in this passage, at least in the small socioeconomic "middle group"[31] of the ancient world, were people with some discretionary spending money, so that

25. See Martin, *James*, 167, for support of this interpretation.

26. Johnson (*The Letter of James*, 297) offers "in your pretentiousness you are boasting," thus supporting this second reading. He interprets this phrase as a description of the stock character of the braggart in Greco-Roman literature.

27. Moo, *The Letter of James*, 206 – 7.

28. Martin, *James*, 165.

29. Hiebert (*The Epistle of James*, 280) points out that they should already have understood from Pr 27:1 or Isa 56:12 the duplicity of boasting about that which only God ultimately accomplishes.

30. Contra Johnson (*The Letter of James*, 298), who sees the "good" in this verse as specifically referring to prefacing "one's endeavors with prayer and [placing] one's projects within the will of God," the "only omission to which the *oun* ('therefore') could refer." Moo (*The Letter of James*, 208) points to Jesus' teaching in Lk 19:11 – 27; 12:47; and Mt 25:31 – 46, reminding us that "we have a tendency, when we think of sin, to think only of those things we have done that we should not have done."

31. The term preferred by Meier (*A Marginal Jew: Rethinking the Historical Jesus*, 282) rather than the more anachronistic "middle class" commonly used.

some of James's emphasis here on "doing" or "not doing" (ποιεῖν ... μὴ ποιοῦντι) relates back to ch. 2 with its emphasis on practical religion and the need to help those less well off. If we do not acknowledge God in all that we do and say, and particularly with our material possessions, we fail to live our faith truly and commit sin instead. Kurt Richardson rightly labels 4:13 – 17 "one of the most important biblical sources for a Christian ethic of business,"[32] but this passage also informs an ethic for how we ought to live in general — in humility and in submission to God's will.

Theology in Application

Whereas Western Christians today often take for granted the necessity and even goodness of buying and selling internationally, ancient opinion on seafaring merchants was far more mixed. Whether because of the history of Israelite abuse of wealth (see esp. Am 4 and 6), because of Roman import practices that emptied the provinces of much of their raw material to provide luxury items for the affluent in Italy, or even because of Hellenistic dualism's suspicion of too much involvement with the merchandise of this world in general, many first-century readers of James would have looked with initial suspicion on these travelers with such grandiose plans.[33] Help for the 70 to 80 percent of the empire who lived not far from the subsistence level[34] was conspicuously absent in their scheming (recall the parable of the rich fool in Lk 12:16 – 21). They had estimated a time, a purpose, a place, goals, and a reward (v. 13), never once acknowledging the central role that benefaction played in a world without any overarching government welfare.[35]

The percentage of needy in America today may be noticeably smaller, but worldwide the suffering as a result of a lack of material resources remains staggering, and it is the wealthy West that has replaced Rome as the primary exploiter of the natural resources of poorer countries to sustain our ever-fattening consumer demands. Obesity is at an all-time high in the United States, while millions starve to death elsewhere. Obscenity would be the more accurate word for this disparity! As the film by the same title so powerfully portrayed it, we suffer from "affluenza." Christopher Church calls it "triumphant consumerism" and cites Arthur Simon, president of Bread for the World: "An affluent culture turns our hearts towards fleeting satisfactions and away from God," while "unprecedented prosperity has left our lives full but not necessarily fulfilled." Simon concludes that "the problem is not

32. Richardson, *James*, 201.

33. Uniting all of these contributing factors was life before either capitalism or socialism had ever been invented, in which the theory of what anthropologists call "limited good" dominated, when it was believed that almost all surplus money acquired by any given individual implicitly deprived the poor from having as much as they otherwise might have. See esp. Bruce J. Malina, *The New Testament World: Insights from Cultural Anthropology* (Atlanta: John Knox, 1981), 71 – 93.

34. See Lenski (*Power and Privilege: A Theory of Social Stratification*, 284) for the typical economic pyramid of ancient empires.

35. Cf. Stulac, *James*, 158.

that we've tried faith and found it wanting, but that we've tried mammon and found it addictive, and as a result find following Christ inconvenient."[36]

The transience of life is a commonplace in Jewish wisdom literature. The entire book of Ecclesiastes highlights the fleeting and unsatisfying vanities of earthly pleasure. Pr 27:1; Hos 6:4, 13:3; and Wis 2:1 – 5 are just a few of the texts that make this point, including by means of the metaphors of mist or smoke. Vv. 14 – 15 effectively counter the presumption that we can plan our lives out meticulously for months on end, by reminding us of our ignorance of the future, our frailty as fallen human beings, and our utter dependence on God's will.[37]

The last of these points harks back most immediately to the Lord's Prayer (Mt 6:9 – 13; Lk 11:1 – 4), with its central role for petitioning God that *his* will be done on earth, as it is already being done in heaven. But that requires us to leave enough time to listen to God on a regular basis so that his plans can overrule ours when necessary, so that we can distinguish a divine from a diabolical interruption to our daily schedule, and so that we can make "the most of every opportunity, because the days are evil" (Eph 5:16, TNIV).

The generalizing language of "such-and-such" (v. 13) and "this or that" (v. 15) refutes the claim that adding "if the Lord wills" applies only to certain kinds of prayers, but not to others in which we are taught to "name it and claim it." The latter approach turns prayer into magic — attempting to manipulate God or the gods through ritual or formula — and replaces God's sovereignty with human presumption, precisely what these merchants were doing![38]

Indeed, long-range planning would have stood out as far more unusual in James's world than in ours. The high value we place on such strategizing "is decidedly a modern phenomenon," not typically practiced even by the minority in the ancient Roman empire who *did* have surplus savings or investments.[39] The antidote in our modern world is not to try to recreate some mythically ideal past society, which would prove impossible anyway, but to reflect biblically on what *Christian* planning within contemporary economic systems should look like.

Barton, Veerman, and Wilson suggest five practices to avoid: envisaging retirement as a time merely to enjoy the fruit of *our* labor, seeing work as just a way to make the money we need to buy what *we* want, viewing material prosperity as

36. Church, "James," 390 – 91. Simon's work is *How Much Is Enough? Hungering for God in an Affluent Culture* (Grand Rapids: Baker, 2003).

37. Motyer, *The Message of James*, 161.

38. Bruce Barron (*The Health and Wealth Gospel* [Downers Grove, IL: IVP, 1987], 103) twenty years ago quoted Kenneth Hagin alleging that it was unscriptural to include "if it is the will of God" in prayers for health and wealth. Hagin can still be heard making the same claim on television today. But if James 4:13 – 17 isn't about accumulating wealth, nothing is! Hagin's claim is the unscriptural one. The danger of treating God as an object of manipulation, ironically, accrues also to the overly casual use of "if the Lord wills" in noncharismatic circles as a verbal (or written) amulet to safeguard prayers against the perception of presumption, when in fact one gives but lip service to the principle and continues mindlessly with one's previously arranged agenda. Cf. Hubbard, *The Book of James*, 103 – 4.

39. Keenan, *The Wisdom of James*, 141.

a symbol of *our* independence, imagining God as aloof from mundane cares of money matters, and making financial decisions without consulting Christ for detailed guidance.[40] Christopher Church, conversely, highlights three ways in which we can "do the right thing" as believers, individually, corporately, and even in the secular workplace: caring for orphans and widows (as examples of the most marginalized and dispossessed), avoiding discriminatory practices, and showing mercy to others (e.g., "fair treatment of stakeholders — employees, communities, customers, venders, even competitors, rather than an exclusive focus on dividends for shareholders").[41] One thinks of the models of such twentieth-century Christian entrepreneurs as Milton Hershey, Henry LeTourneau, or James Kraft, who adopted many of these principles and still led successful (and profitable) businesses.

V. 16 recalls our earlier discussions of the background and application of right and wrong forms of boasting (see above, p. 210). Here James removes all doubt that it is not planning per se to which he objects, but the role that arrogance can play.[42] The "proverb" of v. 17 gives another generalizing thrust to the passage. While for these merchants, not to leave room for the Lord's will would be the key sin of omission to avoid in the future, for other believers quite different things that they know they should do but fail to perform may constitute their sins of omission. James may have Jesus' teaching later recorded in Lk 12:47 – 48 in the back of his mind here — "from everyone who has been given much, much will be demanded" (TNIV).[43] Pr 3:27 – 28 and Mt 25:42 – 43 also contain crucial background teaching on sins of omission. And even if we stay with James's illustration of wealth for our contemporary applications of this passage, we need only consider how often the poor and middle groups, in James's day and in ours, have the same desires to become rich, in order to realize how close to home James drives his points.[44]

40. Barton, Veerman, and Wilson, *James*, 112.

41. Church, "James," 395 – 97.

42. "What is rebuked is the arrogant assumption that life consists of doing business and making money, that human calculation can secure the future" (Gench, *Hebrews and James*, 118 – 19). Wall (*Community of the Wise*, 222) calls this "the peril of great price"!

43. Maier, *Der Brief des Jakobus*, 199.

44. Ibid., 215.

CHAPTER 10

James 5:1 – 12

Literary Context

The comparatively mild rebukes of the traveling merchants in 4:13 – 17 quickly give way to the harshest rhetoric of the whole letter. In 5:1 – 12, James condemns the rich non-Christian oppressors of the poor day-laborers in his congregations. While clearly this passage addresses issues of rich and poor, the principles it enunciates apply readily to any trial. Ch. 5, in fact, offers this letter's last word on each of the epistle's key themes, as proper speech reappears in vv. 10 – 12. The focus on prayer in 5:13 – 18 can also be thought of as dealing with speech, even though often prayer was and is silent. Many commentators end the body of the letter at 5:6,[1] but this appears a singularly inappropriate place for so major a break. Vv. 1 – 6, after all, sketch the key trial that has caused all of the others discussed in this book, while vv. 7 – 11 (and, we will argue, v. 12 as well) present the proper response James's audience is to offer to these difficult circumstances. These twelve verses, therefore, belong closely together.[2]

Vv. 13 – 20 are less clearly tied in with the first half of the chapter, but only vv. 19 – 20 can naturally be viewed as a conclusion (see below, p. 237). So how do vv. 13 – 18 fit in? They have nothing whatever to do with the theme of wealth, but sickness *is* unquestionably a trial. In both halves of ch. 5, then, just as in 1:12 – 18, alternative scenarios emerge. In each half chapter the trial at hand can become a test that one passes or a temptation to which one succumbs. In response to the rich oppressors of 5:1 – 6, vv. 7 – 8 and 10 – 11 point to the right response — a tenacious patience, while vv. 9 and 12 warn against the wrong response — grumbling and rash

1. E.g., Wall (*Community of the Wise*, 248 – 49) finds a pair of three-part conclusions in 5:7 – 20, matching the pair of three-part introductions that formed ch. 1. Thus both vv. 7 – 12 and 13 – 20 begin with an exhortation to endure difficult circumstances through patience (vv. 7 – 8) and prayer (vv. 13 – 16a), continue with OT exemplars (vv. 8 – 11, 16b – 18), and conclude with wisdom proverbs (vv. 12, 19 – 20). The first two sets of parallels are clearly present, contra those who would separate vv. 13 – 18 from the preceding material, but the last set of "parallels" is no more similar than numerous other pairs of passages throughout the letter not demonstrably parallel. Sleeper (*James*, 130) likewise argues for vv. 7 – 20 as a discrete section — on "Christian character and community" (but what in the letter *doesn't* fall under this heading?) — while admitting the segments lack tight connection.

2. On keeping at least vv. 1 – 11 together in the same larger section of James, see, e.g., Stulac, *James*, 156 – 57; Martin, *James*, civ; Nystrom, *James*, 29.

vows. In response to severe illness in 5:13 – 18, James contrasts some, but only some, situations in which confession of sin is needed (v. 16b) with all situations in which prayer is appropriate (vv. 13 – 16a, 17 – 18). The use of the verbs for "we call blessed" (μακαρίζομεν) and "endured" (ὑπομείναντας) in v. 11 harks back to the only other combination of words from these same roots in James — in 1:12, explicitly in the context of a blessing for enduring trials. So it seems probable that the primary point of ch. 5 is to unpack the theme of trials and temptations, introduced in 1:2 – 4 and 12 – 18,[3] even as elements of James's other two key themes help tie all the main topics together at the letter's end.[4]

On any outline, 5:1 – 12 contains numerous specific links with the immediately preceding and subsequent passages. The "come now" of 5:1 exactly matches the address beginning 4:13. The "rich" people of 5:1 recall the merchants of the previous pericopae, even though there we argued that these were middle-group Christians, not rich unbelievers as here. Nevertheless, each group has to learn the lesson of the transience of this life, culminating in God's assessment of their behavior (4:14, 16b – 17; 5:2 – 3, 6).

Chapter 5:7 – 12 leads naturally into vv. 13 – 18, as the call to patience in the former naturally leads to prayer in the latter. Just as vv. 7 – 12 present the positive antidote to the trials of oppression and exploitation, vv. 13 – 18 depict the proper response to the trials of sickness and suffering. Just as vv. 10 – 11 appeal to the OT prophets and to Job as examples of persevering speech, telling the truth to those around them who will listen, vv. 17 – 18 utilize the OT prophet Elijah as an example of persevering speech in prayer to God as he besought the Lord to withhold and then to supply rain. This was the rain so desperately needed for a harvest, as in 5:7.

In terms of tying all three of James's main themes together, the temptation to seek wealth without consulting God's will led to wrong speech in 4:13 – 14. The temptation not to seek God's will in responding to persecution by the wealthy leads to wrong speech in 5:12. In each case, a part of the remedy is right speech (see 4:15 and 5:10 – 11). Likewise in 5:16, confession of sins to one another forms part of the proper response to trials of severe physical affliction. But riches and poverty play no role in 5:13 – 18, and wisdom plays no explicit role here, so it remains best to see this material as unified most prominently by the theme of trials and temptations.

Links to other parts of James, of course, appear as well.[5] The closest parallels to the unjust rich of 5:1 – 6 are their counterparts in 2:6 – 7. The disappearance of their riches resembles the disappearance of the rich person in the midst of pursuing wealth back in 1:10 – 11. Fire as an image of judgment (v. 3) recalls 3:6. The patient

3. Cf. Tsuji, *Glaube zwischen Vollkommenheit und Verweltlichung*, 95.

4. For others who see 5:1 – 20 as a self-contained unit, see Baker, "James," 99; Brosend, *James and Jude*, 130 – 31; and Church, "James," 328, 401. For all of 4:13 – 5:20 belonging together, cf. Isaacs, *Hebrews and James*, iv. For the tying together of all three themes, esp. in vv. 7 – 11, see Davids, *The Epistle of James*, 181.

5. Cf. also Church, "James," 401.

endurance that permeates 5:7 – 10 harks back to the endurance that the trials of 1:3 – 4 helped produce. The warning against grumbling in 5:9, like the commands against oath-taking in 5:12, reminds us of the warning against slander in 4:11 – 12, in view of God's coming judgment.

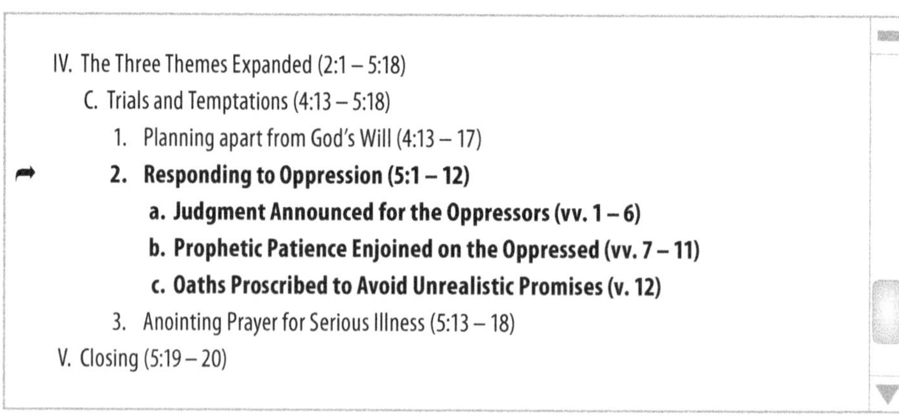

IV. The Three Themes Expanded (2:1 – 5:18)
- C. Trials and Temptations (4:13 – 5:18)
  - 1. Planning apart from God's Will (4:13 – 17)
  - **2. Responding to Oppression (5:1 – 12)**
    - **a. Judgment Announced for the Oppressors (vv. 1 – 6)**
    - **b. Prophetic Patience Enjoined on the Oppressed (vv. 7 – 11)**
    - **c. Oaths Proscribed to Avoid Unrealistic Promises (v. 12)**
  - 3. Anointing Prayer for Serious Illness (5:13 – 18)

V. Closing (5:19 – 20)

Main Idea

Christians should respond to oppression not by usurping God's role as avenger, nor by making unrealistic promises to their oppressors, but with a persevering and prophetic patience. Only God can fully and fairly right all wrongs, and he has promised to do so at the parousia.

Translation

James 5:1-12

1a	Exclamation	**Come now [you] rich**, weep and wail
b	cause	over your tribulations which are coming.
2a	Event	**Your riches have rotted**
b	series	and **your clothes have become moth-eaten**.
3a	Parallel	**Your gold and silver have tarnished**
b	result	and **their rust will be for evidence against you**
c	progression	and **it will eat your flesh like fire**.
d	Series (w 2-3a)	**You stored up treasure**
e	time	in the last days.
4a	Action	Behold **the wages ... from the workers ... cry out**,
b	identification	who mowed your fields
c	description (of a)	which you have stolen

d	sequence	and **the cries of the harvesters have come**
e	place	to the ears of the Lord of Hosts.
5a	Action	**You lived for pleasure** … and
b	place	upon the earth;
		lived luxuriously
c	parallel	**you fattened your hearts**
d	time	in a day of slaughter.
6a	Action	**You condemned**,
b	progression	**you murdered the righteous one**;
c	concession	**(s)he does not resist you**.
7a	Exhortation	**Be patient**, therefore, brothers and sisters,
b	time	until the coming of the Lord.
c	Illustration	**Behold the farmer awaits the precious fruit of the earth**,
d	manner	waiting patiently for it
e	time	until it should receive the early and late rains.
8a	Parallel (to 7a)	**You also must wait**;
b	exhortation	**strengthen your hearts**,
c	basis	because the coming of the Lord is near.
9a	Exhortation	**Do not complain**, brothers and sisters, against one another
b	basis	lest you be judged;
c	expansion	**behold the judge is standing before the doors**.
10a	Example	**Take … the suffering and patience of the prophets**
b	description	**as an example**, brothers & sisters, who spoke in the name of the Lord.
11a	Result	**Behold we call blessed those who endured**;
b	parallel (to 10a)	**you heard the patience of Job** and **you saw the purpose of the Lord**,
c	content	that the Lord is compassionate and merciful.
12a	Exhortation	But above all, my brothers and sisters, **do not swear** either
b	reference	by heaven or by earth or by any other oath;
c	contrast	but **let your yes [be] yes** and **your no [be] no**,
d	basis	lest you fall under condemnation.

Continued from previous page.

Structure

Internally, 5:1 – 12 breaks into three parts. Vv. 1 – 6 present the trials that the rich Roman or Jewish landowners are causing these mostly poor Christian day-laborers. Vv. 7 – 11 provide the proper response. V. 12 rules out one probably frequent contrasting reaction.

The trials emerge as James warns the rich oppressors of their coming condemnation. Vv. 1 – 6 begin with a call to lament for these imminent miseries (v. 1). The unused wealth that they have counted on is already beginning to fail them (vv. 2 – 3a), and it will soon form part of God's judgment against them (v. 3b). Their abuses of material possessions are now enumerated: hoarding, even though time for helping others is short (v. 3c); and not paying their workers their wages (v. 4), yet living in lascivious luxury (v. 5). As a result, some of their workers have been unable to pay their debts and been condemned to prison; a few may even have died there (v. 6).

The antidote does not involve revolutionary violence or supplanting God's role as vengeance-taker, which he will exercise when Christ returns. Rather, these exploited believers must endure their hardships with perseverance. The basic command introduces vv. 7 – 11, along with the brief analogy of the farmer awaiting the rain he needs for his crops to grow. This illustration, like the command in v. 8 to strengthen one's hands, shows that it is no passive inactivity that James has in mind, but an active preparation for God to come and do his part. Negatively, we must not grumble and take out our frustrations on one another (v. 9). Two additional illustrations round out the paragraph — the divinely guided speech of the prophets, which was characterized by denunciatory rhetoric against the injustices of their day (v. 10), and the clearly candid speech of Job, who likewise showed patience to be active rather than passive with his complaints to God (v. 11)!

What James's church members should *not* do, however, is make vows. These likely involved promises to pay off debts if only they could be given more loans or more time, in ways that probably often simply exacerbated the problem (see below, p. 231). Christians should be people of such integrity that their words may simply be trusted (v. 12).[6] By introducing this verse with "above all," James demonstrates that it is the climax of this treatment of proper responses to oppression.[7] Once again, it is speech that forms the heart of how one behaves, rightly and wrongly. Indeed, we may think of vv. 7 – 12 as even more tightly knit together: vv. 7 – 8 command

6. Apart from this interpretive grid for understanding the placement of v. 12 here, it is easy to view the verse as unrelated to the context. Cf. Perkins (*First and Second Peter, James, and Jude*, 134), who labels it "a separate piece of tradition" that has somehow just "found its way into the text," as if there were no guiding hand of any author at all! Others link v. 12 with vv. 13 – 20 (e.g., Isaacs, *Hebrews and James*, 243; Edgar, *Has God Not Chosen the Poor?* 209), on which see further below, p. 230.

7. Paul S. Minear ("Yes or No: The Demand for Honesty in the Early Church," *NovT* 13 [1971]: 1 – 13) demonstrates that in a culture dependent on and dominated by oral speech for communication, the intrusion of an intent to deceive pollutes society at its very source.

patience; v. 9 warns against the wrong use of the tongue (grumbling); vv. 10 – 11 then illustrate patience; and v. 12 again warns against the wrong use of the tongue (oaths). But this time, the positive flipside appears as well. Most important of all is verbal integrity.[8]

Exegetical Outline

- IV. The Three Themes Expanded (2:1 – 5:18)
  - C. Trials and Temptations (4:13 – 5:18)
    - 1. Planning apart from God's Will (4:13 – 17)
    - ➡ **2. Responding to Oppression (5:1 – 12)**
      - a. Christians should not try to wreak vengeance on their oppressors because God has promised to take care of that (vv. 1 – 6).
        - i. The rich oppressors are called to lament their coming miseries (v. 1).
        - ii. Their judgments are enumerated (vv. 2 – 3b).
        - iii. Their sins of oppression are illustrated (vv. 3c – 6).
      - b. Christians should respond to oppression with a persevering and prophetic patience (vv. 7 – 11).
        - i. Christians can remain patient because the judgment day is near (vv. 7 – 9).
        - ii. Christian patience must be persevering and prophetic (vv. 10 – 11).
        - iii. Christians must persevere in faith until they see God's great compassion (v. 11).
      - c. Christians should not be tempted to fend off creditors with unrealistic promises (v. 12).
        - i. They should not promise what they can't deliver (v. 12a).
        - ii. They should be individuals of impeccable integrity (v. 12b).

Explanation of Text

James 5:1 Come now [you] rich, weep and wail over your tribulations which are coming (ἄγε νῦν οἱ πλούσιοι, κλαύσατε ὀλολύζοντες ἐπὶ ταῖς ταλαιπωρίαις ὑμῶν ταῖς ἐπερχομέναις). James continues his denunciation of those whom he does not believe are behaving as they ought. While this section begins in a manner parallel to the preceding one, James becomes more vitriolic in his attack, pressing his addressees to weep about upcoming disasters.[9] While some have argued that both 4:13 – 17 and 5:1 – 6 address rich unbelievers (see above, p. 206), and a few have tried to make both passages refer to believers,[10] the overall tone of the two passages and the content of James's

8. Cf. Motyer, *The Message of James*, 174. Gilberto Marconi ("La debolezza in forma di attesa: Appunti per un'esegesi di Gc 5,7 – 12," *RivBib* 37 [1989]: 176) notes that vv. 7 – 12 can be viewed as falling neatly into two parts, vv. 7 – 9 and 10 – 12. Each section begins with two verses with an imperative or example involving patience based on the Lord's return, while the last verse in each section includes a warning against wrong speech because God will judge when Christ comes back.

9. Johnson (*The Letter of James*, 298) states that "the tone of straightforward hostility is remarkable, matched only by some strands within the Jewish tradition … and within the gospel tradition."

10. E.g., Richardson (*James*, 204 – 6), who thus sees an implicit call to repentance in the commands to cry. Cargal (*Restoring the Diaspora*, 180 – 81) thinks the miseries themselves may produce repentance. But if the miseries include

rebukes point to a different understanding. While in the previous passage James encouraged a Christian group with the aim of correcting their misbehavior, in this passage he attacks "the rich" (οἱ πλούσιοι) without offering them any redemptive options.[11] Here the "come now" (ἄγε νῦν) of direct address most likely exemplifies that figure of speech from rhetorical discourse known as "apostrophe" — speaking to people who are not present, for the benefit of those who are.[12] This way James's listeners will know the certainty of the coming demise of their oppressors.

These oppressors are identified by their economic status (cf. Mt 19:23–24). They are the financially wealthy in a world where the rich occupied a miniscule percentage of the population. James does not call them to change their behavior. Instead, he warns them of impending disaster in their lives by commanding them to mourn their coming fate. The first verb, "weep" (κλαύσατε), is an imperative; the second, "wail" (ὀλολύζοντες), a participle.[13] The two verbs should both be interpreted as commands, however, because the latter is a participle of attendant circumstances, allowing it to function in the same way as the main verb in the sentence.[14]

"Wail" appears in the LXX of the Prophets in contexts of judgment and can refer to inarticulate shrieks of terror.[15] Moo explains that "this background makes clear that *the misery that is coming upon* the rich refers not to earthly, temporal suffering, but to the condemnation and punishment that God will mete out to them on the day of judgment."[16] A. T. Robertson powerfully captures the force of this verse: "Burst into weeping (ingressive active imperative of *klaiō* as in 4:9), howling with grief."[17] The noun for "tribulation" (ταλαιπωρία) means "wretchedness, distress, trouble, misery,"[18] and James makes it clear that these rich people are going to undergo a terrible ordeal. These people probably viewed their wealth as a way to avoid pain and suffering, living lives of ease and comfort, but James declares that their wealth will not save them at this time.

James 5:2 Your riches have rotted and your clothes become moth-eaten (ὁ πλοῦτος ὑμῶν σέσηπεν καὶ τὰ ἱμάτια ὑμῶν σητόβρωτα γέγονεν). James pursues his indictment of the unjust rich. He writes in the perfect tense, the most heavily marked tense, here perhaps used in a prophetic sense.[19] In James's mind it is a certainty that these riches *will* go bad, and so he speaks of it as already having occurred. But there may be a more standard way to read the perfects as well.

final judgment, this will prove impossible. Moreover, Perkins (*First and Second Peter, James, and Jude*, 131) points out that calls to cry in apocalyptic contexts regularly seal people's doom rather than summoning them to repentance. Church ("James," 405) labels them "pseudo-believers" — community members who wrongly think they are saved. Cf. esp. Christine Prieto, "Malédiction des mauvais riches de la communauté — Jacques 5,1–6," *FoiVie* 102.4 (2003): 73–81.

11. Maier (*Der Brief des Jakobus*, 201–2) reminds us, however, that even the sternest prophetic texts of judgment can be used to call people to repentance. James is not, therefore, precluding the rich unbeliever repenting and turning to Christ. It is just not likely that he is addressing anyone he thinks is currently a true believer.

12. See, e.g., Felder, "James," 1799.

13. The latter is a beautiful example of onomatopoeia, a word that means what it sounds like (cf. the English "ululate"; so Sleeper, *James*, 121).

14. So most commentators and translations. It is possible, however, to see it as modal, specifying the particularly intense manner in which these people should weep (cf. Kistemaker, *James and the Epistles of John*, 156).

15. Popkes, *Der Brief des Jakobus*, 302.

16. Moo, *The Letter of James*, 211.

17. A. T. Robertson, *Word Pictures in the New Testament*, vol. 6 (Nashville: Broadman, 1933), 57.

18. BDAG, 988. James uses the related verb in 4:9 in the context of mourning and repentance, but here the context speaks of judgmental misery.

19. See Ropes, *A Critical and Exegetical Commentary on the Epistle of St James*, 284; Isaacs, *Hebrews and James*, 236.

This wealth that they are counting on has already become useless to them in any meaningful sense.[20] These riches and garments have decayed specifically because they are not being used. As Caesarius of Arles put it in the sixth century, "Riches cannot harm a good person, because he spends them kindly. Likewise they cannot help an evil person as long as he keeps them avariciously or wastes them in dissipation."[21]

Mayordomo-Marin makes the strongest case for seeing v. 2 as referring to inappropriate hoarding that has already occurred. Conceptually vv. 2 – 3 go more with vv. 4 – 6; when James unambiguously speaks of the future he uses the future tense (as in v. 3b), and the harsh judgment makes more sense if the rich can see that they have simply wasted material possessions by putting them to no good use for anyone.[22] The image of clothes becoming moth-eaten harks back to Job 13:28 – 14:2, in which humans are compared to moth-eaten garments, and to Jesus' teaching in Mt 6:19 – 20 (par. Lk 12:33) regarding treasures on earth versus treasures in heaven where they cannot be moth-eaten.

James 5:3a Your gold and silver have tarnished and their rust will be for evidence against you and it will eat your flesh like fire (ὁ χρυσὸς ὑμῶν καὶ ὁ ἄργυρος κατίωται καὶ ὁ ἰὸς αὐτῶν εἰς μαρτύριον ὑμῖν ἔσται καὶ φάγεται τὰς σάρκας ὑμῶν ὡς πῦρ). James now becomes even more specific. This verse presents a puzzling image, because technically gold does not rust. Many commentators assume James is referring to the common, impure mixtures of metals that could at least easily tarnish.[23] But the image may be deliberately jarring and all the more powerful if it reflects the metaphorical meaning of becoming useless. In other words, not even the gold, which the rich think they can count on to save them and provide them with the security of wealth, will last to safeguard them.[24]

The word "rust" (ἰός) also proves intriguing, because it can mean both rust and poison or venom (as in 3:8). In some ways the latter definition fits best with the flesh-eating fire of the second half of the verse.[25] Either way, James's declaration sags under the weight of waste. These people have retained so much unused wealth that even the untarnishable has tarnished in God's eyes, and this waste testifies against them. Unused wealth does the kingdom no good and condemns those who refuse to use it for God.

The prepositional phrase beginning with "for" (εἰς) gives the result of this literal or metaphorical rusting. It will result in "evidence" (μαρτύριον, "witness, testimony") against these rich people. We can translate the dative personal pronoun (ὑμῖν) as "against you," a dative of disadvantage. While it could be taken as a dative of reference, with the understanding that this wasted wealth witnesses "to" the rich person so that they might repent (i.e., presenting them with evidence of their folly), the

20. Cf. Sleeper, *James*, 123 – 24; Popkes, *Der Brief des Jakobus*, 303.

21. Quoted in Bray, *James, 1 – 2 Peter, 1 – 3 John, Jude*, 54.

22. M. Mayordomo-Marin, "Jak 5.2 – 3a: Zukünftiges Gericht oder gegenwärtiger Zustand?" *ZNW* 83 (1992): 132 – 37. Cf. Tidball, *Wisdom from Heaven*, 70; Moo, *The Letter of James*, 214.

23. E.g., Baker and Ellsworth (*Preaching James*, 124), who plausibly add that James may have thought of "rust" because its reddish color resembled that of the fire he was about to mention.

24. Cf. esp. Christfried Böttrich, "Vom Gold, das rostet (Jak 5.3)," *NTS* 47 (2001): 519 – 36. Ropes (*A Critical and Exegetical Commentary on the Epistle of St. James*, 284 – 85) argues that the future tenses of "will be" (ἔσται) and "will eat" (φάγεται) mitigate against the position that the decay has already set in and confirm the use of the prophetic perfect in vv. 2 – 3. But what is future is the judicial role this decay will play, not when it first begins to occur.

25. Cf. Wolfram Weiser, "Durch Grünspan verdorbenes Edelmetall? Zur Deutung des Wortes 'IOS' im Brief des Jakobus," *BZ* 43 (1999): 220 – 23.

general consensus holds that James instead presents a threat "that the corruption is seen as evidence against them."[26] The imagery comes from a law court, all the more ironic in that the wealthy typically counted on being able to manipulate the courts through bribery.[27]

The second half of this sentence supports the dual translation of ἰός as both "rust" (in regards to the metals) and "poison" (in regards to its effects on these people).[28] James basically curses these people with both eschatological judgment and present pain because of their greed and wealth. The venom that has tainted their wealth will poison their bodies as well (cf. also NLT: "The very wealth you were counting on will eat away your flesh like fire."). It is just possible that the last two words of this half verse, "like fire" (ὡς πῦρ), may modify the subsequent verb, yielding "like fire you stored up treasure." In other words, the possessions all burn sooner or later or, perhaps, the point is the unbeliever's own coming punishment in hell.[29] But the comparative clause goes much more naturally with "eat your flesh," as in most all translations and commentaries.

James 5:3b You stored up treasure in the last days (ἐθησαυρίσατε ἐν ἐσχάταις ἡμέραις). V. 3 proceeds to explain why these rich are to be punished. Here is where it becomes essential to understand the eschatological worldview of the NT. We live in the last days and have done so since Pentecost (cf. Ac 2:17). Christ can return at any point. Where is our treasure? Are we laying it up on earth so that we might live in comfort, planning for a long life here (see cf. Lk 12:13 – 21), or do we focus more on amassing treasure in heaven with God, being merely grateful for the blessings he has given us here and now? The condemnation is not for owning wealth per se, but for hoarding rather than using it for kingdom purposes. As Johnson observes, " 'the last days' ... are not the anticipated retirement years of the rich, but the time of God's judgment."[30] Martin draws out the probable intended irony that what James has "in mind is not their vaunted riches but the misery that awaits them."[31] Our view of eternity will affect how we live today.

James 5:4 Behold the wages which you have stolen from the workers who mowed your fields cry out, and the cries of the harvesters have come to the ears of the Lord of Hosts (ἰδοὺ ὁ μισθὸς τῶν ἐργατῶν τῶν ἀμησάντων τὰς χώρας ὑμῶν ὁ ἀπεστερημένος ἀφ' ὑμῶν κράζει, καὶ αἱ βοαὶ τῶν θερισάντων εἰς τὰ ὦτα κυρίου Σαβαὼθ εἰσεληλύθασιν). Now James's accusation becomes much more specific. This verse functions in two ways. It levels the charge against those rich who have extorted, defrauded,[32] and cheated their workers — in this case the day-laborers employed

26. Laws, *The Epistle of James*, 199. Cf. *1 En* 94:6 – 9 for a similar threat against the rich. Martin (*James*, 177) identifies the similar sentiments in Eze 7:19 and the relation of wealth to God's judgment there.

27. Guthrie, "James," 262. Cf. Andria, "James," 1515.

28. Johnson (*The Letter of James*, 300) brings out the interesting parallel that gold is tested by fire, and thus "since the rich have placed their trust and their very sense of worth in their gold and silver, the same poison/rust that destroys the metals destroys them as well. Neither they nor the metals are refined, only destroyed."

29. Ropes, *A Critical and Exegetical Commentary on the Epistle of St. James*, 287.

30. Johnson, *The Letter of James*, 300 – 301. Stulac (*James*, 164) itemizes three miseries for these rich persons: despair from losing their wealth, guilt from the evidence against them, and horrible pain from being devoured in the judgment on them.

31. Martin, *James*, 178.

32. The textual variants here represent subtle differences in meaning. The oldest attested option, the rare word for "withhold" or "keep back" (ἀφυστερημένος) has only the support of ℵ and B* and carries the meaning of regarding wages owed. Due to the extremely limited support, this was most likely an Alexandrian refinement. The other two options are different forms of the verb "defraud" (ἀποστερεῖν).

on an as-needed basis to help bring in the harvest (cf. Mt 20:1–16). It also provides comfort for the suffering workers that God does see them and cares about their situation.

James paints a graphic two-part picture: in the first half of the verse it is the stolen wages that cry out to heaven; not until the second half of the verse is it actually the cries of the workers that reach heaven's ears. Even the inanimate wages tell a story to God; when personified, they themselves cry out to him, for they testify against the landowners, demanding judgment (cf. Abel's blood crying out to the Lord from the ground in Ge 4:10).[33] A literal Greek translation of what we have rendered as "the wages which you have stolen ... cry out" would yield the awkward, passive construction, "the wages that have been defrauded by you cry out." This is on the assumption that the prepositional phrase (ἀφ' ὑμῶν) means "by you" and modifies "defrauded." Although "from" (ἀπό) can denote agency, it more commonly indicates source. One wonders why only a few commentators have suggested that the preposition denotes an origin and that the prepositional phrase modifies "cries out," yielding the translation, "the wages ... that were defrauded cry out *from* you."[34] If the wages were not paid, they remain in the pockets, as it were, of the landowners and can be viewed as crying out from that location; after all, they don't belong there but in the possession of the workers.

On either reading James counters any thoughts that someone might be too downtrodden ever to experience justice. Such a notion fails to recognize the character of God as one who loves righteousness and has a passionate concern for the poor and helpless. James chooses the title Lord *Sabaoth*, the Hebrew title for "Lord of Hosts,"[35] in which the image is of God (or Jesus) leading an army in defense of his people. Here it becomes clear that James is not directly addressing the rich but providing comfort for the poor within his congregations, insisting that God does see and hear their precarious situations and that he will bring justice. James uses the perfect tense "have come to" (εἰσεληλύθασιν) because it shows that God has *already* heard their complaints and stands ready to act. Believers need not try to usurp God's unique role in exacting this vengeance.[36]

James 5:5 You lived for pleasure and lived luxuriously upon the earth; you fattened your hearts in a day of slaughter (ἐτρυφήσατε ἐπὶ τῆς γῆς καὶ ἐσπαταλήσατε, ἐθρέψατε τὰς καρδίας ὑμῶν ἐν ἡμέρᾳ σφαγῆς). James persists in his indictment of the rich. This extreme view of life lived only for wanton, personal pleasure shows that James does not necessarily condemn the "capitalist" work ethic per se, but the selfishness that can pair with any economic philosophy. In some ways these people have experienced their "heaven" on earth; they have received their reward in this life.

A present tense ἀποστερήμενος is supported by K and L (see Metzger, *A Textual Commentary*, 614). The UBS committee chose the perfect tense (ἀπεστερημένος), supported by A, B² and Ψ, etc., partially because of its widespread support, partially also because of the consistent use of the perfect tense in this passage, and because of its stronger implications of stealing and defrauding rather than just withholding.

33. On which, see esp. John Byron, "Living in the Shadow of Cain: Echoes of a Developing Tradition in James 5:1–6," *NovT* 48 (2006): 261–74. Many translations add "against you" to clarify this judicial nature of the cries (cf., e.g., NASB, which puts these two words in italics to show they are implied but not actually in the Greek text).

34. E.g., Guthrie ("James," 263), who notes both possibilities without indicating a preference.

35. This word is unrelated to the Hebrew word for Sabbath (*šabbāt*) and should not be confused with it. The Hebrew word underlying this title is *ṣᵉbāʾôt*.

36. George Reyes, "El grito del salario: ensayo de lectura literaria y sociológica," *RevistBib* 66 (2004): 85–86. Reyes plausibly outlines vv. 1–11 as a chiasm: vv. 1 and 7–11 announce judgment on the rich oppressors; vv. 2–3 and 5–6 detail their sins; and v. 4 forms the central, climactic section in which God hears the cries of those oppressed.

Thus they may arrive at the judgment day content but condemned.

The irony is that they have brought about their own demise by living for themselves, producing a downward spiral of ever-greater hedonism and culminating in utter self-absorption. On the last day, the day "characterized by slaughter" (σφαγῆς—a descriptive genitive), they will find themselves facing punishment, while those who have not "fattened" themselves in this life will be invited to the great wedding banquet of the Lamb.[37] "Fattening one's heart" (καρδία) may simply refer to the inward desire for riches. But καρδία at times could refer to a person's midsection more generally, so the expression may mean much the same as "fattening one's stomach."[38]

The first two verbs in this verse (ἐτρυφήσατε and ἐσπαταλήσατε) clearly refer not just to an affluent lifestyle but to debauched self-indulgence. The NAB translates, "you lived in wanton luxury"; the NLT, "satisfying your every whim"; and Moffatt, "you have reveled on earth and plunged into dissipation." Weymouth speaks of "profligate lives"; Goodspeed, of living "luxuriously and voluptuously"; and Rotherham, of having "luxuriated upon the land and run riot." While some might argue that this situation is hyperbolic and not necessarily an actual scenario in James's church,[39] and others might dismiss its applicability to themselves because of the extreme language, it is important to hear the warnings of Maynard-Reid and Tamez that, compared to much of the Majority World, this is precisely the way in which many Western Christians live. Nor dare we soften James's condemnations of the rich to make ourselves feel more comfortable.[40] Indeed, it is perhaps better to translate the closing phrase of this verse as "*in* a day of slaughter" rather than the common "*for* a day of slaughter.[41] V. 6 will make plain that killing—judicial, literal, or both—is going on in James's day, and that these rich are often responsible.[42]

James 5:6 You condemned, you murdered the righteous one; (s)he[43] does not resist you (κατεδικάσατε, ἐφονεύσατε τὸν δίκαιον, οὐκ ἀντιτάσσεται ὑμῖν). James's indictment of the rich oppressors ends abruptly with a sentence full of asyndeton. Here the wealthy usurp the role of God as judge. Because of their status, they feel they have the right to condemn whomever they choose. The staccato style juxtaposing the two aorist tense verbs with a third verb in the present tense, without any connecting conjunctions, heightens the emphasis of James's charge. These victims are innocent!

In a different context, this verse could plausibly read as a condemnation of the Jewish leaders who tried Jesus, the ultimate "Righteous One," and handed him over to Pilate, calling for his crucifixion.[44] In this context, however, the ones James confronts are the rich landowners who have de-

37. While the description "upon the earth" (ἐπὶ τῆς γῆς) may refer merely to living off the land (so Johnson, *The Letter of James*, 303), James tends to contrast things earthly with things eternal, with the former being a negative in his eyes (see 3:15–17).

38. Ernst Lerle, "Καρδία als Bezeichnung für den Mageneingang," *ZNW* 76 (1985): 292–93.

39. So, e.g., Davids, *The Epistle of James*, 178.

40. See Maynard-Reid, *Poverty and Wealth in James*; Tamez, *The Scandalous Message of James*; both *passim*. Perkins (*First and Second Peter, James, and Jude*, 132) observes that the excessive personal consumption demonstrates that these people had the means to help the less fortunate, making them all the more culpable for not doing so.

41. The TCNT captures both halves of this verse succinctly and powerfully: "you have indulged your fancies in a time of bloodshed."

42. Dibelius, *James*, 239; cf. Stulac, *James*, 165.

43. This is a rare occasion where substituting a generic plural does foreclose the interpretive options that take the third-person singular as referring only to one specific male person, so we have opted for the slightly less elegant "(s)he."

44. Cf., e.g., Scaer, *James*, 122–23.

frauded their workers in order to gain more wealth for themselves. Therefore, "the righteous one" (τὸν δίκαιον) must be a generic singular for any righteous person who is thus defrauded.[45] Jesus, nevertheless, does stand at the head of the group as a model of how to respond.

Some scholars, discontent with fatal nonresistance, have tried to turn v. 6b into a question, "Does (s)he not resist you?" or even, "Should (s)he not resist you?"[46] This alternative also allows for the "he" to be interpreted as God as well as a human being.[47] But the clause makes perfectly good sense as a statement, and there is no natural way to turn a Greek "does" into a "should." God is not a near antecedent to readily become the subject of the resistance, and there was little opportunity for the oppressed to rise up and rebel.[48] The asyndeton between the two clauses of this verse could mask an implied concession — "although (s)he does not resist you"[49] — but to translate the text this way destroys the rhetorical force created by the abrupt juxtaposition of clauses without a connective. It remains best to take the clause as an ironic and sad observation — the oppressed person does not resist the oppressor because he or she is in no position to do so.

The murder here most likely is judicial, whereby the wealthy landowners take smaller, poorer indebted farmers to court, stripping them of their land and thus of their source of income, and then hiring them back again to work their former property as sharecroppers. With dirt-poor wages, unpaid debts might then lead their new landlords to throw them into debtors' prison, where they could rot for the rest of their lives.[50] In the Jewish world, to deprive a person of their support was the same as murdering them (see Sir 34:21 – 22). Daniel Doriani explains:

> As before (James 4:2), the murder is probably figurative. Yet by withholding their wages, the rich condemn the poor to poverty, even starvation.
>
> The word "condemn" suggests the law court. It is likely that the rich used the legal system to deprive the poor of their wages and lands.... Those who had power and wealth on their side won in court, not those who had justice.[51]

The rich would have had the access and power in the courts, with the ability to carry their own desires in legal form. Meanwhile, following the example of Christ, these righteous ones await

45. So most commentators. Martin (*James*, 182) argues that the later redactor also alludes to James and his martyrdom but, while James may have become an example of a righteous person unjustly murdered, nothing along those lines appears in this passage that deals with rich landowners and poor workers. Theophylact, in his eleventh-century *Commentary on James*, had already tried to take the text to refer to the poor, to Jesus, and to James, all at once (cited in Bray, *James, 1 - 2 Peter, 1 - 3 John, Jude*, 55).

46. E.g., Maynard-Reid (*Poverty and Wealth in James*, 74), for whom resistance could even involve violent revolution if necessary. But this fits poorly with James's emphasis on peacemaking.

47. E.g., Johnson (*The Letter of James*, 305), following Schökel ("James 5,2 [*sic*] and 4,6," 73 - 76). Cf. TCNT: "Must not God be opposed to you?"

48. Indeed, one has to then take this as the less common futurist use of the present tense, "will (s)he not resist you?" — i.e., through the witness borne on the judgment day. Thus Burchard, *Der Jakobusbrief*, 195.

49. Roger L. Omanson, "The Certainty of Judgment and the Power of Prayer: James 5," *RevExp* 83 [1986]: 429.

50. On the horrid conditions of prisons in the first-century Roman empire, see Brian Rapske, *The Book of Acts and Paul in Roman Custody* (Grand Rapids: Eerdmans, 1994), esp. 195 - 225. Making money to pay one's debts was usually not an option, so unless some better financially situated friends or relatives "bailed one out," that person often died in jail.

51. Daniel C Doriani, *James* (Phillipsbug, NJ: Presbyterian & Reformed, 2007), 172. Omanson ("The Certainty of Judgment and the Power of Prayer," 429), however, finds support in parallel texts like Sir 34:21 - 22 and Wis 2:6 - 24 for understanding this text merely "to mean that the wealthy have so exploited the righteous poor that the latter have no way to support themselves."

God's justice to be enacted on their behalf (recall 2:2 – 4).

James 5:7a-b Be patient therefore, brothers and sisters, until the coming of the Lord (Μακροθυμήσατε οὖν, ἀδελφοί, ἕως τῆς παρουσίας τοῦ κυρίου). James returns his attention to his immediate audience. Having just finished revealing how the oppressive rich will undergo judgment and how God is aware of the cries of his faithful, James calls his congregation to continue to persevere. He stresses his relationship to his audience in this section, calling them "brothers and sisters" (ἀδελφοί) three times in four verses (vv. 7, 9, 10; cf. also v. 12).[52]

The verb "be patient" (μακροθυμέω) contains two nuances. Like James's more common verb "endure" (ὑπομένω), this term calls his listeners to wait and not become overly zealous, turning to violence to further the cause of Christ in the face of oppression. But μακροθυμέω is not as passive as ὑπομένω, for it also calls the believers under affliction to persevere and not give up despite the persecution.[53] They must wait faithfully and patiently, realizing that the Lord of vast armies does hear them and does see their suffering. Again we refer to Tamez's idea of "militant patience."[54] They can wait because they recognize Lord Sabaoth's coming justice. Meanwhile, they can prophetically denounce injustice (vv. 10 – 11) and promote fair treatment of the poor laborers. The oppressed should not take justice into their own hands with violence, but should wait for the appearing of their Lord.

In the early church, "coming" (παρουσία) quickly took on the fixed meaning of Jesus' return in glory and as judge.[55] James probably raises this topic here because the only perfect comfort that people can find in the midst of injustice is the realization that God will bring complete justice in his time. James has just threatened the wicked with God's opposition on the day of judgment, which Christ's return ushers in. Here the same appearing of Jesus brings comfort to the believers.

James 5:7c-e Behold the farmer awaits the precious fruit of the earth, waiting patiently for it until it should receive the early and late rains (ἰδοὺ ὁ γεωργὸς ἐκδέχεται τὸν τίμιον καρπὸν τῆς γῆς μακροθυμῶν ἐπ' αὐτῷ ἕως λάβῃ πρόϊμον καὶ ὄψιμον). James proceeds to give an example of what it means to wait. Farmers form an ideal illustration because, once they have planted their fields, they can do nothing to *make* their crops grow and produce their fruit, a principle especially true in the first century. So they must wait until the proper time for harvesting comes.

The early and late rains[56] were standard climatic features of the eastern half of the Mediterranean basin, familiar to the readers. The early rains nor-

52. It is also interesting to note the sudden, frequent use of "behold" (ἰδού), as in 5:4, 7, 9 and 11. Previously it appeared only in 3:4 and 5. Once an imperatival form of an obsolete form of "to see" (εἴδω), it became equivalent to a simple adverb, used particularly to call special attention to either positive or negative behavior.

53. See Johnson (*The Letter of James*, 312 – 13) for an extensive list of LXX and classical texts that reveal the complex meaning of μακροθυμέω.

54. Tamez, *The Scandalous Message of James*, 43 – 46. Recall above, p. 47. Cf. Deiros, *Santiago y Judas*, 241 – 44, 246 – 50.

55. Johnson (*The Letter of James*, 314) supports this understanding and gives helpful background in the OT and LXX as well as from classical literature, showing how this understanding of "coming" (παρουσία) as referring specifically to Christ's return in James "reflects a virtually technical Christian usage." Laws (*The Epistle of James*, 208 – 9) adds that this term, in James at least, probably refers to Jesus' arrival as judge.

56. The textual variants here represent understandable attempts to give an object to the verb "receives" (λάβῃ), i.e., to supply a noun that both "early" and "late" would modify. The variant chosen is both the hardest and shortest reading and is supported by 𝔓[74] and B. The second variant adds the more explicit object — "rain" (ὑετόν) — and is supported by A and Ψ, while the third variant, supported by א (the original and

mally lasted from mid-October to mid-November, while the late rains spanned key portions of March and April.[57] Thus the two main harvest (and planting) seasons came in fall and spring. Farmers, however, hardly sat idle in between, but rather worked hard in weeding, hoeing, fertilizing, and doing whatever they could to bring their crops to full fruition.[58] James's analogy would have resonated deeply with his audience, many of whom were clearly farmers.

We, too, easily recognize that, just as the farmer can do nothing to force God's hand in the sending of rain or the process of growth, so we cannot compel Christ to return according to any timetable other than God's. Meanwhile, we must busy ourselves with kingdom work, contributing all that we can to the outworking of God's purposes in our world. Johnson notes the odd designation for the fruit as "precious" (τίμιον), commenting that "this is certainly the only time in the biblical literature that something so lowly as produce has been given a designation usually associated with jewels and crowns."[59] For farmers who had to work and wait with no guarantee that the crop would come to full harvest, the produce would indeed be "precious" (recall Mt 7:16 – 20). We, who *do* have the guarantee of Christ's return, should count that as well worth the work of waiting. Christians are called to "wait well" for Christ's return.

James 5:8 You also must wait; strengthen your hearts, because the coming of the Lord is near (μακροθυμήσατε καὶ ὑμεῖς, στηρίξατε τὰς καρδίας ὑμῶν, ὅτι ἡ παρουσία τοῦ κυρίου ἤγγικεν). James pursues his theme of "active" waiting. Clearly, he wants to impress on his readers that they *must* wait and be patient with the Lord, for he repeats the exact imperative that he used in v. 7. However, again contrary to the concept of passive, "lazy" waiting, James urges them to "stand firm." As the farmer waits for the crops to ripen, doing everything in his power to ensure a healthy harvest, so we also must wait, enduring patiently through hard times but also seeking every way we can to strengthen our hearts, our trust in God, and our relationship with him.[60]

In the LXX, this idiom of "strengthening the heart" can mean "to gain physical strength, as for a journey (Jdg 19:5, 8; Ps 103:15), or courage that comes from trust in the Lord (Ps 111:8), or firmness of intention (Sir 6:37; 22:16; see also 1 Thess 3:13)."[61] We do all this because of a constant awareness of God's imminence.[62] James here refers not only to the return of Christ, to which the term "coming" (παρουσία) lends itself, but also to Jesus' teaching regarding the kingdom of God.[63] The

corrector have slight variants on the same reading), makes the object to be the fruit — thus making the more dramatic change that the *farmer* receives the early and late *fruit*, missing the implied "rain" in the "early and late" pairing.

57. Winter rains (and, on rare occasions, snow) also occurred in late December and early January, leading some commentators to try to fit these into James's scheme too. But in Dt 11:14 LXX, the same words for "early" and "late" more clearly mean "autumn" and "spring," so this is probably the correct understanding here, too (Moo, *The Letter of James*, 222 – 23). Cf. Keener, *The IVP Bible Background Commentary*, 702.

58. Hartin (*A Spirituality of Perfection*, 64 – 65) contrasts passivity and perseverance at this point.

59. Johnson, *The Letter of James*, 314.

60. Baker ("James," 103) notes that this stands in direct contrast to the actions of the rich in 5:5, who have "fattened [their] hearts" at this time of judgment.

61. Johnson, *The Letter of James*, 315 (cf. ESV, "establish"; NAB, "steady"). The term also continues James's theme of single-mindedness (Sleeper, *James*, 133).

62. This ὅτι most likely introduces a causal clause, giving the reason why they ought to strengthen their hearts, hence our translation "because" rather than "that," which would have indicated a content clause.

63. Cf. Mt 3:2: "Repent, for the kingdom of heaven is near" (Μετανοεῖτε, ἤγγικεν γὰρ ἡ βασιλεία τῶν οὐρανῶν). Note the verbatim parallelism of the perfect tense form ἤγγικεν.

verb "is near" (ἤγγικεν) is in the perfect tense, an intensive use emphasizing the ongoing results in the present. With that verb, James implies that the coming of the Lord already *is* near because it has, over time, drawn near. But of course, this is nearness in God's time, in light of eternity (cf. Ps 90:4; 2Pe 3:8 – 9). From our earthbound perspective, we strengthen our hearts "to keep hoping when the delay seems interminable," "to keep trusting when God's timing seems questionable," and "to keep working for righteousness when results seem meager."[64]

James 5:9 Do not complain, brothers and sisters, against one another lest you be judged; behold the judge is standing before the doors (μὴ στενάζετε, ἀδελφοί, κατ' ἀλλήλων ἵνα μὴ κριθῆτε· ἰδοὺ ὁ κριτὴς πρὸ τῶν θυρῶν ἕστηκεν). In light of the Lord's imminent return, James again seeks to correct his congregants' behavior. As before, sins of speech cause problems for his audience.[65] In 4:1 – 3 they were quarrelling, whereas here they are only complaining against others in the community.[66] But fights often start out just as complaints. Here their whining contrasts with the patience James has just been trying to instill. Criticizing others implies judging them — hence, James's reminder about God's judgment. This concept of "grumbling" (NIV; cf. Williams, "muttering") recalls the Israelites who tested God's patience again and again, murmuring and complaining about their circumstances and against their leaders.

What gripes does this congregation have? Perhaps they project their frustrations at the landlords onto each other.[67] Or perhaps they disagree on how they ought to deal with the oppression, and the different factions complain about each other in their anger. Maybe they are blaming one another for the problems they are facing as a congregation, or maybe they are accusing each other to avoid problems themselves (cf. NTLT: "Don't blame your troubles on one another"). But now their complaints threaten them with judgment. The expression ἵνα μή can be literally translated "in order that ... not," but "lest" is a smoother, if older, translation that communicates the same idea. James again uses an intensive perfect, this time of the verb "stand" (ἕστηκεν), to portray Jesus' continually imminent return, as the Lord prepares to carry out judgment against his enemies and salvation for his people.

Christians often act as though judgment remains far off, a distant future possibility. James argues, however, that Christ's return lies close at hand, on the threshold of the doorway, so that we ought to behave as people ready for a judgment that has already begun in this life and will culminate quickly at his return. This verse probably refers back to the discussion in 4:12 regarding the "one lawgiver and judge"; the two texts prove remarkably parallel. Jas 4:11 – 12 warned against slandering one another. Here people are complaining against each other, and again James has to remind them about the judge who is over them.[68] The exact form of this complaining may be unclear, but their attitudes to one another within the con-

64. Hubbard, *The Book of James*, 119 – 20.

65. Luke T. Johnson ("The Use of Leviticus 19 in the Letter of James," *JBL* 101 [1982]: 396) finds in this comment about complaining "the most tenuous of the possible allusions to Leviticus 19 in James.... I suggest that it is a thematic allusion to Lev 19:18a, which immediately precedes the 'Law of Love.'" While his logic is well spelled out, it does require several associative steps to arrive at that conclusion. A clearer parallel is to Jesus' teaching in Mt 7:1 regarding judging.

66. Johnson (*The Letter of James*, 316) argues that the "against" (κατά) intensifies the "confrontational character of the 'groaning.'"

67. Moo, *The Letter of James*, 224. In times of stress, we tend to take out our frustrations on those closest to us.

68. Davids (*The Epistle of James*, 185) argues that this judge is most likely Christ, in light of the parousia references. But the allusion to the "one lawgiver and judge" in 4:12 leads Hartin (*James*, 243) to conclude that God is in view.

gregation obviously do not meet with God's approval (cf. Mt 7:1 – 6). Whatever one's views on the disputed concept of degrees of eternal reward in heaven, *at the very least* these believers risk more severe censure and less hearty praise from Christ on the judgment day (cf. 1Co 3:14 – 15; 2Jn 8).

James 5:10 Take as an example, brothers and sisters, the suffering and patience of the prophets who spoke in the name of the Lord (ὑπόδειγμα λάβετε, ἀδελφοί, τῆς κακοπαθίας καὶ τῆς μακροθυμίας τοὺς προφήτας οἳ ἐλάλησαν ἐν τῷ ὀνόματι κυρίου). In order to illustrate his point, James offers OT examples of people who had to both suffer and wait patiently, and who did not complain in inappropriate ways. The noun "example" (ὑπόδειγμα) derives from the verb "to show" (δείκνυμι) and represents a pattern or model intended for imitation.[69] This "example" that James gives is not meant merely for intellectual discussion and pondering but should be the model for the lives of all the congregants. As the prophets suffered, they still sought the glory of God in what they said and did.[70]

The prophetic model that James puts forward steers a middle ground between pacifism and violence, swinging to neither extreme. Tamez highlights the heroism of the prophets: "because of their deeds they suffer oppression and martyrdom and because of those same deeds in defense of the oppressed and the weak they are declared blessed."[71] Church adds the observation that a key part of the way the prophets "spoke in the name of the Lord" involved rhetoric denouncing injustice, even when the perpetrator was the king.[72] They always, however, stopped short of violent reprisal or of inciting revolution. As the prophets spoke in the name of the Lord, so all Christians, bearing a reference to Christ in their very name, represent him to the world in all they say and do, so that they ought to act accordingly and not bring him shame.

James 5:11 Behold we call blessed those who endured; you heard the patience of Job and you saw the purpose of the Lord, that the Lord is compassionate and merciful (ἰδοὺ μακαρίζομεν τοὺς ὑπομείναντας· τὴν ὑπομονὴν Ἰὼβ ἠκούσατε καὶ τὸ τέλος κυρίου εἴδετε, ὅτι πολύσπλαγχνός ἐστιν ὁ κύριος καὶ οἰκτίρμων). James continues with his analogies. The first section of this verse discloses an interesting irony: We are more than willing to call others blessed for enduring suffering, even though we have no interest in undergoing it ourselves! The aorist substantival participle rendered "those who endured" (ὑπομείναντας) implies those who remained faithful to the end.

Second Temple Jewish literature expands on the suffering of Job, claiming that it lasted for many years before God restored him, so that he becomes the prime exemplar of endurance.[73] Indeed, perseverance is the *only* character trait for which

69. Note the double accusative within this verse: "[as an] example … the prophets" (ὑπόδειγμα … τοὺς προφήτας). The word "prophets" forms the direct object; the "example," the predicate object.

70. The expression "the suffering and the patience" (τῆς κακοπαθείας καὶ τῆς μακροθυμίας) probably forms a hendiadys ("one [concept] through two"), in which one or both of two coordinate nouns actually help to define the other, thus yielding "patience in suffering" or even "patient suffering" as acceptable translations (see Kistemaker, *James and the Epistles of John*, 170). Johnson (*The Letter of James*, 318) points out the difficulty that people had in distinguishing true and false prophets who spoke in the name of the Lord and uncovers a tradition that "true prophets came to be perceived as those who suffered hardship, especially that of not being heard and of being rejected by those to whom they spoke," a tradition grounded in Jeremiah and Ezekiel. He adds, "the very experience of such persecution helps solidify the community's sense of being in the line of the true prophets who also so suffered" (319).

71. Tamez, *The Scandalous Message of James*, 30.

72. Church, "James," 407.

73. In the biblical text, Job was not "a silent party to his suffering; rather, he was one who complained bitterly to God

Job is explicitly praised in the *Testament of Job*.[74] Whether his testing lasted months or years, Job remains the prime biblical illustration of patience in trials. He did challenge God's justice, but he never gave up and cursed God, and in Job 42:7 God praises the way Job spoke. The REB thus prefers the translation that "Job stood firm," lessening the difficulty somewhat that attaches to "patience."[75]

Here τέλος seems to mean "end" in the sense of the Lord's "purpose" or "goal" in allowing these calamities to befall Job. The other option is to view the term as describing the "outcome" of Job's life when his fortunes were restored.[76] It is likely that the use of "Lord" (κύριος) here refers not to Jesus but to God himself and that "the readers are reminded of the purpose/result worked out by God" in the life of Job, which would encourage them in their suffering.[77] James does not leave us ignorant of God's purpose, but explains that it occurs in order that we might see his grace. God *will* shower mercy and compassion on those currently oppressed. Here the ὅτι-clause functions as the explanation not only for this verse and Job's suffering but also for all of 5:7 – 11, giving a theological grounding of our suffering in the character of God.

James 5:12 But above all, my brothers and sisters, do not swear either by heaven or by earth or by any other oath; but let your yes [be] yes and your no [be] no, lest you fall under condemnation (Πρὸ πάντων δέ, ἀδελφοί μου, μὴ ὀμνύετε μήτε τὸν οὐρανὸν μήτε τὴν γῆν μήτε ἄλλον τινὰ ὅρκον· ἤτω δὲ ὑμῶν τὸ Ναὶ ναὶ καὶ τὸ Οὒ οὔ, ἵνα μὴ ὑπὸ κρίσιν πέσητε). James finally arrives at some kind of climax with his "above all" (πρὸ πάντων) — but the climax of what? One possibility is that 5:12 introduces the last and culminating section of the entire letter, so that v. 12 should be taken with vv. 13 – 20.[78] But oath-taking has no direct bearing on prayers for physical healing other than as a part of general concluding exhortations. The other option is that v. 12 forms the culmination of vv. 7 – 12 as the proper response to economic exploitation, or as the summation of an even larger stretch of text,[79] perhaps going all the way back to the beginning of ch. 3 with its emphasis on right speech. Baker argues that "James

because of his dire circumstances," a context that makes it less likely that James took his picture of Job solely from the canonical text (Martin, *James*, 194). Tamez (*The Scandalous Message of James*, 44), supported by Church ("James," 408 – 9), plausibly argues that James's point may well be to *include* Job's passionate complaints, since a bitter denunciation of injustice can be appropriate when paired with a willingness to await God's vindication. For the minority view that the parallels in and dates of this literature are not close enough, see Patrick Gray, "Points and Lines: Thematic Parallelism in the Letter of James and the *Testament of Job*," *NTS* 50 (2004): 406 – 24.

74. Cees Haas ("Job's Perseverance in the Testament of Job," in *Studies on the Testament of Job*, ed. Michael A. Knibb and Pieter W. van der Horst [Cambridge: CUP, 1989], 117 – 54) elaborates on this theme under the four subheadings of "standing firm in battle," "stubbornness or toughness," "patience," and "endurance of evil." Supporting "endurance" as the best overarching category is Christopher R. Seitz, "The Patience of Job in the Epistle of James," in *Konsequente Traditionsgeschichte*, ed. Rüdiger Bartelmus, Thomas Krüger, and Helmut Utzschneider (Göttingen: Vandenhoeck & Ruprecht, 1993), 373 – 82.

75. So also Townsend, *The Epistle of James*, 100. Hillel A. Fine ("The Tradition of a Patient Job," *JBL* 74 [1955]: 28 – 32) thinks Job 27 – 28 discloses a patient Job, but in so doing acknowledges that this is too different from the dominant portrait of Job in the rest of the book to have been written at the same time.

76. Perhaps some of both meanings of "end" are intended, because the Lord does indeed bring about that which he purposes. Cf. Edgar, *Has God Not Chosen the Poor?* 207; Robert P. Gordon, "Καὶ τὸ τέλος κυρίου εἴδετε (Jas. v. 11)," *JTS* 26 (1975): 91 – 95. Either way, "of the Lord" (κυρίου) remains a subjective genitive.

77. Johnson, *The Letter of James*, 320.

78. So, e.g., Davids, *The Epistle of James*, 189; Laws, *The Epistle of James*, 203; Martin, *James*, 203.

79. See, e.g., the varying approaches of Ropes, *A Critical and Exegetical Commentary on the Epistle of St. James*, 300; Adamson, *The Epistle of James*, 194; and Johnson, *The Letter of James*, 327.

probably considers swearing the most serious" of the sins of speech because "a broken oath directly involves God in falsehood."[80] Contextually, Baker suggests that James puts this verse where he does because the poor Christians might be "tempted to use oaths to fend off creditors or to obtain credit for food and other necessities," even knowing that prompt payment would be possible only with a miracle.[81]

The Venerable Bede cross-referenced the image of Herod Antipas, saying that "this is the judgment to which Herod fell victim, so that he found that he had either to break his oath or commit another shameful act [executing John the Baptist] in order to avoid breaking it."[82] Given that Job was encouraged to "curse God and die" (Job 2:9), which he never did, it is easy to understand a warning against rash speech following immediately after the use of Job as a positive example of endurance.[83] Oaths can force us into behavior that does not glorify God. Not only can our speech bring either honor or dishonor to God; we ought also to be people whose word is accepted as trustworthy, without needing to swear by anything for others to trust us. We should live, speak, and act with integrity in all we do. James's unifying motif of simplicity versus duplicity continues.[84]

Theology in Application

Judgment Announced for the Oppressors (5:1 – 6)

For Jewish and Christian background on the danger of riches, see above, pp. 63 – 64.[85] In addition, Jer 25:34 employs strikingly similar language to that of Jas 5:1 – 6: "Weep and wail, you shepherds; roll in the dust, you leaders of the flock. For your time to be slaughtered has come; you will fall like the best of the rams." *1 Enoch* 87:8 – 10 denounces those who have grown rich by unjust means, warning them both of the transience of wealth and of coming judgment. In Luke 6:24, Jesus notifies the rich that they have already received their reward. Job 13:28 speaks of human beings wasting away "like something rotten, like a garment eaten by moths"

80. Baker, "James," 105. Keener (*The IVP Bible Background Commentary*, 702) adds that "the fullest form of an oath included a self-curse, which was like saying, 'May God kill me if I fail to do this.'"

81. Baker, "James," 106. Baker adds here the important reminder that "swearing" in this context does not mean using bad language, but rather "using God's name or an unaccepted substitute to signify truthfulness or credibility." Stulac (*James*, 176 – 77) offers a variant on Baker's explanation of why the church members are taking oaths: perhaps they are making rash vows to *God* about what they will do if he extricates them from their plight.

82. Bray, *James, 1 – 2 Peter, 1 – 3 John, Jude*, 59. Leander (in ibid.) adds that "the need of an oath comes from an unsure conscience. It is necessary to extract an oath from one whose sincerity is in doubt, but why should you bind yourself by an involuntary oath when you are bound to show with your lips the sincerity of your heart?" Baker ("James," 105) gives the telling story from Cicero of a man who testified at a trial, and the jury protested that he did not have to take an oath to swear to tell the truth: "Cicero says, 'The Greeks did not wish it to be thought that the credibility of a man of proven honesty was more strictly secured by a ritual observance than by the truthfulness of his character.'"

83. Moore, "Affinities of the Epistle of James with Synagogue Homily and Midrash," 34 – 77.

84. Hartin, *James*, 263.

85. Situating 4:13 – 5:6 particularly in the world of the Essenes and of the Gospel of Thomas, though with some exaggeration, is Bent Noack, "Jakobus wider die Reichen," *ST* 18 (1964): 10 – 25.

(cf. Jas 5:2). Sir 29:10 enjoins using one's money for one's friends and relatives rather than allowing it to rust "under a stone" (again, cf. Jas 5:2).

In Jesus' teaching one thinks especially of his commands to lay up treasures in heaven rather than on earth, "where moth and rust destroy" (Mt 6:19). The personified cries of the laborers' wages in Jas 5:3 remind one of the equally personified cries of Abel's blood in Ge 4:10. The image of rust and poison eating one's flesh like fire is reminiscent of Ps 21:9, in which God's enemies will be consumed by fire. Once again a verse from Lev 19 (Lev 19:13, on not defrauding) seems to lie behind a key teaching of Jas 5:4.[86] An even closer parallel (Dt 24:14 – 15) commands the Israelites, "Do not take advantage of a hired worker who is poor and needy, whether that worker is an Israelite or is a foreigner residing in one of your towns. Pay them their wages each day before sunset, because they are poor and are counting on it. Otherwise they may cry to the LORD against you, and you will be guilty of sin" (cf. also Ge 4:10; Ps 18:6; Mal 3:5).

One of the sins of Sodom is said to involve indulgent living (Eze 16:49 LXX, employing the same verb, σπαταλάω, as in Jas 5:5). The classic NT example is the rich man in the parable of Lk 16:19 – 31, who, despite feasting sumptuously all the time, refuses to give even his table's crumbs to the lame beggar Lazarus (cf. also the rich fool in Lk 12:15 – 21). References to a day of slaughter have appeared already in Isa 30:25; Jer 12:3; and Eze 7:14 – 23. Sir 34:21 – 22 contains a particularly close parallel to the judicial murder of Jas 5:6, with echoes of other details of Jas 5, too: "Bread is life to the destitute, and to deprive them of it is murder. To rob your neighbour of his livelihood is to kill him, and he who defrauds a worker of his wages sheds blood" (REB). Of course, one remembers 1Ki 21 and the example of Jezebel stealing Naboth's vineyard for no better reason than her dislike of seeing Ahab pout over the matter![87]

It is easy to find examples today of the non-Christian rich who exploit the poor and who sometimes go extra hard on believers. Many individual Christians have poignant stories to tell about just such behavior by their employers. But the problem goes far beyond the individual level. Governments around the world almost by definition claim to make decisions based on "national interest," which usually translates into a disproportionate interest in the richest classes of that nation.[88] Multinational corporations may look for the cheapest overseas labor so they can

86. Wall, *Community of the Wise*, 230.

87. For a thorough presentation and analysis of the prophetic genre of and background to this and related sections of James, see Mark H. Taylor, "The Voice of the Prophets in the Letter of James" (M.A. thesis: Denver Seminary, 2008).

88. Cf. Deiros, *Santiago y Judas*, 230 – 37. For workable alternatives, see esp. Bob Goudzwaard and Harry de Lange, *Beyond Poverty and Affluence: Toward an Economy of Care* (Grand Rapids: Eerdmans, 1995). More focused on Christian rather than government or societal responses is Bruce J. Nicholls and Beulah R. Wood, eds., *Sharing the Good News with the Poor: A Reader for Concerned Christians* (Grand Rapids: Baker, 1996). This anthology presents numerous practical steps that have made significant differences in countless lives around the world.

make the greatest profit, whether or not they pay a fair and decent wage and irrespective of the impact on the job market in the communities in which their headquarters or major Western plants are based. In many parts of the Majority World, they (or wealthy indigenous private owners, the local equivalent of the Mafia, or the government itself) own vast tracts of land that are cultivated by "guest workers" at substandard wages.

Migrant workers in the U.S. often face similar injustices, made all the more complicated by the fact that some — but only some — of them are also illegal aliens. Even among full-fledged American citizens, the buying power of workers (i.e., wages evaluated based on cost of living in any given location) varies greatly from one part of the country to the next, with inequities based on race, country of origin, gender, and marital status still alarmingly sizable.[89] Wall's words are worth pondering: "If James's brand of piety is taken seriously and at face value ... a substantial portion of the North American church would become quite uncomfortable with the ease by which it has accommodated the upward economic mobility of liberal democracy while trying to follow after its downwardly mobile Lord."[90]

But there are even more uncomfortable applications that should be made. How many upper- or middle-class Western Christians have so many extra, largely unused clothes, so that, were it not for mothballs or their equivalent, they *would* have become moth-eaten? How many have other needless possessions, even investments, that are not being used for much of anything, and certainly not for the Lord's work, that would be better off given to the needy? How many, if they were to be ruthlessly honest, live a lifestyle perilously close to that of v. 5 — of luxury and self-indulgence? Then there is the enormous waste of food left uneaten and thrown away in restaurants, of the quantities of garbage thrown out that could be recycled, of planned obsolescence of products so that entirely new ones must be bought rather than old ones repaired (or the prohibitive cost of repairs making it cheaper just to buy a new item).

A generation ago it was almost unheard of to raze an entire building just to put another one on the same site, or to level a whole shopping center to replace it with a new one, or to tear down an entire athletic stadium just to build a larger, fancier one; but today all of these are common occurrences. How many churches think that the only realistic option when they outgrow one facility is to build a bigger, more upscale one, with perhaps millions of dollars diverted from truly helping the world's

89. For sample statistics, see Church, "James," 414 – 15. On "the vital link between your possessions and your soul," see the book thus subtitled by Wesley K. Willmer with Martyn Smith, *God and Your Stuff* (Colorado Springs, CO: NavPress, 2002).

90. Wall, *Community of the Wise*, 246. From a Latin American perspective, see esp. René Krüger, "Antisociales, anticomunitarios y asesinos (Santiago 5:1 – 6)," *Cuadernos de teología* 20 (2001): 55 – 75. From an urban North American vantage point, see Robert Lupton, *And You Call Yourself a Christian: Toward Responsible Charity* (Chicago: CCDA, 2006).

destitute, physically and spiritually? One shudders to think of the potential judgment of God being stored up by so many examples of profligate waste.[91]

Of course, one dare not minimize the differences between a largely capitalist world today and the ancient Mediterranean economy of "limited goods" (the belief that there was a fixed amount of wealth in the world such that, if one person had more, someone else necessarily had less). Many investments today are highly beneficial when their earnings continue to increase and are regularly used for God's kingdom work at home and abroad.[92] A little bit of research can enable investors to determine companies that make reasonable efforts not to defraud workers, exploit the poor, or rape the environment. Similar research can enable consumers to make godlier, wiser choices when deciding which of several brands of some product to purchase. In 5:1 – 6 James is not condemning saving or investing but rather hoarding.[93] But he comes down hard on that selfishness and then even harder on lavish expenditures for self-indulgence.[94]

Prophetic Patience Enjoined on the Oppressed (5:7 – 11)

One might have expected the purveyor of such fiery invective to proceed to champion all-out class warfare on these wicked bourgeoisie. Instead, at first glance, it would appear that James remains completely passivist, if not pacifist! In essence, "just wait, be patient, stand firm, don't complain." It is true that a tenacious endurance does dominate the response James desires from his churches in this paragraph.

But two qualifications prove crucial. First, James can take this tack because of his theodicy — his solution to the problem of evil. Christ is coming back, he is coming back soon (at least from God's perspective),[95] and he will wreak vengeance on the wicked — with absolute justice and equity — something sinful mortals could

91. "This section of James should send tremors through many American Christians, for the culture in which we live is fundamentally oriented toward leisure. Whether people say they live to 'play' or that they 'worship the game,' all such living represents a massive investment of one's worldly possessions primarily for pleasure.... These selfish tendencies in every culture must be fiercely assaulted with the Word of God in order to expose their gross sinfulness and harm to others" (Richardson, *James*, 213). Cf. Motyer, *The Message of James*, 171: "We must keep the tightest hold on all luxury spending." For a full-orbed, positive antidote, see R. Scott Rodin, *Stewards in the Kingdom: A Theology of Life in All Its Fulness* (Downers Grove, IL: IVP, 2000). For specific suggestions, see Brian Rosner, *Beyond Greed* (Kingsford, NSW: Matthias Media, 2004). Cf. now esp. Wesley K. Willmer, ed., *Revolution in Generosity: Transforming Stewards to Be Rich toward God* (Chicago: Moody Press, 2008).

92. As helpful as any book in general supporting capitalism as an economic philosophy, but critiquing it from a thoroughgoing Christian framework, is Fred Catherwood, *The Creation of Wealth: Recovering a Christian Understanding of Money, Work, and Ethics* (Wheaton, IL: Crossway, 2002).

93. See the helpful chart in Barton, Veerman, and Wilson (*James*, 121) on distinguishing between saving and hoarding.

94. On these three points, see Baker and Ellsworth, *Preaching James*, 113 – 15. Cf. esp. Deiros, *Santiago y Judas*, 218 – 23.

95. On James's "thoroughgoing eschatology," see Brosend, *James and Jude*, 146.

never do and therefore should not try to do![96] For a similar blessing on those who wait and endure until the end, see Da 12:12. The most important NT background text is the Olivet Discourse, especially Mt 24:33, in which Christ stands near, at the very door, about to return and usher in judgment.

Other intertextual connections to vv. 7 – 9 involve the early and late rains, well-known from a host of OT texts (Dt 11:14 – 15; Jer 5:24; Hos 6:3; Joel 2:23; Zec 10:1). Lack of grumbling will separate James's congregations from the numerous times that many of the children of Israel murmured and protested: in the wilderness, at God's leaders, at his prophetic rebukes, and in eventually rejecting Jesus himself. It will also spare them judgment, just as Christ himself warned against a judgmental spirit, "or you too will be judged" (Mt 7:1). In a time of so many hardships imposed from outside, these Christians cannot afford to be squabbling with each other; now of all times they must be supporting and encouraging one another.[97]

The second qualification that demonstrates James is no passivist appears in vv. 10 – 11. He may never condone violent resistance, but he offers two bizarre models if his point is nothing but quiet acceptance of oppression — the prophets and Job! What is more, he calls special attention to the prophets' divinely inspired *speech*. Old Testament prophetic rhetoric with respect to injustice was always blunt and denunciatory. While Yahweh's prophets did not usurp God's role in enacting vengeance on the unjust, they certainly made clear God's displeasure and coming judgment, even if they had to rebuke monarchs in the process![98] Job's endurance, too, was scarcely quietist. From his finite perspective, he correctly perceived (unlike all his "friends") that he had done nothing to deserve this intense suffering, and he demanded that God explain himself. When God finally did speak, Job responded with appropriate humility.

Thus James adopts a middle ground between the revolutionary Zealots and the monastic Essenes of his day. Like Job, the prophets, and Jesus before him, he calls on believers to fight injustice through wise speech. Both physical separation from and physical attack against the fallen world prove misguided.[99] God can be trusted to right all wrongs, in his perfect timing, because he is merciful and compassionate (cf. Ex 34:6; Ps 103:8; 111:4). But God's people are called to warn others of this impending judgment of evil and vindication of the righteous.[100] Solomon Andria notes an additional *via media* here: "Patience will help us to avoid both the feverish speculation about the date of his return that characterizes some groups and the

96. Reyes, "El grito del salario," 85 – 86. Cf. Tidball, *Wisdom from Heaven*, 32.

97. Townsend, *The Epistle of James*, 99.

98. See Keenan (*The Wisdom of James*, 147) for a long list of sample texts.

99. Davids, *The Epistle of James*, 182.

100. Indeed, Susan R. Garrett ("The Patience of Job and Jesus," *Int* 53 [1999]: 263) argues that the only time one patiently endures without any kind of protest is "wherever suffering can be avoided only by making a grievously wrong choice, or wherever suffering cannot be avoided at all."

lack of concern shown by those with divided hearts who say that the Lord will never return."[101]

Oaths Proscribed to Avoid Unrealistic Promises (5:12)

Here appears the closest thing to a direct quote from the Jesus tradition in any text in James. Jesus in the Sermon on the Mount likewise forbade oaths, commanding one's affirmative or negative statements to represent such a commitment to truth-telling that they can always be taken at face value (Mt 5:34 – 37).[102] Once again, Lev 19 also looms large in the background, as it did for Jesus when he contrasted the Torah's prohibition of swearing falsely with his insistence not to swear at all. At the same time, these verses form part of a larger segment of the "Antitheses" in Matthew (Mt 5:21 – 48), all of which need to be interpreted against their historical and cultural horizons. Jesus probably had no intention of banning oath taking in a court of law, for example. In context, the problem was the Pharisaic casuistry, in which one could swear by something lesser than God himself and then claim that the oath was less binding (cf. also Mt 23:22). After all, in quite different contexts Paul called God to be his witness that what he said was true, and he did so as part of inspired Scripture (2Co 1:23; Gal 1:20), while Hebrews stresses that even God made oaths and swore by himself (Heb 6:13 – 18).

In James's context, the problem appears to be rash or unrealistic vows that were often broken, thus impugning the oath taker's character and Christian witness. It is sad to see how American culture has deteriorated in less than three generations. Before World War II, a "gentleman's handshake" could often substitute for a written agreement. In much of the last half century, formal contracts were needed before one could trust a businessperson's word, but then one could usually count on it. Today, even written contracts are frequently broken, to such an extent that in some circles people do not even perceive the process to be unethical. Societies ultimately collapse when too many people lose their verbal integrity, so Christians must remain at the forefront of those whose word can be trusted unquestioningly.[103]

101. Andria, "James," 1515. Bill Moyers cites the view of some, though wrongly attributing it to James Watt: "After the last tree is felled, Christ will come back" (www.commondreams.org/views05/0211-22.htm, accessed 8/20/08). Attempts to hasten Jesus' return through destroying the environment directly contradict the teaching of Ge 1:28 – 30, where we are put in charge to steward the earth, and also Rev 11:18, where we are told God will destroy "those who destroy the earth." Carelessness with God's creation does not hasten God's timetable; it merely brings judgment on those who are careless.

102. See Isaacs (*Hebrews and James*, 245) for a helpful chart, in parallel column form, showing the close similarities in wording at each point.

103. See further William R. Baker, "'Above All Else': Contexts of the Call for Verbal Integrity in James 5:12," *JSNT* 54 (1994): 57 – 71.

James 5:13 – 20

CHAPTER 11

Literary Context

The last passage in James has often been seen as the conclusion to this epistle, even though it reads more like the last topic of the letter body than a standard epistolary closing.[1] If our proposals about James's outline are on target, 5:13 – 18 fits very nicely as the final subsection of James's unpacking his theme of trials and temptations.[2] For those in his congregations who have not personally experienced economic exploitation, chances are good they or someone close to them *has* experienced serious illness. Or if they have not done so yet, sooner or later they will. Disease and disability ran rampant in the ancient Mediterranean world, without the kinds of medicine we in the modern West have come to take for granted.[3] These Christians would need to know how to respond to such suffering.

Indeed, even vv. 19 – 20 can be seen as James's exhortation concerning yet another temptation — to stray from the faith. At the same time, even though they do not form a conventional letter closing, these two verses do form a fitting end to the epistle, after the body of the letter has concluded with v. 18. Either they prove analogous to an "epilogue in Greek speeches, giving a short thematic recapitulation" — in this case, of the "addressees' inconstancy"[4] — or they form a brief exhortation summing up the proper response to the recipients' key problems (cf. also the end of 1 John).[5] In either event, the exhortation to fraternal correction remains "in perfect sympathy with all that is written by James, pervasively, concerning a constant preoccupation to avoid the bad and to stimulate good works."[6] Even if they don't suddenly all mature at once, at least they must not give up the faith.

Connections between 5:13 – 20 and the earlier two subsections on trials (4:13 – 17

1. The ambiguity appears because it includes instructions for providing for people's health, just as letter closings often offer wishes or prayers for the recipients' health. Cf. Edgar, *Has God Not Chosen the Poor?* 210. But the latter form does not involve prescriptions for a ritual to secure that health.

2. On 5:13 – 18 continuing the theme of trials, cf. also Wendell G. Johnston, "Does James Give Believers a Pattern for Dealing with Sickness and Healing?" in *Integrity of Heart, Skillfulness of Hands*, ed. Charles H. Dyer and Roy B. Zuck (Grand Rapids: Baker, 1994), 169 – 70.

3. See esp. Bolt, "Life, Death, and the Afterlife in the Greco-Roman World," esp. 56 – 59.

4. Edgar, *Has God Not Chosen the Poor?* 213 – 14.

5. See esp. Francis, "Form and Function of the Opening and Closing Paragraphs of James and 1 John," 125 – 26.

6. Giovanni C. Bottini, "Correzione fraterna e salvezza in *Giacomo* 5,19 – 20," *SBFLA* 35 (1985): 135 (translation ours).

and 5:1 – 12) include the general uncertainties of health and wealth (here today, gone tomorrow), as well as more specific similarities between prayer (the main appropriate response to suffering in this passage) and patience (the key to the response to exploitation in vv. 7 – 11). Calling on the name of the Lord for healing (v. 14) parallels turning to the Lord for vindication and justice (vv. 8 – 9). The possibility that sin was part of the cause of sickness (vv. 15 – 16) mirrors the possibility that the sin of failing to take God's will into account could lead to the love of transient riches (vv. 13 – 17) and that the sin of exploiting the poor could lead to even harsher judgment (vv. 1 – 6). The illustration of Elijah (vv. 17 – 18) recalls the appeals to OT prophets and to Job (vv. 10 – 11), and the reference to his prayers against and then for rain reuses the imagery of the farmer waiting for early and later rains (v. 7).[7]

The next biggest cluster of conceptual or verbal parallels in the book occurs, not surprisingly, in James's opening treatments of trials and temptations. Just as the general call to rejoice in trials (1:2 – 4) led to the command to pray for wisdom (v. 5), so too prayer is the proper response to suffering in sickness.[8] Just as the one other use in James of the verb for "wander" (πλανάω) occurs in 1:16 in James's second segment on trials and temptations as he calls his listeners not to be deceived, so also those who wander away should be brought back (5:19 – 20). Just as those who endure trials will receive the crown of life (1:12), so those who are led back from their wandering will be saved from death. Just as one's own sin regularly plays a central role in succumbing to other forms of temptation (1:13 – 15), so likewise sin can at times be part of the cause of illness. God, however, gives only good gifts (1:17 – 18), which include, at least at times, physical healing.

Finally, "the truth" as a synonym for the way of the gospel (5:19) parallels "the word of truth" as a similar shorthand in 1:18. More allusively, one discerns echoes of other portions of the epistle in "the prayer of faith" (5:15), comparable to the good works that flow from faith more generally (2:14 – 26), and in the literal "fruit" that Elijah's prayer for rain helped to produce (5:18) and the fruit of righteousness produced by the wisdom from above (3:13 – 18). Key teaching about prayer occurs also in 4:2 – 3.

IV. The Three Themes Expanded (2:1 – 5:18)
- C. Trials and Temptations (4:13 – 5:18)
  1. Planning apart from God's Will (4:13 – 17)
  2. Responding to Oppression (5:1 – 12)
  3. **Anointing Prayer for Serious Illness (5:13 – 18)**

V. Closing (5:19 – 20)

7. Stulac (*James*, 179) takes v. 12 as the introduction to vv. 13 – 20 and adds, therefore, that prayer (vv. 13 – 18) is the alternative to swearing (v. 12).

8. Cf. Hartin, *James*, 272 – 73. He finds an inclusio around the whole letter via these references. Cargal (*Restoring the Diaspora*, 46) finds another inclusio via the references to the dispersion in 1:1 and to someone wandering from the faith here, but this seems more tenuous.

Main Idea

Christians should deal with suffering, sickness, and sin by intercession with God and intervention in the lives of fellow believers. Sometimes sin will be one of the direct causes of suffering or sickness and sometimes it will not. When it is, confession becomes crucial. In all situations, prayer proves powerful.

Translation

(See next page.)

Structure

Two brief questions form the equivalents of conditional clauses to introduce this text. If one is suffering or if one is happy, one should pray (v. 13). V. 14 introduces a similar question-condition, which is the more specific focus of the rest of the pericope. If anyone is sick, that person should likewise pray, but in severe instances also call on the church's eldership for ritual anointing with oil (v. 14). James's promise, stated twice in parallel fashion, insists that the combination of the faithful prayer and the Lord's power will produce the desired healing (v. 15a). In some instances, sin may also have been involved in the sickness, in which case this process will lead to forgiveness as well (v. 15b). The appropriate inference from this latter consequence is that believers should freely confess their sins to each other, along with praying for one another, in hopes of the most holistic healing possible (v. 16). With the motivational illustration of Elijah's prayers for drought and rain, James brings the letter body to a close (vv. 17–18).

If vv. 19–20 form the conclusion to the entire letter, however unusual it may be, then it is somewhat artificial to keep them joined to vv. 13–18. Nevertheless, it is difficult to be completely sure this is how these two verses are functioning, and there are natural links with the preceding pericope, most obviously with the theme of restoration from sin and its consequences. So it is possible to keep vv. 19–20 together with vv. 13–18 as two parts to a passage of preachable length. This final, shorter section will then present an additional response to sin. If the sinner is not initiating confession, other believers can pursue them in hopes of restoration. When successful, they will have helped produce God's forgiveness of sin and helped save the person from eternal death.[9]

9. Cf. Hartin, *James*, 282: "'My brothers [and sisters]' ... indicates ... that this is a separate section. This does not mean it is unconnected to what has preceded it, but it may be James's way of indicating that he is concluding the letter (see, e.g., 1 John, which ends similarly: 'Little children, keep yourselves from idols' [5:21])."

James 5:13-20

13a	Condition	**Is anyone suffering among you?**
b	Exhortation	**Let them pray.**
c	Alternative (to a)	**Is anyone happy?**
d	Exhortation	**Let them sing praise.**
14a	Gen/Spec (w 13a)	**Is someone sick among you?**
b	Exhortation	**They should call together the elders of the church**
c	sequence	and **they should pray for that one**,
d	manner	anointing the person with oil
e	association	in the name of the Lord.
15a	Promise	And **the prayer of faith will save the sick**,
b	parallel	and **the Lord will raise them up**;
c	condition	and if they have committed sins,
d	result	**they will be forgiven them.**
16a	Inference	Therefore **confess [your] sins to one another**
b	sequence	and **pray on behalf of one another**
c	purpose	so that you may be healed.
d	Basis (of a-c)	In many ways, **a prayer of a righteous person is strong**
e	time	when it is exercised.
17a	Illustration	**Elijah was a man with the same nature as us**,
b	expansion	and **he prayed fervently** that it would not rain,
c	result	and **it did not rain** upon the earth three years and six months.
18a	Contrast (to 17b)	And **again he prayed**,
b	result	and **the heavens gave rain**
c	result (of b)	and **the earth produced its fruit**.
19a		My brothers and sisters,
	Condition	if someone among you should stray from the truth and
b	sequence	someone should restore them,
20a	promise	**let that person know** that the one returning a sinner ...
b	separation	from the error of their ways
		saves their soul from death and
c	restatement (of a)	covers a multitude of sins.

Exegetical Outline

IV. The Three Themes Expanded (2:1 – 5:18)

C. Trials and Temptations (4:13 – 5:18)

➡ **3. Christians must always pray and, when necessary, confess their sins, in order to deal with suffering and sickness (5:13 – 18).**

a. Christians should respond to all situations of life with prayer (v. 13).

b. Christians should respond to sickness with prayer and anointing with oil (vv. 14 – 15a).

c. If the sickness is the result of sin, Christians should confess their sin in order to receive physical and spiritual healing (vv. 15b – 16a).

d. The prayers of righteous people are powerful, like Elijah's (vv. 16b – 18).

V. Christians must intervene in the lives of fellow believers who are sinning (vv. 19 – 20).

A. Successful intervention (that which brings repentance) saves that person from the consequences of possible apostasy (vv. 19 – 20a).

B. Successful intervention can bring forgiveness even when that person has committed many sins (v. 20b).

Explanation of Text

James 5:13 Is anyone suffering among you? Let them pray. Is anyone happy? Let them sing praise[10] (κακοπαθεῖ τις ἐν ὑμῖν, προσευχέσθω· εὐθυμεῖ τις, ψαλλέτω). James changes abruptly from the trials of riches and poverty to those of illness and sin. In doing so, he returns to his earlier discussions on prayer. This verse provides a general introduction to this section, highlighting the two extremes of suffering and joy and outlining the appropriate responses. The first verb for prayer (προσεύχομαι) is the broadest of the Greek verbs that denoted "speaking to God" in James's day. The verb for singing praise (ψάλλω) is cognate to the English word "psalm." The two imperatives are in the third person, reflecting a cross between "let" and "must," but closer to "must."[11] In modern English, "what we *should* do" may come closest to capturing the sense. The present tenses may suggest that we should pray and sing praises repeatedly (cf. NLT: "they should keep on praying about it" and "should continually sing praises to the Lord").[12]

We should view prayer as another revolutionary tactic, *not* a passive resignation to a situation.[13] In prayer, we enlist the aid and ear of "the Lord of Hosts" (recall 5:4), our God who is more than capable of righting our wrongs and helping us in our pain. The use of "among you" (ἐν ὑμῖν) may

10. Davids (*The Epistle of James*, 191) argues that the question and answer form of these sentences parallels a conditional sentence, thus allowing the translation: "If someone ... then they should...." It is also possible to translate each as a statement: "Someone is ... they should," though this seems less natural a way of speaking.

11. Wallace, *Greek Grammar beyond the Basics*, 486.

12. Alternately, we may think of v. 13 as containing the two *general*, present-tense commands that apply in all situations and v. 14 the two *specific*, aorist-tense commands that apply to severe illness. Cf. Porter, *Verbal Aspect in the Greek of the New Testament*, 359.

13. Martin (*James*, 205) comments that "it may be that his exhortation is an attempt to defuse a volatile situation, suggesting that to pray is much better than to fight.... If this piece of advice is followed, then some (but not necessarily all) suffering that is the lot of the afflicted church could be avoided."

suggest "that James was not thinking primarily of private, personal prayers, but of prayers within the believing community."[14]

James 5:14 Is someone sick among you? They should call together the elders of the church and they should pray for that one, anointing the person with oil in the name of the Lord (ἀσθενεῖ τις ἐν ὑμῖν, προσκαλεσάσθω τοὺς πρεσβυτέρους τῆς ἐκκλησίας καὶ προσευξάσθωσαν ἐπ᾽ αὐτὸν ἀλείψαντες [αὐτόν] ἐλαίῳ ἐν τῷ ὀνόματι τοῦ κυρίου[15]). James now supplements his directions on prayer. Seemingly following the same pattern of identifying a situation and then prescribing a remedy as in the previous verse, he describes an appropriate response to illness. The first question this verse raises is whether the sickness is physical or spiritual. While Paul often uses "to be sick" (ἀσθενέω) spiritually, always in the Gospels (and almost everywhere else) the verb refers to physical illness. Given an early date for James, his dependence on Jesus' teaching, and the fact that the other sufferings mentioned in his letter have referred to concrete physical problems, the latter connotation is more likely here.[16]

Motyer draws out five points from these verses that imply how serious an illness James is here discussing, suggesting that this sick person is bedridden and potentially helpless even to pray for him- or herself: (1) the elders are called *to* the sick person; (2) the elders do all the praying; (3) the person is called "worn out" or "exhausted" in v. 15 (his understanding of κάμνω); (4) the faith is also that of the elders, not of the sick person; and (5) the elders pray "over" the person as if that one were confined to a prone position.[17]

In striking contrast with the traditional Catholic sacrament of extreme unction, or last rites, the purpose of this prayer and anointing is for physical healing in this life, not spiritual cleansing before one dies.[18] Moreover, the call from the sick person is not to a priest (or any solitary church leader), but to the elders who represent the entire local Christian community.[19] The most distinctive part of the command is that they ought to anoint the sick person with oil. Two main interpretations compete for acceptance. Some see the oil as symbolic, in the sense that the anointing of kings in the OT symbolized God's presence with them. Moo discusses at length the uses of oil in the ancient Mediterranean world, both medicinal and ritual, and concludes that "anoint" here "refers to a physical action with symbolic significance.... As the elders pray, they are to anoint the sick person in order to symbolize that the person is being set apart for God's special attention and care."[20]

14. Baker and Ellsworth, *Preaching James*, 143.

15. Here the textual variant originates from an attempt to clarify who the "Lord" might be, or, conversely, through scribal omissions. The reading τοῦ κυρίου has the broadest support base, including א and Byz., so that the UBS committee granted the reading an {A}. Metzger (*A Textual Commentary on the Greek New Testament*, 614) argues that the omission of either the article or the phrase "of the Lord" "probably arose through inadvertence in transcription." Finally, the addition of other modifiers to "Lord" such as "Jesus" or "Jesus Christ" are most likely scribal glosses to clarify James's ambiguous uses of "Lord" (κύριος).

16. Sigurd Kaiser, *Krankenheilung: Untersuchungen zu Form, Sprache, traditionsgeschichtlichem Hintergrund und Aussage zu Jak 5,13–18* (Neukirchen-Vluyn: Neukirchener, 2006), 29–41.

17. Motyer, *The Message of James*, 193–94.

18. Perkins (*First and Second Peter, James, and Jude*, 137) notes that liturgical renewal within Catholicism is starting to apply this ritual more broadly to settings of physical healing, too.

19. Here it is important to note that the word "church" (ἐκκλησία) appears rather than "assembly" (συναγωγή), as in 2:2. James clearly is referring to *Christian* communities only. On the holistic interplay between physical and spiritual healing in the religious and medical communities of a society, see Martin C. Albl, "'Are Any among You Sick?' The Health Care System in the Letter of James," *JBL* 121 (2002): 123–43.

20. Moo, *The Letter of James*, 238–240. The quotation comes from p. 242.

Note that the grammar in this clause indicates the need for prayer as the primary reason for the elders' visit, represented by the main verb "they should pray" (προσευξάσθωσαν). The participle "anointing" (ἀλείψαντες) indicates concurrent[21] but subordinate action. The oil is the symbol of God's presence, but prayer is the mechanism for tapping into his power.

Some scholars, however, understand the oil as a medicinal substance,[22] though partial parallels in Jewish circles to ritual anointing for physical healing make this view less probable.[23] It is true that the verb for "anoint" (ἀλείφω) here is not the uniformly symbolic one (χρίω — as in "Christ," the anointed one), but still it is one that implies a ritual anointing in eight out of its nine NT occurrences.[24] This observation scarcely precludes seeking medicinal help; it just means that is probably not what James has in mind here.

Given the overall teaching of the NT, in which healing is not consistently paired with anointing, we should not take this one verse as mandating that oil must accompany *all* prayers for the sick. At the same time, there is no reason not to implement a practice like this one for some of the most chronic or life-threatening illnesses that church members face. Neither does this verse refer to a specific "gift" of healing, but rather assigns the task of anointing the sick to the elders, the duly commissioned church leaders responsible for the leadership and nurture of the body as a whole.[25] The descriptive phrase "in the name of the Lord" reminds us that the healing is done solely by the will and power of God.[26] Given the use of the formula "in the name of Jesus" throughout the early church, especially in Acts, the Lord here may specifically be Christ.

James 5:15 And the prayer of faith will save the sick, and the Lord will raise them up; and if they have committed sins, they will be forgiven them (καὶ ἡ εὐχὴ τῆς πίστεως σώσει τὸν κάμνοντα καὶ ἐγερεῖ αὐτὸν ὁ κύριος· κἂν ἁμαρτίας ᾖ πεποιηκώς, ἀφεθήσεται αὐτῷ). This verse makes the bold claim that if we pray in faith, God will heal the person for whom we pray.[27] The verbal roots for "sick" (κάμνω) and "raise up" (ἐγείρω)

21. The aorist participle, when it appears *later* in the sentence than the main verb that it modifies, in a significant minority of instances, refers to action simultaneous rather than prior to that of the main verb. Cf. Ropes (*A Critical and Exegetical Commentary on the Epistle of St. James*, 305), and the ancient literature there cited.

22. See the actions of the good Samaritan in Lk 10:34. Davids (*The Epistle of James*, 193) provides a helpful list of literature showing the medicinal use of oil in the ancient world.

23. The closest parallels come in the later rabbinic literature (cf. *Eccl. Rab.* 1.8.4 with *b. Bab. Bat.* 116a); pre-Christian precedent *may* appear in *Life of Adam and Eve* 36; *Apoc. Mos.* 9:3. 13:1.

24. The sole exception is Mark 6:13. Robertson (*Word Pictures in the New Testament*, 6:65) thus drastically overstates matters by following Trench and alleging that ἀλείφειν is a "mundane and profane" word, so that "at bottom in James we have God and medicine, God and the doctor." Gary S. Shogren ("Will God Heal Us — A Re-Examination of James 5:14 – 16a," *EvQ* 61 [1989]: 99 – 108) presents a useful examination of four different interpretations: (1) medicinal use; (2) extreme unction; (3) psychological reinforcement; and (4) a symbol of divine favor — opting for a combination of (3) and (4). For a vigorous defense of (1) see Daniel R. Hayden, "Calling the Elders to Pray," *BSac* 138 (1981): 258 – 66. For (2), cf. Charles Pickar, "Is Anyone Sick Among You?" *CBQ* 7 (1945): 165 – 74.

25. John Christopher Thomas (*The Devil, Disease and Deliverance: Origins of Illness in New Testament Thought* [Sheffield: SAP, 1998], 21, 23) notes that James "does not advocate calling for those who possess the charism of healing, which would have been likely in the Pauline community (as 1Cor. 12 might imply)." Instead, "the elders were to be called because they were recognized leaders in the church. As such they represent the community and its ability to minister to those who are physically ill." Cf. his earlier work, "The Devil, Disease and Deliverance: James 5:14 – 16," *JPT* 2 (1993): 25 – 50.

26. Cf. Stulac, *James*, 181 – 82; Tidball, *Wisdom from Heaven*, 194, 197.

27. Mark A. Seifrid ("The Waiting Church and Its Duty: James 5:13 – 18," *SBJT* 4 no. 3 [2000]: 32 – 39) notes that "the greatest part of the closing instructions deals with sickness

can be used for both physical and spiritual afflictions and their cures, but in the context of anointing most likely refer at least primarily to physical illnesses.[28] "Raising up" thus refers to their getting out of bed after they are well again.

The promise of healing for the sick offers a much needed corrective for those of us who have trouble praying boldly, for we fear or even assume that God will *not* do what we ask of him. Instead, we ought to pray boldly, believing that he is a God of power and love and that he listens to the prayers of his people. A necessary caveat, however, requires us to remember that he chooses how and when he heals, as Paul lays out clearly in 2Co 12:8 – 10, and that complete healing never occurs in this life. In fact, every other time James uses "save" (σῴζω), it refers to spiritual salvation. While this passage most likely refers to physical healing, we must remember that ultimately God is more interested in eternal, spiritual life than temporal, physical health.

Somewhere in our prayers we must find a balance between never expecting God to heal and requiring him to heal on demand. Trying to identify an exact definition of the "prayer of faith" is perplexing, but perhaps the best explanation appears already in 1:5 – 8, where we are instructed to pray "with the confident expectation that God will hear and answer the prayer."[29] Still, these commands also assume the proviso of 4:15 in which everything for which we hope remains contingent on God's will.[30] Thus Keith Warrington concludes that "the prayer of faith is best identified as knowledge of God's will for a particular situation when no scriptural guidance is available." Warrington nevertheless recognizes that such a knowledge of God's will is often absent, in which case we are still to pray, but in a way that acknowledges God's right to supersede our desires.[31]

The second half of the sentence forms a third-class condition, which counters the assumption that there *must* be some sin, or lack of faith, that needs God's forgiveness (recall the recurring, errant counsel of Job's friends).[32] James does not, however, exclude the option that past sins may well have caused current illness.[33] Christopher Thomas notes that confession is required in cases where illness is a direct result of sin, but that "there is no indication that the sick believer is to be preoccupied with discovering some secret sin that may have been committed; rather the implication is that the sick believer would know full well the nature of the sin. There is also the impression left that confession should be a normal part of the worshiping community's life." We must remember, however, that "certain illnesses are simply the consequence of living in a sinful world."[34]

Some have argued that these verses indicate an activity valid only in apostolic times, so that we do not have the right to expect supernatural healings any longer.[35] But James does not place any restrictions on how long or to whom his command applies, and inasmuch as miraculous healings have occurred throughout the Bible and church history

and sin within the congregation. We often allow such matters to be pushed to the periphery of our life as a church. James places them at the center, undoubtedly because he sees in them the primary expression of the Gospel and its power" (33).

28. Kaiser, *Krankenheilung*, 41 – 48, 77 – 84.

29. Thomas, *The Devil, Disease and Deliverance*, 30.

30. See Moo, *The Letter of James: An Introduction and Commentary*, 182. The parallel situation occurs in the Sermon on the Mount, where the seemingly blank check of Mt 7:7 – 11 ("Ask and it shall be given to you ...") must be read in light of Christ's command in 6:10 to pray that *God's* will be done.

31. Keith Warrington, "James 5:14 – 18: Healing Then and Now," *IRM* 93 (2004): 358, 359.

32. Guthrie, "James," 271; Popkes, *Der Brief des Jakobus*, 340.

33. Indeed, in this event, he places noteworthy emphasis on the commission of the sin by virtue of the periphrastic construction with the perfect participle. Cf. Hartin, *James*, 269.

34. Thomas, "James 5:14 – 16," 36, 37.

35. Classically, B. B. Warfield, *Counterfeit Miracles* (New York: Charles Scribner's Sons, 1918).

for good and godly ends,[36] we dare not restrict such activity to any given time period.

James 5:16 Therefore confess [your] sins to one another and pray on behalf of one another so that you may be healed. In many ways, a prayer of a righteous person is strong, when it is exercised (ἐξομολογεῖσθε οὖν ἀλλήλοις τὰς ἁμαρτίας καὶ εὔχεσθε ὑπὲρ ἀλλήλων ὅπως ἰαθῆτε. πολὺ ἰσχύει δέησις δικαίου ἐνεργουμένη). James clarifies that the forgiveness of sins comes in a context of confession. His flow of thought here makes us wonder whether the illness under discussion comes as a direct result of unconfessed sin. As just noted, however, the third-class condition of the previous verse precludes the allegation that all sickness results from personal sin. Communal confession of sin, however, remains important for the life and health of the community, even if our own sins have not had obvious physical consequences in our lives.

James uses here yet another verb for healing (ἰάομαι), which can refer to physical or spiritual cures as the context dictates. Here it seems to refer to restored spiritual well-being due to confession and forgiveness.[37] We ought to have people close enough to us whom we allow to inquire into our spiritual state, whether formally as with a pastor or elder, or more informally as with an accountability group, partner, or mentor. James makes it clear that the Christian life should not be lived apart from community. Martin explains that "though the elders are still responsible for the prayer of intercession on behalf of the ill (5:14), the text here widens to make prayer and confession and so pastoral responsibility the 'privilege and responsibility' of all in the congregation."[38]

God intended prayer to bring the body together, so that when one person falls ill, physically or spiritually, others in the community may intervene redemptively. Likewise, confession is not merely a mental activity as we talk to God in our individual prayer times, but a corporate activity that involves the people we have hurt or offended. Whether to bring humility and unity to a body of believers or to effect reconciliation between estranged parties, God clearly intended confession to be as much a part of life together as prayer.

The participle we have rendered as "when it is exercised" (ἐνεργουμένη), by taking it as adverbial and temporal, might instead be adjectival and attributive ("the effective [prayer of a righteous person is strong]"). But then James's statement borders on tautology. One can avoid this by translating the participle as "energetic," but then one probably commits the anachronistic fallacy. The English word "energy" derives historically from this Greek root, but it reflects the scientific understanding of a much later date.[39] In context, James is more likely trying to encourage his congregations to *exercise* or "work at" their option of prayer more consistently. Indeed, the form could even be middle ("when they exercise it [for] themselves"). More probably, though, it is passive, indicating God as the ultimate agent in activating his people's prayers.[40]

James 5:17 Elijah was a man with the same nature as us, and he prayed fervently that it would

36. See throughout Kate Cooper and Jeremy Gregory, *Signs, Wonders, Miracles: Representations of Divine Power in the Life of the Church* (Woodbridge, Suffolk: Boydell & Brewer, 2005).

37. Burchard, *Der Jakobusbrief*, 212; Ruckstuhl, *Jakobusbrief; 1–3 Johannesbrief*, 31.

38. Martin, *James*, 211. Thomas ("James 5:14–16," 26) points out that even in this context, close to v. 14, prayers for healing do not necessarily require anointing with oil.

39. Translations involving the English word group of "energy, "energize," and "energetic" do not appear in BDAG, *EDNT*, or *NIDNTT* under entries for this Greek root.

40. See Davids (*The Epistle of James*, 196–97) for an outline of the various interpretations of this participle. For the approach we have adopted, cf. Ropes, *A Critical and Exegetical Commentary on the Epistle of James*, 309–10; Mayor, *The*

not rain, and it did not rain upon the earth three years and six months (Ἠλίας ἄνθρωπος ἦν ὁμοιοπαθὴς ἡμῖν, καὶ προσευχῇ προσηύξατο τοῦ μὴ βρέξαι, καὶ οὐκ ἔβρεξεν ἐπὶ τῆς γῆς ἐνιαυτοὺς τρεῖς καὶ μῆνας ἕξ). Like a good Jewish preacher, James supports his arguments for prayer with an example from the OT. He sets up his illustration carefully, making it clear that Elijah was simply a representative human being rather than a larger-than-life hero, somehow holier than us. His ability to pray and obtain results did not stem from his differing from us in any way. Rather, Elijah was a fallen, stubborn person "just like us," but one who on these occasions was in touch with the Spirit.[41] Thus his prayers did not arise from arrogance or a selfish desire to prove a point; rather, they came from trust and confidence in God. By the expression "a man with the same nature as us" (ἄνθρωπος ἦν ὁμοιοπαθὴς ἡμῖν), James makes it clear that we have this same ability to pray powerfully.

As James goes on to explain Elijah's prayer, he uses the Semitic method of emphasis, employing two of the same words or roots next to each other as a way of intensifying the original action.[42] Thus a woodenly literal translation for the two cognates (προσευχῇ προσηύξατο) would be "he prayed with a prayer," but the better understanding is the emphatic rendering, "he prayed intensely" or "fervently."

But why appeal to *this* incident from Elijah's life? Why not the more dramatic encounter with the prophets of Baal (1Ki 18:16–40) or the more directly relevant episode of the resurrection of the son of the Zarephath widow (17:17–24), given James's context of physical healing? Elijah's prayer for drought is not as amazing as a prayer for resurrection, and in the original context (1Ki 17:1) it is not even obvious that Elijah *does* pray.[43] One possible answer involves the sinfulness of ancient Israel, epitomized in King Ahab, whose overt rebellion and apparent repentance brought about Elijah's prayers. The example of Elijah illustrates not only the power of prayer in a righteous person, but also the restoration of a leader of God's people who has fallen away, as in the closing little paragraph of James (5:19–20).[44] Indeed, Elijah's

Epistle of St. James, 177–79. The root meaning of the verb is "to be at work"; hence, "to be exercised" seems closer to the origins of the word than "to be effective," though both are possible. The other NT uses of this verb in a middle or passive participial form appear in 2Co 1:6; Gal 5:6; Eph 3:20; and Col 1:29. In each of these contexts, "being exercised" or "exercising itself" yields better sense than any alternatives. The word order, with the participle at the end of the clause, separated from the noun with which it agrees, favors the adverbial over the adjectival classification. Cf. Hiebert, *The Epistle of James*, 327.

41. Johnson (*The Letter of James*, 336) comments that "James' language could be taken as a counter to the tendency to elevate the status of Elijah.... emphasizing the humanity of Elijah functions to affirm the possibilities available to them in their prayer." Keith Warrington ("The Significance of Elijah in James 5:13–18," *EvQ* 66 [1994]: 217–27) argues, however, that Elijah's righteousness may have been the trigger for James to include him, since James has just stressed the effectiveness of prayer from a righteous person. The two theories seem complementary not contradictory, for in this example James shows the power of prayer, highlights the relationship between righteousness and prayer, which is available to any Christian, and also helps to show the importance of God's will in prayer.

42. Kistemaker (*James and the Epistles of John*, 182) argues that here we have an aorist-tense verb with a dative noun of manner, and that "the translation of this particular dative is adverbial to express the intensity of the verb." Older grammars often categorize it simply as a cognate dative. The expression may represent a Semitism, given the corresponding form in Hebrew known as an infinitive absolute.

43. Barclay (*The Letters of James and Peter*, 132) points out that it is the expressions "before whom I stand" (1Ki 17:1, RSV) and "bowed himself down upon the earth" (18:42, RSV) that probably led to the understanding that Elijah was praying on these two occasions.

44. Moo (*The Letter of James*, 248) comments that "one explanation for the unusual choice [of this illustration] might be that James intends us to see an analogy between the sickness of a believer restored to health and the deadness of the land brought back to life and fruitfulness." Johnston ("Does James Give Believers a Pattern for Dealing with Sickness and Heal-

prayers had the goal of bringing repentance and confession to the whole nation, thus restoring the people to a proper relationship with God.[45] A secondary reason for choosing these incidents from Elijah's life may involve the lag time between the prayers and their answers. One obviously cannot tell if a prayer that it *not* rain has been answered until a lengthy period of drought has occurred (1Ki 17:1). So, too, believers' prayers may often require persistence and patience.

James 5:18 And again he prayed, and the heavens gave rain and the earth produced its fruit (καὶ πάλιν προσηύξατο, καὶ ὁ οὐρανὸς ὑετὸν ἔδωκεν καὶ ἡ γῆ ἐβλάστησεν τὸν καρπὸν αὐτῆς). James's illustration of the power of prayer continues as he shows that Elijah's stunning petition was not merely a one-time event. The prophet was also able to beg God later on for a lifting of the restrictions he himself had imposed. With this prayer *for* rain, Elijah had to persevere and not doubt, waiting for his servant to go seven times to look toward the sea before he saw even a cloud the size of a person's hand (18:41 – 46).[46]

This verse contains several connections with what has come before, the most obvious being 5:7 with the farmer waiting for the rains to come in order for the "fruit" to grow. The less obvious link, but clear from James's general theology, is with the idea that all good gifts come from above, from heaven (see 1:17; 3:17). Quite literally, rain comes down from above, but more importantly, this rainstorm came as a specific answer by God to his prophet's prayer that the drought might be ended. So often in our cynical Western world, when something miraculous does happen, we chalk it up to luck and fail both to give God the recognition he deserves and to ingrain that pattern of gratitude into our lives. But James shows Elijah praying again and God lifting the entire curse of the famine.

We should not assume that Elijah did not pray at all during that entire three-and-a-half-year period, but it was not until the end of that time that Elijah *did* pray that God might end the famine. Nor did Elijah ineffectively pray to God after, say, two years, with God hearing him only after three and a half years. Instead, James insists that as soon as Elijah asked, God acted, both with the initial famine and then with the final coming of the rains. Still, as noted above, there was a period of time required for Elijah to continue to exercise his faith as the requested events unfolded; more importantly, Elijah knew that he was acting within God's will in both the initial pronouncement and the final prayer.

James 5:19 My brothers and sisters, if someone among you should stray from the truth and someone should restore them (Ἀδελφοί μου, ἐάν τις ἐν ὑμῖν πλανηθῇ ἀπὸ τῆς ἀληθείας καὶ ἐπιστρέψῃ τις αὐτόν). James chooses to touch on one last awkward subject as he closes his letter. Here he deals with the problem of someone inside the congregation wandering away from the faith.[47] The root of the verb "should stray" (πλανηθῇ)

ing?" 172 – 73) thinks the analogy concerns a punishment for sin (Ahab's in the OT and the sick person's here).

45. The period of three and one-half years most likely comes from Jewish tradition, since it is not specifically outlined in the OT. But Jesus cites the same number (Lk 4:25), so presumably it was an accurate figure. Davids (*The Epistle of James*, 197), however, introduces the intriguing idea that it "is probably a symbolic round figure, half of 7, for a period of judgment (Dn. 7:25; 12:7; Rev. 11:2; 12:14)."

46. Keenan, *Wisdom of James*, 167. Hartin (*James*, 280 – 81) sees Elijah's humanity, fervency, and effectiveness all behind the choice of this particular illustration.

47. Johnson (*The Letter of James*, 337) points out that "the situation is cast in a future conditional sentence, with the aorist subjunctive being used for both verbs in the protasis and the indefinite pronoun *tis* being used for both subjects: the condition could not be more generalized."

produced the English term for "planet," because a planet does not appear fixed in the sky as a star but "wanders" (or "strays") through the night sky. When this verb (πλανάω) appears in the passive, it conveys the idea of being led astray or deceived. This use of the verb can either reflect a true passive ("be led astray") or perhaps an implied middle ("one goes astray" of one's own accord).[48] The word for "if" (ἐάν) makes the protasis a third-class condition. James does not assume that people within the congregation *have* wandered away; perhaps no one has yet acted in this fashion. But the fact that he raises this issue makes it seem probable, whether in his own congregations or within the larger church, that he does know of people leaving the faith.

James again uses the indefinite pronoun "someone" (τις), referring first to the wanderer and then to the restoring member of the congregation. He may not be discussing complete apostasy here, because the person has "wandered," not disowned the faith, and also this person willingly returns to the faith upon having their error pointed out to them.[49] The stronger believer is said to have "turned the person back" (lit. trans.), indicating that they have "restored" that person to the faith.

But from what has the wanderer strayed? Johnson argues that "'truth' in this context does not mean theoretical correctness, but rather the proper 'way' of behaving,"[50] while Martin thinks that "straying from the truth could easily be characterized as one who emphasizes orthodoxy (as in 2:19) more than orthopraxis."[51] Given James's stress on the practical aspects of faith and truth, it seems reasonable to conclude that this is a public falling away, whether in speech or action, rather than merely a private change of theology or thought.

James 5:20 ... let that person know that the one returning a sinner from the error of their ways saves their soul from death and covers a multitude of sins (γινωσκέτω ὅτι ὁ ἐπιστρέψας ἁμαρτωλὸν ἐκ πλάνης ὁδοῦ αὐτοῦ σώσει ψυχὴν αὐτοῦ ἐκ θανάτου καὶ καλύψει πλῆθος ἁμαρτιῶν).[52] This verse finishes the thought of the previous one, explaining the results of turning the sinner from their path.[53] The confusion here lies, however, in who actually receives the ben-

48. Kistemaker (*James and the Epistles of John*, 185) observes that "both explanations are possible and acceptable at the same time." We might argue that both explanations are possible and acceptable, but probably not at the same time, since they require quite different categorizations of the verb. See also BDAG, 821 – 22.

49. Moo (*The Letter of James*, 249), however, argues that "since James suggests in v. 20 that the 'wandering' Christian is saved from spiritual death, the deviation from the faith here must be a very serious one, tantamount to apostasy." Omanson ("The Certainty of Judgment and the Power of Prayer," 435) seems more open to balancing the two views, but highlights the dangers of persecution for the early Christians, making it more likely for them to turn away from the faith. But he emphasizes that "the focus is not upon the action of the Christian who wanders from the truth. It is on the responsibility of other Christians to seek actively to restore the sinner."

50. Johnson, *The Letter of James*, 337.

51. Martin, *James*, 219.

52. This verse has two sets of textual variants in the UBS[4]. The first includes changing the third person singular imperative into the second person plural, both in conformity with the vocative "my brothers and sisters" (ἀδελφοί μου) and also "to avoid the ambiguity of who is to be regarded (the converter or the converted) as the subject of the verb" (Metzger, *A Textual Commentary on the Greek New Testament*, 615). The external support, however, for the third person singular is significantly greater, and it represents the harder reading that would have most likely been changed by a later scribe. The second variant involves the ambiguity of "their soul" (ψυχὴν αὐτοῦ), which led scribes either to transfer the αὐτοῦ to the intensive position after "death" (θανάτου) or to omit it altogether. This reading is supported by ℵ and A, among other manuscripts.

53. Moo (*The Letter of James*, 250) notes here the allusion to Pr 10:12, an identification supported by 1Pe 4:8, suggesting "that the phrase had become a traditional way of denoting God's forgiveness of sins."

efit of these actions. The subject of the clause is the substantival participle, "the one returning" (ὁ ἐπιστρέψας) — the faithful Christian who helped to shed light on the path of the sinner. Of this person James declares that they both save someone's soul and cover someone's sins, without specifying whose in either instance.[54]

The first question is the simpler one. Whose soul is saved by this action? The answer seems clear because of the parallel uses of αὐτοῦ in both "the error of *his/her* ways" and "saves *his/her* soul."[55] It makes more sense that the soul in danger of being lost belongs to the person who strays from the truth. Meanwhile, the soul of the person who did the restoring would not be saved by this action, as we would assume that such a person already does believe, thus making them want to restore the wanderer. This restoring is more a work that *shows* their faith than one that creates their salvation. The implication of "saves their soul" may well be that the wanderer never truly believed, and it is in this restoration that they come to their own saving faith. Or James may be using "saved" here in the sense of final, eschatological salvation — they have now been brought safely to the end of the process that their earlier belief initiated.

The second, and harder, question is that of whose sins are covered in this act. The most obvious person would be the one who has strayed.[56] Yet, "Jewish sources are quoted to the effect that the one who turns a sinner to repentance is deserving of forgiveness himself."[57] But perhaps James left that description purposely ambiguous, so that while the one who strayed appears to have the more immediate need of forgiveness, it does not hurt us to remember that we are all sinners in need of God's grace, all "prone to wander" given the opportunity and right inducement. Thus, in this one act of righteousness in turning another person who has wandered farther astray, we find ourselves drawn back closer to God's grace and righteousness.[58]

54. Several scholars actually split the two, where the one saved is the wanderer, while the sins covered are those of the converter (see Laws, *The Epistle of James*, 239; Ropes, *A Critical and Exegetical Commentary on the Epistle of St. James*, 315–16; Adamson, *The Epistle of James*, 204).

55. In this situation the use of inclusive plurals does mask a grammatical issue and so we have chosen to go with the less elegant but still inclusive pronouns.

56. Davids, *The Epistle of James*, 201; Johnson, *The Letter of James*, 339.

57. Martin, *James*, 220. See also Dibelius, *James*, 259–60.

58. Moo (*The Letter of James*, 251) concludes: "if James is indeed something of a sermon in epistolary form, these last two verses are an appropriate conclusion. Not only should the readers of James 'do' the words he has written; they should be deeply concerned to see that others 'do' them also." An alternative reading sees Pr 17:9 with its concern about gossip in the background. There, "covers" (κρύπτει) refers to one who refrains from spreading gossip about another, and how that encourages love, while one who spreads slander only brings about further alienation. Perhaps James means to indicate that when a person turns another from their sinful way, it is not that God somehow covers their sins, but the one restoring covers the restoree's sins by not gossiping about them within the larger congregation (this explanation retains the subject [ὁ ἐπιστρέψας] given in the sentence).

Theology in Application

Anointing Prayer for Serious Illness (5:13 – 18)

The faithful Jew in the first century prayed several times a day. James's commands to pray in good times and in bad would hardly cause any surprise. How to deal with illness proved more complicated. The same range of interpretations that competed to explain wealth and poverty (see above, pp. 63 – 64, 231 – 32) attach themselves to health and sickness. A study of Jesus' miracles, even just of his miracles of healing, shows that about half of the time he is responding to someone's faith and the other half of the time he is trying to induce or strengthen faith where it is weak or nonexistent.[59] Sometimes personal sin seems to have caused an illness or chronic malady (Jn 5:1 – 16); other times it clearly has not (9:1 – 5). Sometimes Jesus healed everyone who was brought to him (Mt 4:24); sometimes he left almost everyone sick around him and healed just one person (Jn 5:3 – 9). James would have recognized all of these possibilities.

Calling on the elders to pray keeps the sick person closely related to the local Christian community. Elders already formed part of a Jewish synagogue's leadership, just as Greco-Roman municipal governments often included elders as well. The close links between age, maturity, wisdom, and leadership in the ancient patriarchal world meant that the key social and spiritual leaders of a community usually came from among the older men, hence the title "elder."[60] Acts 14:23 notes how Paul and Barnabas appointed elders in all their newly planted churches. First Timothy 5:17 and Tit 1:5 refer to elders in the contexts of those who teach and exercise authority in church and exhibit characteristics of godly, mature Christian living. There would be no reason not to allow someone with a proven track record of having gifts of working miracles or healings (1Co 12:29 – 30) to pray over a sick person, too. But even then God offers no guarantees and not every Christian fellowship will have such an individual. A ceremony of anointing with oil and prayer by the elders, however, can be implemented in any scripturally organized congregation.

Anointing with oil was widely used for both medicinal and ceremonial purposes.[61] Those who see ritual or symbolism primarily in view may then debate whether application should limit itself to physical maladies or include situations of intense spiritual or emotional weakness and suffering as well.[62] On any of these

59. Craig L. Blomberg, *Jesus and the Gospels: An Introduction and Survey* (Nashville: Broadman & Holman, 1997), 267 – 75. The best recent, detailed study of all of Jesus' miracles of Jesus is Graham H. Twelftree, *Jesus the Miracle-Worker: A Historical and Theological Study* (Downers Grove, IL: IVP, 1999).

60. The key study is R. Alastair Campbell, *The Elders: Seniority within Earliest Christianity* (Edinburgh: T&T Clark, 1994), which, however, overly downplays the role of elders as an "office."

61. See, respectively, Baker and Ellsworth, *Preaching James*, 158; and Tidball, *Wisdom from Heaven*, 191. For a detailed understanding of the text in light of ancient medicine, see John Wilkinson, "Healing in the Epistle of James," *SJT* 24 (1971): 326 – 45.

62. Arguing for a both-and approach to this question on

understandings of this passage, the key application question is how to deal with the majority of cases in which prayers for healing do not yield their desired effects, at least not so instantaneously as to demonstrate that the ceremony itself had the desired effect. As long as the "prayer of faith" is defined so as to leave room for God's will to overturn ours (see above, p. 224), the problem is resolved. But we must not lose sight of 4:2 – 3: sometimes God has chosen to give us certain good gifts if and only if we (or others) pray for them.

While God certainly can and does answer prayer, even for healing and apart from a ritual like anointing with oil, we risk losing out on a blessing God wants to give us if we refuse to include opportunities within our church's life for the seriously ill to request the elders to lead them in this kind of anointing ritual.[63] At the same time, whenever we come anywhere close to claiming we can declare what God *must* do in response to our prayers, we compromise his sovereignty and risk lapsing into idolatry.[64] Above all, we dare never assume we can *know* that it is someone else's lack of faith that has prevented their healing. When we are wrong with such accusations, we risk piling such guilt on the ones not cured, and on those who love them, that we may scar them emotionally or spiritually forever.[65]

More difficult to apply is James's command to confess our sins to one another. Catholicism elevated this procedure to a sacrament but limited it to a private encounter between church members and clergy.[66] The Lutheran and Anglican/Episcopalian liturgies include a public confession of sins at the start of each service, followed by the pastor's pronouncement of absolution. Still, neither of these practices is quite the same thing as going to the person against whom one has sinned to acknowledge one's failure and seek forgiveness. Mt 18:15 – 18 lies in the background. When sin has estranged two parties, one of them needs to take the initiative to restore the relationship. If that fails, then other Christian helpers must be brought into the process. If at all possible, the confession should not be made any more or less public than the original sin.[67] And "any confession should be offered in the presence of those who have been harmed by the sin or in the presence of the leaders of that community rather than a wider context, so that wise counsel may be offered."[68]

Community life can be powerfully strengthened by sensitive application of appropriate confession, whereas cavalier and irresponsible application can do great damage. If a person does not know that another has sinned in their thoughts against

James's part is Robert J. Karris, "Some New Angles on James 5:13 – 20," *RevExp* 97 (2000): 207 – 19.

63. Cf. Mark A. Seifrid, "The Waiting Church and Its Duty," 36 – 37. For elaboration on how a church can faithfully apply this procedure today, see Hughes, *James*, 356 – 57.

64. For a balanced articulation of both of these points, see Barton, Veerman, and Wilson, *James*, 139 – 40. Cf. also Mt 17:20 for how little a quantity of faith may be necessary on those occasions when God *does* want to heal.

65. Deiros, *Santiago y Judas*, 271.

66. For a Protestant equivalent of sorts, see C. J. Collins, "James 5:14 – 16a: What Is the Anointing For?" *Presb* 23 (1997): 79 – 91.

67. See esp. Doriani, *James*, 200.

68. Warrington, "James 5:14 – 18," 353.

them, it can probably only work harm if the latter confesses sinful thoughts, thereby creating an unnecessary fracture in the relationship. But when people are aware of offenses, even when two parties are each partly to blame, it is almost always healthy to take the initiative in apologizing.[69]

Prayer, anointing with oil, and confession of sin (when appropriate) are, of course, not put forward as alternatives to medicine. Even in James's world, his audiences would have known of Sir 38:1 and 4, which declared, "Honor the physician with the honor due him, according to your need of him," and "The Lord created medicines from the earth, and a sensible man will not despise them," while at the same time insisting that "healing comes from the Most High," so that we should "pray unto God for he will heal" (vv. 2 and 9). Nor is James limiting to the elders the circle of those who can pray for the sick. Rather, he is presupposing that elders will illustrate the principle of 5:16b, exemplifying the righteous people whose prayers prove powerful when exercised.[70] If righteousness by itself cannot guarantee healing, "sin in the camp" can certainly squelch it.[71] For the full canonical account of Elijah as a righteous person, who still had doubts and sins like every "saint," see 1Ki 17–2 Ki 2.[72]

Wilkinson deduces five cross-cultural principles from this passage irrespective of one's stance on the nature of the sickness and its healing or the specific purpose of the oil: (1) The church must be concerned for the sick; (2) healing is part of the normal work of the church; (3) healing most appropriately occurs within the context of Christian community; (4) the healing ministry of the church encompasses a multiplicity of methods; and (5) spiritual health is always more important than physical well-being.[73]

Closing (5:19–20)

Helping bring back wayward Christians securely into the "fold" may constitute one of the most neglected responsibilities of the church today.[74] One thinks of God's heart for such "little ones," as disclosed in Matthew's account of the parable of the lost sheep (Mt 18:10–14). Many churches, particularly growing ones, count only the number of visitors, new members, converts, those baptized, and so on, but never notice how many disappear out "the back door." Some, of course, get well assimilated into other fellowships, but many do not. Without keeping track of such people, we will never know how many truly fall into each category. This passage scarcely

69. For excellent practical advice, see Hughes, *James*, 264–67.

70. Warrington, "James 5:14–18," 361.

71. Nystrom, *James*, 317.

72. For subsequent biblical and postbiblical traditions about Elijah, see Hartin, *James*, 271–72.

73. Wilkinson, "Healing in the Epistle of James," 344–45. For an expanded and updated treatment, cf. idem, *The Bible and Healing: A Medical and Theological Commentary* (Grand Rapids: Eerdmans, 1998), 236–60.

74. Cf. Baker and Ellsworth, *Preaching James*, 147; with Brosend, *James and Jude*, 162.

resolves the classic Calvinist-Arminian debates; restoring a wanderer is consistent with one who might have lost salvation, one who was merely backsliding, and one who had never truly believed to begin with.[75]

Love covering a multitude of sins alludes to Pr 10:12 and will reappear in 1Pe 4:8. But the really serious issue at stake here goes back to Mt 18:15 – 18. So often when a person drifts away from active involvement in church and even from the faith, it is due to unresolved personal offenses within the congregation. Because we have so little accurate teaching on Jesus' process for conflict resolution and even fewer healthy models of implementing it,[76] estrangement remains. If Christians spent even half the time taking their concerns about other people directly to them in gentleness and love (recall Gal 6:1) rather than complaining about them to others, we would all be far healthier, individually and collectively.

So if James's closing remains abrupt, it cannot be fairly accused of being inappropriate or trivial! Perhaps James means to return to the unifying thread of God's single-mindedness versus human duplicity one final time, stressing the need to help restore those who have taken important steps to imitate God in this respect but then have "backslidden."[77] All of us should constantly be striving to allow God to remake us increasingly into his consistent, faithful, *truly* human image-bearers that he initially created humanity to be.

75. Cf. Stulac, *James*, 188.

76. For an excellent exception to both of these generalizations, see Ken Sande, *The Peacemaker: A Biblical Guide to Resolving Personal Conflict* (Grand Rapids: Baker, rev. 1997). Among groups, cf. esp. Stassen, *Just Peacemaking: Ten Practices for Abolishing War.*

77. Gilberto Marconi, "La malattia come 'punto di vista': esegesi di Gc 5,13 – 20," *RivBib* 38 (1990): 72.

The Theology of James

Now that we have studied the epistle in detail, we are in a good position to summarize its major theological contributions. We will use headings that emerge from an inductive study of the text rather than imposing some preexisting grid of doctrines on which we might hope to find teaching. We will also arrange our topics roughly in an order that proceeds from the most central to the most peripheral, and then ask if there is a unifying theme or thread running through the entire letter.

Wealth and Poverty

If our suggested structure of James is at all on target, then the theme of wealth and poverty, at the center of the chiasm of three key topics, emerges as this letter's most important issue. Despite some who have argued that for James one cannot be both rich and Christian, we have seen that 1:9 – 11 and 2:1 – 4 are best understood as depicting rich Christians, while 4:13 – 17 treats believers who are at least "middle-group" if not more well-to-do. But it is true in these texts that James strongly warns followers of Jesus not to trust in material resources (4:13, 15 – 16), nor forget their transience (1:10 – 11; 4:14). We should not expect wealth to buy us preferential treatment (2:2 – 3). Rather, we should use our surplus possessions to help the world's neediest (1:27a), especially impoverished fellow believers (2:14 – 17). If true Christians do perform good works (2:18 – 26), then stewarding resources to maximize one's ability to perform acts of mercy takes center stage. It may well be true that it is impossible to be both rich and Christian unless one is generous in giving from one's riches.[1]

For the non-Christian rich, James has only scathing denunciation. Unless they repent, those who hoard wealth, withhold fair wages from others, or live in luxury and self-indulgence will have only God's wrath on Judgment Day to which to look forward (5:1 – 6). Given James's theology of works, when professing Christians too consistently act like these non-Christians, their salvation may be called into ques-

1. "James might ask, Did you in fact realize that the meeting of needs is not peripheral, nor optional, but central and obligatory to your faith?" (Motyer, *The Message of James*, 16).

tion (2:14).[2] Some unbelievers, of course, clearly distinguish themselves from Christians by persecuting and slandering them (2:6–7).

On the issue of the poor, James declares that God has chosen those who are poor by the standards of the world (2:5). This includes but is not limited to material poverty (1:9). This is not salvation by socioeconomic bracket, because the poor in question are "those who love him." But it does reflect a reality apparent in the first-century and every era since that the poorer classes prove more open to the gospel because they are less tempted to depend on themselves and their possessions to meet all their needs.[3] At the same time, some poor people are consumed with the desire to get rich and, when they cannot obtain what they want, they fight and quarrel (4:1–2). Even short of this outward show of the sins in their heart, they may harbor lusts and desires for gain that demonstrate basic self-centeredness rather than commitment to Christ (4:3).[4]

Trials and Temptations

The frames or outermost parts of an extended chiasm are the second most stressed portions of the structure. Since the oppression that the largely poor Christians in James's audience are suffering forms the central trial from which his exposition begins, it makes sense to see this theme as the next most important. James's fundamental challenge hits us immediately after his greeting, as he calls us to consider difficult situations as grounds for rejoicing (1:2), not because they are good in and of themselves, but because God will bring good out of them — at the very least in the maturing of our character (1:3–4). James does not ask the impossible — that we should *feel* exuberant — but rather commands us how to think, how to "consider" hardship. We remind ourselves that glory awaits us on the other side of suffering when we persevere and respond properly, a crown promised if not in this life then definitely in the life to come (1:12).[5]

2. "The propensity of the rich to ignore the poor is not only an ethical but also a religious matter. To truly confront the plight of the poor would disturb the rich in their comfortable cocooning of themselves against the realities of life. It would challenge the superficial and easy atheism (whether practical ignoring of God, as in biblical societies, or practical ignoring of God supported by a thoughtless theoretical atheism, as often today) which rarely exists apart from affluence" (Bauckham, *James*, 190).

3. Cf. Nystrom, *James*, 25: "The poor whom James knows of have been placed at the margins of society — widows and orphans, and those victimized by economic conditions as well as the dishonesty of their employers. The poor are the pious because they throw themselves on the mercy of God in the face of injustice. It is this inclination that James extols."

4. Alicia Batten ("Ideological Strategies in the Letter of James," in *Reading James with New Eyes*, ed. Webb and Kloppenborg, 26) thus sees that James is trying "to preserve the community from the negative influence of wealth and all of the problems that such influence could bring."

5. Cf. further Peter H. Davids, "Why Do We Suffer? Suffering in James and Paul," in *The Missions of James, Peter, and Paul: Tensions in Early Christianity*, ed. Bruce Chilton and Craig Evans (Leiden and Boston: Brill, 2005), 434–44, 451–53.

The topics of trials and riches intersect in 4:13 – 5:12. The pursuit of wealth can become a trial when we do not leave room for God's will to overrule ours (4:15).[6] The rich unbeliever can wreak considerable havoc for the believer, precisely because of what money can buy or deprive one of when it is promised and then withheld (5:1 – 6). The appropriate Christian response is patience, leaving vengeance to the Lord (5:7 – 11), who alone will judge righteously (4:12). One must avoid rash vows that may merely exacerbate problems (5:12). But one may well imitate the prophets and Job, who in nonviolent fashion vigorously denounced the injustice of their worlds (5:10 – 11). Sickness can also become a significant trial, with prayer a crucial antidote (5:13 – 15a).

When we respond improperly to trials that were intended by God to build our character, they become temptations, used by the devil to seduce us to sin (1:13 – 15; 4:17). But we dare not blame God; his power to resist temptation is always available and adequate (1:13; 4:8 – 10). Nor may we blame Satan, because we have enough free will to choose to resist. Thus we have only ourselves to blame when we decide not to (1:14 – 15).[7] As with those who too consistently demonstrate no stewardship or concern for the poor, so also those who never demonstrate any change of life in resisting temptation may no have genuine, saving faith at all. Those whose lives remain characterized by intimate involvement with sin make themselves God's enemies (4:4).

Wisdom and Speech

James's third key theme appears to be the broadest. God's wisdom is endless and he wants to give it to us freely and without berating us, if only we will ask him (1:5). But we must believe that he is the one from whom true wisdom comes rather than from any other source (1:6 – 8). The doubt that we are to avoid in this context is not realistic uncertainty about the *contents* of his will. The precise contents are often opaque to us, and so to "name it and claim it" can reflect gargantuan arrogance. The true prayer of faith (5:15) is by definition the one that acknowledges "if the Lord wills" (4:15, echoing "Your will be done" in Mt 6:10). The doubt we must banish is that which questions whether God in Christ is the one to whom we are ultimately loyal, to whom we pledge allegiance.

Christian wisdom plays itself out particularly in action or "good conduct" (3:13b).[8] Jas 1:19 outlines the three main points of vv. 20 – 26: "quick to listen, slow to speak, slow to anger," but it becomes clear that true listening means not hearing

6. Nystrom (*James*, 22 – 23) identifies "three major sources of adversity afflicting the community James is addressing." Two are regularly noted: the "evil impulse" inside of each person and external temptation by Satan. The third is frequently missed: "money and status." Cf. Peter H. Davids, "The Test of Wealth," in *The Missions of James, Peter, and Paul*, ed. Chilton and Evans, 354 – 84.

7. Cf. Painter, *Just James*, 252 – 54.

8. For detail, see James B. Adamson, *James: The Man and His Message* (Grand Rapids: Eerdmans, 1989), 363 – 91.

and forgetting but hearing that leads to obedience (vv. 22 – 25). Godly wisdom may be summed up with the countercultural trait of humility (3:13b; 4:6). It begins with purity and culminates in peace (3:17 – 18). Overall, wisdom functions for James much like the Spirit does elsewhere, which may explain why there is no unambiguous reference to the Holy Spirit in the book (4:5 is the disputed passage).[9] The world will make many competing claims to wisdom, but they will all distinguish themselves by being ultimately self-centered and thus envious of others, and by denying Christian truth (3:14 – 16, 4:11). Instead of promoting peace, worldly wisdom only produces violence (4:1 – 2).

Speech ethics represent "exhibit A" of godly wisdom, much like stewardship does for good works.[10] If people could remain sinless in their speech, all other forms of self-control would follow (3:2). Teachers, who make their living by their tongues, as it were, must exercise particular caution (3:1). Malicious speech can cause grave damage (3:5b – 8) and highlight hypocrisy (3:9 – 12). But lest all believers become afraid ever to speak, James also stresses the tongue's great power for good (3:3 – 5a). If we listen to others carefully, think before we talk, and save our anger for rare occasions in which it is truly justified (1:19), we will be wise indeed.

Prayer

Just because one can account for a letter's structure under the headings of three main themes does not mean that its theological contributions are exhausted. A close fourth among James's major topics is prayer.[11] We gain God's wisdom by praying (1:5). We pray believing that God can and will answer our prayers (1:6 – 8).[12] When we lack the necessities of life, we must ask God for them. When it seems as if he has not given us what we ask for, we need to persist in prayer, but also recheck our motives (4:2 – 3). Sometimes, however, certain things we request simply are not God's will (4:15).

Many times God showers his good gifts on us even when we haven't prayed for them (1:16 – 18), for which we remain profoundly grateful. But because God in his sovereignty has chosen to reserve certain good gifts for us contingent on our asking,

9. See above, pp. 178 – 79. Bruce Chilton finds similar parallels and distinctives between wisdom in James and grace in Paul in his "Wisdom and Grace," in *The Missions of James, Peter, and Paul*, ed. Chilton and Evans, 307 – 22.

10. At a technical level, see esp. Baker, *Personal Speech-Ethics in the Epistle of James*, 84 – 104, 123 – 38, 175 – 86, 222 – 48, 278 – 90. At a popular level, cf. idem, *Sticks and Stones*, *passim*.

11. For an excellent overview, see C. Richard Wells, "The Theology of Prayer in James," *CTR* 1 (1986): 85 – 112.

12. Again, we cannot sufficiently stress that this does *not* mean that he will answer them the way we initially desire. God is single-minded in knowing and initiating/allowing that which, in his inscrutable but omniscient understanding, will produce the greatest eternal good for his people, even when it least seems that way in this life. Our prayers, however, often stem from our duplicity, a double-mindedness sometimes hidden even to ourselves. See, in rich detail, Adrian Wypadlo, *Viel vermag das inständige Gebet eines Gerechten (Jak 5, 16): Die Weisung zum Gebet im Jakobusbrief* (Würzburg: Echter, 2006).

we should persevere in prayer (4:2). Indeed, prayer is appropriate in every circumstance of life, but especially when we suffer (5:13 – 15a). Prayers of confession when we sin lead to forgiveness and restoration (5:15b – 16a). Prayers of the (relatively) righteous prove particularly powerful (5:16b – 18), including those for the restoration of others who have sinned or wandered away spiritually (5:19 – 20).[13]

Faith and Works

Contrary to what the extent of the discussion of the topic might suggest, faith and works is not the main focus of James's letter. It is a subordinate point that grows out of his concern for the poor and dispossessed (2:14 – 26; cf. 2:1 – 13). James is not the "odd person out" in the canon, teaching salvation by works, but rather he teaches the demonstration by works of one's salvation. Of course, the theme of good conduct permeates the whole letter, but that is precisely what one expects in an epistle of this form — exhortation flowing from proverbial-like wisdom. But the emphasis in James is that sheer monotheism alone is inadequate (2:19). Faith is inseparable from action (2:18); indeed, it represents belief *through* action, as with Abraham and Rahab in OT times (2:20 – 26).

But this action, these deeds or works, are not put forward in any attempt to merit God's favor but as the natural, spiritual outgrowth of one's faith (2:18).[14] And the works that formed part of what came to be called the ceremonial and civil portions of the law never appear in James as incumbent on Christians. Instead, language that once applied to issues of ritual purity repeatedly is transferred to matters of moral purity (see esp. 1:27, 4:8 and 5:14).[15]

Law and Word

James's attitude to the law thus appears in a consistently positive light.[16] But his qualifiers suggest he is often speaking of more than Mosaic legislation, of more even

13. "Prayer has always been difficult, but the difficulty of prayer in the modern western world has its own specific profile. The fundamental reason why prayer became difficult in the modern period was humanity's modern self-image as those who, especially through technology, have gained control over the world. Rather like affluence, this assumed position of mastery over the world has deluded modern people into trusting their own capacity to achieve all human ends and has promoted a sense of autonomy and self-sufficiency to which prayer is alien" (Bauckham, *James*, 207).

14. For a concise summary of faith and works in James, see Andrew Chester, "The Theology of James," in *The Theology of the Letters of James, Peter, and Jude*, by Andrew Chester and Ralph P. Martin (Cambridge: CUP, 1994), 20 – 28. Unpacking the implications, especially for the so-called "lordship salvation" debate, is John F. MacArthur, "Faith according to the Apostle James," *JETS* 33 (1990): 13 – 34. For an encouraging and nearly equivalent Latter-day Saint perspective, see Robert L. Millet, *Grace Works* (Salt Lake City: Deseret, 2003).

15. Cf. esp. John H. Elliott, "The Epistle of James in Rhetorical and Social Scientific Perspective: Holiness-Wholeness and Patterns of Replication," *BTB* 23 (1993): 71 – 81.

16. See, most fully, Matt A. Jackson-McCabe, *Logos and Law in the Letter of James* (Leiden: Brill, 1999), who unfortunately does not adequately perceive the balancing points made in the rest of this paragraph.

than the OT. In 2:9 – 11 he may be thinking purely of the Hebrew Scriptures as he explains how breaking any individual law makes one guilty before God, no matter how many others one may keep. For precisely this reason, it is hard to envision "the (perfect) law of liberty" (1:25; 2:12) or the "royal law" (2:8) as referring to the OT without remainder. Particularly because the command to love one's neighbor in 2:8 appears in both the Torah and Jesus' summary of the law, and because "royal" could also mean "kingdom," we assume that the new covenant joins with the old — indeed is the grid through which the old must be filtered — to create the sum total of God's will for believers.[17]

Something similar must be implied in James's use of "word" as well.[18] This "word" is true, producing rebirth (1:18); it helps get rid of moral filth and guides people through to final salvation once it is implanted (1:21). The word must include at least the gospel, but the seeming interchangeability of "the word" in 1:22 – 23 with "the perfect law of liberty" in 1:25 suggests that it too represents all of God's special revelation to humanity up to that point in time. As a result, James can cite approvingly both Torah (Ge 15:6; Ex 20:13 – 14/Dt 5:17 – 18; Lev 19:18) and the Writings (Pr 3:34), while quoting or alluding to all three major parts of the Hebrew canon, including the Prophets,[19] even while constantly alluding to Jesus' teachings.

God

It seems strange to put God so far down on a list of James's doctrines, arranged in roughly descending order of importance. Doubtless, belief in Yahweh is a fundamental presupposition for James, but God is not as central or direct a focus for doctrinal reflection in this letter as the six preceding themes. Nevertheless, James teaches us that God dispenses wisdom (1:5) and reward (1:12). He cannot do evil but only good (1:13 – 18). He chooses those who turn to him as their only hope (2:5). He is one, both in his existence as the only true God and in his unwavering constancy (2:19). God is Creator and Redeemer (1:17 – 18), Lawgiver and Judge (4:12),[20] compassionate and merciful (5:11). His righteousness requires us to be righteous (1:20), but this can be accomplished only by faith (2:23). He embraces those who humble

17. Cf. esp. Mary J. Evans, "The Law in James," *VE* 13 (1983): 29 – 40.

18. Scot McKnight, "A Parting within the Way: Jesus and James on Israel and Purity," in *James the Just and Christian Origins*, ed. Bruce Chilton and Craig A. Evans (Leiden: Brill, 1999), 129. Cf. Dockery, "True Piety in James: Ethical Admonitions and Theological Implications,"69: "James pictures true piety as the direct application of the implanted word in the life of the believer. The result vertically is the submission to and worship of God. The result horizontally is concern for the poor, widows and orphans in distress. The result relationally is living peaceably with others in the church. The result inwardly is the humility, purity and gentleness of character that comes from heavenly wisdom."

19. The best apparatus of OT quotations and allusions in the NT appears in the bottommost segment of footnotes on each page of the UBS editions of the Greek NT.

20. On which, see Marianne Sawicki, "Person or Practice? Judging in James and in Paul," in *The Missions of James, Peter, and Paul*, ed. Chilton and Evans, 385 – 408.

themselves before him while he resists the proud (4:4–8). He may be viewed as a benefactor (one who gives freely and graciously) but not as a patron (requiring reciprocity).[21] He is Father (3:9), not in any authoritarian sense but as a nurturer of widows and orphans, a caregiver to the most dispossessed (1:27).[22]

Christology

At first glance, Jesus appears to play a surprisingly minor role in this NT document. He appears explicitly only in 1:1 and 2:1, though given the full title, "Lord Jesus Christ," in both instances. James knows that Jesus is both the Messiah and the Master of the universe. He also appears to be the very *shekinah* glory of Yahweh (2:1). The numbers of verbal allusions to his teachings, however, disclose an even more thoroughly Christian composition. The clearest appear in 1:6, 17, 22; 2:8, 10, 11, 13, 14; 3:18; 4:13–14, 17; 5:1, 2, 9, while 5:12 deserves to be called an actual quotation. For James, Jesus is obviously the authoritative teacher. While "Lord" in 1:7; 3:9; 4:10; 5:4, 10, 11 appear to refer to God the Father, "the coming of the Lord" in 5:7 and 8 clearly refers to Christ's return. "The name of the Lord" (5:14), given the frequency of early church prayers in Jesus' name, likewise points to Christ, which then makes "the Lord" in 5:15 Jesus also. Although less certain, all this makes the reference to leaving room for "the Lord's will" in 4:15 more likely a specific reference to Jesus than just to God.[23]

Eschatology

Although it is not a major theme either, eschatology, like Christology, emerges more frequently than a superficial reading of James might suggest.[24] The "great reversal" of rich and poor in 1:9–11 occurs only fully on the judgment day. At that time, faithful Christians will receive their reward of eternal life (1:12), but those who remain controlled by their evil desires will face eternal death (1:15). The merciful, by contrast, will be blessed, because mercy triumphs over judgment, a judgment that will be merciless to those who themselves have been merciless (2:13). Even as God alone is perfectly merciful, he is likewise alone truly just. Because he will be the judge with these twin traits (4:12), we must not prematurely judge our neighbors in the sense of speaking evil of them (4:11). The unbelievers who mistreat the weak and vulnerable can expect only frightful judgment in their futures (5:1–6).

21. Alicia Batten, "God in the Letter of James: Patron or Benefactor?" *NTS* 50 (2004): 257–72.

22. Esther Y. L. Ng, "Father-God Language and Old Testament Allusions in James," *TynBul* 54 no. 2 (2003): 41–54.

23. Cf. further esp. William R. Baker, "Christology in the Epistle of James," *EvQ* 74 (2002): 47–57.

24. See esp. Todd C. Penner, *The Epistle of James and Eschatology: Re-reading an Ancient Christian Letter* (Sheffield: SAP, 1996).

From God's perspective, final judgment ushered in by Christ's parousia remains near (5:8).[25]

Other Themes

Sin for James is pervasive, afflicting even the redeemed more than we would like (4:1 – 4).[26] However, the unsaved still reflect some measure of God's image (3:9). Salvation for James is clearly a process, begun with faith in Christ but not completed until the end of one's life, after one has faithfully persevered (2:18 – 26). Growth in maturity comes as we increase in Christlike attributes and multiply good deeds, especially acts of mercy toward the most dispossessed of our world (1:27; 2:14 – 17). This mercy is how love of neighbor is fleshed out (2:8). James assumes the Christian communities he addresses will gather together as an assembly, either for worship or as a court or both (2:2). He knows the church has elders, who represent the body in praying and anointing the seriously ill with oil (5:14), and teachers, of whom there may be too many aspirants (3:1). Despite all his emphasis on right behavior, James acknowledges God's grace as what keeps us from staying his enemies (4:5). Repentance is not something we do only once, at the beginning of the Christian life, but throughout it (4:7 – 10).[27]

A Unifying Motif?

We suggested above that James's theology of God seems more of a presupposition than a major emphasis in his letter. But when we examine the attribute of God's simplicity or single-mindedness and the way in which Christians ought to imitate it, we discover a potentially unifying motif or subtheme running throughout the epistle.[28] Because God never wavers in his character or purposes, believers should shun all duplicity or vacillation in their allegiance and obedience to Christ and emulate God's trustworthy consistency. In short, they should become people of integrity.

25. As Moo (*The Letter of James*, 30) explains, "The sense of 'nearness' that James and the other early Christians felt stemmed from two convictions: (1) now that the Messiah had come and the new age had dawned, the end of history was the next event in the divine timetable; and (2) that culmination of history could happen at any time. James, in other words, motivates his readers to godly living not by insisting that the Lord *would* come at any time but by reminding them that he *could*."

26. In this, "James is no different from all the other teachers God has given us in the Bible. But he is different from teachers who have arisen and still arise, saying that there is an easy way to holiness — an experience, a technique or a blessing which will waft us effortlessly, even if not necessarily painlessly, to permanent loftier heights of living" (Motyer, *The Message of James*, 14). Cf. Davids, "Why Do We Suffer?" 452 – 60, 462 – 64.

27. For a comprehensive list of themes, topics, keywords, technical terms, and the like, in (German) alphabetical order with relevant verse references in James for each, see Burchard, *Der Jakobusbrief*, 19 – 20.

28. Cf. esp. Laws, *The Epistle of James*, 29 – 32; Tamez, *The Scandalous Message of James*, 46 – 56; Bauckham, *James*, 177 – 85; and, in detail, Nic Scherer, "The Unity of God and the Duplicity of Humanity in the Letter of James" (M.A. Thesis: Denver Seminary, 2007).

Thus in 1:2 – 4, we are to consider trials purely as grounds for the joy that comes from knowing our character can mature. In 1:5, God gives to us single-mindedly, but we must believe in him unswervingly (vv. 6 – 8). The reversal of rich and poor in vv. 9 – 11 reflects the transience of this life compared with the constancy of the life to come. V. 12 then repeats the need for perseverance under trial. Vv. 13 – 18 stress that God gives only good gifts, so that we have only ourselves to blame for yielding to temptation. Vv. 19 – 27 point out the futility of hearing God's word without obeying it, enjoining the consistent follow-through of doing what we learn is right.

Favoritism and discrimination are sinful because they do not treat everyone equally (2:1 – 4). The unsaved behave that way; believers should not (vv. 5 – 7). The law is a unity — not because each sin is as bad as every other, but because even one violation of God's commands brings judgment (vv. 8 – 11). Reliance on God's unswerving mercy, which makes his people merciful, is the only salvific alternative (vv. 12 – 13). Claiming to have faith but ignoring the most desperate needs of fellow believers whom one is in a position to help proves the height of hypocrisy (vv. 14 – 17). Because God is single-minded in purpose and action, true faith is inseparably linked to good works (vv. 18 – 26).

Speech ethics likewise follow from single-mindedness. One ought to use one's tongue only for good and not evil (3:1 – 8). Human conversation will then avoid the unique duplicity of which it is capable, so different from the rest of creation (vv. 9 – 12). This is why "wisdom from above" is first of all "pure" or unmixed and "impartial" or not hypocritical (v. 17), in contrast to the false demonic wisdom that brings "disorder" or rebellion (v. 16). Jas 4:1 – 6 brings this theme to a climax with its sharp rebuke for those who think they can be friends of God and the world at the same time. The principle of single-mindedness forces us to conclude that to be a friend of the one makes us an enemy of the other. Double-minded people must repent of their ways and change (vv. 7 – 10). Slander reflects especially egregious duplicity in speech, which again denies the unity of God and of God's people (vv. 11 – 12).

At first glance, planning for the future could appear to be a good way to avoid frequent changes of mind. James does not discourage planning, but he does call us to leave room for God's will. Even though God's will may at times overturn our plans, it unfailingly reflects what is best for our lives, at least in light of the uncertainty of the future (4:13 – 17). The wicked who withhold the poor's wages while living in the height of luxury represent extreme duplicity, and God will be relentless in his judgment of them (5:1 – 6). Christians, by contrast, ought to model patience and perseverance and speak trustworthy words (vv. 7 – 12). Prayer is always appropriate throughout all the ups and downs of life (vv. 13 – 18), while the one who "wanders" from a consistent path of truth should be restored (vv. 19 – 20).

Perhaps the teaching of Jesus presented in Mt 6:24 and Lk 16:13 best summarizes this unifying thread of James in a nutshell: we cannot ultimately serve two masters, for we will always finally love one and hate the other. Coming in the Sermon on the Mount in Matthew's version, this teaching would almost certainly have been familiar to James. Perhaps his epistle is a conscious elaboration of it, as seen especially in 4:4. If we flesh out this summary in narrative fashion, a "pattern of salvation" like that proposed by Wall results: "(1) the sovereign God (2:19), who is able to save and to destroy (4:12), (2) sends forth the 'word of truth' (1:18), (3) which saves those who humbly receive it (1:21), (4) at the coming triumph of God's reign."[29] We should probably add, in between (3) and (4), that increasing purity leads to the maturity God desires.[30]

29. Wall, *Community of the Wise*, 28.
30. See esp. Lockett, "'Unstained by the World,'" 49–74.

Scripture Index

1 Chronicles

2 Chronicles

Job

Psalms

Proverbs

Ecclesiastes

Isaiah

Jeremiah

Mark

Luke

John

Acts

Romans

Titus

Hebrews

James

1 Peter

2 Peter

1 John

2 John

Revelation

Apocrypha

Wisdom of Solomon

Sirach

1 Maccabees

2 Maccabees

Subject Index

Author Index